Critical Feeling

How can we develop the sensitivity necessary to play music or make objects requiring craftsmanship? How can teachers make their lessons interesting? In what ways can consumers avoid undue influence? How do we acquire refined tastes or come to believe what we want to believe? Addressing these issues and providing an account of how to tackle personal and societal problems, Rolf Reber combines insights from psychology, philosophy, and education to introduce the concept of *critical feeling*. While many people are familiar with the concept of critical thinking, critical feeling denotes the strategic use of feelings in order to optimize an outcome. Reber discusses the theoretical and empirical foundations of critical feeling and provides an overview of applications, including well-being, skill learning, personal relationships, business, politics, school, art, morality, and religion. This original and thought-provoking study will interest a broad range of researchers, students, and practitioners.

Rolf Reber is Professor of Cognitive Psychology at the University of Oslo and Adjunct Professor in the Department of Education at the University of Bergen, Norway. With his colleagues, Reber developed and tested the processing fluency theory of aesthetic pleasure; example choice, which is a new teaching method to increase student interest at school; new accounts of mathematical intuition and of the aha-experience; a new solution to an old paradox in Confucianism; and the psycho-historical approach to research on art appreciation. He has held visiting professorships and is an award-winning teacher and author of two popular science books in German.

Critical Feeling

How to Use Feelings Strategically

Rolf Reber

CAMBRIDGE
UNIVERSITY PRESS

CAMBRIDGE
UNIVERSITY PRESS

University Printing House, Cambridge CB2 8BS, United Kingdom

Cambridge University Press is part of the University of Cambridge.

It furthers the University's mission by disseminating knowledge in the pursuit of
education, learning and research at the highest international levels of excellence.

www.cambridge.org
Information on this title: www.cambridge.org/9781107629769

First published 2016

Printed in the United States of America by Sheridan Books, Inc.

A catalogue record for this publication is available from the British Library

Library of Congress Cataloguing in Publication data
Names: Reber, Rolf, author.
Title: Critical feeling : how to use feelings strategically / Rolf Reber.
Description: Cambridge, United Kingdom : Cambridge University Press,
2016. | Includes bibliographical references and index.
Identifiers: LCCN 2015046519 | ISBN 9781107060197 (hardback)
Subjects: LCSH: Emotions. | Critical thinking. |
BISAC: PSYCHOLOGY / Cognitive Psychology.
Classification: LCC BF531.R424 2016 | DDC 158–dc23
LC record available at http://lccn.loc.gov/2015046519

ISBN 978-1-107-06019-7 Hardback
ISBN 978-1-107-62976-9 Paperback

To my parents: Edi and Heidi Reber

TABLE OF CONTENTS

PREFACE

After walking my younger kids to school, I mounted the Vancouver SkyTrain at Sapperton Station on the morning of Monday December 14, 2009. As always, I took my current reading out of my backpack – on that day the book *Effortless Action* by Edward Slingerland (2003a), which analyzes the metaphorical nature of Confucian thought. I began thinking about what I read; my mind was wandering when all of a sudden an insight struck me: What Confucius wrote some 2500 years ago is critical feeling. Much has been written about critical thinking, but to my knowledge not one scholar has ever written a comprehensive work about how feelings can be used to improve personal or societal outcomes. The deficiencies of critical thinking have also been extensively covered, and recent decades have seen an increasing number of works on the rationality of emotions. Despite these insights, we lack an overview of strategies that realize the potential of feelings to improve outcomes. Feelings go beyond emotions and encompass moods, preferences, metacognitive experiences, and bodily states, as will be defined in due course. This book introduces the concept of critical feeling and provides an overview of applications in various areas, from personal well-being and skill learning to the acquisition of artistic tastes and religious creeds.

Writing such a book is often a solitary affair but at the same time impossible without a host of colleagues and friends who take time to collaborate, discuss, criticize, and encourage. Within the five years since my decisive aha-experience, I have had the privilege of working with and discussing ideas with many people, some of whom I would like to mention by name. At the University of Bergen and later at the University of Oslo, I met wonderful colleagues and students who gave input from various perspectives relevant to the project; among these people were Michael Stausberg (who provided input on parts of Chapter 10), Morten Brun, Kevin Cahill, Per Olav Folgerø, Marina Hirnstein, Lasse Hodne, Sigve Høgheim, Kenneth Hugdahl, Christoph Kirfel, Geir Overskeid, Francisco Pons, Ole Martin Skilleås, Karsten Specht, and Matthias Stadler. Some of my research relevant to critical feeling has been made possible by grants from the Research Council of Norway (#166252 and #212299) as well as by a fellowship from the Leiv Eirikssons mobility program.

I had the privilege to work with many fabulous scholars and students on projects that were all relevant to critical feeling. Among them are Nicolas Bullot, Sascha Topolinski, Edward Slingerland, Teresa Garcia-Marques, Rita da Silva, Christian Unkelbach, Rainer Greifeneder, and Ara Norenzayan. Ara was also the host of a one-year sabbatical visit at the University of British Columbia. Judith Harackiewicz (University of Wisconsin), Ellen Langer (Harvard University), Daphna Oyserman, and Norbert Schwarz (both University of Southern California) hosted shorter research visits and generously spent time discussing issues that all were relevant to critical feeling. Jan Landwehr (who provided input on parts of Chapter 7), Julia Annas, Martin Fortier, Joëlle Proust, Iain Robertson, Klaus Scherer, Stephen Stich, Lawrence Ward, Wendy Wood, and many others spent their time discussing aspects of critical feeling. Audiences at the University of Southern California, the Metacognitive Diversity Conference at the École Normale Supérieur in Paris, and the University of Oslo provided me with invaluable feedback on the book's plan and the concept of critical feeling. My wife, Hélène, improved the book by encouraging me to clarify issues or to illustrate statements with better examples. She also helped with the references and the index. I am grateful that my daughter Viviane read the book and provided feedback, mainly on English language but also on content. She told me this was the first time she had been able to do something meaningful with her education. Shouldn't we give every student such opportunities? Hetty Marx, Carrie Parkinson, and many others on the editorial team of Cambridge University Press shepherded the book with great care and benevolence.

Finally, I thank Hélène and my children – David, Viviane, Eric, and Anne-Sophie – who were a source of loving support and encouragement.

The book contains adapted excerpts from the following sources:

Reber, R. 2012. "Critical feeling: The strategic use of processing fluency," in *The experience of thinking*, C. Unkelbach and R. Greifeneder (eds.). Hove, UK: Psychology Press, 169–184.

Reber, R. 2014. "Mindfulness in education," in *Handbook of mindfulness*, A. Ie, C. Ngnoumen and E. Langer (eds.). Oxford: Wiley-Blackwell, 1054–1070.

Reber, R. and Norenzayan, A. 2010. "The shared fluency theory of social cohesiveness." http://papers.ssrn.com/sol3/papers.cfm?abstract_id=1702407.

Reber, R. and Slingerland, E. G. 2011. "Confucius meets cognition: New answers to old questions," *Religion, Brain & Behavior* 1: 135–145.

Part I
THE BASICS OF CRITICAL FEELING

INTRODUCTION

Ever since Plato introduced his allegory of the charioteer, where one horse is passion, the other is motivation, and the charioteer is reason, thinkers have captured conduct of life as a conflict between passion and reason. Theorists distinguished between human nature, which acts on impulses, and acts derived from reason-based morality (see Dewey 2012/1922). Humans often act on impulses that do not comply with what they themselves think would be best. Some eat too much, drink too much, or have romantic adventures they later regret. People who forget about the consequences of their actions and act based on their feelings may experience unsatisfactory results. For example, couples divorce due to a shattered relationship despite the shattered finances that follow suit. On the other hand, decision makers sometimes know that a course of action may have disastrous consequences if they follow their gut feeling. That is why employees do not walk away from their job when they are angry at their boss. Sometimes, however, it is good to act on gut feelings. For example, job applicants *feel* negatively about an option they *think* would be best. That is why people may reject a job offer that would yield a higher income and better career prospects; they feel uncomfortable at the job interview, a sign that the job has some drawbacks. Finally, although attitudes have been defined as consisting of cognitive, affective, and behavioral components (Krech, Crutchfield, and Ballachey 1962; Rosenberg and Hovland 1960), there is ample evidence for a lack of correspondence among these components of attitudes (Wicker 1969; Zanna and Rempel 1988). For example, people think of themselves as environmentalists but drive cars, produce unnecessary garbage or fly to distant conference destinations to give speeches about how to curb climate change.

This lack of agreement between thought and feeling that precede action raises several questions. How can we keep our impulses in check? When can we trust our gut feelings, and when not? How can we align feeling with thought and vice versa? Finally, how could we learn to use our feelings in order to act according to our values and the values of our community? These are the questions I address in this book.

Historically, this problem has been solved in two different ways. The most dominant solution in the West since the Enlightenment has consisted of excluding feelings as a guide to actions (see Lerner, Li, Valdesolo, and Kassam 2015; the notable exception was David Hume 1888/1738). According to the Western standards of optimal thought, people must analyze the consequences of an action in order to arrive at a reasoned decision. Cutting feelings out and acting on what reason tells us are preferred to acting impulsively based on feelings. This led to normative rules of inference and moral reasoning (e.g., Kant 2011/1785; Mill 2002/1863; Rawls 1971) and to models of moral development based on reasoning capacities (e.g., Kohlberg 1981). This solution denies the possibility that feelings ever lead to better outcomes than thinking. However, as we shall see by the end of Chapter 1, this approach is insufficient because feelings are always with us, and they have adaptive functions that we can exploit. Feelings can be seen as a source of information that may assist thought in determining the best course of action.

A second solution for optimizing the outcomes of actions was developed by the Chinese philosopher Confucius (551–479 BCE). His thoughts are collected in the *Analects* (Slingerland 2003b). Confucian ethics assumes that people have a natural inclination toward moral behavior that has to be refined through repeated practice of traditional cultural forms, including rituals, music, and readings of moral maxims. According to Confucian thought, repeated practice leads to information being processed more easily and to the feeling that that information is correct and pleasant (Reber and Slingerland 2011). These observations suggest that Confucian virtue ethics is psychologically feasible. Similarly, Aristotle (384–322 BCE), most prominently in his *Nicomachean Ethics* (Aristotle 2004/ca. 350 BCE), emphasized that virtuous action does not only include proper thought but also the right feeling (see Sherman 1989). For example, the act of giving money to the poor while feeling contempt for them would not qualify as virtuous.

Based on this old solution to the problem of how to spontaneously perform the right action, this book introduces the term *critical feeling* as a complement to critical thinking. In analogy to critical thinking, which is the strategic use of reasoning in order to optimize an outcome, critical feeling denotes the strategic use of feelings in order to optimize an outcome. Such outcomes may be happiness, mastery of a skill, true love or friendship, profit, the best outcomes for a community or state, or the realization of a spiritual or religious ideal. Critical thinking is aimed at bringing thought and action in line with each other. Yet people do not only want to do what they think is best; they want to feel good when they think and act well. A good life therefore means that thought, feeling, and action are in harmony with each other (Annas 2011; Fowers 2005) and with personal and communal values. That is why we need to introduce critical feeling.[1]

The main purpose of the book is to outline the theoretical foundations and some practical examples of how people can optimize feelings in order to act in accordance with their personal or community values. When individuals are able to achieve this feat, thought, feeling, and action are brought into agreement, and people enjoy doing the right thing (see James, 1985/1902).

The examination of critical feeling requires contributions from three disciplines: philosophy, psychology, and education. When the philosopher Kristján Kristjánsson (2013) discussed the virtue-ethical underpinnings of positive psychology, he compared the tasks of the three fields in providing excellent virtue education to three neighbors who go on a duck-hunting party. One neighbor owns the gun, another brings the ammunition, and the third has hunting expertise. In Kristjánsson's view, the virtue ethicists provide the gun (the overarching theory), the psychologists the ammunition (the empirical evidence necessary to implement virtue ethics), and the educators the know-how about hunting techniques (the knowledge of how to impart moral practices). He claimed that the psychologists have been the weakest member of the hunting party. The same analogy can be applied to critical feeling. Philosophers provide an overarching theory; they theorize about educational aims, values in science, morality, and the epistemology of thinking and feeling. Psychologists provide the empirical evidence for the effectiveness of strategies that employ feelings to optimize outcomes. Finally, education researchers provide the know-how on how educators, both parents and teachers, can instruct students regarding critical feeling. Educators need to assess how critical feeling might enter school curricula; how to implement various educational aims, such as improving results on standardized tests, educating for the economy, and educating for care; how critical feeling fits school as an institution; and whether critical feeling would change educational policy. Finally, educational psychologists could provide evidence-based means to teach critical feeling to students of all ages. This provides a distribution of tasks where communities determine the desired values. Philosophers examine the normative issues, such as the nature of values or the nature of understanding emotions. Philosophers therefore explore, based on the values of a community, the right things to do. Psychologists deliver empirical evidence for how to achieve the desired ends with the right means. They explore how to do things right. Finally, educators put the implementation of values through evidence-based strategies into practice. They teach people both what the right thing is and how to do it right. This procedure to achieve optimal outcomes applies to both critical thinking and critical feeling.

As a psychologist, I shall focus on the psychological aspects of critical feeling. However, I cannot write a book on evidence-based practices in the use of feelings without considering critical thinking, raising questions about values in science and in education, discussing the rationality of feelings, or asking how critical feeling could be implemented at home and at school. Despite my focus on psychological research, I shall develop the connections of the concept of critical feeling to the other members of the imaginary duck-hunting party. Philosophy and education, however, will only be discussed to the extent needed to embed or to apply the findings from psychology.

This approach has a positive side effect: If we embed empirical psychology in the philosophy of education, theory of science, and ethics, we get a more broadly supported psychological science than when psychologists work in isolation. Some colleagues in humanities tell me that most psychological studies are insipid and uninspiring. Often enough, psychologists cite nobody other than psychologists, which leaves their work uninformed by broader scholarship. It is a "psychological science illusion" to think we can conduct research in moral psychology without a background in moral philosophy; political psychology without political science; educational psychology without educational theory or history; empirical aesthetics without philosophical aesthetics; or cognitive science of religion without religious studies. Some scholars in the humanities conclude that psychology has nothing to offer to their field; an early example is George Dickie (1962), who claimed that empirical aesthetics has no relevance to art. One reason, to be discussed in more detail later, lies in the fact that psychologists examine supposedly universal laws of the mind when it might be more relevant to consider the historical and cultural context.

While I can understand the lack of enthusiasm in the humanities for some of the research that goes under the flag of psychological science, I think empirical studies in psychology – if embedded in an appropriate theoretical framework – have much to offer the humanities and arts (see Slingerland 2008). This is an emerging trend, as shown by new journal titles such as *The Review of Philosophy and Psychology* (founded 2010) and *Religion, Brain & Behavior* (founded 2011); edited books that bring together scholarship from philosophy, the arts, psychology, and neuroscience (e.g., Currie, Kieran, Meskin, and Moore 2014; Schellekens and Goldie 2011; Shimamura and Palmer 2012); and thematic issues of journals in the humanities, such as a special issue of the journal *Religion* on "Evolutionary Approaches to the Study of Religion." Some of my own work in the past few years has been aimed at embedding psychological findings in a wider theoretical context (Bullot and Reber 2013a; Reber 2008; Reber and Slingerland 2011; Reber and Unkelbach 2010). In this spirit, I will outline in rough strokes both the philosophical background in which the empirical studies relevant to critical feeling are situated and the implications of these observations for educational practice.

The book has two parts. The first part deals with the basics of critical feeling. Chapter 1 is dedicated to critical thinking. Critics of the critical thinking movement lament the absence of moral values as a criterion for good thinking. I therefore sketch arguments for how such values can be connected to critical thinking. This outline will prepare the ground for the discussion of similar problems when it comes to critical feeling. The chapter ends with ten reasons why critical thinking is not enough and why we need critical feeling as a complement. Before critical feeling can be introduced, we need to review the different kinds of feeling, and this is done in Chapter 2. The chapter ends with a discussion of the rationality of feelings, which is the foundation of the proficiencies that constitute critical feeling. Chapter 3 is the core chapter of this book in that it introduces critical feeling, defines its proficiencies and different strategies, delineates how it could serve values, and distinguishes critical feeling from other concepts, such as the rationality of emotion, emotional competence, emotional intelligence, positive psychology, and mindfulness.

The second part of the book, Chapters 4 to 10, will discuss the different domains in which critical feeling can be applied, such as well-being, skill learning, social interaction, business and politics, school, art, and religion and morality. When describing strategies of critical feeling, I rely on empirical evidence, mainly from psychology but sometimes also from sociology, political science, or history. Where there are gaps in empirical evidence, I discuss predictions derived from theory or from empirical evidence for a related phenomenon.

Woven into some chapters is a discussion of fundamental ideas relevant to critical feeling. The chapter on well-being discusses the notion that many desired states are by-products of actions performed for their own sake. Such states cannot be achieved strategically. The chapter about sensory and bodily feedback reviews evidence that every cognitive process is affectively colored – there is a feeling behind every thought. The ubiquity of feelings reveals the importance of making use of them through critical feeling. The chapter on business and politics touches critical theory – how could critical feeling be used to effect the emancipation of the disadvantaged and oppressed? This perspective complements perspectives seen in textbooks and marketing journals that provide recommendations on how businesspeople can persuade customers. The chapter on art discusses a recent framework for research on art appreciation that has deep consequences for how we understand feelings related to art. The final chapter asks how we could reverse disenchantment stemming from the progress of understanding the workings of nature. Such re-enchantment might be gained by reinvigorating literal belief in holy scriptures, as evangelical churches do (see Luhrmann 2012). Yet many people reject forms of re-enchantment that are based on ignoring the scientific worldview. Therefore, we have to ask which strategies help believers find a sense of awe and sanctity.

The chapters in Part II begin with a short introduction of a viewpoint – often derived from philosophy – that demarcates the values that will be considered. It follows a review of empirical findings about strategies we could use to optimize outcomes through the use of feelings. Each chapter ends with a short coda on the implementation of critical feeling for the domain covered in the respective chapter.

1 CRITICAL THINKING

It is a narrow mind that cannot look at subjects from various points of view.

(GEORGE ELIOT 1994/1871, P. 54)

Reasoning as a basis for judgment and decision making is a keystone of modern Western culture. Modern society aims to educate an intellectually mature citizenry that overcomes fallacies, biases, superstition, and adherence to unquestioned authority. One offshoot of this emphasis on reasoning is the critical thinking movement that emerged in the 1960s in the philosophy of education. This movement responded to the observation that even well-educated people possessed inadequate reasoning skills (Pritchard 2014). Philosophers argued that one objective of school and college education should be the training of critical thinking. Students should be able to form beliefs or to make decisions by proper reasoning. These proficiencies can be applied to the subjects taught at school and be transferred to everyday life (see Fisher 2011). Critical thinking goes beyond the reasoning abilities examined in cognitive psychology: It relies not on descriptions of how people actually think but on prescriptions for how they should think. Such prescriptions cannot be determined by empirical research because they derive from norms and values that are beyond scientific scrutiny; they are therefore often neglected in scientific discourse (see Wecker 2013 for an interesting discussion on prescriptive statements in education).

In this chapter, the main focus will be on the prescriptive part of critical thinking because critical feeling serves similar objectives to critical thinking. It is necessary to unveil the objectives of critical thinking and why it is insufficient to serve these purposes. Together with the next chapter (on the psychology of feelings), this discussion will set the stage to introduce critical feeling. In this chapter, I first consider critical thinking as a skill and examine its strengths before looking at how critical thinking may serve values. At the end of the chapter, I discuss the neglect of feelings in critical thinking and why critical thinking is not enough.

Critical thinking as a skill

Critical thinking has been defined as "correct assessing of statements" (Ennis 1962, p. 83) and as "reasonable, reflective thinking that is focused on deciding what to believe or do" (Fisher 2011, p. 4). Critical thinking is *thinking* because it utilizes reasoning capacities and abilities to decide what to believe and what to do. These reasoning capacities and abilities consist of accurate procedures (in the sense of methods, techniques, and application of rules) to scrutinize beliefs and optimize judgments and decisions. Critical thinking is *critical* because it involves careful and judicious reflection, analyzing and questioning the thinker's own assumptions. One may wonder how critical thinking differs from intelligence. The latter is a trait of a person that is assumed to be stable over time whereas critical thinking is an activity embedded in a situation. Intelligence is something people *have* whereas critical thinking is something people *do*.

Most philosophers have defined critical thinking in a narrow sense that does not take moral considerations into account. The decisive criterion for whether or not thinking is critical is logical coherence and the correspondence of one's premises with reality (Fisher 2011). The ideal critical thinker is one who is in command of reasoning skills that enable him/her to apply the laws of logic, to observe and assess facts and events in the environment, and to connect those facts and events with prior knowledge. Critical thinkers ideally exhibit certain proficiencies, such as grasping the meaning of a statement, finding contradictions, classifying observations, making inferences and judging their quality, conceiving and stating assumptions and alternatives, offering a well-organized or well-formulated line of reasoning, evaluating statements and chains of reasoning, and detecting problems and open questions (Ennis 1987; Noddings 2012). This kind of critical thinking could be in the service of both cognitive and strategic rationality. Robert De Sousa (1987) introduced this distinction to denote the difference between rationality as fitting mental representations to facts in the world and rationality as maximization of expected utility. *Cognitive* rationality aims at *truth*; *strategic* rationality aims at *utility*.

Critical thinking in terms of cognitive rationality uses the proficiencies proposed by Ennis to create an adequate representation of the state of the world in the mind of the observer. Truth of a claim essentially boils down to two criteria (Fisher 2011; Moore and Parker 2012). First, consistency: Is the set of propositions on which an argument is based consistent? If there is any contradiction in the set of propositions, the argument as a whole cannot be true. Consistency or coherence of propositions is therefore a derivative criterion for the justification of the truth of a statement as being true (Goldman 1986). Second, correspondence to reality: Does a set of beliefs correspond to facts in the outside world? If it corresponds only weakly with external facts, it is doubtful whether the argument as a whole is true, and we should not decide based on these beliefs.

Critical thinking in terms of strategic rationality aims to optimize decisions by trying to maximize personal utility. Although expected utility is often expressed in terms of monetary value, it could refer to any outcomes, goods, or inner states valued by a person.

Going beyond the mere use of appropriate reasoning skills, Paul and Elder (2002) distinguished critical thinking in the "weak" sense from critical thinking in the "strong" sense. The former is the use of proper reasoning *without* being able to take the perspective of the other side so that discussants are not able to challenge their own opinions. Critical thinking in the strong sense means that discussants can challenge their own opinions and reflect their own arguments. Similarly, some proponents of critical thinking have proposed neutrality of viewpoint in presenting arguments (Vandenberg 1983).

The strengths of critical thinking

Critical thinking has several advantages. By invoking rules of logic and evidence, critical thinking helps to achieve both cognitive and strategic rationality. Rules of critical thinking provide standards for best practice for exchanging arguments, where logic and evidence win against blunt attempts at attacking the person, appealing to fear, or building up a straw man to attack. People are forced to argue and act reflectively instead of impulsively (for the difference between reflective and impulsive modes of thought, see Strack and Deutsch 2004). Critical thinkers are supposedly able to arrive at better judgments and make better decisions because their thinking is less likely to be biased by sources that disrupt reasoning, such as passions, unfounded beliefs, or unquestioned authority. One might question whether even the best thinkers have always been independent of any authority. Yet one could imagine that such thinkers emancipate themselves from the educators they have listened to and that they develop the ability to distinguish accurate teachings from the inaccurate teachings they received during their youth.

Another reason why critical thinking is undisputed lies in the fact that coherent thinking – thinking logically – is a necessary condition for getting an argument right. Even if one accepts emotions, motives, and feelings as part of a good argument, one can hardly accept blatant contradictions (but see Nisbett 2003 for dialectical modes of thinking in

East Asian cultures). For example, it is not acceptable from a logical point of view that someone rejects abortion on the grounds that we do not have the right to kill but at the same time supports the death penalty, as many voters do (see Cook 1998; Jones, Cox, and Navarro-Rivera 2012). Although Christian church fathers such as St. Augustine and Thomas Aquinas defended the death penalty, it is nowadays theological common sense that these arguments contradict basic assumptions in theology, thus resolving the contradiction (Jones 2007). Logical coherence and the requirement that our judgments correspond to the facts in the outside world are necessary conditions for appropriate thinking.

Critical thinking in the strong sense goes further and considers that critical thinkers can take the perspective of others. Critical thinkers are expected to adhere to virtues that are held to be important in evaluating arguments such as impartiality, intellectual humility, and intellectual integrity (Paul and Elder 2002). *Impartial thinking* means that we take the perspective of an opponent and try to see the arguments in favor of the opposite position. As a further step, we may try to take the perspective of an impartial third party. If I have a conflict with a colleague at work, how might a noninvolved person who does not take sides see it? Such a position allows us to see the conflict from a neutral viewpoint and might allow us to weigh the arguments in a nonpartisan way. *Intellectual humility* is the virtue of knowing the limits of your own knowledge. I do not claim to know more than I indeed know and I am aware of the fact that my opinion could be influenced by egocentrism and prejudice. Finally, *intellectual integrity* leads us to recognize that we have to meet the same standards of thinking as we apply to others. We require others to think rigorously; we therefore should require the same rigor of thought from ourselves. It is certainly right to be an impartial, fair, and humble thinker who possesses a repertoire of correct and reliable reasoning skills. A human being who possesses these intellectual skills certainly has strength of character. However, a definition of critical thinking in the strong sense is not enough. Although it adds to the strength of critical thinking as a skill, virtues such as impartiality, intellectual humility, and intellectual integrity remain within the intellectual realm. Outside this realm, critical thinking is morally blind.

In addition, proponents of critical thinking assume that people who have acquired the competence to reason critically use this competence to act accordingly (Glaser 1942; see also Fisher 2011). This would require not only that critical thinkers in the strong sense possess the ability to take the perspective of the opposing or a third party but also that the consideration of others' viewpoints guides their action. Let us assume that I have easy work, and I see that a colleague has a higher workload than me. Taking his perspective tells me that he would appreciate it if I could lighten his burden. This reasoning should elicit a moral attitude concerning helping others that leads me to take on more work. If moral attitudes automatically elicited moral behavior (see Kristjánsson 2013 for a discussion) the outcomes of critical thinking in the strong sense would be sufficient to elicit moral action. Yet this is not the case. Consistent with observations that the link between attitudes and behavior is notoriously weak (see Ross and Nisbett 1991; Wicker 1969), it has been difficult to ascertain that moral beliefs lead to moral action. Behavior is not only determined by attitudes but also by perceived social pressure and the controllability of the situation, further weakening the attitude–behavior link (see Ajzen 2001). As moral attitudes do not automatically motivate moral behavior, we have to question whether critical thinking even in its strong sense achieves its purpose.

A person could therefore be perfectly capable of thinking critically in the strong sense but lack moral guidance from this ability. Let me illustrate this with an example: The owner of a paper mill may use her critical thinking skills for purposes such as outsmarting competitors, keeping employees' salaries low, and opposing laws against environmental pollution. One could object that a critical thinker who is not egocentric and takes the perspective of the other into account would not do these things. Nevertheless, we have to distinguish two levels of egocentrism: The first is egocentrism in thinking; the other is egocentrism in action. The owner of the paper factory may be perfectly able to overcome egocentrism in thinking by taking the perspective of her competitors, her employees, environmental activists, and the national legislators. She may present her arguments as if they came from a neutral viewpoint. However, she may use the outcomes of her thoughts to outsmart the other parties and hence act egoistically. In other words, she would possess all the reasoning skills that make up critical thinking in the strong sense, but she would use her skills to promote her own interests. Good critical thinkers do not necessarily act well.

This is exactly what philosopher Jane Roland Martin (1992) criticized when she elaborated on the definition of critical thinking, using experts on nuclear war as an example. When such experts discuss nuclear armament, they may use arguments that perfectly obey rules of reasoning, and they may even be able to take each other's perspective. However, such discussions often drift into debates about technicalities without considering moral issues, such as the possibility of the extinction of human life by nuclear war (Erickson, Klein, Daston, Lemov, Sturm, and Gordin 2013; see Kahn 1960 for an example of such a technical discussion). Martin's example of a skillful critical thinker was Wernher von Braun, who was a leading figure in the Third Reich's rocket program during World War II. However, Von Braun and his engineers apparently did not consider the fact that they served an immoral system or that they might prolong a war long lost. Critical thinking in the service of values does not isolate a given purpose – building a rocket or building nuclear arms – from the big picture. Virtuous thinkers need to consider the values they serve. While critical thinking as a skill helps in doing things right, critical thinking in the service of values asks first about the right thing to do.

Critical thinking in the service of values

I am going to present a sketch of arguments to improve the concept of critical thinking. This outline paves the way for similar arguments concerning critical feeling. The purpose of this section is to demarcate the key philosophical points on which the concept of critical thinking and later critical feeling will be founded. It is not the purpose to discuss each of these issues in detail; more thorough discussions are often presented in the literature cited in this section. The outline in this section remains short but will suffice to situate the empirical findings within the conceptual framework of critical feeling.

We start from the idea that psychologists can conduct value-free research in value-rich domains and we then proceed to the notion of value-laden practice. I endorse moral realism, not because I claim that it must be right but because it seems to be a fruitful starting point for the psychology of critical thinking. Moral realism has explanatory power regarding what happens in the real world because children do not grow up in a moral vacuum, and most people see their values as objective facts. Moral realism does not preclude value pluralism. Philosophers, psychologists, and educators alike are tempted to assume that there is one and only one right action in a given set of circumstances. Beyond some minimal moral standards that seem to be universal, I prefer to assume that situations afford more than one right action. In contrast to virtue ethics and positive psychology, which aim at character education, critical thinking aims to find an appropriate action in a given situation. Finally, mainstream psychology claims that basic psychological processes are the same for all human beings and therefore universal. However, the conditions that trigger such processes and the environments in which these processes are embedded differ widely. For example, what is appropriate thought and behavior in a certain situation differs across cultures (e.g., Nisbett 2003), social classes (Bourdieu 1984/1979), historical epochs (Elias 1969), and personal histories. We have to understand the personal history of an individual in order to decide what would be the best course of action when it comes to, for example, lending money. To enable such understanding, psychology needs to describe cognitive ecologies (Brunswik 1955, 1957; Reber and Unkelbach 2010) or to introduce psycho-historical frameworks (Bullot and Reber 2013a; see also Chapter 9) that put the psychological processes involved in critical thinking and critical feeling into context.

Value-free science

Within critical thinking, especially in science, there are so-called epistemic values. For example, we try to be unbiased in the collection of data that help us to decide whether an assumption holds true – this is a value inherent to scientific practice. Given that science aims to find truth, epistemic values are justified. Science is supposed to be neutral regarding nonepistemic values, such as instrumental, political, social, aesthetic, moral, or religious ones. The concept of value freedom was introduced by Max Weber (1949/1917) and states that scientists who do research should proceed from a neutral viewpoint. Although Paul and Elder's impartiality and Weber's value freedom look alike, there is an important difference. Whereas Paul and Elder address every person who thinks, Weber's principle of value freedom encompasses only scientific research. However, there is a crucial distinction between scientists examining thinking and people who use critical thinking in education and in their daily life.

Scientists often discuss applications of their research for everyday life. For example, many marketing researchers describe applications of their research from the viewpoint of the marketer, who tries to persuade an audience of a product's desirability (but see Cialdini 2006). Does this discussion of applications of research outcomes not contradict the value freedom of science? Not necessarily. Morton White (1965) discussed a common fallacy among historians who think that, when researchers conduct their studies from a certain viewpoint, they have to endorse it. We should not confuse looking at a matter from a certain angle with endorsing this view. White noted that a historian may discuss the American Civil War from the perspective of the Confederate states without having to endorse slavery. Conditional statements clarify that a historian does not necessarily endorse a viewpoint. In the case of the American Civil War, a scholar could state, "If one took the viewpoint of the Southern states, it would follow that …" By making conditional statements, scientists are able to conduct impartial research despite taking a viewpoint.

That means that the scientist can take a viewpoint from which to examine an issue without accepting this viewpoint (see Schurz 2013;

White 1965). For example, a psychologist may examine how suicide bombers tick without having to endorse suicide bombing. In fact, most researchers who conduct research on this topic want to understand the mind of a suicide bomber in order to prevent future terrorist attacks (Atran 2006; Kruglanski, Chen, Dechesne, Fishman, and Orehek 2009). Similarly, when marketing researchers describe implications of their research from the viewpoint of business, the use of conditional statements should indicate that the applications of their research are discussed under the assumption that one takes the standpoint of the marketer. This would open up research to discussion from the standpoint of consumers, as for example Cialdini (2006) does. Unfortunately, the viewpoints of psychologists too often remain implicit, and only rarely do psychologists discuss their research in the light of more than one normative viewpoint. As an overwhelming majority of psychologists endorse liberal political values, recommendations are often given from only this perspective (Duarte, Crawford, Stern, Haidt, Jussim, and Tetlock 2015). Duarte et al. propose more political diversity among psychology faculty. Although this would solve some of the problems, political screening of job candidates to increase political diversity seems both unfeasible and undesirable. Instead, psychologists have to learn to use conditional statements to disclose the values they address.

However, just using conditional statements, as Schurz (2013) and White (1965) propose, would be insufficient. If a marketing researcher states that, in order for sales to increase, consumers have to be exposed to a product repeatedly (the well-known *mere exposure effect*; see Bornstein 1989; Zajonc 1968), readers do not necessarily know what the alternative values are, and, even if they know them, the values often do not readily come to mind. Therefore, scientists have to try to come up with at least the values that are relevant to the discussion. In the case of marketing, scientists should discuss such ends as maximizing sales, providing consumers with the products they need, protecting consumers from undue influence, minimizing social costs, and maintaining a clean environment.

Value-laden practice

While the aim of science is to conduct value-free research, the aim of education is to transmit values and implement them. Critical thinking serves the purpose of implementing values in action. When educators want critical thinking to serve values, they have to make clear which values they are going to endorse and teach.

A value is a prescription for what to do (Rokeach 1973). Various value systems have been proposed. The first to be used broadly was established by Eduard Spranger (1928/1914) and later taken up by Allport, Vernon, and Lindzey (1960), and Triandis and Gelfand (1998). Spranger distinguished six value domains: knowledge, economic values, aesthetic values, living together with others, power, and meaning. Later, Rokeach (1973) developed a classification of 18 terminal and 18 instrumental values. Terminal values refer to the purposes of life and include, among others, true friendship, happiness, freedom, wisdom, a world of beauty, and an exciting life. Instrumental values refer to desirable attributes of behavior; examples are ambition, love, courage, honesty, independence, obedience, and forgiveness. Finally, Schwartz (1992) tested a system of universal values and found that they have similar content and structure across different countries and cultures. He classified values under primary motivational types. In this system, the motivational type *spirituality*, for example, subsumes the values of *a spiritual life, meaning in life, inner harmony*, and *detachment*. For the purpose of this book, we do not need a sophisticated classification of values.[1]

The essential point is that critical thinking serves values and therefore goes beyond mere skills. When my examples are inspired by Spranger's classification of values, it is due to the simplicity of his system. Later research may connect critical thinking and critical feeling with more complex value systems.

As discussed earlier, critical thinking does not only serve values but also includes values itself, such as impartiality, adherence to the rules of logic (instead of personal interest) when assessing a result, and intellectual humility. Indeed, the capacity to reason rationally comes close to prudence, one of the cardinal virtues. A virtue is the disposition to act in accordance with a desirable trait or value, such as honesty, courage, or temperance. However, a given virtue cannot be seen in isolation; it is not sufficient to demonstrate one virtue to the exclusion of all others (see Annas 2011 for a detailed discussion). Virtuous action requires the consideration of the situation as a whole, including an understanding of the moral implications; otherwise, critical thinking would be a mere skill. According to Annas, an action is not virtuous if done for the wrong reasons or if done mindlessly, without proper understanding of why it is necessary to employ a virtue in a given situation. In the example introduced above, the owner of the paper mill would lack critical thinking in the service of values if she had not taken the perspective of the other parties or of the environment into account. In contrast, as I shall discuss later, when it comes to critical feeling, there are situations where we can trust our feelings without having to fully understand the situation, as such an understanding follows from the feeling.

In short, value-laden practice means that people who apply critical thinking in their everyday life have to decide which value to endorse and to act on. In order to serve values, critical thinking needs to be considered in the context of the whole situation – one cannot pursue one value at the cost of more important ones. Another necessary condition is that critical thinking needs to meet minimal moral standards. Such moral standards cannot come from within; they come from a source outside the person.

Value realism

Psychologists, it seems, often tailor the philosophical foundations of their research in accordance with their needs. In moral psychology, the easiest and therefore predominant solution is *moral internalism*, which denotes the assumption that humans use their mental capacities to construct moral norms. Internalism is a convenient solution because psychologists do not need to make assumptions that are outside their realm of expertise. Psychologists often endorse what is called *emotivism*, as Brinkmann (2011) illustrates. In this view, moral values are constructed as a result of procedures of the mind, and decision makers feel whether or not a value is right (Eisenberg 2000; Hoffman 2001). However, such an internalist view of moral values risks being relativistic and does not require that a person is accountable to anybody except their own conscience.

A solution to the problem of relativism and lack of accountability is moral realism. Moral realism assumes that values are "out there." The normative aspect of moral realism may be disputed, but, descriptively, moral realism is real. Values are not the outcome of deliberation but exist before minds can think about moral problems. Children grow up in a culture where moral values already exist (e.g., Bellah, Madsen, Sullivan, Swidler, and Tipton 1985; Rakoczy, Warneken, and Tomasello 2008; Selznick 1992). Cultures result in mindsets that define which values are important and fluent (see Oyserman 2011). It is an illusion to think that moral action is the result of individual development of the inner workings of the mind (see Brinkmann 2011 for a thorough discussion). Children are brought up to follow the norms and conventions of a given community before they are able to decide for themselves how to act appropriately in a given situation. Such inculcation of values is the purpose of education. The desire to enhance the education of American students was the origin of the critical thinking movement. Education is aimed at enabling people to lead a good life within the natural and social environment in which they live. School has always been in the service of some purpose, such as educating students to become faithful members of the church, loyal citizens of the state, or valuable workers in the economy (Kvale 2003; Olson 2003). Later construction of values presumably originates in the values learned at home and at school.

Such a realist account of moral values counters the well-known instrumental and procedural theories of moral judgment. Instrumental or utilitarian theories assume that right and wrong depend on the greatest happiness of the greatest number (in Bentham 1988/1776, classical formulation). People derive morally appropriate action by computing the greatest subjective utility for themselves, their community, or society at large. Procedural or deontological theories assume the existence of rules that help us to derive the right action in a given situation; the Kantian categorical imperative ("act only according to that maxim through which you can at the same time will that it becomes a universal law" Kant 2011/1785, p. 34) is one such rule. Despite their differences, both instrumental and procedural theories assume that moral judgments are the result of mental procedures in order to find the right action in a given situation. However, it is often too complicated to calculate the expected utility of an action, as an instrumental account would require (see Simon 1956), and decision makers hardly ever go through the workings of the Kantian categorical imperative, as procedural accounts would presuppose (see Brinkmann 2011). Even if decision makers went through all the necessary procedures and computations, it may be questioned – to say the least – whether such calculations would lead to optimal moral outcomes. Note that realist accounts do not have to deny the role of understanding the moral implications of situations, which is a prerequisite for arriving at good decisions according to instrumental, procedural, and virtue theories. Good educators are not satisfied with just inculcating the values of their community but aim at their students' understanding of the value-related questions inherent to the situations they encounter.

Based on work by MacIntyre (1985), Rouse (2002), and Taylor (1989), Brinkmann (2011) defends a view of morality based on practices. Communities around the world build up and execute sets of actions that are derived from uncontested norms and values. For the members of a community, the values are given; they are affordances that can be directly perceived (Gibson 1979). Although claims that moral values can be perceived in the same way as a physical object are controversial (see Audi 2013 for a modern defense of such a view; Mackie 1977 for a critique of the resulting moral realism), I assume that moral values can in principle be recognized or at least inferred by our feelings. In contrast to an emotivist account of moral judgment, moral value is not derived from feelings; these are just indicators of an objectively existing value. Feelings have to be trained properly in order to accurately assess whether an action is right. I shall discuss how practices could result in people being able to assess the morality of an action in Chapters 3 and 10. Here, it suffices to state that feelings do not constitute a moral value but serve as indicators of whether actions follow its lead.

To sum up, an externalist approach to morality is in better agreement with educational practice than internalist views, and therefore suits the needs of critical thinking and critical feeling. Schools implement norms of society, and children are exposed to the values of the community from an early age. One challenge for moral externalism is the plurality of values, one of the hallmarks of democratic societies in the West. However, different communities, while they converge on some foundational values, develop different practices that lead to variability in values and therefore to value pluralism.

Value pluralism

Nel Noddings (2003) argued that, if there were no individual differences in personality characteristics, "we could seek and recommend one best way of raising all children" (p. 181). The hidden assumption behind this belief in finding one best way to educate children is that we educate them to adhere to the same set of values and to act accordingly. As soon as we acknowledge that we may convey different values to our children, there is no longer *one* best way to educate them, even if personality differences were minimal. This point is important because reading the literature reveals that many psychologists think like Noddings; she simply made this point explicit. Psychologists lack Noddings' care to spell out the values they start from; they seem to assume that there is one best way to do things, as practical recommendations in journals ranging from marketing to special-needs education testify. Such recommendations are often derived from hidden values favored by the authors.

Value pluralism, together with the notion that moral attitudes are built on practices, seems to preclude universal values and therefore to support relativism. However, there seem to be at least some universal values, based on both religious and secular foundations (see Brinkmann 2011 for a thorough discussion). The Universal Declaration of Human Rights by the United Nations is one attempt at defining and enforcing universal values on a secular basis. Although practices vastly differ, they seem to converge on some basic values that are common to virtually all moral systems. For example, to kill people without justification or excuse seems to be universally abhorred (Mikhail 2009). With this minimal definition,

I exclude controversial issues such as abortion, doctoral-assisted suicide, killing soldiers in war, and death penalty, despite the fact that I have clear personal convictions on each of these issues.

Endorsing the plurality of values (see Berlin 1969) – in contrast to the value universalism characteristic of positive psychology (e.g., Peterson and Seligman 2004) – allows us to look at critical thinking from alternative perspectives. For example, distributional justice can be examined from the perspective of performance orientation (who deserves the funds) or from the perspective of need orientation (who needs the funds; see Forsyth 2009). In line with Brinkmann, I start with the assumption that there are practices that demarcate the appropriate values and actions in a given community. While many values are context-dependent, some practices converge on similar values across communities; the core of such values is universal and can be seen as foundational. Although there are both religious and secular foundations of such minimal values such as the prohibition of killing, I am not going to discuss these foundations further. Most importantly, we should be aware that critical thinking most often involves a plurality of values, and we have to clarify what these values are.

Value pluralism challenges character education and therefore dispositionism because there is often more than one right action in a given situation. Instead of instilling stable traits that guide action invariably across situations, a more fruitful approach to educate for critical thinking might include flexible responses, depending on the situation. This means educators are supposed to teach people to think and act appropriately in a given situation.

Dispositionism versus situationism

In recent years, some theorists and researchers, especially in positive psychology, have begun to rely on Aristotelian virtue ethics to ground their research on a moral foundation (see Kristjánsson 2013). As noted earlier, virtue is defined as the disposition to act in accordance with a given value, such as bravery, justice, or generosity. Virtues were seen as the building blocks of character, or rather as a disposition to act in accordance with a set of overarching values. This presupposes that people possess character traits that remain stable over time. If a woman is generous, she is generous in situations where generosity is relevant. If a soldier is brave, he is brave in situations where bravery is relevant. However, we have already seen above how attitude and behavior are only weakly correlated (Mischel and Shoda 1995; Ross and Nisbett 1991; Wicker 1969). Some theorists go as far as to claim that the conception of character traits is empirically inadequate (Doris 2002; Harman 1999). Still others observe critically that character educators seem to see virtue as a possession; these theorists doubt that such stable inclinations can be taught at all (see Noddings 2003). A situationist account captures what critical thinking is about more accurately. Indeed, Annas (2011; see also Hursthouse 1999) makes clear that virtuous action requires practical reasoning in order to choose the virtue in a given situation. Likewise, Confucian ethics offers strategies not only to expand character traits over time but also to manage a variety of situational forces (Slingerland 2011). For example, lying is morally bad, but, when a family hid their Jewish neighbor from the Nazis, it was, of course, appropriate to lie to a Gestapo officer who inquired about the whereabouts of their neighbor. Virtues have to be applied flexibly, which means that it might be more fruitful to ask about the right action in a certain situation than about the right dispositions educators should instill in children. A critical thinker knows the right course of action in a given situation.

A dispositionist might argue that critical thinking is about building a critical, thoughtful character by teaching the right actions in situations that people might encounter in their life. First and foremost, however, critical thinking is about finding and applying appropriate arguments in a given situation. Teachers provide students with the know-how of proper reasoning to arrive at the right arguments. Only when a student applies this knowledge regularly can she be said to be a critical thinker. However, this trait is an incidental outcome of finding the right arguments; the regular application of critical thinking determines the trait, and not the trait the regular application of critical thinking. In a similar vein, a person has the virtue of being generous because she has repeatedly helped people by giving money even when she was short of money herself; she does not give money because she is generous. I am advocating a situationist account of performing the right action that does not entail the dispositionism in virtue ethics. Reliable behavior in a given situation, including virtuous acts, is an incidental outcome of a person's learning history, not a character trait.

Universalism versus contextualism

Another characteristic of mainstream psychological research is its assumption of universal laws of the brain and mind that guide thought, feeling, and behavior. Such universalism pervades psychology and neuroscience, for example from laws of vision to laws of art appreciation. While laws of vision at a molecular level certainly apply to humans universally (see Palmer 1999), general laws of art appreciation are hotly disputed. While some theorists who adhere to universalism have claimed that such laws exist (e.g., Ramachandran and Hirstein 1999; Zeki 1999), theorists who advocate contextualism have rejected this view. Contextualists argue that art appreciation depends on the history of the creation of an artwork, something that cannot be captured by laws of the brain or mind (Bullot and Reber 2013a; Dickie 1962; Hyman 2006; see Chapter 9 for a detailed discussion).

Correspondingly, psychologists look at cognitive heuristics and biases as universal mechanisms. Early on, the key figures in this field admitted that such heuristics could be ecologically valid but they did not offer an analysis of when heuristics are reliable and when they lead to bias. Many psychologists in the heuristics and biases tradition therefore saw intuition as faulty and biased (see Kahneman and Klein 2009). One of the most prominent critics of the heuristics and biases tradition did not criticize the implicit universalism of the biases but claimed the universal adaptiveness of heuristics (e.g., Gigerenzer, Todd, and ABC Research Group 1999). What we need is an analysis of the cognitive ecology in which people live in order to find out whether a certain heuristic is adaptive or leads to bias in a given situation (see Fiedler 2013).

Finally, psychologists tend to see morality and the underlying cognitive processes and feelings as universal. Whether they adhere to Kantian moral psychology, as Kohlberg (1981) did, or to virtue ethics, like the positive psychology movement (see Kristjánsson 2013), psychologists start their moral psychology from the assumption that people the world over are ruled by the same laws of mind and brain. As I outlined above, some moral values may be universal, such as the prohibition to kill, and abhorrence of killing may be based on universal processes of the mind. However, most moral values are bound to their community, and their interpretation depends on the social and institutional context.

The alternative to universalism in perception, thought, and moral behavior is contextualism, which comes in at least three forms: indigenous psychologies, psychological ecology, and psycho-historical theories. We may advocate that psychology is not a unitary enterprise but includes various psychologies, as proposed by the indigenous psychologies movement (Allwood 2011; Kim and Berry 1993). While I sympathize with the movement's aim to break the monopoly and hegemony of mainstream Western psychology, it mostly deals with higher-order processes and therefore does not distinguish between universal mechanisms of the mind that are inherent to human nature and their triggers determined by human culture. We need a more careful analysis of the relationship between natural and cultural determinants of thought, feeling, and action.

Such a more fine-grained analysis may come from a psychological ecology that analyzes the appropriateness of mental processes in different biological and cultural environments (see Cosmides and Tooby 2013; Nisbett 2003). Reber and Unkelbach (2010) provided such an analysis of the phenomenon that people are more likely to judge a statement as being true when they have heard the statement before. This phenomenon is partially caused by the fact that individuals can more easily process such statements, and statements are more likely to be judged as true when they can be processed easily (Reber and Schwarz 1999; Unkelbach and Stahl 2009). This mechanism is adaptive when people are in an environment where most statements are true, but maladaptive when they are in a manipulative environment, such as a totalitarian political system that indoctrinates its population with propaganda. Although not outlined in this book, similar ecologies could be delineated for perception (Brunswik 1956; Rosch 1996), desires (Rosch 1996), the validity of heuristics (Fiedler 2013), and moral reasoning (Dewey 2012/1922; Hertzke 1998). Bronfenbrenner (1979) provided a classification of ecological systems according to the proximity of the system to the person. In terms of Bronfenbrenner, we shall deal with microsystems (activities, roles, and interpersonal relations experienced by individuals in their immediate environmental setting), but critical thinking and critical feeling could certainly be used to improve mesosystems, which refer to interactions of two or more settings in which the individual participates, and macrosystems, which denote characteristics of institutions at the cultural level, for example the German versus the US high school system.

Instead of analyzing the appropriateness of mental processes and actions in given environments, as in a psychologically inspired ecology, the psycho-historical approach assumes that historical understanding is a necessary component to assess how adequate a thought, a feeling, or an action is. An example of such a psycho-historical approach, to be discussed in more detail in Chapter 9, is the psycho-historical framework for the research on art appreciation introduced by Bullot and Reber (2013a).

Critical thinking in the service of values: summary

Let us bring the threads together. While scientific research can be value free, life is value laden. That is why the research question often has moral implications. In order to situate critical thinking – and later critical feeling – we assume value realism because people grow up within communities that transmit values from generation to generation. Some values seem to be ubiquitous – for example, the prohibition on killing or causing suffering. Regardless of whether a value is global or local in scope, people experience them as real and not as inner mental or social constructions. Despite value realism, different values exist, mainly as

a consequence of the existence of different practices across communities and groups. Value plurality has two consequences. First, critical
thinking aims to find an appropriate action in a given situation instead
of educating character; there often is more than one right action in a
situation, and thinkers have to respond flexibly. Second, we assume that
critical thinking does not follow universal laws of the mind but depends
on context. Only when we know the values within a given situation
can we make sure that the universal processes underlying reasoning are
the right ones to apply. There is no "one-size-fits-all" kind of critical
thinking.

Now that we have outlined some basic tenets of critical thinking
embedded in values, we can address critical thinking's main weakness,
which lies in the neglect of feelings.

Critical thinking and feelings

Feelings are only rarely mentioned in the philosophical literature on critical thinking. David Hitchcock, for example, mentioned that we "have
to rely on our instincts, on authority, on emotion, and so forth. This
means that you should receive some practice in the rational assessment
of such guides to belief" (Hitchcock 1983, p. 8). However, Hitchcock did
not further elaborate on emotions or instincts, and he discussed reliance
on authority only briefly. There are exceptions, such as Lipman (2003),
who advocates the teaching of an emotion vocabulary as part of critical
thinking education, and Lafortune and Robertson (2006), who reflect on
how critical thinking might help us to understand our emotions and how
emotions might serve as an input in critical thinking. However, the tenor
in works on critical thinking is that you should ensure that your judgments and decisions are not influenced by feelings. Moore and Parker
(2012) devoted ten pages of their book *Critical Thinking* to fallacies that
involve appeals to emotion and provided detailed examples. Let us discuss arguments from outrage and scare tactics as they play a role in our
later discussion on critical feeling.

Argument from outrage can be illustrated with the example of
gay marriage. Supporters of gay marriage may put on an angry expression and exclaim that they are outraged at the prospect of fundamentalists looking into what people do in their bedrooms. Opponents of gay
marriage may state that they are outraged at homosexuals demanding
"special rights" and violating basic tenets of religion. In a face-to-face
discussion, I may be so impressed by this outrage that I forget to examine
the facts and acquiesce to the argument of the outraged other.

Scare tactics include threats or appeal to harmful consequences. For example, politicians sometimes paint in the darkest colors the dire consequences for the jobs and earnings of the middle and lower classes if taxes were to be raised for the rich. This is done to persuade voters to oppose a tax increase. Another example from personal communication includes simple threat. A popular tactic to prevent a discussion about a disliked topic is to threaten that bringing up this topic will have nasty consequences. Often the discussion immediately stops, not because the person who brought up the topic thinks that she is wrong but because she fears the repercussions if she insists on continuing to speak about it.

Even proponents of critical thinking in the strong sense do not have much good to say about emotions and feelings as factors that influence our thinking (Paul and Elder 2002). In their view, emotions and motivations (Paul and Elder talk of "wants") do not correct themselves. According to proponents of critical thinking, the only way to prevent undue influence by emotions is through reasoning.

This suppression of feeling or its subordination under the orbit of thinking is typical of the tradition of Western thinking. Feelings, emotions, and drives were seen as the animal side of human nature that had to be eradicated, a tradition that goes at least as far back as Plato's chariot allegory, where the charioteer has to control two horses, especially the black one, which is related to passions that distract from higher goals (see Hackforth 1972). That emotion is inferior to reason is deeply rooted in the metaphors of Western languages. In their seminal book *Metaphors We Live By*, George Lakoff and Mark Johnson document how people use spatial metaphors to express the idea that emotion is inferior to reason; for example, "The discussion *fell to the emotional* level, but I *raised* it back *up to the rational* plane" (Lakoff and Johnson 1980, p. 17, italics in the original). Not incidentally, these authors found similar spatial metaphors for moral judgments. There exists a correspondence of *up* for virtue and *down* for depravity. Indeed, the bottom line in the critical thinking tradition has been that decision makers can only arrive at accurate moral judgments when they reason properly; feelings are epiphenomenal at best and harmful at worst.

This lack of feeling in critical thinking has been criticized by Lafortune and Robertson (2006) and Martin (1992). According to Martin, critical thinkers are often distanced spectators of what is going on in the world without caring for the subject of their thought. Showing love, care, concern, and commitment would involve feelings; critical thinking is not enough.

Why critical thinking is not enough

We all know of examples where everything happened in accordance with reason, the protagonists showed the proficiencies of critical thinking listed by Ennis (1962), but, nevertheless, their arguments and actions felt wrong. Let us look at an example.

Adolf Sauerland, a father of three children and former mayor of the city of Duisburg in Germany, wanted to lift his hometown from a dozy city with dated industry to a modern center of entertainment. Hence, an offer to host the Love Parade came along just at the right time. Plans were made to channel the hundreds of thousands of people through the city and through a tunnel to a large field that was intended to be the center of the parade. The city administrators were so enthusiastic about the opportunity that they wanted to realize the event at any price. However, the price turned out to be too high: Thousands of people pressed into the tunnel, and panic broke out. Twenty-one participants of the Love Parade died, more than 500 were injured, and many more were traumatized. This was a horrible event, not least for Mayor Sauerland. How should he react? Should he take the responsibility and resign? From his standpoint, he did not bear any legal responsibility for the disaster because he was not involved in the planning and safety procedures of the event. According to the law, he should be viewed innocent until proven guilty; and, indeed, even at the time of writing, more than four years after the event, his juridical guilt has still not been proven. The situation was complicated by the fact that, if he had decided to step down, he would have lost his whole pension; he could only claim his retirement pension if he was voted out of office. If he apologized for the horrible outcome of the event, he would indirectly admit that he was guilty. He therefore said that he "deplored" that this disaster had happened, without admitting any personal responsibility. From the viewpoint of critical thinking, this strategy is fine and maybe the only viable possibility. However, from the public and especially from the families of the victims, the mayor's reaction earned bitter criticism because they felt that he did not take them seriously. Protests erupted, and even politicians from Sauerland's own party did not want to be seen with him. He became an outcast in his own city, even though he had acted according to the law. About one and a half years after the disastrous Love Parade, a referendum was held in the city of Duisburg and Mayor Sauerland was voted out of office. He lost his reputation, but he could save his pension.[2] This is only one of many examples where people have acted rationally yet been criticized for their behavior. The common denominator of such examples is that the action in question seems reasonable but looks insensitive and cold. Such examples show that critical thinking is not enough. There are at least ten reasons why critical thinking alone is deficient.

First, there are arguments that can rarely be solved by logic and evidence alone – for example, disputes over values (see Weber 1949/1917), moral disagreements (Doris and Stich 2005), and contradictions between experiential goals (Hsee and Hastie 2006). Is capital punishment justified? Should abortion be a legal option? What about immigration? Other decisions are at least partly based on feelings – for example, "Do I want to marry this person?" or "What would I like to eat for lunch?" Rational decision makers encounter limits as soon as a course of action is based on values or on personal preferences. It is difficult to find the right answers using critical thinking alone.

In line with critical thinking, some arguments derived from values are amenable to logical scrutiny or empirical test. I discussed above the case where a pro-life activist contradicts her own logic if she argues that she is against abortion because she is against the idea that humans can take the lives of other humans, but at the same time endorses capital punishment. If a conservative politician argued against adoption rights for gay couples, reasoning that the adopted children would be harmed, he would have to present evidence for his argument (see Kendler 2006). When arguments are logically consistent and built on verifiable claims about consequences, we can achieve an unequivocal solution if people agree on the desirability of the consequences. In our example of adoption rights for gay couples, the answer would depend solely on the evidence if everybody agreed that harm to children should be the crucial factor. If children were harmed, no adoption rights should be granted. If there were no harm, nothing would speak against adoption rights.

Yet how do we assess these moral propositions if the pro-life activist is consistent in her logic and if the conservative politician argues on the basis of family values instead of consequences that can be assessed by empirical research? Although critical thinking constrains the ways opponents can argue, it rarely leads to unequivocal solutions because values based on religion or social norms come into play. People educated to adhere to religious or social norms develop moral views that – if violated – may lead to negative feelings such as outrage or fear.

The major task for critical feeling is to monitor the sources of such feelings and check whether they are appropriate. From this perspective, it is wrong to argue against abortion, for example, out of fear of sanctions; it would be justified to argue against abortion based on outrage at killing people, or from a feeling of awe caused by the sanctity of life. This religious argument is subjective and cannot be derived logically from premises. "Justified to argue" therefore does not mean that the argument is accurate – it just means that the feeling pertains to the argument. In the same vein, it would be wrong to be in favor of abortion to please one's liberal friends but justified to argue in favor of abortion based on a sense of outrage about other people making decisions concerning an individual woman's pregnancy. Again, outrage is a feeling genuinely tied to the argument and not to issues outside the argument. The feeling tells us something about the importance of the attitude. There are feelings that are justified and feelings that are as wrong as illogical arguments. Like critical thinking, critical feeling does not lead to unequivocal solutions to an issue, but it further constrains the scope of justified arguments.

Second, and related to finding the right answers, McPeck (1981) noted that one skill critical thinkers should possess is asking the right questions. Although reasoning certainly helps to avoid unjustified questions, asking the right question may depend on feelings that guide our attention. There are questions we would never ask without the guidance of our feelings. For example, fear is a signal of danger. Whenever we feel fear whose justification is doubted, we should ask ourselves what the danger is. This is the right question to ask when the source of the fear is not obvious; just suppressing the feeling would be fatal when danger is imminent. In conclusion, there are questions that only come up when we take our feelings seriously.

Third, research has shown that thinkers can deliberate too much. Spontaneous decisions may be more satisfying in the long term than decisions made after deliberation (e.g., Wilson, Lisle, Schooler, Hodges, Klaaren, and Lafleur 1993; see Newell and Shanks 2014 for a review of findings and a critique). These findings contradict the notion that more thinking leads to better outcomes, for example better information or better decisions. It seems that we need a criterion regarding when to stop. As it would be difficult to establish such a criterion on logical grounds (see Langer 1994), feelings may well play a role in creating stop rules. Martin, Ward, Achee, and Wyer (1993) have shown, for example, that people in a good mood persist longer when asked to collect information as long as it is fun than when required to collect information until they know enough about the topic. People in a negative mood, on the other hand, persist longer when required to collect information until they know enough than when told to collect information for as long as they enjoy doing so. This finding suggests that stop rules can be built on feelings instead of reasoning.

Fourth, psychologists have observed that, where there is thought, there is feeling. It is an illusion to think that we can separate thought and feeling, as would be the ideal from the point of view of a rational thinker. For example, the fact that a thought is fast or slow, easy or difficult has by itself an affective quality, as we shall see in the next chapter. Moreover, moods serve as backgrounds for our thoughts. Some thoughts influence the quality of our moods and some moods influence what we think and how we think (see Schwarz and Clore 2007). In Chapter 5, I defend the claim that all cognitive activity is accompanied by feelings and that feelings are more than a mere epiphenomenon. They turn out to be crucial in skill acquisition.

Fifth, critical thinkers can be completely detached and disinterested, like Mr. Casaubon in *Middlemarch* (Eliot 1994/1871). Martin (1992) used this example to demonstrate that we would wish people to care for their subject and that a distanced critical thinker disinterested in his subject, like Mr. Casaubon, differs from a critical thinker who cares about the subject he examines. Moreover, the distance critical thinking provides prevents a thinker from getting involved in the subject. Martin (1992) described examples of writers and professors whose ability to think critically allowed them to circumvent getting involved with the subject, in one case the oppression of black people and in another the rape of a student. Critical thinking in these cases kept feelings at bay where it would have been appropriate to let feelings guide thoughts and actions, from the standpoints of both the emancipation of the oppressed and compassion with a victim.

Sixth, if critical thinking were sufficient, it would not matter whether a person were a happy critical thinker or a grumpy critical thinker. However, this difference matters a lot. Gracian (1991/1653), a Spanish Jesuit, wrote in his book *The Art of Worldly Wisdom* that we should eschew unhappy company because misery is contagious. Modern research supports the notion of mood contagion (Neumann and Strack 2000). In addition, people who experience positive emotions on a regular basis enjoy a broader outlook that helps them to build psychological resources (Fredrickson 2013). Such people are more resilient and more skillful, have more positive social relationships, and receive more social support. These positive attributes feed back into the experience of positive emotions, completing the circle postulated in Fredrickson's broaden-and-build hypothesis (see Chapter 4). It might be better to be a good critical thinker than to be a bad critical thinker in order to find more adaptive responses to problems that can be solved through reasoning. However, functioning in an environment depends on resources that go beyond reasoning, and these resources depend on the experience of positive emotions. Critical thinking may make us smart;

positive emotions make us more social, more interested, and more curious, which leads to explorative behaviors that make us even smarter.

Seventh, human beings are masters at tailoring rational arguments in order to justify a decision they have already taken. People think that they weigh moral options, take a decision, and then act. Often enough, however, people act and then try to find post-hoc justifications for why they acted as they did (Haidt 2001) in order to alleviate threat to their moral self (Shalvi, Gino, Barkan, and Ayal 2015). Part of the problem seems to be the lack of transparency of our mental processes (Carruthers 2011); that is, we often do not know why we did what we did. It seems that people first decide spontaneously on the basis of their feelings and then try to find rational reasons for their actions after the fact (see also Mercier and Sperber 2011). Such post-hoc rationalization contradicts the tenets of critical thinking. Ironically, it has been shown that more intelligent people who presumably possess superior reasoning abilities are better at constructing arguments in favor of the side they prefer a priori (Perkins, Farady, and Bushey 1991). Instead of avoiding error, critical thinkers presumably misuse their superior skills to justify their feeling-based decisions.

Eighth, one reason for post-hoc reasoning may lie in the fact that people rationalize actions after having followed natural needs and impulses. The best-known classification of needs stems from Maslow (1943) who distinguished five levels within a hierarchy that ranges from basic needs essential for survival at the bottom to self-actualization at the top. Maslow assumed that when needs lower in the hierarchy are satisfied people strive for the next higher class of needs. Deci and Ryan (1985; Ryan and Deci 2000) introduced a more modern and empirically better tested classification of needs within their self-determination theory. They distinguished three needs – competence, autonomy, and relatedness – whose fulfillment promotes well-being and a sense of agency, which are at the heart of intrinsic motivation. Deci and Ryan followed Maslow in that they claimed that these needs are based on natural inclination. It is not important for the sake of the present argument what these natural needs are. However, if we assume that such natural needs and impulses exist, we have to ask how people handle them.

Critical thinkers may see them either as necessary for survival or as nuisances that distract individuals from more important tasks. Of course, food and safety needs are essential, and critical thinking has to follow them up. In the end, success in our activities serves to cover these needs. Hence, we need to employ strategic rationality in order to maximize expected utility when trying to satisfy those needs. Other needs and impulses are seen as nuisances. For example, the need for recognition – included in Maslow's esteem needs – may shroud the sense of impartiality that is a prerequisite of critical thinking; the pleasure of drinking that glass of wine may obscure the grim fact that we should abstain from anything that impairs our ability to drive home; the impulse of yelling at a workmate may spoil a relationship instrumental for further progress in a project; the impulse to watch the news on the Internet impedes progress on the work that needs to be done. The way critical thinking deals with such nuisances is to dismiss human nature and put reason in its place. As already mentioned in the Introduction, I pursue another path in this book, one drawn by Confucius some 2500 years ago (see Slingerland 2003a, 2003b). Instead of denying human nature and therefore needs, desires, and impulses, Confucius proposed refinement of the "native substance" (Slingerland 2003a, p. 59). Human nature needs not to be undone but rather to be shaped in order for individuals to prepare for a good and virtuous life. If we can achieve this feat, it does not matter that human thought lacks transparency (see Carruthers 2011) because we would not need it if properly trained.

Ninth, from the viewpoint of development, children at an early age may not have the capacity to reason critically. In his *Politics* (Lord 2013), Aristotle recognized this problem. He divided the soul into alogical and logical halves and claimed that the former comes into being earlier in development than the latter (see Fortenbaugh 1975). This basic idea has found support in Piaget's (1970) research on cognitive development. Formal thinking is not developed until early adolescence, and studies have revealed that inhibitory control is not fully developed until early adulthood (e.g., Fischer, Biscaldi, and Gezeck 1997; Velanova, Wheeler, and Luna 2008). Such inhibition would be necessary to inhibit impulses and come to reasoned decisions. Late development of reasoning capacities yields the problem that children cannot be taught to reason about morality; however, even children need to be taught about the moral norms of a community and society. Aristotle solved this intricate problem by concluding that moral education should not be based on reasoning about morality but on habit (see Fortenbaugh 1975 for further discussion). Confucius followed a similar strategy (see Slingerland 2010). Therefore, critical thinking is not sufficient to inculcate morality. I shall give a detailed account of how to instill moral habits in Chapter 10.

Tenth, critical thinking does not cover all aspects of worldviews or domains of value for which human beings can strive. We have seen earlier that there are more values than just truth, which amounts to cognitive rationality, and subjective utility, which amounts to strategic rationality (De Sousa 1987; see also Chapter 1). Beyond cognitive and strategic rationality, people may strive for values such as experiencing beauty or the sublime, finding meaning in life, taking responsibility by assuming leadership, or caring for others (see the earlier discussed value domains of Spranger 1928/1914). Psychology as a science has to aim at a comprehensive overview of how people may achieve their most valued goals. If we go beyond cognitive and strategic rationality, critical thinking is not enough. It may help to think critically when we live with and care for other people, but it seems obvious that a mere thinker would not make a good nurse or a good parent. The finest moments in the history of statesmanship were those where politicians could give their people a sense of purpose, hope, and identity; one example is Winston Churchill during World War II. Although some theorists in art claim that aesthetic feelings play a subordinate role in understanding art (Carroll 2002; Gopnik 2012), feeling certainly plays a role in art's experience and evaluation (see Chapter 9). Moreover, we can look at everyday objects from an aesthetic perspective that differs from one focused on gaining information or making money. Again, critical thinking may help but cannot cover all aspects of aesthetic appreciation. Finally, religion seems at times to oppose both cognitive and strategic rationality. In fact, Gervais and Norenzayan (2012) have found that, the better people are at critical thinking, the less religious they are. Moreover, religious people rely more on intuition, and therefore presumably more on feelings, than nonreligious people. From the fact that literal interpretation of religious scripture does not accord with cognitive rationality (e.g., creation instead of evolution; miracles instead of natural explanations), some scholars have concluded that religion must be wrong (most prominently Dawkins 2006). However, from the perspective that cognitive rationality is one but not the only value people may pursue, we have to consider how people may succeed at finding enchantment in religion (see Chapter 10).

In conclusion, despite the advantages that critical thinking brings to the life of individuals and society, it is not sufficient. Critical thinking does not keep its promises even in core areas of rationality, such as finding appropriate information and making good decisions. In addition, critical thinking is not suited to success in the pursuit of central human activities such as skill acquisition, aesthetic experience, or finding enchantment and meaning in life; this is why we need critical feeling. However, before we can introduce this concept, we need to outline the scope of feelings discussed in this book, including emotions, moods, preferences, bodily states, and metacognitive feelings, and then discuss the rationality of these feelings.

2 THE PSYCHOLOGY OF FEELINGS

The heart has its reasons, which reason does not know.
(BLAISE PASCAL 1995/1660, §277)

What is a feeling?

What is a feeling? A good way to arrive at a working definition of feeling is to proceed as psychologists of emotion have done (see Reisenzein 2007). They first compiled a list of what has been called emotion in everyday life, such as joy, sadness, anger, and disgust. From this list of emotions, they derived some characteristics common to emotions. Norbert Schwarz provided a list of subjective experiences that encompass feelings. "Human thinking is accompanied by a variety of subjective experiences, including moods and emotions, metacognitive feelings (like ease of recall or fluency of perception), and bodily sensations" (Schwarz 2012, p. 289). We may add to this list affective preferences that take the form of likes and dislikes. Affective preferences are neither emotions nor moods but are based on comparisons between two or more objects. Preferences will therefore be introduced here in their own section, after emotions and moods but before metacognitive feelings and bodily sensations. From this list we can derive characteristics common to all feelings. The most obvious common feature of all feelings is their subjectivity, as noted by Scherer (2005) and Schwarz (2012). Feelings are bound to the person who feels. Although I can infer what you feel or even empathize with you, *I* never can have *your* feeling.

Another characteristic of feelings is that their experience is conscious (Laird 2007). We must distinguish between two kinds of consciousness, which Block (1998) called *access consciousness* and *phenomenal consciousness*. A feeling is access conscious when a person can both experience the feeling and is aware of it. In this case, we can label or at least circumscribe the feeling. Feelings are phenomenally conscious when a person experiences them without necessarily being able to reflect or even verbalize them. When a person is access conscious of the feeling, the experience is in the foreground, or the focus of attention. If the feeling is phenomenally conscious without being accessible, the experience is in the background, or at the fringes of consciousness (James 1890).

A definition of feelings would be too inclusive if it included sensations (see Overskeid 2000). Seeing red or hearing a musical instrument play a high C are sensations but lack a feeling component – I do not feel red or the high C. It is therefore essential to find a final attribute that demarcates feelings from sensations. Carl Gustav Jung (1971/1921) noted that feelings always have an evaluative component. Feelings fulfill their evaluative function by being the output of a comparator and thus are essential in monitoring thought and action (Proust 2014). Although I shall argue – based on empirical evidence – that all evaluations include affect, affect is not included in evaluation by definition. For example, people may have a feeling that a statement is true independent of the affective valence of the statement (Unkelbach, Bayer, Alves, Koch, and Stahl 2010). Judgments of truth include a non-affective evaluation. In a similar vein, a decision maker who weighs the pros and cons of an option performs an evaluation that could be affectively cold – at least in principle.

To summarize, a feeling is a subjective experience of mental or bodily states that includes an evaluation. Different qualities of feelings include emotion, mood, affective preferences, metacognitive feelings, and bodily sensations. This excludes pure sensations – such as seeing red, hearing a High C, tasting the sweetness of chocolate, or smelling ammonia – as feelings.

Tasting chocolate and smelling ammonia do in fact include feelings, but these supplement the sensation. If you taste chocolate and say "I feel the sweetness on the tongue," there is a sensation part (the sweetness) and at the same time an evaluation part (it's good, assuming you like sweetness). The pure sensation can be separated from its evaluation. The same applies to pleasures of the eye and of the ear. Although we can demarcate in these cases sensation and feeling, let me repeat that most, if not all, sensations are accompanied by feelings of some sort.

The types of feelings I will review are emotions, mood states, preferences, metacognitive feelings, and bodily sensations. The discussion of sources or determinants of feelings is inspired by a wonderful article in which Juslin and Västfjäll (2008) discuss six kinds of connections of emotions in music to their source. As they describe rather general mechanisms and use emotion in a broad sense, we can base the discussion on their analysis. Moreover, the present analysis extends to domains other than music and to non-affective feelings, which broadens the scope of possible mechanisms. The review of the effects of feelings is rather cursory and selective because there is too vast a literature to consider all effects in this chapter; the chapters to come elaborate on the effects that are relevant to the application of critical feeling.

Emotions

Despite much effort to define emotion, the question "What is an emotion?" has not found a definitive answer ever since it was asked by William James (1884; see Prinz 2004 for an overview of proposed answers). What scholars of emotion agree upon is that there are several qualities of experience that can be seen as emotions. The list of emotions includes joy, hope, anger, fear, sadness, and disgust, which are sometimes seen as basic emotions, and self-conscious emotions such as shame, guilt, and regret. It is not clear whether surprise is an emotion in itself or – due to the novelty of the event to which it responds – just has emotional consequences: negative ones when the news is bad; positive ones when we, for example, receive an unexpected gift. From this list of unequivocal emotions, theorists have derived a working definition of emotion (Reisenzein 2007): An emotion is usually a short-lived state that is directed toward an object and has various components, such as a physiological component; an experiential component, which is the feeling the emotion provides; a cognitive component, which is the appraisal of a situation; and an action tendency (see Frijda 1986; Scherer 1984).

Let us take a closer look at the appraisal and action tendency components and illustrate them by examples. Which of the different emotions a person experiences depends on the appraisal of a situation. For example, if Nina sees that her camera is broken and makes Mike responsible for this mishap because he let it fall, she is likely to feel anger. Note that these are not objective facts but appraisals: Nina is the person who appraises the outcome as harmful, and she judges that the other person, in this case Mike, is responsible. Therefore, she is angry. Basing emotions on appraisals may lead to different emotional outcomes in very similar situations: Mike may feel guilt because he appraises the situation as harmful for Nina and believes he caused that harm, whereas another person, let's call him Joshua, in the same situation may think that he is not responsible for the harm Nina has experienced. The experience of an emotion determines action tendencies. If Nina feels anger, she is disposed to be aggressive. If Mike feels guilt, he is inclined to apologize and offer the victim some form of compensation for the harm he has done. Appraisal theory can also describe the cognitive antecedents of more complex emotions (see Roseman, Antoniou, and Jose 1996). Silvia (2005) analyzed the appraisal structure of interest as a positive emotion. He postulated that interest consists of two so-called evaluation checks of a stimulus. First, is it novel? Second, can I cope with the stimulus? If the stimulus is novel, but the person can cope with this novelty, then the emotion of interest will be felt. In Chapter 8, we shall turn to interventions to increase the positive emotion of interest at school.

In short, appraisals determine what kind of emotion a person experiences, and reappraisal of situations will be a keystone of critical feeling. Appraisals as the determinants of emotions seem to be so evident that this has been the dominant theory for decades. However, there are at least two alternative mechanisms that could account for the elicitation of emotions: specialized emotion modules in the brain and simulation.

Specialized modules for the activation of basic emotions have been proposed by neuroscientists and evolutionary theorists. The best-known such module is the fear module (Öhman and Mineka 2001). The basic idea is that we do not need to interpret a situation in order to feel an emotion. If a snake is in front of us, we will lack the time to run through all computations necessary to analyze the situation. Instead, through the long process of evolution, humans have acquired prepared-ness for objects that are dangerous. This is best demonstrated by an experiment on fear conditioning (Hugdahl and Kärker 1981): It is easy to condition fear of potentially dangerous objects that are either bio-logically relevant (snakes; mushrooms) or biologically irrelevant (elec-tric appliances; loose electric cables) by associating pictures of these objects with mild but painful electric shocks. Later, the researchers tried to remove these associations by showing the pictures without provid-ing electric shocks, a process called *extinction*. Supporting the biological preparedness hypothesis, it was easy to extinguish fear of loose electric cables and other human-made artifacts, but it was difficult to extinguish fear of biologically relevant stimuli. Although such modules may not account for more complex emotions such as regret or interest, they are handy theoretical tools to explain some of the basic emotions, such as disgust, anger, and fear.

Simulation is a mechanism that enables communicators to feel empathy without having to analyze the emotions of others. When we see a child fall and subsequently cry, we pity the child. Part of this pity stems from the fact that we can remember how it hurt when we once fell ourselves. We are therefore able to simulate the fall and the pain of the child. The plausibility of such simulation mechanisms has been sup-ported by the discovery of mirror neurons in monkeys and birds that fire not only when these animals perform an action themselves but also when they observe the same action in another animal of the same species. Although the existence of mirror neurons in human beings is debated

(Hickok 2009), ample empirical evidence exists that human beings simulate behaviors of others (e.g., Lakin and Chartrand 2003 for gestures; Bavelas, Black, Lemery, MacInnis, and Mullet 1986 and Meltzoff and Moore 1977 for facial expressions). Hence, part of the debate is about whether actions by others could lead to simulation processes that do not need mirror neurons. Simulation is a powerful mechanism. It helps us to understand the facial expressions, postures, and actions of another person because we spontaneously feel what the other person feels, though with weakened intensity. We do not need time-consuming analytical processing to interpret another person's expressions and actions; we can derive the feelings of the other person directly by assessing our own feelings. This is akin to the feelings-as-information theory, discussed at the end of the following section.

Moods

There are three differences between emotions and moods (see Frijda 1994). First, in contrast to the short duration of emotional states, moods are more long lived. We are rarely angry for longer than an hour or two, but we could be in a bad mood all day. Second, mood states are not directed toward an object. We may be angry at a thief who stole our money or fear a snake that lies on the hiking trail in front of us. Moods, by contrast, may have diffuse causes, but they are not directed at the misdeed of the thief or at the snake on the trail. Finally, emotions tend to induce actions, such as fight in anger or flight in fear. Conversely, moods do not possess characteristic action tendencies. From these differences between moods and emotions, we can derive a working definition: Moods are affective states that have a long duration, are not directed toward an object, and do not elicit specific action tendencies.

Psychologists have devised several techniques to bring people into a certain mood state, and most of those techniques were inspired by how we come into a mood in everyday life. These techniques are interesting because they can help people to regulate their mood or to influence the mood of others. There is a distinction between overt and covert mood-induction techniques.

When working with overt techniques, an experimenter instructs participants to attempt to get into a certain mood. Participants do so with the help of statements or music. The so-called Velten technique includes 60 positive statements about oneself for the induction of a positive mood, such as "If your attitude is good, then things are good, and my attitude is good." To induce moods, study participants are instructed to read those statements aloud and to try to reach a positive mood. In order to induce a negative mood, participants read 60 negative statements – for example, "I have too many bad things in my life" (Velten 1968) – and try to arrive at the instructed state. In another overt mood-induction technique, experimenters instruct participants to listen to music that sounds either happy or sad, and to bring themselves into the happy or sad mood when listening to it.

When using covert techniques, experimenters do not tell participants that they are aiming to induce a positive or negative mood. While mood induction through music is most effective when people consciously try to attain a certain mood (Eich and Metcalfe 1989), playing happy or sad movie clips induces moods very efficiently even if participants do not know the intention of the experimenter (Westermann, Spies, Stahl, and Hesse 1996). Another covert mood induction is derived from the well-known fact that success makes us upbeat whereas failure brings us down. Psychologists work with bogus positive feedback in order to induce a positive mood and with bogus negative feedback to induce a negative mood.

Mood-induction techniques tested in the laboratory have taught us quite a bit about the sources of moods. If performers interpret their performance as a success, they get into a positive mood; if they interpret their performance as failure, they get into a negative mood. People usually do not recite happiness-inducing sentences to bring about positive mood – and they even more rarely recite depressing statements to bring their mood down. However, people may have positive self-esteem, which increases happiness (Baumeister, Campbell, Krueger, and Vohs 2003). On the other hand, depressed people may think (though not with the intention to bring their mood down) that they feel tired or that there are too many bad things in their life. Positive thoughts or memories result in positive mood, negative thought and memories in negative mood. Other sources of positive mood are sunshine and beautiful interior decoration; sources of negative mood are rain or clouds and a shabby or smelly interior (Schwarz and Clore 1983).

People may strategically use music to regulate their mood. A commonsense hypothesis would state that we always prefer happy music to sad music because people aim to attain happiness. However, the relationship between emotion and music is more complicated. Listeners in a happy or neutral mood indeed like happy music better than sad music, but this preference is eliminated when people are in a sad mood, suggesting a shift toward the kind of music that is congruent with the listener's mood (Hunter, Schellenberg, and Griffith 2011; Menninghaus 2003). Although it remains unclear how music influences mood, it is possible that sad music leads to mixed emotions – that is, that it provides a kind of bitter-sweet mood state not yet captured in the scientific literature (Hunter, Schellenberg, and Schimmack 2008).

Using mood-induction techniques, psychologists have observed effects of mood on memory, judgment, and thinking styles. We tend to retrieve memories that correspond to our moods. If we are in a positive mood, we tend to recall joyful memories; if we are in a sad mood, we tend to recall sad memories. This is called *mood-congruent memory*. We also tend to judge people more positively when in a good mood and more negatively when in a bad mood (Forgas and Bower 1987). A job applicant may be judged as more competent and friendly after an employer has had a pleasant lunch with his wife than after he has had a nasty dispute with an employee.

Why does mood color our memories and judgments? Schwarz (2012) argues in his *feelings-as-information theory* that when we have to evaluate a situation, including another person, we ask ourselves, "How do I feel?" and then base our evaluation on this feeling. The feelings-as-information heuristic is a shortcut that often serves us well because the feeling we assess stems from the current situation. However, in the situation above, the evaluation of the job applicant may depend on whether the employer had a pleasant lunch or a nasty dispute. As neither the lunch nor the dispute is related to the competence of the job candidate, it should not affect the employer's final evaluation. In general, we do not want feelings that stem from sources unrelated to the current situation influence our judgments or decisions. When this happens, we need to become aware of the fact that our feeling is based on the wrong source, and we have to correct our judgment. What seems to be a straightforward strategy, however, is quite difficult to achieve, as we shall see in the next chapter.

Moods not only color our thoughts and memories; they also influence how hard we think. Let us start with the observation that if everything goes fine, we are in a good mood, but if things go awry, we are in a bad mood. However, we often do not exactly know whether the current situation is positive or negative; in this case, our mood becomes a signal for the quality of our interaction with the environment. There is ample evidence for this prediction from the feelings-as-information theory. Negative moods signal that something is wrong and that we need to pay close attention to the situation; we therefore employ an analytical processing style in order to assess and improve the situation. A positive mood, by contrast, signals that everything is fine and that we can carry on without much thinking; we therefore employ a heuristic processing style (Mackie and Worth 1989; Schwarz 1990).

Preferences

If I taste Pepsi and Coke and spontaneously like Pepsi better than Coke, I show a preference. A characteristic of preference is that we attribute our affective state to the object: If I like Pepsi more than Coke, I attribute my feeling state to the drink, not to myself. Preferences are therefore neither emotions nor moods. If I prefer Pepsi to Coke, I think that the former is better than the latter and not that I feel a more positive emotion toward the one, nor that Pepsi brings me into a more positive mood than Coke (even though this may in fact be the case).

Some scientists, especially economists, use the term *preference* to denote that a person makes one choice rather than another. For example, if people can choose between two lottery options, they more often "prefer" one option over the other (Denes-Raj and Epstein 1994). In these choice situations, "preference" may denote a purely reason-based evaluation that could be performed by a computer. Such preference does not qualify as feeling because it lacks the subjective experience component. However, human preferences are rarely based on reason alone and often rely on feelings in order to arrive at a comparative judgment. Unlike some scholars in psychology and behavioral economics, I use the term *preference* to refer to an evaluation based on affect. Preference results from a comparison between two options on the basis of affective feelings.

Food preferences belong to this category, as do affective preferences studied in empirical aesthetics, social psychology, and marketing. Let us look at empirical aesthetics as an example. Researchers in this field have often studied visual preferences (see Palmer, Schloss, and Sammartino 2013; Reber, Schwarz, and Winkielman 2004 for overviews). In general, people seem to prefer objects that have high figure–ground contrast (Reber, Winkielman, and Schwarz 1998), are symmetric (Jacobsen, Schubotz, Hofel, and von Cramon 2006; Reber and Schwarz 2006), have a smooth surface (Bar and Neta 2006; Reber and Schwarz 2006), are of medium complexity (Munsinger and Kessen 1964), and are prototypical (Winkielman, Halberstadt, Fazendeiro, and Catty 2006). A rich literature shows that people prefer average faces (Langlois and Roggman 1990). However, exaggerated features are preferred to average faces when they emphasize the differences between the sexes. Particularly, feminine faces are seen as being more attractive if they have attributes that distinguishes them from male faces, such as high cheekbones and a small chin (Perrett, May, and Yoshikawa 1994; see also Rhodes 2006).

In addition, people seem to entertain affective preferences for objects they have been exposed to before (Zajonc 1968). This mere exposure effect can be obtained even when people cannot recognize the stimuli they have been repeatedly exposed to (Kunst-Wilson and Zajonc 1980; Lee 2001; see Bornstein 1989 for a meta-analysis). Beyond implications for marketing, where a new brand logo or name can be made attractive by presenting it repeatedly to the target audience (see Chapter 7), this finding has important implications for the development of taste (see Chapter 9). Now that the meaning of the term *preference* has been clarified, we can look at innate and learned preferences.

Innate preferences

Innate preferences are alike for all humans. For example, newborns like attractive faces (Slater, von der Schulenburg, Brown, Badenoch, Butterworth, Parsons et al. 1998). Amusingly, chickens have the same preference for attractive human faces as do human newborns (Ghirlanda, Jansson, and Enquist 2002). In the auditory domain, newborn infants have been shown to prefer the voice of their mother to the voice of a female stranger (DeCasper and Fifer 1980). *Innate* does not mean genetic transmission. It has been found that fetuses in the last three months of pregnancy can hear sounds and voices from the outside world. In one study, pregnant mothers were instructed to read a story to their unborn child during the last six weeks before birth. After birth, the infant preferred the story heard before birth to new stories (DeCasper and Spence 1986). This result suggests that inborn preferences can be acquired before birth and do not need to be genetically determined. Other studies on music preferences in infants found a general preference for consonant music over dissonant music (Zentner and Kagan 1996). As these infants were already four months old when tested, it is not certain whether this preference is genetically transmitted, acquired in utero and therefore existent at birth, or acquired at an early age after birth. These examples show that innate or at least very early preferences exist.

   Such preferences can sometimes have undesired consequences. For example, as soon as babies are able to differentiate strangers from their parents, they no longer smile at everybody; they begin to show fear (Sroufe 1977). This results in an inborn preference for one's own group. In adults, such preferences may contribute to prejudice toward strangers that influences our thinking or behavior. One study has observed that a stereotype can unconsciously activate negative prejudice in people who do not want to have racist attitudes. Only if the influence is made obvious and therefore becomes salient can people circumvent the influence of race-related prejudice (Devine 1989).

Associative learning

A powerful mechanism underlying preference formation is the association of formerly unrelated stimuli. If you drink a new beverage and get sick, you probably will not drink that beverage again. If high school students see two youths in love drinking from a bottle of Pepsi, they associate Pepsi – which itself may be neutral – with the arousing picture of a young man kissing a young woman. The same logic underlies many phenomena where attitudes are conditioned through instrumental learning (De Houwer, Thomas, and Baeyens 2001). For example, parents may provide nonverbal affirmation or rejection of their children's expressions of taste. Although academic parents may not tell their children that they should prefer classical music to country songs, they may respond to the child's listening to Lynn Anderson's "Rose Garden" with a facial expression that immediately but unobtrusively informs the child that this is below Mom and Dad's expectations. On the other hand, if the child is listening to Schubert's *Trout Quintet*, they may put on a smile that obviates the need for words to signal that this is the road to take. The same logic applies to the taste for certain clothes. By such associative learning mechanisms, parents can convey *their* preferences to the child without having to say anything. Later on, the peer group takes over the role of the parents in rewarding or punishing expressions of taste. Such conditioning could account for a large part of the education of taste that Pierre Bourdieu (1984/1979) described in his book on distinction.

Metacognitive feelings

In everyday language, "I feel" often refers to affective states, such as emotions, moods, or preferences. The states we have discussed so far are therefore *affective feelings*. However, there are feelings that are not affective states. Some of them pertain to thinking, to memory, or to our state of knowledge, and we refer to them as *metacognitive feelings* (see Schwarz 2012). They are feelings in accordance with our definition because they are subjective experiences that include an evaluation. This evaluation is based on metacognitive states, such as the state of our knowledge or learning, or on epistemic concerns, such as whether a statement is true or whether a story is coherent. Although these feelings are not necessarily affective, they are likely to have affective consequences down the road.

Psychological research has unraveled at least five types of such non-affective states and I will discuss these in more detail. First, the *feeling of familiarity* is the feeling that we have encountered an object before.

Second, I may feel that a statement I hear is true; this is a *feeling of rightness*. Third, I may have a feeling that I will be able to come up with an answer to an exam question even though I do not know the answer right now, which is called the *feeling of knowing*. States related to the feeling of knowing are judgments of learning, which are predictions of learning outcomes, and the tip-of-the-tongue phenomenon, which is the feeling that I do not only know a word but also know roughly how the word sounds. Fourth, we sometimes have the feeling that all things fit together, known as a *feeling of coherence*. All these feelings depend on a fifth, more elementary, feeling, the feeling that information is processed with ease, or *processing fluency*.

Feeling of familiarity

Metacognitive feelings have been the object of much research in the past decades (Schwarz and Clore 2007). This research began with the feeling of familiarity. Familiarity can have several meanings (see Whittlesea and Williams 2000 for an analysis) but the one relevant here is the feeling of having encountered somebody or something before, regardless of whether the encounter indeed took place. We sometimes feel that a person is familiar without remembering his or her identity or where we met this person before. Imagine you regularly go to a butcher's shop to buy meat and one day you see the butcher on the bus. You know you have met this person before, but you do not know where because the butcher on the bus is out of his usual context. Only after some time, maybe even after you have left the bus, you may realize, "Oh, it was the butcher!" (Whittlesea 1993).

An important branch of research has been conducted on the effects of reading text or hearing utterances. Repeated exposure to statements increases not only their familiarity but also the feeling that they are right.

Feeling of rightness

The feeling that a statement is true, or the feeling of rightness (Mangan 1993), is the experience that a statement seems right without knowing that it is true. These could be factual statements, such as "Osorno is in Chile," whose factual truth can be determined, but also beliefs and value statements, such as "God is omnipotent" or "you should respect the elderly," where factual truth cannot be determined (Reber and Unkelbach 2010). A wealth of research, beginning with a seminal study by Hasher, Goldstein, and Toppino (1977), has shown that familiarity with a statement after repeated exposure increases the probability that this statement will be judged as true. There are two possibilities for why a listener may judge a repeated statement as being true: First, the listener may remember the statement and think that it is probably true. Indeed, people judge a statement to be more probably true if they remember having heard the statement before. They may think that people normally tell the truth and hence can trust a statement they have heard before. Second, people sometimes judge a repeated statement as being true even when they cannot remember it. One hypothesis is that repeated exposure increases processing fluency, which in turn increases the probability that a statement will be judged as true (Begg, Anas, and Farinacci 1992; Brown and Nix 1996; Garcia-Marques, Silva, Reber, and Unkelbach 2015). Indeed, ease of processing influences judgments of truth even when it is generated from sources unrelated to repetition, such as high figure–ground contrast (Reber and Schwarz 1999). This mechanism helps to explain why laypeople are more convinced of a finding in brain research when the scientific text is accompanied by a fancy image of a brain that does not add relevant information than when the text is presented alone (Keehner, Mayberry, and Fischer 2011; McCabe and Castel 2008). Newman, Garry, Bernstein, Kantner, and Lindsay (2012) obtained a similar finding with trivia statements, such as "giraffes are the only mammals that cannot jump." Participants judged a statement as being more likely to be true when it was shown together with a thematically related but uninformative photograph.

Feeling of knowing and related phenomena

Nelly, an undergraduate student, is preparing for an exam and tries to answer a question about the main export products of Kenya. She crammed the facts about the economy of Africa some days ago and pertinent information, such as terms or fragments of knowledge, comes to mind when she tries to recall some facts. She feels that she will be able to produce the answer; she experiences a *feeling of knowing* (Hart 1965; Koriat 1993). Two other phenomena are related to feelings of knowing. One is the *judgment of learning*: Nelly has just learned the name of the capital of Burkina Faso and has to predict whether she will know the answer in the exam tomorrow (e.g., Koriat 1997; Nelson and Dunlosky 1991; Schwartz 1994). The other is the *tip-of-the-tongue effect* (Brown and McNeill 1966). Nelly sits in the exam and indeed gets a question asking what the capital of Burkina Faso is. She not only knows that she has learned the answer; she also knows that it is a complicated name with many *oo* and *ah* sounds. She even thinks it begins with an *oo* sound and includes the letter *d*, but she is unable to write it down. Sadly, only half an hour after the exam, the answer suddenly appears to her: Ouagadougou!

Feeling of coherence

Sometimes, we experience a sudden insight when solving a difficult problem. All the elements fall into place and everything seems to fit together. In intuitive problem solving, we may even have the feeling that things fit together, or a feeling of coherence, without having arrived at the solution yet. In studies to examine this phenomenon, Bolte and Goschke (2005) and Bowers, Regehr, Balthazard, and Parker (1990) presented their participants with word triads, such as SALT, DEEP, FOAM. This word triad converged on a common solution word (SEA) that was associated with all words in the triad. Some of the triads, such as DREAM, BALL, BOOK, did not have such a common associate and therefore had no solution. Participants were instructed to find the solution word within fifteen seconds. This was a difficult task, and the participants could on average solve only about 30 percent of the triads. Surprisingly, for those word triads where participants could not find a solution, the participants were able to determine whether the word triad had a solution word or not. That is to say, participants were able to know whether the word triads were coherent or incoherent without knowing the solution word. Bowers et al. observed the same phenomenon with picture fragments where participants were able to decide with above-chance accuracy whether a picture depicted an object or not, even if they did not guess the object.

Processing fluency

We have discussed four kinds of metacognitive feelings: familiarity; the feeling that a statement is true; the feeling of knowing, including some related phenomena, such as judgments of learning and the tip-of-the-tongue phenomenon; and the feeling of coherence.

There is one subjective experience that has been shown to be related to all these metacognitive feelings: processing fluency (henceforth *fluency*), which is the ease with which a mental operation can be performed. People are mentally active when they are awake, and all mental acts have a certain speed; this speed is experienced as fluency (Reber, Wurtz, and Zimmermann 2004). In other words, every percept, every memory, every thought is accompanied by an experience of how easily it can be performed. Fluency is often in the background of our thinking, or – as William James (1890) has put it – at the fringes of consciousness.

Only rarely does the degree of fluency come into our conscious awareness. This is most likely to happen when mental processing does not go smoothly and the person experiences disfluency.

None of the four feelings discussed first – feelings of familiarity, rightness, knowing, or coherence – is the same as fluency. However, fluency has been shown to influence each of these feelings because experienced ease underlies the experience that an object or name is familiar, that a statement is true, that we have some piece of knowledge, or that a text is coherent.

It took a series of ingenious experiments by Bruce Whittlesea and his colleagues (Whittlesea, Jacoby, and Girard 1990) to show that fluency influences the experienced familiarity of an object. The basic paradigm was to present a series of words in a rapid sequence. After the presentation of the words, another word, the test item, was shown, and participants had to decide whether or not that word had been presented in the preceding list. So far, this is a recognition experiment. In one experiment, the authors manipulated the clarity with which the test item could be seen by manipulating the background to render the test word more or less readable. Participants were more likely to judge that the test item had been presented before when it was presented with high contrast to the background and therefore could be processed more fluently than when the test item was presented with low contrast to the background and therefore could be processed less fluently (Whittlesea, Jacoby, and Girard 1990). Processing fluency in this experiment was assessed through pronunciation latency, which was faster when the test item was seen clearly than when it was seen less clearly.

Other experiments revealed that it is *surprising fluency* that makes words look familiar. Surprising fluency means that it is difficult to recognize a plausible source for fluency, and this may lead to misattribution of the experience of ease. In an experiment by Whittlesea and Williams (2000), the list of items included words that were easy to pronounce ("STATION"), as indicated by fast pronunciation latencies; orthographically regular pseudowords ("HENSION") that were easy to pronounce; and orthographically irregular nonwords ("STOFWUS") that were more difficult to pronounce, as indicated by slower pronunciation latencies. In sum, words and pseudowords could be processed fluently while nonwords were disfluent. In the subsequent test, participants had to provide recognition judgments for words, pseudowords, and nonwords that had either been presented or not presented in the previous list. The most surprising effect emerged when an item had not been presented in the previous list. In this case, respondents claimed to recognize pseudowords more often than words and nonwords. In more technical terms, pseudowords produced more false alarms than the other two item classes. The researchers argued that nonwords were processed disfluently; that is why they were not seen as familiar. Words, on the other hand, were processed fluently, but this did not come as a surprise as they were known from before and had meaning. That is why participants did not misattribute the experience of ease to familiarity and therefore did not produce false alarms. Fluent processing of unknown pseudowords, however, came as a surprise because the pseudowords were meaningless but could be read with ease nonetheless. In this case, participants used surprising fluency as information and concluded that they must have seen the pseudoword earlier in the experiment. Therefore, surprisingly fluent processing of a stimulus may result in a feeling of familiarity.

Besides familiarity, processing fluency influences judgments of truth, as mentioned earlier. This does not seem surprising, given that fluency increases the experience of familiarity and familiarity increases the probability that a statement will be judged as being true. It has just to be shown that fluency increases judged truth in a situation where familiarity does not play a role. For this purpose, Reber and Schwarz (1999) manipulated the readability of statements of the form "Osorno is in Chile." These statements were shown just once. Participants had to decide whether the statement was true or not. Half of the statements were shown in dark colors (dark blue; red) that had high contrast to the white background of the computer screen and were therefore easy to read. The other half of the statements were shown in bright colors that had lower contrast to the background (colors such as yellow and light blue). Participants could still read statements with low figure–ground contrast but not as easily as statements with high figure–ground contrast. The rationale of this manipulation was simple: If the effect of familiarity on judged truth is mediated by fluency, any manipulation that increases fluency should also increase judged truth. The researchers indeed found a small but reliable effect of figure–ground contrast on judged truth. The findings were replicated (Unkelbach 2007), sometimes with more effective manipulations than figure–ground contrast (Parks and Toth 2006). Akin to Whittlesea and Williams' (2000) observations on familiarity, it is not fluency per se that increases judged truth, but surprising fluency. Let us assume participants read a series of statements that are all easily readable. In this case, it would come as no surprise if the next statement could be read fluently as well. On the other hand, if all statements were shown with low contrast and therefore were difficult to process, a highly fluent statement would come as a surprise. In one study, figure–ground contrast had virtually no influence on judgments of truth where a statement shown in high figure–ground contrast appeared after another statement shown in high figure–ground contrast. However, participants judged a statement shown in high figure–ground contrast as more likely to be true if it followed a statement shown in low figure–ground contrast (Hansen, Dechêne, and Wänke 2008). In sum, high fluency increases the probability that a statement will be judged as being true, especially when high fluency comes as a surprise.

Processing fluency plays a crucial role in feelings of knowing (Koriat 1993). When assessing their knowledge, learners assess how easily bits and pieces of the answer come to mind. This becomes even clearer when we look at answering essay questions. At the final exam of the introductory course in psychology at the University of Oslo, undergraduate students can select six of ten essay questions. How can Ragnhild know which of the ten questions she will answer best without already having answered them? From what we know about the feeling of knowing, Ragnhild will retrieve a few relevant materials for each question and then choose those questions where it has been easiest to retrieve some basic facts.

This research about feeling of knowing can be generalized to how people draw inferences from processing experiences about their traits and current states (see Schwarz 1998, 2004). In a study testing the availability of heuristic (on which see Tversky and Kahneman 1973), Schwarz, Bless, Strack, Klumpp, Rittenauer-Schatka, and Simons (1991) asked people to list six or twelve instances where they had behaved self-assertively. In pilot studies, these authors had found that it is relatively easy to recall six instances of self-assertive behaviors but it is quite difficult to recall twelve such instances. Participants who listed six behaviors judged themselves as being more assertive than those who listed twelve behaviors, supporting the notion that participants based their answer on the ease of recall and not the amount of recalled information. By employing misattribution manipulations, Schwarz and colleagues could show that processing fluency is the mechanism underlying the ease of recall effects. Specifically, if they played music that purportedly facilitated the recall of assertive events, participants no longer relied on ease of recall for their judgments of assertiveness. Ease of recall has been shown to have an impact on frequency estimates (Wänke, Schwarz, and Bless 1995), product preferences (Wänke, Bohner, and Jurkowitsch 1997), health-related judgments (Rothman and Schwarz 1998), and assessments of performance (Reber, Meier, Ruch-Monachon, and Tiberini 2006).

The effects of ease of recall can be moderated by naïve theories that are commonsense assumptions about the world (see Schwarz 2004). In an experiment by Winkielman and Schwarz (2001), participants had to recall four or twelve childhood events. They were then led to believe that either pleasant or unpleasant memories fade from memory. When retrieval of memories was easy, participants judged their childhood as being happier when told that unpleasant memories fade away, showing that assumptions about memory influenced their judgments.

When examining the feeling of coherence, Topolinski and colleauges (Topolinski, Likowski, Weyers, and Strack 2009; Topolinski and Strack 2009a, 2009b) found that coherent word triads were processed faster than incoherent word triads. This difference in processing fluency led to a more positive affective reaction toward coherent rather than incoherent triads, and the feeling of coherence, as expressed by the response of the participants, depended on this affective reaction. In other words, the effect of coherence in the word triads on coherence judgments was mediated by positive affect derived from processing fluency.

Fluency and affect

I earlier mentioned the mere exposure effect, which denotes the fact that people prefer a stimulus simply because they have been exposed to it before (Zajonc 1968). A meta-analysis by Bornstein (1989) showed that liking after repeated exposure increases for a wide array of stimuli. Among the many explanations that have been offered (see Harrison 1977), I focus here on an account of the mere exposure effect that postulates a two-step account. Repeated exposure of a stimulus facilitates the perception of the stimulus, or its perceptual fluency (Jacoby and Dallas 1981). This increased fluency is in turn affectively positive (Reber et al. 1998; Seamon, Brody, and Kauff 1983). Although an explanation in terms of uncertainty cannot be excluded and actually is compatible with the fluency account, I focus on the fluency account because there is evidence that processing fluency is affectively positive even when it is not caused by repetition. For example, symmetric patterns or stimuli shown with high figure–ground contrast are both fluent to process and preferred (Reber et al. 1998; see also Reber, Schwarz, and Winkielman 2004). Importantly, it is the subjective feeling of fluency, not the objective ease of processing of the stimulus, that influences affect (Forster, Leder, and Ansorge 2013). The link between fluency and affect has been shown to be relevant in various domains, such as marketing (e.g., Labroo, Dhar, and Schwarz 2008; Landwehr, Labroo, and Hermann 2011; Lee and Labroo 2004) and prejudice (Rubin, Paolini, and Crisp 2010; see also Lick and Johnson 2015).

What is the function of the link between processing fluency and affect? If everything is running smoothly and processing is fluent, our interaction with the world is fine; this is positive. In contrast, when things are not going easily and we have difficulties processing the information at hand, there may be a problem we have to deal with. A problem that slows or even disrupts processing is negative. Like negative moods, disfluency therefore elicits an analytical processing style (Alter, Oppenheimer, Epley, and Eyre 2007). As we shall see in Chapter 9, some artists exploit the fact that disfluency results in analytical thinking by strategically building difficulties into their artworks to make their audience think.

From what research has found about processing fluency, we can assume that high processing fluency is positive by default (Winkielman, Schwarz, Fazendeiro, and Reber 2003); the fact that ease of processing has an inherently positive affective quality links the experience of fluency to evaluation, which is a defining feature of feeling. It remains an empirical question whether the feelings related to processing fluency – familiarity, rightness, knowing, coherence – have an inherent affective quality. Regardless of the outcome of this future research, each of these feelings gauges the state of the person and his or her interaction with the environment.

An offshoot of the research on ease of processing is the fluency theory of aesthetic pleasure (Reber, Schwarz, and Winkielman 2004). According to this theory, beauty is derived from the interaction of the perceptual system with its environment. The more fluent people can process an aesthetic object, the more aesthetic pleasure they experience. Importantly, the experience of beauty is supposed to be at its pinnacle if a pattern or a detail within an object can be processed with surprising ease, in line with the research findings reviewed above. Although this theory has had its critics (see Silvia 2012) and has been extended to cover intense emotions in art appreciation (Armstrong and Detweiler-Bedell 2008) and interest in exploring the aesthetic object (Graf and Landwehr 2015), the fluency theory has done well in explaining mild affective reactions in low-level perception.

As fluency is common to positive affect and to judged truth, we would expect that positive affect – for example, derived from aesthetic pleasure – signals truth. This seems to be the case. When mathematicians solve a problem or prove a theorem, they sometimes take the beauty of a solution or a proof as an indication of its correctness (Chandrasekhar 1987). This is difficult to understand, given that mathematics is seen as the basis and pinnacle of rational thinking. However, the fluency theory accounts for this surprising phenomenon in that fluency seems to be the common mechanism underlying both beauty and truth (Reber, Brun, and Mitterndorfer 2008; Reber, Schwarz, and Winkielman 2004). As I shall discuss in Chapter 8, these observations open the path to the strategic use of intuitive judgments.

In the same way, research may open the path to induce the aha-experiences that accompany sudden insights. Such experiences are characterized by four defining attributes (see Sternberg and Davidson 1995): First, they are sudden and often appear as a surprise after a long phase of an apparently unproductive incubation period. Second, after a long period of processing difficulties, sudden understanding facilitates the processing of information that is relevant to the solution of the problem. Everything seems to come together, to fit in. Third, a sudden insight yields positive affect (see Muth and Carbon 2013 for a recent study). Problem solvers often feel joy or an aesthetic experience while solving a problem. Fourth, a person who has an aha-experience is convinced that the solution is correct. Traditionally, these four characteristics were seen as independent attributes of the aha-experience. More recently, Sascha Topolinski and I presented an account that combined those four attributes (Topolinski and Reber 2010). As we have seen, fluently processed information is liked more and is more likely to be judged as true. In fact, people are even more strongly convinced that a statement is true if it can be processed with surprising ease (Hansen et al. 2008). Therefore, we can summarize the account of the aha-experience as an experience where information related to a solution can be processed with sudden ease; this surprising fluency results in both positive affect and the conviction that the solution is true. First evidence has shown that aha-experiences during mathematics lessons may result in a more positive attitude toward mathematics (Liljedahl 2005). This observation suggests that aha-experiences might be useful in increasing interest in mathematics at school.

We must also consider fluency in the description of the mechanisms underlying critical feeling. With this knowledge at hand, we can use processing fluency strategically. Research has shown that synchronous movement between people facilitates communication and increases liking, presumably due to increased interpersonal fluency (this term was introduced by Ackerman and Bargh 2010), suggesting ways in which people can connect to each other (Reber and Norenzayan 2010). Moreover, repeated exposure to a work of art increases its appeal (Cutting 2003), suggesting ways to develop taste (Chapter 8). Finally, learners often take fluent reading of the learning materials as an indication that they will remember well what they have learned. Surprisingly, as discussed in Chapter 5, difficulties in reading learning materials often result in better learning. This finding will be relevant both to learning at school and to the acquisition of norms.

Bodily feedback

Beyond senses such as seeing, hearing, smelling, and taste, the body has various sensors that provide us with information from both the outer and inner worlds. They include receptors in the skin for touch, pressure, temperature, and pain; specialized receptors that tell us about the state of our food and water intake; and stretch receptors in the muscles that may help us assess effort, to name just a few examples. From the definition of feeling outlined earlier, it becomes clear that the sensation of qualities such as touch or temperature are not feelings in themselves; a sensation is only a feeling if it includes an evaluation, such as *too* hot or *too* cold. Sensing that we have an empty stomach would not in itself qualify as a feeling. Only the evaluation that we lack food intake makes the sensation of an empty stomach a feeling of hunger. The same applies to proprioception, the sensation of feedback from one's muscles. It provides us with a sense of balance, movement, and effort. The feeling component comes in when we evaluate our bodily sensations. We monitor our balance, our movements, and the expenditure of effort all the time, and we often respond affectively when this monitoring shows that we are out of balance, that our movements are not leading to the intended position, or that we are expending too much effort. For example, when we learn to ride a bicycle, we learn from bodily feedback whether we are still upright, in which direction we are moving, and how fast. This bodily feedback is not mere sensation but includes all kinds of evaluations and affective states. It is quite unpleasant, for example, to lack balance on a bicycle; it is nice to know, by contrast, that we are moving in the right direction; and we may have a feeling of rightness when the speed is neither too fast nor too slow.

By aligning the notion of bodily feelings to our definition of feelings in general, we can limit the discussion to those bodily states that include an evaluation. We exclude pure sensations such as vision, hearing, smelling, taste, or touch.

Other feelings

Having discussed a whole array of feelings, let me mention other experiences that may qualify for this list. The first that comes to mind are experiences of being in control. Research has mostly conceptualized such experiences as control beliefs, in line with a purely cognitive view (e.g., Skinner, Chapman, and Baltes 1988). However, well-being and control expectancies are positively correlated (Grob, Little, Wanner, and Wearing 1996) and mood is related to both control beliefs and a sense of agency (Reber and Flammer 2002). Like fluency, the experience of control could be inherently positive. As experiences of control not only include beliefs but also evaluations, we may subsume them under the concept of feelings. However, we should not confuse affect as an inherent part of the experience of control and affect as a consequence of control beliefs. It is an empirical problem to decide between these two hypotheses.

Other potential feelings include experiences related to traits such as competence, dominance, and power. There is growing evidence that these traits and affect are grounded in bodily experiences. For example, warmth and competence are the two main dimensions used when judging another person (Cuddy, Fiske, and Glick 2007). Freddi, Tessier, Lacrampe, and Dru (2013) observed that these two dimensions were related to bodily experiences: warmth to approach and avoidance, competence to upward and downward motion. The vertical dimension is also related to dominance and power, which are two closely related concepts. Dominance and power are connected to the upper part of the space, and submission and powerlessness are connected to the bottom part (Schubert 2005; Schubert, Waldzus, and Seibt 2008).

Again, we encounter the question of whether these experiences necessarily include evaluations and therefore can be subsumed into the list of feelings. It remains an empirical question whether bodily states inherent to warmth, competence, and dominance feed back into affective states. If so, and if these processes are automatic, it may well be that evaluation is inherent to the experience of these dimensions, and that judgments of warmth, competence, and dominance are feelings. While the assessment of warmth certainly is related to feelings and can hardly be determined by mere thinking, we theoretically could determine competence and dominance analytically, without any contribution of affect. The question then becomes whether an evaluation based on analytical judgments is always accompanied by a subjective experience that includes an evaluation.

As it is not clear whether or not the experiences discussed in this section are feelings, they will not be included further in this book. However, one cannot underestimate the importance of those experiences for critical feeling if they turn out to be feelings. For example, the finding that many Wall Street bankers and criminals have similar personality traits (Babiak and Hare 2006) suggests that there is something very wrong with the process by which bankers are promoted to the top level. Critical feeling would have to disentangle dominance and affective evaluation in order to spot the narcissists among the hopefuls for promotion.

In this book, we are interested in how feelings can be used strategically. It is therefore important to delineate, first, how feelings can contribute to the optimization of outcomes through experience, as exemplified in the somatic marker hypothesis, and, second, to what degree feelings are rational.

The somatic marker hypothesis

Phineas Gage has become a paradigmatic case study of decision making that lacks an emotional basis. Gage was a railway worker who prepared explosives to clear the way for construction. One day, the explosives detonated while he was still preparing them, and an iron rod entered his face and passed through his skull, injuring frontal parts of his brain. His wounds healed, and at first Gage did not seem to have any brain damage that would have prevented him from leading a normal life (see Damasio 1994). However, Gage led a restless life, became friends with people he would have avoided before the accident, and made disastrous financial decisions. He retained his intelligence, but something went wrong with his feelings. From this and other case studies, neurologist Antonio Damasio and his colleagues (Bechara, Damasio, and Damasio 2000; Damasio 1994, 1996) derived the somatic marker hypothesis, which goes as follows: You make decisions all the time. After making a decision, you observe the outcome. You will not be able to remember the outcome for every decision you have ever made. However, this is not necessary because every outcome is recorded as a somatic marker that is associated with the decision you made; positive decision outcomes result in somatic markers that differ from markers associated with negative outcomes. Later, when you have to make a similar decision, you can simply check how you feel and use this feeling as information that helps you to make the decision. Experiments have shown that healthy people can acquire attitudes implicitly (Bechara, Damasio, Damasio, and Anderson 1994; Bechara, Damasio, Tranel, and Damasio 1997; Betsch, Plessner, Schwieren, and Gutig 2001), supporting a key assumption of the somatic marker hypothesis.

Two characteristics distinguish people with damage in the orbitofrontal cortex from healthy subjects: Their emotions are flat, and their decision making is suboptimal. This observation suggests that gut feelings do not oppose cognitive mechanisms underlying rational decision making but are instead a very part of it. Although these two characteristics may be mere coincidence, and although the experimental evidence gathered from groups of patients and of healthy people is not without problems (Newell and Shanks 2014), the interpretation of the case studies with patients in terms of the somatic marker hypothesis provides a plausible and parsimonious explanation.

What implications does the somatic marker hypothesis have for critical feeling? We may be tempted to conclude that decision makers should trust their gut feelings. These feelings are, after all, based on information acquired over a lifetime (see Brinkmann 2006 for a thorough discussion). Yet can we trust these gut feelings? Not unconditionally. There are at least two points to consider. First, the reliability of gut feelings depends on whether earlier encounters provided veridical information or not. For example, if we have encountered shy car dealers who were incompetent, our gut feeling might tell us not to trust shy dealers any more. If there were indeed a negative correlation between shyness and competence, we could rely on our intuition. However, if the car dealers we encountered were unrepresentative, and shy dealers typically are competent, we might get an erroneous gut feeling we cannot rely upon (see Fiedler 2000 for an analysis of such biased distributions). To trust feelings, we need to have stable and predictable environments. Derived from this reasoning, we could predict that people who live in environments that are familiar to them – where they grew up or have lived for a long time – would fare better in trusting their gut feelings than migrants in foreign environments. Although this seems plausible, one could also conceive of the possibility that strangers are more distanced and may see clues to erroneous feeling that people within a community do not. Another interesting question pertains to the learning history of a person. What factors in a biography determine whether individuals can trust their gut feelings in a purchase decision or in the choice of a partner? These are open questions that await further research.

A second reason not to blindly trust gut feelings is the observation that such feelings may be biased by all kinds of undue influences (see Schwarz and Clore 2007). As mentioned earlier, an employer might judge a job applicant more positively after a cozy meal than after a nasty quarrel. In Chapter 7, we shall see how marketers and campaigners try to influence our feelings to make us buy their products or vote for their candidate. We often do not need these products, and we often do not know what a candidate stands for. To trust our gut feelings blindly is therefore as wrong as to categorically exclude them as a source of our daily decisions.

Both reasons for not unconditionally trusting our gut feelings have to do with the fact that we might not understand our feelings properly. Recent work on the epistemic role of emotional experience suggests that we need to understand the reasons that give rise to our feelings in order to respond properly (Brady 2013; Deonna and Teroni 2012). Based on the analysis of these authors, a feeling is only justified if it refers to real underlying causes in the environment, which is when it is cognitively rational. Although the somatic marker hypothesis provides a plausible account of how feelings might make for rational judgment, information from the past might be unreliable; either because there was no fixed relationship between a type of decision and its outcomes within the previous few years or because carry-over effects of feelings experienced within the past few minutes result in undue influence of judgments and decisions.

Feeling and rationality

This final section of this chapter combines the psychology of feelings with critical thinking. We have seen that good reasoning is the foundation of critical thinking, which enables human beings to base their judgments and decisions on rational arguments and to optimize outcomes. Let us conclude this chapter with the question of how feelings can be rational. A good starting point is the already mentioned distinction between cognitive and strategic rationality discussed by De Sousa (1987). The question is to what purposes we reason. People assess the rationality of reasoning according to two essential purposes: Cognitive rationality aims to obtain an adequate mental representation of the state of the world around us. Strategic rationality aims to optimize valued outcomes and is characteristic of rational decision making.

What is the purpose of feelings? How can they be rational? De Sousa (1987; see also Frank 1988) answers these questions for emotions. He claims that the purpose of emotions is neither to align mental representations to reality, like cognitive rationality, nor to maximize the utility of outcomes in a given situation, like strategic rationality; emotions have the function to guide attention. In contrast to reason, whose rationality is measured at the end of an event, the rationality of emotion is assessed according to whether it guides our attention to salient events at the beginning in order to help us to decide which lines of inquiry to pursue. Emotions thus become an indicator of the importance of an event or object. The insight that emotions guide attention dovetails with research on the interruption as an elicitor of emotion (Mandler 1975; Simon 1967). Disruption of the usual routines guides attention to the action and to the potential causes of its interruption. For example, if we turn a car key and nothing happens, our attention is now directed at starting the car – usually an automatic activity. We may try again and get angry or distressed. Negative emotions narrow down our attention, which becomes more focused than when we feel positive (see Easterbrook 1959). We have already seen that moods (Schwarz 1990) and processing fluency (Alter et al. 2007) determine how hard we think. In the same way that negative emotions focus our attention on the ongoing event, negative moods and disfluency focus our thoughts to enable us to analyze the situation.

The last few sentences form a bridge between De Sousa's notion of the rationality of emotions and the rationality of feelings. Like emotions, all feelings may serve to guide our attention. Emotions provide us with information about the nature of our interaction with an object (see Leventhal and Scherer 1987). Is it something new? Is it positive or negative? Is its outcome certain or uncertain? Can we cope with it? We can assess the rationality of emotional feelings by the degree to which they guide our attention in a direction that later results in aligning our mental representations with the state of the world or maximizing expected utility. Similarly, we have seen that positive moods inform people that everything is fine and that they do not need to focus attention whereas negative moods inform people that trouble may be ahead and that they have to watch out for problems. The same applies to fluent versus disfluent processing of information. Feelings that depend on fluency may provide some specific information. For example, lack of familiarity tells us that incoming information is likely to be novel and therefore deserves close attention. A student may choose to believe the most plausible of two versions of the same rumor about a fellow student. On the other hand, a warning bell rings when a fellow student's claim does not feel right, and the original student may begin to scrutinize future statements by the fellow student. Feeling of knowing may tell the student that he does not need to learn more, whereas a lack thereof directs attention to the topic he does not know or understand. Finally, feelings of coherence may guide a mathematician's choice of the problem he is going to solve. Why should he pursue an unsolved problem that is not accompanied by a feeling of coherence when there is an unsolved problem that elicits such a promising experience? Preferences based on affect guide our attention in choice situations. Finally, bodily states tell us something about what we should do next. When we feel pain, our attention is directed automatically to the source of pain and to withdrawal of the inflicted body part. As a consequence, we learn to avoid this source in the future. When we feel thirsty, we aim to find water; when hungry, we seek food. To summarize, it looks like we can nicely transfer De Sousa's idea of the rationality of emotions to the rationality of feelings in general.

However, why should feelings not have functions related to cognitive and strategic rationality? Having accurate knowledge about our interaction with the environment amounts to cognitive rationality, and feelings contribute information. When we use feelings in order to implement values, feeling states contribute to strategic rationality in that they enable spontaneous action that is right.

Feelings serve as information about our interaction with the environment. Negative mood and processing difficulties tell us about problems we need to address; preferences not only guide our attention toward an object but also inform us about its quality. They may form part of an evaluation of the object; feelings of knowing and related feelings inform us about what we know and what we need to learn more deeply, and the experience that a statement does not feel right provides us with the information that we should not uncritically believe it.

When we want to assess the hedonic, aesthetic, or epistemic aspects of an object, we have to distinguish good from bad, true from false, or coherent from incoherent. How can we prefer Pepsi to Coke when we do not taste the difference? How can we benefit from feelings of knowing if we are insensitive to subtle differences of fluency that indicate how easily we can retrieve the relevant information? As we shall see in the next chapter, it is advantageous to educate our senses through discrimination learning in order to be able to distinguish sensations and to refine our assessment. This refinement ranging from artistic taste to the recognition of emotions of others is an important part of extracting information from feelings and therefore may serve cognitive rationality.

Sometimes we dream of achieving a state where we can spontaneously do the right thing by just following our feelings, and where we can accurately assess what we have done not by thorough analysis but just by assessing the feelings that inform us about the progress of our thought or action. The first part, the use of knowledge about feelings to determine the right thing, amounts to strategic rationality; the second part, assessing the progress of an action, pertains to cognitive rationality. Such states make for a richer life. Yet achieving this feat may be hard work and prone to biases, as we shall see in the next chapter and in Chapter 10, where the acquisition of moral habits are discussed. With these general remarks about the rationality of feelings in mind, we are now ready to examine the idea of critical feeling.

3 CRITICAL FEELING

Men are admitted into Heaven not because they have curbed &
govern'd their Passions or have No Passions, but because they have
Cultivated their Understandings.

(WILLIAM BLAKE 1972/1810, P. 615)

What is critical feeling?

In Chapter 1, critical thinking was defined as "reasonable, reflective thinking that is focused on deciding what to believe or do" (Fisher 2011, p. 4). Combining the concise definition of critical thinking with what we know about the rationality of feelings, we can now define critical feeling as the reflective use of feelings that is focused on guiding attention, evaluating information, and guiding action according to the values we like to implement. Feelings we use in critical feeling can be either ends or means. For example, when we want to alleviate fear, we use means to achieve a feeling as an end. When we use feelings as information to evaluate a job applicant or to assess what we know, we use them as means. Sometimes, feelings are used as both ends and means, for example when therapists use feelings connected to relaxation in order to alleviate fear.

According to Ennis (1962), critical thinkers ideally exhibit certain proficiencies such as observing; inferring; generalizing; conceiving and stating assumptions and alternatives; offering a well-organized or well-formulated line of reasoning; evaluating statements and chains of reasoning; and detecting standard problems. Could we find a similar list of proficiencies for critical feeling that supplements the short definition given above? Although there are no rules of feeling like there are rules of logic and rules of inference from empirical evidence, there are some capacities and abilities related to feelings that seem to be advantageous. They are summarized in Table 3.1, with strategies that pertain to the individual proficiencies.

The first proficiency is interrupting feelings. It is certainly adaptive to interrupt feelings that are inappropriate to a situation. Beyond simply suppressing feelings, this includes timeouts, distraction, and

Table 3.1 The three proficiencies of critical feeling and their strategies (rational functions of proficiencies in parenthesis)

Proficiency (rational function)	Strategies
Interrupting inappropriate feelings (guiding attention)	Suppressing inappropriate feelings Timeouts and distraction Stop and think Reappraisal Meta-awareness
Extracting information (accurate information)	Use of feelings as information Correcting wrong information Discrimination learning Using knowledge about feelings

Changing context (implementing values)
    Changing external context
 	
    Changing inner states
	
	Changing the environment
	Selecting optimal environments
	Sharing information
	Planning
	Mental imagery and simulation
	Conditioning
	Changing values
	Changing aspiration level
	Shaping appropriate behavior

stop-and-think rules to calm down affective responses and prevent impulsive action. Another method of interrupting inappropriate feelings is meta-awareness in that people become aware of the fact that, for example, anger is their *personal* feeling and not an objective feature of the situation. Finally, people may reappraise a situation to not only interrupt but also revise the inappropriate feeling.

Second, critical feelers are able to extract accurate information based on their feelings. We may use feelings as information but we also have to be able to correct inaccurate information based on feelings that come from an irrelevant source. Discrimination learning is a powerful tool through which we can shape our feelings and refine our tastes. Alternatively, people may simply use knowledge about feelings. Such knowledge, acquired from one's own experience or from literature, is useful in social interaction. On the other hand, marketers can exploit such knowledge to influence our likes and wants. In a similar vein, consumers can use this knowledge to circumvent these attempts at persuasion.

A third proficiency of critical feeling is changing the state of the context. I distinguish between changing the external context and changing our inner states. We could change the external context in a direct manner either by actively changing the environment we live in or by selecting environments that optimize the desired outcomes. An indirect method of changing the environment exploits the fact that providing information to others may change their behavior and therefore our interpersonal context. Changing internal states is the sub-proficiency that includes by far the most strategies, including: planning; mental imagery and simulation; classical and instrumental conditioning; changing values; changing aspiration levels; and shaping appropriate behavior to implement values. Shaping appropriate behavior means that people take the right measures to achieve a state where they can act both spontaneously and accurately. If they are proficient at using feelings to extract accurate information (the second proficiency of the list above), they may assess their spontaneous, feeling-based actions.

Essentially, critical feelers can interrupt inappropriate feelings, use feelings to extract information about the state of another person or of the environment, and are able to change the external environment and internal states in order to be able to spontaneously perform appropriate actions by following the lead of feelings.

Each of the three proficiencies is loosely related to one of the rational functions of feelings. Interrupting feelings draws attention away from current feelings. Reappraisal, which is one strategy to interrupt feelings, draws attention away from emotions deemed inappropriate to emotions deemed appropriate. Extracting information is related to cognitive rationality in that it serves the function of obtaining accurate information about our interaction with the environment. Finally, shaping behavior is related to strategic rationality in that it serves the function of maximizing the utility of personal outcomes in terms of implemented values, as stated earlier. While I claim that a certain kind of proficiency primarily serves a particular rational function, this is not to say that this proficiency could not serve a different function as well. For example, we may use reappraisal to interrupt inappropriate feelings in most cases, thus guiding attention to more appropriate feelings. Yet interrupting *inappropriate* feelings always includes a value component. Although guiding attention is the primary rational function, interrupting inappropriate feelings may maximize utility and therefore serve strategic rationality. Hence, proficiencies are only loosely tied to rational functions.

The proficiencies of critical feeling are related to the specific strategies. Table 3.2 lists all strategies with some examples that will be discussed in different chapters. In the remainder of this chapter, we first review each strategy, ordered according to the proficiencies to which they belong. The discussion then turns to the function of values introduced in Chapter 1 and analyzes how critical feeling goes beyond mere skill and

Table 3.2 Strategies of critical feeling with examples and chapter where example is discussed

Strategy	Examples	Chapter
Suppressing inappropriate feelings	Critical thinking	1
	Suppressing emotion	3
Timeouts and distraction	Calming down	3
Stop and think	Alleviating aggressive impulses	4
	Alienation effect in art	9
Reappraisal	Therapy of social phobia	4
	Shame and guilt	4
	Appreciating romantic art	9
Meta-awareness	Accepting one's own feelings	4
	Preventing negativity bias	6
	Resisting temptations	10
Feelings as information	Feedback in skill learning	5
	Reading the feelings of others	6
	Feelings of knowing	8
	Surrogates (Gilbert)	10
Correcting wrong information	Wrong rumors	3
	Lie detection	6
	Correcting undue influences of adverts	7
Discrimination learning	Skill learning	5
	Classification of styles in art	9
Using knowledge about feelings	Peak-end rule	4
	Commitment and intimacy in marriage	6
	Overcoming pluralistic ignorance	7
	Marketing and politics	7
	Making stuff interesting	8
	Cultivating intuition and aha-experiences	8
Sharing information	Telling others about negative experiences	4
	Overcoming pluralistic ignorance	7
Selecting optimal environments	Cultivating intuition	5
	Exposure to violent sports	6
	Selective exposure to cultural forms	10

(continued)

Table 3.2 (cont.)

Strategy	Examples	Chapter
Changing the environment	Changing physical environment (e.g., lighting)	4
	Control of food intake	4
Planning	Implementation intentions	4
Mental Imagery and simulation	Posing emotional expressions (simulation)	5
	Satisfaction with performance (imagery)	7
Classical and instrumental conditioning	Relaxation therapy	4
	Marketing and politics	7
	Associating values to feelings	10
Changing values	Consumer attitudes	7
	Re-enchantment	10
Changing aspiration level	Less is more in happiness	4
	Winning the silver medal	5
Shaping appropriate behavior	Synchronous movement	5
	Desirable difficulties	5
	Adopting artistic taste	9
	Adopting moral norms	10

serves values. Finally, we expound what critical feeling is not, how we study critical feeling, and how critical feeling may be taught before we pass to the applications of critical feeling in Part II.

Interrupting feelings

The first proficiency is interrupting feelings. This proficiency can be seen as a virtue in societies that cherish self-control, for example in Prussia (derived from pietistic values; see Clark 2006; Haffner 1980) or in East Asian cultures (as a means to achieve harmony; see Nisbett 2003). There are five strategies for interrupting feelings: suppressing feelings, timeouts and distraction, stop-and-think, reappraisal, and meta-awareness.

Suppressing feelings

The most obvious way to stop feelings is to suppress them (Gross 1998). For example, if we feel fear that is unjustified, inappropriate, or embarrassing to reveal in a given situation, we may simply try not to experience this feeling. Suppression of feelings is sometimes an efficient way to get rid of them. It has, for example, been shown that it is an effective method of alleviating grief and helping to overcome severe loss (Bonanno, Keltner, Holen, and Horowitz 1995). In addition, suppression of emotional expression may help – via facial feedback – to weaken the experience of an emotion. However, Gross (1998) has shown that suppression may reduce the expression of a negative emotion without reducing its experience. A boy who suppresses fear when being harassed by an older boy may not reveal his fear to the bully, but he still experiences fear.

Moreover, evidence shows that suppression of emotions may come at a cost. First, thoughts about personal emotional events are more difficult and thus more effortful to suppress than thoughts about everyday events (Petrie, Booth, and Pennebaker 1998) and therefore require self-control. As exercise of self-control has been shown to deplete cognitive resources (Muraven and Baumeister 2000), suppressing undesired feelings may result in lower cognitive performance in subsequent tasks.

Second, there is ample evidence that suppressing thoughts backfires in that the thoughts often bounce back after people have suppressed them (see Wenzlaff and Wegner 2000). Most famously, trying not to think about a white bear in the next five minutes makes the concept of a white bear more accessible in subsequent tasks (Wegner, Schneider, Carter, and White 1987). Trying to suppress stereotypes makes them thereafter more accessible than not trying to suppress them at all (e.g., Macrae, Bodenhausen, Milne, and Jetten 1994). Suppressing negative feelings, like suppressing thoughts, may backfire when we can no longer control them, for example after watching a distressing movie (Davies and Clark 1998). When trying to suppress their current mood under cognitive load, people have been shown to be more likely to end up with the mood they wanted to suppress than people who did not suppress their current mood (Wegner, Erber, and Zanakos 1993). Wenzlaff and Bates (1998) found that higher levels of self-reported suppression of depressive thoughts over a four- to six-week period were associated with a worsening of depressive symptoms. These findings, and many more reviewed by Wenzlaff and Wegner, suggest that suppressing emotions is not only costly but ineffective.

Third, and most importantly, suppressing emotions is maladaptive because it can be shown that a repressive coping style increases physiological measures that indicate stress (Gross 1998; Weinberger, Schwartz, and Davidson 1979) and health costs in the long run (Bonanno and Singer 1990). Although suppressing feelings may be part of the arsenal of critical feeling, we have to apply this strategy with caution.

Timeouts, distraction, and "stop and think"

Three behavioral measures have been proposed to direct attention away from inappropriate emotions and to prevent behavior based on impulses derived from such feelings: timeouts, distraction, and stop and think.

Timeouts have been a popular means for parents to calm down angry or aggressive children (e.g., Allison and Allison 1971). For example, your daughter learns to go to her room or another suitable place where she can be alone and is told to stay there for five minutes. Timeouts interrupt the ongoing course of inappropriate action and cool down the hot feelings causing it. This effect of timeouts fits well with the empirical observation that arousal from an event declines over time (Zillmann, Katcher, and Milavsky 1972).

Another strategy to interrupt inappropriate feelings is distraction from the emotion-eliciting situation by finding an alternative focus of attention (Parkinson and Totterdell 1999). Examples include relaxation, positive thinking, and doing some work such as cleaning up one's apartment.

Whereas timeouts rely on the effect of decreasing arousal as time passes and distraction on attention shifts, so-called *stop-and-think rules*, mentioned in John Dewey's book *Education and Experience* (Dewey 1938), add a problem-solving step to the interruption of feelings in that a person is instructed to think about the causes of the feeling. The idea is that, when "bad" feelings are coming up, a person must stop spontaneous action and switch to analytical thinking. There are several possible outcomes of this thinking phase. First, like timeouts, thinking may take time and therefore simply calm down inappropriate feelings. Second, thinking about the situation and its affordances may replace feelings in guiding action. Finally, thinking about the causes of the feelings may lead to a reassessment of the situation, or reappraisal, another strategy used to interrupt feelings.

Stop-and-think rules can also be used when people try to persuade us by appealing to our feelings. As discussed in Chapter 1, some people argue from outrage. The arguments aim to elicit outrage and hence to prevent thinking. Such attempts at persuasion can be countered by stopping to automatically process the incoming information and think about what one's counterpart in the argument wants to achieve. Stop-and-think rules aim to calm down a feeling and to activate knowledge about techniques of influence in order to be able to think critically. Stop and think is an opportunity to pause and think about the appropriate response in a particular situation. There may be situations where outrage is a fully appropriate response that we may feel even after a round of stop and think. Alternatively, we may find that the feeling is based on an inaccurate source, that we have misjudged the situation, and that we must correct our judgment. In a similar vein, our feelings may be the product of erroneous interpretations. When we then stop instead of impulsively give in to our feelings, we may think about how to reinterpret the situation and reappraise it.

Reappraisal

People often become angry because they have misunderstood another person's intentions, only to find out that their anger was misplaced. For example, an employee does not tell his supervisor that something has gone wrong in a production plant. When the supervisor hears about the mishap from a third person, she may get angry because she immediately thinks the employee withheld information with intention. When she hears that the employee knocked at her office door instead of calling her because he wanted to inform her in person, or when it turns out that he sorted out the mistake himself and did not need to communicate the mishap, her anger immediately wanes. She reappraises the intentions of the employee, and this reappraisal results in a change of emotions. This example follows the logic of the appraisal theory discussed in the previous chapter. In short, different interpretations of events lead to different emotions. Appraising the situation in a new way does not suppress negative feelings but rather supplants them with other feelings. Indeed, Gross (1998) provided evidence that reappraising situations, compared to suppressing emotions, results in less sympathetic activation, a hormonal response that indicates stress (see Koole 2009; Ochsner and Gross 2008 for reviews of cognitive emotion regulation).

Employing critical feeling means to look at events from different angles in order to arrive at different potential explanations. For instance, if a supervisor hears about an employee's mishap from a third party, she may stop short her spontaneous reaction and search for further information. Even if further information is not available, she may try to look at the problem from different perspectives (Langer 1997). Such a mindful approach of looking at situations enables a person to reappraise the causes of events. Reappraisal can be a powerful tool for critical feeling: A short intervention of twenty-one minutes to reappraise conflict has been shown to increase marital satisfaction during the following year (Finkel, Slotter, Luchies, Walton, and Gross 2013). No wonder psychotherapists have begun to use reappraisal as a tool to change the thoughts of their clients in order to alleviate feelings that impede normal life and healthy psychological functioning (see Troy, Shallcross, Davis, and Mauss 2013).

As reappraisal is such a successful strategy in alleviating inappropriate feelings, we may think that it is a widely used strategy to keep our emotions in check. Yet this is not true. Suri, Whittaker, and Gross (2015) presented participants with negatively valenced images and gave them an opportunity to reappraise them to decrease negative effect. The researchers found that people reappraise a negative situation less often than one might expect. The reason is that doing nothing in the face of a negative event seemed to be the default option, at least in the laboratory situation created by the authors. It would be interesting to examine whether this observation replicates in everyday life. If so, critical feeling would include overcoming the default option of doing nothing.

Reappraisal of the situation thus prevents impulsive responses and has also been shown to lead to more elaborate and hence less intuitive moral judgments (Feinberg, Willer, Antonenko, and John 2012). Individuals can combine a stop-and-think rule with reappraising the situation. Whereas the think part of the stop-and-think technique remains unspecified, the think part in reappraisal is specific in that people reinterpret the situation in order to change their emotions. As emotions have specific action tendencies, a change of emotions through reappraisal is likely to change subsequent behavior (see Frijda 1986). Another strategy that includes thinking after stopping impulsive responses is meta-awareness.

Meta-awareness

Meta-awareness refers to the fact that people not only are aware of *what* they think but also can become aware of *that* they think. If depressive patients think that they are worthless, they are aware of this thought, and they believe it. Depressive patients are often not able to decenter, or to become aware of the fact that they think this thought, and that it is not necessarily reality (Hargus, Crane, Barnhofer, and Williams 2010; Teasdale, Moore, Hayhurst, Pope, Williams, and Segal 2002). Meta-awareness is similar to the stop-and-think technique in the sense that it stops impulsive thoughts and ruminations. Yet meta-awareness differs from the unspecific stop-and-think rule in that we reflect on the contents of our thoughts and feelings. In contrast to reappraisals, which change the interpretation of a situation, achieving meta-awareness by decentering helps us to see a thought as a thought. There is certainly potential for meta-awareness to be used for various applications, for example when solving interpersonal conflict by becoming aware that *I* think of this person in a negative way; or when coping with negative feelings such as embarrassment, envy, or intense grief. Despite such promising prospects, I have not found much relevant research on the application of this method. I shall mention meta-awareness in passing when we discuss accepting emotions in Chapter 4 and fighting temptations in Chapter 10.

We have discussed suppression of feelings, timeouts and distraction, stop-and-think rules, reappraisal, and meta-awareness as strategies connected to interrupting feelings. We have noted that interrupting feelings redirects attention. Now that our attention is focused on what really is important to us, we can begin to collect information about the state of our interaction with the environment.

Extracting information

There are four strategies when it comes to extracting information from the environment. First, we may use feelings as information. Second, we must correct biased information stemming from erroneous sources of feelings. Third, discrimination learning enables us to make distinctions based on feelings. Finally, we may use knowledge about feelings to influence them, especially the feelings of others.

Feelings as information

How adaptive it would be if we could extract information about the interaction with the environment by tapping our feelings! The basic idea of such a feelings-as-information heuristic (Schwarz 2012) is that the interaction with the environment provides us with cues that we can evaluate by asking how we feel. This heuristic, compared with a thorough analysis of a situation, is advantageous because it often provides sufficient information much faster. The drawback of the feelings-as-information heuristic is its proneness to bias judgments because the feeling may stem from the wrong source. For example, if students have to judge life satisfaction, moods due to transient contextual conditions may inform the judgment even though these cues are not relevant to the judgmental dimension at hand (e.g., Schwarz and Clore 1983).

When interacting with the environment, we may benefit from getting information about ourselves, about others, and about the environment. Extracting information about the state of ourselves becomes important when we have to "listen" to our body. People sometimes do not know when to stop doing an activity, whether it is eating, drinking alcohol, or working hard. Interrupting their ongoing action and asking themselves how they feel may help them to stop an unhealthy activity and thus improve well-being. However, as we shall see in Chapter 4, it is sometimes easier to change the external context, for example serving sizes, when it comes to regulating excessive eating. We "listen" to our body not only to stop unhealthy activities but also to learn a skill. We shall discuss in Chapter 5 how a cybernetic model of action planning and execution called the TOTE model (by Miller, Galanter, and Pribram 1960) can be grasped in terms of feelings gained from bodily feedback.

Another benefit of using feelings as information consists in gaining knowledge about how other people feel. This helps us to assess the state of social interaction. In some cases, the feelings of others are obvious because their facial expressions and posture are distinct. Clear cases of joy, pride, sadness, or anger are examples. A more subtle route to know the affective states of others is the simulation of another person's expression of feelings, as mentioned in the previous chapter. There is ample evidence that adults coordinate their behavior with others (see Wilson and Knoblich 2005), including mimicking gestures and postures (Bernieri 1988; Lakin and Chartrand 2003), facial expressions (Bavelas et al. 1986; Meltzoff and Moore 1977), vocal expressions (Neumann and Strack 2000), and linguistic characteristics in communication (see Garrod and Pickering 2004). Other findings show that one's expression and posture feed back to one's own feeling state (Laird 2007; Strack, Martin, and Stepper 1988). When I smile, I become happier than when I express sadness; when I express sadness, I become sadder than when I smile. Taken together, the findings about imitation of emotional expression and the effect of facial and postural feedback on emotions mean that you can influence how I feel by expressing your feelings. If you smile, I may imitate your smile and feel better; if you express sadness, I may imitate your sad expression and become sadder myself. Such states may come about automatically, without intervening thoughts or interpretations, and without us noticing them. This is different from knowing my son to be proud after having won a game of chess because he shows an unambiguous facial expression and posture. Facial expression of feelings by others influences our feelings because we imitate their facial expression, which leads to genuine feelings due to the feedback from our facial expression.

Given that people simulate feelings of others, we could use our feelings strategically to influence the feelings of others. There certainly are situations where the use of critical feeling seems to be appropriate, at least if we share the value that we should not cheat others. In my opinion, it would be inappropriate if I behaved cheerfully with the intention to bring you into a cheerful mood because I want to persuade you to buy my rusty bicycle. In some situations, however, the strategic expression of feelings in order to influence emotional reactions of others might be appropriate. For example, if we were to get stuck in an elevator together with young children, we might try to put on a calm expression for the sake of pacifying the children.

The third benefit of using feelings as information is the extraction of information from the environment. We saw in the previous chapter that the metacognitive feeling of fluency influences other feelings, among them the feeling of rightness. Sometimes, we may look up the truth of a statement in an encyclopedia or another source upon hearing it. However, this is not always possible, it is often time-consuming, and, in many cases, it is not important enough to justify the effort. The question arises whether fluency as an indicator of truth is epistemically justified and can be used strategically when we do not know the objective truth of a statement. Can we judge the truth of a statement with above-chance accuracy on the basis of the experienced ease with which the proposition can be processed? If this were the case, we could either infer the truth of a statement from the ease with which we process it or at least demonstrate that feelings of rightness go along with the factual truth of a statement we have heard, which would bring inferences from the analysis of facts and from the assessment of feelings into agreement with each other.

Fluency might indicate truth, as shown in a formal analysis by Reber and Unkelbach (2010). Essentially, fluency is a reliable indicator of the truth of a statement we have heard if more than 50 percent of all statements we hear are true. "Reliable" here means an above-chance probability that the statement indeed is true. Whether fluency is a reliable indicator therefore depends critically on whether the sources we are exposed to are reliable.

Critical feeling means that we expose ourselves to sources that we believe are reliable. However, *believing* that a source is reliable does not mean that it indeed *is* reliable. Nevertheless, there is evidence that even preschool children are quite good at distinguishing credible from incredible sources (Koenig, Clément, and Harris 2004). Moreover, there is good reason to assume that statements we hear in everyday life are more probably correct than incorrect: Preliminary evidence for the high probability of the truth of statements comes from research about the accuracy of encyclopedias, such as Wikipedia. One study examined the accuracy of both Wikipedia and a peer-reviewed web site, the patient-oriented National Cancer Institute's Physician Data Query (PDQ) comprehensive cancer database (Rajagopalan, Khanna, Stott, Leiter, Showalter, Dicker, and Lawrence 2010). The authors observed that inaccuracies were very rare (below 2 percent) in both sources. These studies do not of course suffice to make the point that statements are probably true in general, but they mark a starting point for the ecological study of the truth of statements one encounters. Moreover, there may be differences in the truth of statements provided by different outlets. A survey of audiences of various news channels has found that the audience of National Public Radio (now NPR) was best informed about political facts and the audience of Fox News was worst informed (Kull, Ramsay, and Lewis 2003). In summary, the formal analysis by Reber and Unkelbach demonstrates that it would be advantageous to use fluency as a source of judgments of truth. Importantly, people can increase the probability of being exposed to true statements by strategically choosing those sources that have a reputation or even an empirically proven record of being the most reliable. In our example, reviewed above, people will choose to expose themselves to NPR if they want to get accurate information about politics.

However, fluency can sometimes be misleading. A friend of mine who grew up in communist Poland told me that the more often the authorities touted that the economy had grown the more likely it was that the claim was wrong. In this case, we would have to correct for the falseness of the feeling of rightness due to endless repetition (see Unkelbach 2007). Similarly, often repeated advertisements about the health of chocolate bars due to their content of milk provide misinformation to children; it has become the task of parents to rectify the facts. This raises the question of how critical feelers can correct false information stemming from feelings.

Correcting wrong information

A second strategy to extract accurate information is the ability to correct judgments that are biased because people misinterpret feelings and their sources. Feelings provide people with information about their interaction with the environment, and they often base their judgments and decisions on this information (see Schwarz 2012). In many cases, relying on feelings results in accurate judgment. When we have to assess a job applicant, we may have a positive gut feeling because he makes a competent and friendly impression, and our feeling-based judgment may be accurate. If we have a negative gut feeling about him, we may restrain from hiring him. Sometimes, however, our judgments and decisions are biased because the source differs from the genuine object of evaluation. As mentioned earlier, there is the possibility that the outcome of the hiring process might be biased by an irrelevant source of feelings underlying the decision, such as a good meal or a nasty dispute.

Research in cognitive and social psychology has unraveled that people make systematic mistakes as a result of their feelings (see Schwarz, Sanna, Skurnik, and Yoon 2007). For example, teachers give worse grades when an essay is written in bad handwriting than when the handwriting is elegant and readable (e.g., Greifeneder, Alt, Bottenberg, Seele, Zelt and Wagener 2010; James 1929; Markham 1976). There are two possible reasons for this effect: First, teachers may think that bad handwriting goes along with bad performance. However, there are also stereotypes to the contrary: Medical doctors, for example, are notorious for their unreadable handwriting, but this does not harm their reputation. The second possible reason starts from the assumption that essays in good handwriting are easy to read and essays in bad handwriting are hard to read. As we have seen, ease of processing influences affective responses. Thus, teachers like essays that are easy to read better than essays that are hard to read, and this affective preference may carry over to their evaluation of the quality of the essay. As handwriting and essay quality are presumably unrelated, the feelings-as-information heuristic applied to judging handwritten essays leads teachers astray. If they know that handwriting influences their feelings, they may try to correct their biased judgment (Greifeneder et al. 2010). Similarly, listeners are influenced by a foreign accent that is hard to understand; if they are warned that they might not understand utterances because of the foreign accent, the bias decreases (Lev-Ari and Keysar 2010). However, as we shall see throughout this book, the advice to correct biased judgments is easier said than done, because it may be difficult to find out about the influence of our feelings on judgments in the first place (Nisbett and Wilson 1977). Even if we determine in what direction our feelings are influencing our judgments, it may be difficult to find out to what degree they do, resulting in over- or under-correction (see Schwarz et al. 2007).

A variation of the same theme is the observation that "mud sticks." Let us assume you hear a negative rumor about your neighbor that later turns out to be wrong. Although the rumor is unfounded, people do not fully correct for their mistaken knowledge and an odd feeling remains. Social psychologists explain this "mud sticks" phenomenon by the fact that, when we hear a negative rumor about a person, we not only register the uncomfortable fact but also try to explain why this person could have done what she did, especially if the behavior in question comes as a surprise (Heider 1958). This is important because, next time, we like to try to predict such behavior before it happens instead of having to explain it after the fact. After hearing the rumor, we look for information that could help to explain the surprising fact but neglect to search for contradicting information. For example, if a person behaved aggressively, we commit a confirmation bias (Klayman and Ha 1987) by looking for instances of prior aggressive behavior but not for instances of prior friendly behavior. We integrate each piece of information that helps to make the rumor plausible into our representation of the target of the rumor. From this search for information plus its integration into existing representations results a tightly knit web of knowledge about the target. This makes it difficult to disentangle whether the information was integrated before or after we heard the rumor. When we later hear that the rumor is wrong, we revise the information that the target person did commit the deed in question but we are unable to correct all the information that accumulated as a consequence of our search for an explanation of this behavior. That is why mud sticks. Most of the information accumulated to explain the rumored behavior remains uncorrected and leads to more negative judgments of the character of the target person (Ross, Lepper, and Hubbard 1975). Critical feeling means that we reflect on the fact that our feelings might be biased by information integrated after hearing the rumor and that we attempt to correct this one-sided information. Again, we cannot be sure whether or not we have corrected our feelings and our judgment of the person to the right degree.

Discrimination learning

Experiences pervade our daily lives. Whether we perceive art, listen to music, taste wine, attend to the sound of an engine, or monitor our own movements when learning a new skill, the common denominator is that we can feel the quality of the experience, and we often feel it automatically. This gives rise to the third strategy to extract information from the environment. Experts in certain domains can experience fine differences that people without proper training or extensive experience cannot. In fact, in one study, the superiority of wine experts over novices in recognizing wine-related odors did not depend on enhanced semantic memory or linguistic capabilities but on superior perceptual skills (Parr, Heatherbell, and White 2002). Once people are able to tell different tastes from each other, they neither have to consciously recall the taste differences nor be able to verbalize their experience by giving different labels to the different tastes. They have simply learned to experience the new tastes. This learning takes time and people may need extensive training to be able to perceive the finer nuances.

Why is discrimination learning important for critical feeling? There is a simple reason: Thorough analysis of experiences or critical evaluation of tastes is logically impossible without being able to discriminate between different experiences and therefore between different underlying stimulus structures. Having the ability to feel the finer distinctions has two consequences: First, the feeling becomes richer in itself. Enjoying a piece of music without being able to distinguish between a good and a bad performance may be fine. The learned capacity to hear the difference between a presentation with superb expression and one that is flat lets us enjoy the expressive performance, but with the disadvantage that we may no longer enjoy the flat piece. As a second consequence, being able to experience the difference between two performances of music – or between two objects of sensation in general – has further consequences down the road. If Julie learns to play the flute, she has to learn to find the right notes. However, she can only do that if she has learned to distinguish the right note from other notes. She must therefore first train her musical ear before she begins to practice. As outlined in the previous chapter, pure discrimination as a cognitive phenomenon is not yet a feeling, which depends on Julie's ability to evaluate the distinct tones.

To apply this idea, let us return to expertise in wine tasting. There are at least two capacities that make a wine expert: the ability to identify a wine and the ability to evaluate it (see Burnham and Skilleås 2012). Identifying different wines depends first and foremost on discrimination learning that improves perceptual discrimination between different flavors and odors. Better discrimination makes for richer experiences and therefore for more fine-grained distinctions when it comes to evaluations. Being able to identify wines and classify their tastes results in refined evaluations and therefore more differentiated feelings. True connoisseurs have superior taste because they base their evaluations on richer sensations. In Chapter 5, I elaborate on the notion that each perception includes evaluation; that is why discrimination affects not only cognitive processing related to the distinct content but also feelings.

Discrimination learning may lead to ironic effects. For example, two guests in a restaurant both order samples of the same two wines. Let us assume that one, let's call him Andrew, cannot taste any difference between the samples whereas Colleen has enough expertise to discern the difference in taste. The consequence may be that Andrew chooses the cheaper wine because he feels there is no difference whereas Colleen goes for the superior, but more expensive, wine. We can change this example a bit to illustrate the ironic effect: If the cheaper wine is the better one, we may even observe that Andrew chooses the more expensive wine despite not feeling any difference because he uses the price as a cue to quality and wants to show that he is a connoisseur. Colleen, in contrast, orders the cheaper wine because she has the experience to know that it is the better one (see Plassmann, O'Doherty, Shiv, and Rangel 2008 for a related study).

The examples I gave for discrimination learning not only apply to supposedly upper-class examples of wine, art, and music but also to hands-on activities such as tuning the engine of a car (see Dewey

2005/1934). Good mechanics can distinguish between distinct sounds and immediately evaluate whether all is well with the engine.

Using knowledge about feelings

Research in psychology and the social sciences has amassed a huge amount of data about what makes people happy. There are at least two ways in which we can use this knowledge. We may consult the evidence and initiate the action with the highest probability of making us happy. For example, we may read that marrying makes us happier than remaining single (see, for example, Myers 1993; Seligman 2002). Apart from the problems inherent in interpreting statistics – for example, when we compare people who are married with singles, excluding divorced and widowed people who were once married (DePaulo and Morris 2006) – there is a problem in making one's decisions according to such knowledge. Let us assume that marrying indeed does make people happier: Does this mean that you should marry if you have not already done so? Certainly not; a decision based on such data would not qualify as critical feeling but would amount to the uncritical adoption of a way of life based on probabilistic outcomes (see Annas 2011, p. 129). We have to remember that not all married individuals are happier than singles; the happiness of married people and singles form two overlapping Gaussian distributions (or "bell curves"). It is possible for an individual single person to be much happier than an individual married person. Another way to use the same information is to imagine marriage as an option. This will qualify as critical feeling if you act mindfully, open to every possible outcome. In this case, information about the probability of becoming happier does not seduce you into marriage but just into playing with your thoughts, weighing your options and reasons both in favor of and against the pursuit of a way of life. You do not only think about whether marriage would make you happier; this would relegate your future spouse to an instrument of your happiness. You must also think more broadly about what your values are and whether marriage would fit or contradict such values and whether you are willing to commit yourself to a long-term relationship. Such thoughts are certainly accompanied by feelings you would have to listen to. This would be critical decision making without exploiting marriage to one's own goals. The same logic applies to having children or being religious; such decisions should not be in the service of making us happy. As we shall see in the next chapter, happiness is a by-product of what we do, and the conscious pursuit of happiness may backfire.

Besides using knowledge about their own feelings, people often use knowledge about the feelings of others in order to influence them.

I discussed above the simulation of feelings of others and how they can be used to extract information. Knowledge about another person's feelings gained through feedback from our own feelings is only possible if we have direct contact. Even hearing a voice on the phone does not provide the direct access to an interlocutor's expressions that face-to-face contact does. Often, we do not rely on our knowledge about the feelings of an individual to influence him or her but on knowledge about the feelings of people in general. Of Beethoven, for example, it was said that he knew exactly how to compose music to bring listeners to tears but that he laughed at them (see Carroll 1999). Marketers and salespeople use knowledge about their customers' feelings to sell their goods. Political campaigners try to persuade voters by appealing to the emotions of the masses, as Le Bon (1960/1895) described.

We use knowledge about other people's feelings not only to influence their behavior to our benefit but also to understand and help them. For example, students who attribute failure in an exam to the difficulty of the task may react with hopelessness, while those who attribute it to lack of effort may respond with guilt, and those who attribute it to lack of talent with shame (see Weiner 1985). If a teacher knows about emotional responses to attribution, he may try to change the suboptimal attributions of his students. As long as a student does not lack talent and as long as the task is really not too difficult, attribution to effort leads to the best outcomes in terms of greater persistence and higher learning outcomes.

Changing external context

Changing the physical environment

It is a human tendency to attribute a mishap to victims and to think that *they* have to change in order to improve a situation. In a study about counterfactual reasoning, the experimenters presented a scenario where the driver of a car died after an accident caused by a drugged teenager (Kahneman and Tversky 1982). When asked about how this accident could have been prevented, the participants focused on what the victim of the accident could have done, not on how the teenager could have acted differently. Even relatives of victims who died in a car accident reacted in the same way and rarely considered other parties involved or the circumstances. Similarly, when a person feels bad, or when she wants to feel better, we often look for how this person could change her thoughts or attitudes in order to attain a more positive state. We sometimes ask ourselves whether a little gift might help, which is a small external change, but we rarely ask how we could change the environment or the circumstances to make the person feel better. This is unfortunate because changing the external context is a powerful proficiency of critical feeling.

Among the few researchers who have examined optimal contexts to optimize well-being are environmental psychologists interested in which conditions result in positive affective states. Factors that have been found to influence affect in working environments are noise, temperature, the quality of air, light, colors, whether an office has a window, and spatial arrangement (see Gifford 2002 for a summary). It is easy to recommend changes in the environment to match the needs of workers. However, beyond the money that employers would have to invest in office and production settings, such an adaptation of the work environment is sometimes prevented by what Gifford calls *environmental numbness*. When it comes to spatial arrangements, employees may be insensitive and do not realize that their workplace is suboptimal. They therefore do not report their feelings, and no measures are taken to improve the situation (Gifford 1976). Overloaded or overworked employees may be even less sensitive to environmental factors, such as temperature or density, than employees with normal workloads (Sutton and Rafaeli 1987).

Changing the arrangement of stimuli in the environment can also help to overcome momentary feeling states that prevent the achievement of long-term goals. An early-morning dilemma experienced by most students sometimes – and by some students most of the time – lies in the conflict between the long-term goal of passing an exam and the short-term pleasure of turning over and getting two hours' more sleep. Most of the time, passing the exam is the prioritized value. However, just when one should tumble out of bed at seven o'clock to get ready for one's lectures, the momentary value of getting more sleep is greater than the long-term value of passing the exam (for a summary of this phenomenon and how to cope with it, see Mazur 2006, p. 341–342.). As soon as one gets up at nine o'clock, the priority of the values is dramatically reversed; overflowing with regret about the missed lecture, students at that very moment promise never to snooze again – until the next time they wake up, too tired to cope with the problems of the dawning day.

Learning theorists recommend changes in the physical or social environment to overcome the impulse to give in to such momentary pleasures. For example, when my alarm clock is in the next room, I have to get up to stop the alarm. Another effective method is to ask a reliable friend to pick me up in the morning. It should be a friend I would feel ashamed to greet in my pajamas. Such behavioral measures are realistic in the sense that they rely neither on reasons to get up (which I know already but without effect) nor on my will-power in the early morning (which has proven to be weak); we should instead set some external obstacles to staying in bed. The hope is that, after some time, such contextual measures will build a habit of getting up early and attending the lectures. Changing the arrangement of the environment is also important in eating behavior, as we shall see in Chapter 4.

The question is, however, what happens when external support is removed – for example, when I no longer put my alarm clock outside my bedroom or when my friend moves to another place and can no longer pick me up. It would therefore be interesting to find internal means to increase the probability of me getting up early and attending at least the lectures I need to attend to pass the exam.

Selecting optimal environments

We can try to avoid situations we dislike. For example, if I feel awkward talking in public, I may simply avoid doing it instead of getting training to overcome my anxiety. This is different from changing the arrangement of the environment because the environment is left unchanged; I just avoid it. People in the Western hemisphere often think that they have to change themselves in order to feel better in a situation. However, why not seek out situations where we feel good and avoid those where we feel bad? This solution is inspired by research about differences in thought between the West and the East (Nisbett 2003). Nisbett argued that Western people try to improve their skills whereas Eastern people may opt to avoid a situation in which they fail to act properly. Learning from the Easterners, Westerners might broaden the scope of their options by selecting the environment that suits them best. Selecting environments can be understood in a broad sense.

However, selecting environments is not alien to people in the West. We all select our friends. Indeed, Aristotle emphasized the role of friends for self-improvement and advised people to choose the right friends for this purpose (see Chapter 10). Choosing friends can be seen as the selection of a social environment that accepts us the way we are; we can share information with them.

Sharing information

People share information with others. Providing information may change the state of the listener in a way that feeds back to the speaker. We shall encounter two instances of this phenomenon in this book. First, people who have experienced the loss of a close person talk to others about their grief (Chapter 4). It has been observed that people who talk about their

negative feelings improve their well-being. It was first thought that talking about negative feelings to friends and therapists is good in itself. If so,
it should lead to a change in our inner state, which we discuss in the next
section. However, research has shown that it is not the change in inner
states from talking about negative experiences that results in relief but
rather changes in the responses of the listeners.

Finally, in Chapter 7 we discuss pluralistic ignorance, which is
the phenomenon in which a majority of people in a group think that the
others in the same group have views that differ from their own when the
majority in fact entertains the same views. For example, adolescents may
believe that most others think cool clothes are important when in fact
most of their peers care as little about clothing as they do themselves.
By sharing the opinion that branded clothes are not important, teenagers may increase the willingness of others to admit that cool clothes
are not important to them. By sharing information about our thoughts
and feelings, we receive information about the thoughts and feelings of
others; this part of the strategy could be subsumed under receiving accurate information. The mutual exchange of information helps to change
the social environment in that it changes collective beliefs. In the case of
pluralistic ignorance, accurate information about others helps to change
feelings that were derived from wrong assumptions. A teenager might feel
less shame over the old-fashioned trousers he "inherited" from his older
brother after hearing that others do not mind what clothes he wears.

Changing inner states

After having reviewed potential strategies to change the physical and
social environment, I address strategies to change inner mental states. I begin
with three tools to influence feelings: planning, mental imagery and simulation, and conditioning. I then continue with more foundational changes
that go beyond mere mental tools and require a person's long-term commitment: changing values, changing aspiration levels, and shaping behavior.

Planning

When momentary impulses are powerful and external support for
overcoming them is lacking, we need to plan how we can achieve our
long-term goals. One promising strategy is to use implementation intentions (see Gollwitzer 1999), which are concrete plans to perform a clearly
defined behavior. For example, instead of saying, "In the future, I will
stand up when the alarm clock rings," the plan is, "Tomorrow, when the

alarm clock rings at 7am, I shall immediately roll back my blanket, sit up, put my feet on the floor, and then stand up." Research has shown for many situations (but to my knowledge not for standing up in the morning) that such implementation intentions are a powerful tool in overcoming momentary impulses in order to achieve long-term goals. Examples are procrastination and health behavior (see next chapter). Sometimes, we do not need planning; it is enough to imagine the future acts in order to achieve our goals.

Mental imagery and simulation

There is a famous finding that the vivid portrayal of an isolated case can be more persuasive than more sober but reliable statistics about the same issue (Hamill, Wilson, and Nisbett 1980). In this study, the statistics showed that the average payment period for social security was relatively short. However, a lively story about one recipient who never got off welfare benefits influenced the attitudes of participants toward recipients of social security more than prosaic statistics. Presumably, the students imagined the story and these images had a stronger impact on their feelings toward welfare recipients than statistical tables; in turn, those feelings influenced their attitudes, even when the vivid story was accompanied by the statistics. Holmes and Mathews (2010) reviewed evidence that mental imagery amplifies emotions and even influences future behavior. When people imagine a future act, especially from an observer perspective, they are more likely to behave accordingly. For instance, appropriate imagery increases the probability of revising for an exam (Pham and Taylor 1999), voting (Libby, Shaeffer, Eibach, and Slemmer 2007), and donating blood (Carroll 1978).

This short review of research suggests that manipulation of mental imagery as a strategy can be used in two opposite directions. First, when we endorse a cause but are too passive to act on it, we may employ mental imagery to heighten the intensity of the feeling toward that cause. Sometimes, however, imagery is overwhelming, and we may wish the inner images would lose some of their vividness. Suicidal patients, for example, often imagine vivid scenarios about their suicide and its consequences – for example, that all is over (Holmes, Crane, Fennell, and Williams 2007). It seems that such imagery distinguishes those who commit suicide attempts from those who have suicidal ideation without executing suicidal actions. In this case, tempering the vividness of mental images might save lives.

Imagining suicidal scenarios is related to mentally simulating events or states. We have earlier seen that automatic simulation of the facial expressions of others leads to empathy. In a similar way, we may try to intentionally simulate emotional expressions through face, posture, or voice in order to get into a desired feeling state (see Laird 2007). However, evidence for the success of such posing is mixed, as will be reviewed in Chapter 5.

Classical and instrumental conditioning

Remember the example of the advertisement that connects Pepsi to kissing. Whereas Pepsi may be a neutral object for young people, kissing certainly is not. The mechanism underlying the effectiveness of this advertisement is classical conditioning, specifically the fact that kissing is an unconditioned stimulus that elicits an unconditioned response, in this case sexual arousal. Pepsi is the conditioned stimulus, which in itself does not arouse anything. However, the pairing of the kiss and the beverage results in the arousal of a positive feeling when seeing Pepsi alone. If advertisers use classical conditioning with apparent success, why should we not do the same? For example, by relaxing when we think of an exam, we may connect the exam to relaxation instead of anxiety. When a woman recalls positive experiences while she thinks of her parents, she may rekindle positive attitudes she has not had for some time.

There is a smooth transition from classical conditioning to instrumental conditioning. For example, when the woman recalls positive experiences while she thinks of her parents, positive experiences are not only paired with her parents but also rewarding and thus tend to be repeated. Reward and punishment are used in education, mostly in the form of praise and reproof. Behavioral therapy builds on reinforcement. There are ample opportunities to do the same in order to persuade ourselves to adopt the behavior we want to establish as routine. For example, eating a small chocolate after having accomplished a difficult task may reinforce the tendency to persist in the face of difficulty in future tasks. In theory, we could also punish ourselves to counter undesired behavior. We shall see in the next chapter, however, that such aversive interventions are not commendable.

Changing values

Instead of using tools that help us in individual situations, we may go for fundamental change, for example by rethinking and revising our values. Such a change of values can happen gradually or abruptly. The best-known abrupt change of values happens in conversion experiences, vividly reported in James' (1985/1902) classic *The Varieties of religious experience*. In a typical conversion experience, non-believers feel miserable or are in a deep personal crisis. They are desperate because they do not see any escape from their misery. All of a sudden, a deep insight occurs out of the blue. From one moment to another, they switch from being non-believers to being believers. We have seen that values guide thought, feeling, and action. Conversion experiences have far-reaching consequences because they fundamentally change the mindset of a person. However, little is known about how much believers, compared to non-believers, change their behavior, except for those actions directed at practicing the new creed. Moreover, there has been little research about whether such experiences really come out of the blue. It may well be that conversion experiences have to meet a prepared mind and that the conversion is more gradual than it seems, in line with empirical observations on intuition (Bowers, Farvolden, and Mermigis 1995; Reber, Ruch-Monachon, and Perrig 2007). Indeed, conversion experiences can be gradual, as James (1985/1902) documents, and they can go in both directions. Not only can an atheist or an apatheist – a person who does not care about religion (Norenzayan and Gervais 2013) – become a believer but a believer can begin to doubt her creed and become a non-believer.

Fundamental change of values is not limited to religious conversion experiences. People may turn from liberals to conservatives; from capitalists to socialists; from car freaks to environmentalists; from lovers of luxury to advocates of the simple life. I shall discuss in Chapter 7 how consumers may avoid the influence of advertisements by building a value system that emphasizes the simple life. These consumers change, among other things, their aspiration levels.

Changing aspiration level

Happiness is much more flexible than we assume. Lottery winners are happier than normal mortals who have to work for an income – but only for about three months (Brickman, Coates, and Janoff-Bulman 1978). Similarly, patients with a chronic illness or disability do not feel as miserable as healthy people think they do. These observations can be explained by the fact that what seems to be unusual today will be normal tomorrow. Both lottery winners and the seriously ill or handicapped forget how life was in the past after some time. Their aspiration level adapts to the new reality and, when they compare their current state with the state they aspire to, the discrepancy is not as large as we assume. The observation that people with a disability adapt their standards to reality and remain happy leads to the question, answered in the next chapter, of whether it is possible to consciously set standards that are lower than the standards we currently adhere to.

Shaping behavior

After changing values, people may not only change aspiration levels but also shape their behavior in order to implement their values. In fact, shaping behavior involves a combination of changing inner states, changing external contexts, and extracting information. People first decide how they would like to behave. They may then use the methods to change inner states discussed above, such as conditioning or planning. An integral part of shaping behavior is repetition, which increases the fluency of executing an action such that it becomes a habit (Dewey 2012/1922). In later chapters I discuss how we may enhance our well-being by mimicking a positive emotional expression; how we can alleviate anxiety; how we may cultivate positive emotions at school; how we can learn styles in art; and, finally, how we may live our religious and moral values by using our feelings. One way to improve our moral life comes from Confucianism.

Confucian training aims at thoughtful execution of moral habits (in the sense Dewey 2012/1922 understands them). If we have trained well enough, we will not only be able to execute an action efficiently but also be able to evaluate a situation spontaneously by using feelings as information. Feeling well after the execution of an action indicates that our action corresponds with our values; feeling bad indicates that the action might not correspond with our values and hence needs improvement. This kind of enactment of norms and values may be applied to such different domains as health behavior, learning at school, and implementing one's norms and values. In sum, successful Confucian training cultivates feelings that serve both the initiation of action and the assessment of its outcomes. In the best case, assessment of an action through feelings corresponds to the assessment of the same action through reason. If it turns out that reason and feelings contradict each other, we should look for improvements in either our reasoning abilities or our feeling capacities.

Taking these factors together, when people want to implement their goals, norms, or values, they ask themselves how they could use their knowledge about feelings in order to achieve the desired outcome. After having implemented the measures, they assess the outcome by asking how they feel. This is in line with what we learned earlier about extracting information from the environment. For example, if a person wants to get into a happy mood and therefore simulates the expression and posture of a happy person, she may assess the success of her measures by asking herself: How do I feel? If she feels well, she has managed to get into a positive mood. Similarly, if an expat worker wants to develop a taste for the food of his new home country, he may know that it is best to expose himself to the native food of the country. After some time of exposure to the new cuisine, he can assess whether he has developed the desired taste by checking how he feels when eating the local food.

Critical feeling in the service of values

After having reviewed the proficiencies and strategies of critical feeling and the rational functions they serve, we have to consider the purposes of critical feeling. So far, we have discussed critical feeling as a skill. We have listed the proficiencies without considering the values they serve. Critical feeling as a skill may help a person to focus on the technical even in the face of cruelties. In a well-known study, participants were shown movies about revolting accidents or bloody rituals and asked to watch the movie from the perspective of a scientist who is interested in the technicalities of these events. The researchers observed that participants who took a technical perspective showed fewer physiological responses to the movies than a control group without such instructions (Speisman, Lazarus, Mordkoef, and Davison 1964). Other research showed that long-term exposure of youth to violent movies or videogames resulted in blunted affect that in turn may lead to a lack of scruples and remorse (Anderson, Berkowitz, Donnerstein, Huesmann, Johnson, Linz, Malamuth, and Wartella 2003).

In line with these studies, critical feeling as a skill can be used to commit abominable atrocities. In her book *Eichmann in Jerusalem: A Report on the Banality of Evil*, Hannah Arendt (2006/1963) described how soldiers of the German SS felt disgust at seeing the blood gushing in streams from the victims they shot. The soldiers could not help feeling disgust – this seems to be a feeling too hard-wired to get rid of easily; it simply cannot be suppressed. Instead, the soldiers transformed themselves into victims (of a sort) who had the unsavory but necessary task of accomplishing the objectives of the Nazi state. Here, the soldiers cultivated the feeling they wanted to experience in order to circumvent a signal that would have shown them how ghastly their deeds were. Another example is the Norwegian terrorist Anders Behring Breivik, who stated that he trained himself to numb his negative feelings in order to be able to kill his young victims at Utøya (Børringbo, Buan, and Johanessen

2012). Again, a villain cultivated a feeling state with the aim of overcoming natural sentiments and moral intuitions so as to be able to descend into a state of savagery.

Examples of misguided critical feeling as a skill do not need to be as nauseating as the examples in the previous paragraph. For example, Côté, DeCelles, McCarthy, Van Kleef, and Hideg (2011) examined the question of whether people who know how to regulate their emotions always use this knowledge in a virtuous way. Their results suggest that this is only the case when moral purposes, such as compassion, honesty, or fairness, are crucial to an individual's sense of self. Only the participants for whom this was the case showed increased prosocial behavior, compared to participants for whom moral purposes were unimportant. This study documents that the abuse of critical feeling for pernicious purposes is not restricted to exceptional cases but seems to be quite common. Other examples include a defendant in a crime case who feigns contrition and repentance in order to get a less severe sentence and a student who feigns agreement with the teacher in order to get better grades.

Critical thinking cannot resolve this issue. Remember how Martin (1992) criticized discussions that could be in accordance with the rules of critical thinking but neglect moral issues. Critical thinking as a skill may limit a discussion to mere technicalities without seeing the bigger picture. I therefore now apply to critical feeling the idea that critical thinking can be employed in the service of values.

We can again distinguish value-free science from value-laden practice. To repeat, science is value free because taking a certain perspective does not mean that the researcher endorses this viewpoint (Schurz 2013; White 1965). Practitioners, on the other hand, have to start from values and then ask how to best implement them. Children grow up in value-laden environments, and educators aim to inculcate (to use a favorite term of Bourdieu 1984/1979) the values of their country, religion, or economy (Kvale 2003). Even the distinctions drawn in the discussion on critical thinking between universalism and contextualism and between dispositionism and situationism apply to critical feeling. Like critical thinking, critical feeling aims to find the best outcomes within a situation and therefore challenges the assumption of the universalism of patterns of thought, feeling, and behavior.

What needs to be discussed is the understanding of the situation; this discussion leads us to the same conclusions regarding value pluralism as in critical thinking, but the epistemological questions concerning the understanding of a situation through affective information are more intricate than understanding a situation through inferences from observation or from prior knowledge.

In the previous chapter, we discussed recent work on the epistemic role of emotional experience. This work suggests that we need to understand the reasons that give rise to our feelings in order to act properly (Brady 2013; Deonna and Teroni 2012). To act properly means that we connect our actions to our values. If understanding feelings is a prerequisite to acting properly, we have to understand how our feelings relate to our values. Only if we understand this relation between feelings and values can we trust our feelings when we assess the outcome of actions. While Goldie (2004) thinks that we can trust our feelings at least in some cases, Brady (2013) argues against unconditional trust in the information our feelings provide and proposes that the virtuous person tries to understand the situation that elicited the emotion. Besides the fact that critical feeling involves looking for the right course of action within a situation and – in contrast to what is argued by Brady – does not primarily aim to build a virtuous character (see Chapter 1), searching for reasons for our emotions would be a time-consuming process and therefore be useful only in theory, not in practice. As we saw in Chapter 2, the somatic marker hypothesis provides a plausible account of how the learning history of a person leads to feelings that reliably anticipate the outcome of a decision. Searching for reasons is only necessary if one is uncertain about whether emotions provide reliable information.

This uncertainty may be greater nowadays than it was in the past. In traditional societies, values, positions within a hierarchy, and behaviors within the community were clearly defined and stable over time (see Weber 1958a). Growing up in a tribal community meant socialization in responding accurately to every situation within the community. Such a community, at least in the idealized case presented here, had fixed pairings of stimuli and their appropriate responses that left little room for interpretation. Individuals in traditional societies could trust their emotions because they had internalized behavioral programs for social situations they had encountered in their community. As most situations left little room for interpretation, the reasons for an emotion were understood spontaneously; elaboration was not necessary. Such traditional patterns reached into the modern era, as an example from Imperial Germany shows. When an officer's sister was defiled, he had no choice but to defend his honor by challenging the sister's lover to a duel, at least if he wanted to maintain his dignity (see Frevert 1995/1991). Humans in traditional societies could be sure that actions derived from their emotions implemented the internalized values of their community.

The open society of modern times leaves much more leeway for interpreting the causes of social behavior. This increases uncertainty regarding whether emotions stem from reliable sources. Consequently, citizens often do not know whether their emotions will result in actions that implement their own values or the values of their society. Modern citizens cannot trust their feelings because social life has become more complex, which means that people cannot spontaneously understand the reasons for their emotions. This lack of understanding means that humans in modern society cannot be sure that spontaneous action based on feelings is appropriate.

How could the modern person regain the trust that traditional people possessed in the reliability of their feelings? One potential response – and the most depressing one – is that times of certainty are gone forever and that there will be no way of knowing about the justification of a feeling except by deeper analysis. Alternatively, one could imagine that modern societies will build a global community that defines and enforces universal values. Some groups may wish their values to become universal. However, given the plurality of values, and the undesirability of force, such unification seems utopic, with the exception of some basic rules of conduct. Finally, modern people might select a community that provides rules of conduct whose internalization would allow immediate understanding of the reasons for emotions and therefore enable spontaneous actions that are deemed right by the community. Typical examples of such communities are religious or minority ones.

Such communities provide a framework within which people can think, feel, and act. Instead of constructing every situation anew from the bottom up, people can retrieve and enact the sanctioned values in a top-down manner. This is advantageous because it saves cognitive resources. People can act accurately as defined by their community – and fast. One could criticize that acting from what we have internalized would lead to pre-programmed behavior and hamper social progress. However, Karl Popper (2002/1963) makes the case that tradition provides us with options for actions, for it "is not possible for you to act rationally in the world if you have no idea how it will respond to your actions" (p. 175–176). Therefore, Popper argues, one has to "consider traditions critically, weighing their merits against their demerits, and never forgetting the merit which lies in the fact that they are established traditions" (p. 178). Basically, traditions help people to orient themselves within their community.

These thoughts do not change the plurality of values discussed in Chapter 1. Akin to the justification of beliefs, people can weigh the same situational facts differently and therefore arrive at distinct conclusions concerning the justification of feelings. Understanding the basics of feelings does not mean that there is only one correct interpretation of the information gathered within the situation. Value plurality does not exclude the possibility, however, that we can define some indicators of when critical feeling is used as a mere skill and lacks virtue. In line with the discussion on critical thinking, moral norms are defined through practices, and virtually all practices converge on some basic moral values that are irrevocable, such as not killing another person. Exceptions to this rule are limited to precisely defined cases.

Even if one advocates moral realism and claims that moral values are not constructions of an individual's mind, some indications signal that people are acting against their own values and the values of their community. First, and almost trivially, most people feel scruples when they do something wrong. If a person is not too scrupulous, a bad conscience is a good indicator that she is not acting virtuously even when she uses her feelings to achieve a personally desired outcome – say, to sell a bad car for a good price by not telling the buyer about its deficiencies.

Second, the car-selling example is not only about having scruples but also about concealing information. If we have the impression that it would be wise to conceal facts that would be relevant in our dealings with another person, we should ask ourselves whether we are acting virtuously. There are some situations where hiding information is appropriate, such as concealing what present I shall bestow on my wife on her next birthday; however, often, hiding information or even providing deceiving information is a sign that we use critical thinking or critical feeling not in the service of values but as a technique to give us a cutting edge.

Third, feelings may come from the wrong source and therefore lead to erroneous action. One kind of wrong source comes from the situation. A father who is angry because he has lost money in gambling should not let off steam at his children. Another kind of wrong source may stem from socialization. When children are made to feel guilty during their upbringing, they may subsequently feel guilt in situations where the community at large would consider this feeling as unfounded. Critical feeling attempts at least to detect such erroneous sources in order to align one's behavior with the values one endorses. In general, however, subsequent correction and thus debiasing has been found to be difficult (see Schwarz et al. 2007 for examples).

These first three indicators all pertain to contradictions between thoughts or actions on the one hand and feelings on the other; the contradictions lie within our own mind. There is a fourth indicator that measures the contradiction between our actions and the norms of the family, community, or society. Actions and feelings may be in perfect agreement, but the action may be wrong nevertheless. Transgressing the norms and values of our group or society may be a sign that we are on the wrong side. Norms have grown from tradition, and we may assume that they have some function. Of course, deliberation may reveal that the norms are no longer topical and hence need to be changed. However, we should not ignore norms lightly because – as we have seen above – traditions may have some rational basis (Popper 2002/1963).

In summary, we can trust our feelings if we have a learning history that provides us with valid information about the environment in a given situation. Moreover, proper understanding of feelings can only be accomplished when we know the values we want to implement. If the environment or the values change, our feelings no longer provide valid information to guide our action. We then need to rely on an analysis of the situation, including its value options. This is why people in modern, pluralistic societies can presumably rely less on feelings than people in traditional societies that have stable routines and practices. As modern humans we could only return to a state where we could again trust our feelings by selecting or building stable communities.

What critical feeling is not

Having defined the term critical feeling, we must examine existing concepts that are similar to critical feeling, and we must delineate the differences. We are going to look at the concepts of rationality of emotion, emotional intelligence, emotional competence, positive psychology, and mindfulness.

Rationality of emotion

I have reviewed Damasio's somatic marker hypothesis (Damasio 1994) and De Sousa's notion of the rationality of emotion (De Sousa 1987; see also Frank 1988). Both lines of work conclude that feelings are rational, a claim that was provocative as late as the 1980s and 1990s. Scientists nowadays admit that heuristics based on cognitive shortcuts or feelings may be adaptive and may optimize a person's dealings with the environment. However, while some philosophers have concluded from the insights about thinking and rationality that we need to teach critical thinking skills, neither Damasio nor De Sousa provide us with a systematic overview of how we could turn from the insight that feelings are rational to the implementation of critical feeling. In the last chapter of his book, De Sousa underlines the importance of emotions to the conduct of life without giving concrete advice on how to use emotions strategically in order to achieve desired outcomes.[1] Critical feeling goes beyond rationality of emotions in the sense that it refers to psychological research on the use of feelings to provide evidence-based advice that improve outcomes.

Emotional intelligence

Opposing the notion that intelligence is a purely intellectual concept, Daniel Goleman (1995) used examples to illustrate that people who are intellectually brilliant can fail because they lack some capacity that Salovey and Mayer (1990) termed *emotional intelligence*. This capacity includes several elements. Emotionally intelligent people feel with others; they can read emotions in the faces of others and figure out how others must feel in a certain situation. Emotionally intelligent people can keep their emotions under control, especially negative ones and those that lead to aggression. In contrast to intelligence in the cognitive domain, where studies have revealed that intelligence can be considered a unitary concept, there is little evidence that emotional intelligence is a unitary concept that can be distinguished from other forms of intelligence (see Waterhouse 2006).

There are obvious similarities between emotional intelligence and critical feeling. Reading and comprehending the emotions of others, using gut feelings to make decisions, and monitoring one's own emotions and checking their consequences are all part of both emotional intelligence and critical feeling. Moreover, Goleman's (1995) book, written for interested laypeople, contains many recommendations that could be seen as instructions akin to critical feeling. Goleman's last chapter also discusses the use of emotions in order to improve life and can be seen, like interventions in psychotherapy (see next chapter), as a precursor of critical feeling.

How, then, is emotional intelligence different from critical feeling? First, critical feeling is more than emotional intelligence in that it includes, but is not limited to, emotions. For example, the experience that a person looks familiar or that a statement feels right are feelings but not emotions. Developing a skill by using bodily feedback or developing artistic taste by selective exposure has to do with critical feeling but not with emotional intelligence. This means that a whole range of metacognitive feelings, preferences, and bodily experiences that are important for critical feeling are not included in the concept of emotional intelligence. The literature about emotional intelligence has reported important insights about emotions in social life; critical feeling goes beyond emotional intelligence by including phenomena related to the individual, such as the notion of desirable difficulties in learning, and feelings and emotions in activities such as learning, or the appreciation of food, wine, art, music, literature, and religion. Some authors also criticize that emotional intelligence does not consider morality and could therefore be seen as a mere skill (Kristjánsson 2013; Saarni 1999), while in critical feeling strategies for the betterment of life are embedded in values.

Moreover, emotional intelligence targets a kind of explanation that differs from the explanatory target of critical feeling. The former aims to describe and measure an isolated aptitude whereas the latter aims to describe ways to strategically use feelings in order to optimize behavioral and personal outcomes. Emotional intelligence has the same relationship to critical feeling as intelligence in the traditional sense has to critical thinking. Although people agree that critical thinking is part of being an intelligent person, hardly anybody would equate critical thinking to intelligence. In Chapter 1 it was mentioned that intelligence is something people *have* whereas critical thinking is something people *do*. Intelligence is person-centered and descriptive; it is an aptitude that can be measured. A person is not responsible for his or her intelligence. Critical thinking, on the other hand, is situation-centered in that it tells people how they should normatively approach a situation. Critical thinking is about *using* the right procedures based on reasoning to optimize judgments and decisions, and people can be made accountable for whether they use their thinking capacities. In analogy to intelligence and critical thinking, emotional intelligence aims to describe the general ability to use emotions in social situations whereas critical feeling emphasizes the use of the right procedures based on emotions and feelings in order to optimize desired outcomes in a given situation. If a medication such as Ritalin increases the emotional functioning of a child, for example by enabling him or her to be better adapted to the classroom, we may say that Ritalin enhances emotional intelligence because the outcome is right. By contrast, we cannot say that Ritalin enhances critical feeling because using the right procedures requires the reasoned intention of a person (the example is inspired by Olson 2003, p. 267–268). Critical feeling means that a person acts intentionally and is held accountable for the strategies used. Moreover, some drugs or hormones may change response bias in that they change the threshold of a feeling, but they do not improve sensitivity. A good example is the observation that oxytocin increases trust (Kosfeld, Heinrichs, Zak, Fischbacher, and Fehr, 2005). It seems that oxytocin only changes response bias by making people trust others more. Critical feeling, however, would require that sensitivity increases in that people can better distinguish whom to trust and whom not.

To summarize, emotional intelligence is something people *have* whereas critical feeling is something people *do*. Emotional intelligence is

a trait of a person that is assumed to be stable over time. We could imagine that a computer could be programmed to be emotionally intelligent.
Critical feeling, in contrast, is an activity that requires what philosophers
call an *intentional agent*. Only a person with intentions can employ feelings strategically. A being without intentions may be able to feel intel-
ligently but cannot feel critically.

Emotional competence

Emotional competence is similar to emotional intelligence but emphasizes the pursuit of values. Similar to emotional intelligence but unlike
critical feeling, emotional competence is restricted to emotions. This is
not the only difference from critical feeling. Saarni (1999) lists eight emotional skills that make up emotional competence: awareness of one's own
emotion; ability to discern and understand others' emotions; ability to
use the vocabulary of emotion and expression; the capacity of empathic
involvement; ability to differentiate internal subjective emotional experience from external emotional expression; the capacity to adaptively
cope with aversive emotions and distressing circumstances; awareness
of emotional communication within relationships; and the capacity for
emotional self-efficacy. What is the relationship between these skills and
the proficiencies of critical feeling? Proficiencies are types of strategies
and may need several emotional skills that make up emotional competence. For example, to extract information, we may need (1) the ability to
understand the emotion of others, (2) the ability to use the vocabulary of
emotion and expression, and (3) the capacity for empathic involvement.
For other proficiencies, such as changing the external context, we need
(1) to be aware of our own emotions and (2) the capacity for adaptive
coping with aversive emotions and distressing circumstances. Note that
these competences do not include the strategic component essential to
critical feeling. Even where competence and strategy look similar, as in
understanding another person's emotions, there is a difference as critical
feeling includes strategies to achieve this goal, such as using our feelings as information or applying knowledge about facial expression to try
to decode whether an emotional expression is genuine. Understanding
another person's emotions as a competence, by contrast, means that people have developed the ability to do so.

Saarni (1999) focuses on the development of emotional skills
during childhood and adolescence while critical feeling focuses on how
these skills can be used strategically. While Saarni describes how capacities and abilities develop naturally or are learned in childhood, critical
feeling starts with a more or less competent adult and asks how these

skills could be applied and refined to guide attention, to extract information, or to implement values. Taken together, emotional competences that develop during childhood relate to proficiencies of critical feeling in the same way as cognitive competences that develop during childhood relate to proficiencies in critical thinking.

Positive psychology

Since the mid-1990s, a movement called *positive psychology* has gained momentum (Kristjánsson 2013; Lopez and Snyder 2011). This movement is a response to the fact that the task of psychology often has been identified with reducing or eliminating negative states, such as anxiety or depression. Why not emphasize the potential of positive states – for example, happiness, hope, or gratitude? How could we make people resilient in order to avoid the negative impact of stressful events? How could educators instill virtue, which has been shown to be associated with happiness (see Diener and Kesebir 2013)? Indeed, various research has pointed to the contribution of positive emotions to a more meaningful and happier life, as we shall see in the next chapter. This movement has been an important corrective to the prevalent clinical orientation in psychology and has contributed a new perspective on happiness and mental health. Interventions developed in positive psychology could indeed be seen as employing the strategic use of feelings to increase happiness.

Despite some similarities, there are crucial differences between positive psychology and critical feeling: First, the objectives of critical feeling are broader. Beyond happiness and virtuous character, critical feeling also aims at veridical representation of the environment and therefore serves cognitive rationality. In contrast to positive psychology, critical feeling deals with negative states and how to avoid or alleviate them. For example, stop-and-think rules are strategies of critical feeling but not of positive psychology. Second, the aim of positive psychology to build positive character points to personality traits instead of flexible use of feelings in different situations (see Kristjánsson 2013). In this regard, positive psychology is akin to emotional intelligence. From the viewpoint of critical feeling, the objective is to perform the right action in a given situation. Goodness of character or happiness would be a by-product of consistently performing appropriate actions in the situations a person encounters. The final difference pertains to the scope of phenomena examined under the notion of critical feeling. Like emotional intelligence, positive psychology mainly deals with emotions, perhaps even moods. Preferences, metacognitive feelings, and bodily states have not been objects of research in the positive psychology movement, even though they have not been explicitly excluded as means to build character. Therefore, research on the role of feelings in expertise and skill, in reading the emotions of others, in creating and appreciating art, and in building and adhering to religious norms would not fall under the notion of positive psychology.

Mindfulness

Another concept that is related to critical feeling is mindfulness. Mindfulness can be defined as directed attention in order to (1) be open to novelty; (2) be alert to distinctions; (3) be sensitive to different contexts; (4) become at least implicitly, if not explicitly, aware of multiple perspectives; and (5) be oriented in the present (Langer, 1989, 1997). A rich body of research documents the success of mindfulness interventions in health and education. Mindfulness, as it is often captured in the literature, is mostly about directing attention and about opening up new perspectives in thinking, but rarely about feelings (see Reber 2014). The concept of mindfulness is fully compatible with feelings. Mindfulness is both more and less than critical feeling. Mindfulness is more in that it encompasses both critical thinking and critical feeling. Indeed, each instance of critical feeling may require mindful attention, but this is not the whole story because mindfulness lacks the strategic moment of critical feeling. The relationship between mindful feeling and critical feeling is analogous to the relationship between mindful thinking and critical thinking. Mindful thinking in itself does not include the strategic use of reasoning capacities, but each act of critical thinking has to be mindful in order to succeed; seeing arguments from different perspectives, for instance, is essential to critical thinking. In the same vein, critical feeling has to be mindful, but it includes a strategic element that mindfulness does not.

Critical feeling: research and educational practice

I have defined critical feeling and elaborated on its relationship to rationality of emotion, emotional intelligence, emotional competence, positive psychology, and mindfulness. In order to go beyond conceptual analysis, and to set the stage for the second part of this book, it is necessary to outline the methods with which critical feeling could be studied and to make some general remarks about how to implement critical feeling in educational practice.

How to study critical feeling

Rozin (2006) noted that current mainstream psychology as an academic field examines processes, for example those of perception, memory, thought, or emotion. This focus on mental processes results in neglect of the really interesting topics in mainstream research, such as food, politics, religion, entertainment, and work. Research on critical feeling differs from research on psychological processes. The latter are supposed to be universal and grounded in the functioning of the brain. Critical feeling, as we have seen, depends on the values we like to pursue. While process-oriented psychology belongs to the natural sciences, critical feeling is best situated within the social sciences, the difference being that the natural sciences search for universal laws while the social sciences consider the context in which behavior is observed (see Kagan 2009). Interventions in critical feeling may be compared with psychotherapy or with interventions in education. While the values seem to be pretty clear in psychotherapy, and discussions pertain more or less to how to improve the mental health of a patient, the goals of education are more frequently disputed (see Noddings 2003).

I agree with mainstream scientific psychologists that there is only one process-oriented psychology, assuming that the healthy human brain is by and large the same across classes and cultures. By contrast, I assume that there is not one uniform psychology when understood as a social science; there are several psychologies, depending on culture, historical background, and the values groups and communities pursue. We may develop separate psychologies for the upper and the lower classes (see Bourdieu 1984/1979 for a sociology of taste for different classes); for Buddhists, Christians, Hindus, Jews, and Muslims (see Weber 1958a, 1958b, 1967, 1968/1916, 1992/1905 for the sociologies of different religions); for northerners and southerners in the United States (see Cohen, Bowdle, Nisbett, and Schwarz 1996 for an example); for employers and employees; for conservatives, liberals, and socialists; and so on.

The main difference between critical feeling and mainstream process-oriented research consists of taking defined values as the criteria for the success of an intervention a priori. This focus on the pursuit of values is in line with educational research where the success of an intervention depends not only on the means but also criteria set by the educator. For example, some teachers may want their students to learn mathematical formulas and apply them in well-defined problems whereas other teachers may want their students to grasp the underlying logic of the algorithm and to apply it in ill-defined practical situations. Using retention-based learning strategies and drill may suffice to perform well on standard textbook tasks but may fail when it comes to practical problems that need deeper understanding of the underlying logic (see Mayer and Wittrock 1996; VanLehn 1990).

In conclusion, identical learning techniques may succeed or fail, depending on the criteria set by the educator. Likewise, the identical intervention in critical feeling could succeed or fail when the outcome criteria differ. For example, research shows that people like things they can process easily (Reber et al. 1998; Winkielman and Cacioppo 2001) but that they learn better if materials are slightly disfluent (see Diemand-Yauman, Oppenheimer, and Vaughan 2011). If a teacher wants her students to have a positive attitude toward a topic, she should present it in a way that can be processed easily. If, by contrast, the learning outcome is central, she might render a text disfluent by presenting it in a difficult-to-read font.

The proper kind of study via which to examine critical feeling is a controlled experiment with random assignment of participants to groups where a critical feeling intervention is compared to a control group that does not undergo the intervention or that undergoes a sham intervention that is not supposed to be effective in order to control for placebo effects. The intervention is effective if critical feeling leads to better outcomes than are experienced by the control group. Intervention studies are common in applied areas of psychology. Indeed, intervention studies that could be subsumed under the umbrella of critical feeling already exist in clinical psychology, where researchers have developed treatments such as systematic desensitization to alleviate anxiety. In Chapter 8, I shall discuss interventions to increase interest in educational psychology.

Often, however, intervention studies are not available. Some empirical studies reveal how feelings bias cognitive processes, and other studies examine mechanisms to correct such errors. I follow the strategy to review such studies and then discuss their consequences for critical feeling. For example, the observation that moods influence judgments about others raises the question of what could be done to prevent undue influence and to arrive at accurate judgments about other people. Sometimes, studies about correction mechanisms are available. When this is the case, we are one step closer to a solution in that we know which debiasing methods might work and which might not (Ross et al. 1975; Schwarz et al. 2007). In such cases, we describe what measures could plausibly be recommended; whether they work in the real world awaits further intervention studies.

At other times, we want to derive a strategy to attain a desired state, such as training a new skill or developing a new artistic taste. While there may be intervention studies on training a new skill, I do not know of randomized controlled studies that examine strategies to develop new tastes. In this case, too, we have to rely on what we know on the development of taste and derive plausible interventions. Such interventions provide us with plausible predictions that need to be tested. By revealing the many gaps in empirical evidence regarding critical feeling, I hope to elicit new research that provides new insights into the potential of interventions in everyday life. Early attempts at finding smart interventions in social psychology show the promise of such a research strategy (Walton 2014).

The role of school in teaching critical feeling

I would like to end this chapter with what I see as the greatest opportunity of critical feeling: to educate a citizenry that is both intellectually and emotionally mature. Universities and schools produce critical thinkers by the thousands thanks to the Enlightenment and the modern educational system. However, the values taught to the students at universities and business schools are often one-sided and restricted to reason-based moral codes specific to the field of study. Even worse, the current educational system, at least in the West, seems to produce some leaders who lack moral values and resemble psychopaths (see Babiak and Hare 2006). School curricula are narrowed down to learning intellectual content and do not provide a broad moral outlook (see Noddings 2003 for a critique), though children's literature may provide an *éducation sentimentale* (see Frevert et al. 2014). School education is often technical. From elementary school to tertiary education, schooling focuses on teaching the intellect, not feelings, with the rare exception of teaching emotion understanding (Ornaghi, Brockmeier and Grazzani 2014; Pons, Harris, and Doudin 2002). Even a painting or a poem can be analyzed in a merely technical manner, "to its ruin," as Noddings (2003, p. 103) noted. Moreover, schools rarely consider feelings when determining how to improve learning and motivation. Even when feelings could be instrumental in interesting students in subject matter and keeping them in school, thinking trumps feeling. In other words, schools not only neglect whole areas of life that arguably do not belong to the core task of school, which is impartation of knowledge, but also fail when it comes to their core task because even conveying knowledge has a feeling component.

In principle, public schools in democratic countries are supposed to teach children *how* to think but not *what* to think. Students learn methods of reasoning and critical examination (how to think) without being told which attitudes are correct and which are wrong (what to think). Teaching how to think needs schooling because parents, besides being at work, may lack the necessary know-how to teach their children how to use their reasoning skills. In the same vein, when it comes to educating critical feeling, the public educational system in democratic countries should draw a fine line between teaching *how* to feel and teaching *what* to feel. As we begin to know more about how feelings work, parents may lack the necessary knowledge to teach their offspring how to use their feelings and how to implement their values. Schools will need well-educated teachers to instruct students in the skill of critical feeling. Alternatively, parents may be offered courses that enable them to convey critical feeling to their children. It will take time until we know enough about feelings to optimize the education of critical feelers. We have to go a long way until parents and teachers know enough about the methods of critical feeling to teach it effectively.

Another open question is whether proficiencies in critical feeling are domain-general or domain-specific. McPeck (1981) noted in his work that teaching critical thinking courses might be wrong because critical thinking is domain-specific. For instance, proper thinking in mathematics is different from proper thinking in history. It is therefore appropriate to educate proper thinking for each subject, as schools already do. In line with this reasoning, I am reluctant to propose domain-general critical feeling courses; critical feeling might be bound to domains and skills. In order to educate critical feeling for making pots, the potter would not need an overarching course in critical feeling but to develop expertise in pottery. Similarly, enhancing intuitive judgment in such different domains as mathematics and evaluating job applicants would require the building up of expertise through experience. The point of critical feeling is not to change the curriculum; the point is to consider feelings within domains where they have so far been neglected.

The remainder of this book provides an overview of applications of critical feeling. Each chapter ends with a coda about the teaching of critical feeling. Beyond an overview of the psychology of feelings aimed at evidence-based interventions, we have to address how these pedagogical tools could be integrated into current school curricula. I do not propose a school reform centered on critical feeling – even if schools tried to implement such a novel curriculum, it would be likely to fail as most school reforms have in the past when they have not fit the institutional traditions that have governed schools for centuries (see Olson 2003; Ravitch 2000). When I outline educational applications of critical feeling, I start with the assumption that schools stick with their core mission in that they convey knowledge that empowers young people to participate in the world of work. Parents, on the other hand, practice how to live in a family and convey values. Future policies might change the share of parents and schools when it comes to teaching about feelings, but for the time being I stick with the traditional distribution of the roles.

Part II
APPLICATIONS OF CRITICAL FEELING

4 HAPPINESS THROUGH CRITICAL FEELING

I have now reigned above fifty years in victory or peace; beloved by my subjects, dreaded by my enemies, and respected by my allies. Riches and honour, power and pleasure, have waited on my call, nor does any earthly blessing appear to have been wanting to my felicity. In this situation, I have diligently numbered the days of pure and genuine happiness which have fallen to my lot: they amount to FOURTEEN.

(CALIPH ABDULRAHMAN III, WHO REIGNED AT
CORDOVA IN THE TENTH CENTURY CE; CITED IN
GIBBON 1995/1788, P. 346)

Well-being as a goal in itself has been propagated at least since Epicurus (341–270 BCE). He stated that a good life is a life of happiness, tranquility, and peace; a life that is free of worry, fear, and pain (Epicurus 2012). Pleasure and pain are the direct measures of such a life: The more pleasure and the less pain, the better. Epicurean philosophy does not go beyond pleasure and pain – that is, expected utility for oneself – to measure well-being. Such an egocentric notion of well-being is seen as deficient by most authors (see, for example, Spranger 1928/1914). Modern philosophical approaches therefore extended the notion of happiness for oneself to the earlier mentioned notion of the greatest happiness for the greatest number (Bentham 1988/1776). Yet this approach would not claim that we have to suffer pain and give up happiness beyond the needs of the well-being of society. Even most religious communities do not require their believers to voluntarily suffer. Ascetic life and self-castigation are accepted only, if at all, as exercises that harden body and spirit in order to be better able to serve society, while suffering for suffering's sake is commonly seen as meaningless in the West (e.g., Noddings 2003). In order to be capable members of society, we have a duty to look for our well-being, which includes both good health and happiness. Toward the end of this chapter, I review research on the positive effects of happiness. Regular experience of positive emotions makes people more broadly attentive, resourceful, and social (see Fredrickson 2013); individuals become better suited to cope with loss (see Bonanno 2004; Kaltman and Bonanno

2003) and to meet the challenges of pursuing social and societal values (Fredrickson 2013). There is no contradiction between happiness for the sake of the person and for the sake of society because a happy person benefits the community and the society at large. In conclusion, well-being is a good in itself; beyond advancing the flourishing of an individual, it benefits the society the individual lives in. Therefore, people may not only possess a right but also a duty to maintain their health and pursue their happiness.

However, there is a basic problem related to the pursuit of happiness, a problem we do not encounter with the pursuit of proper reasoning. If Laura wants to increase her reasoning abilities, she can pursue this goal, acquire the appropriate skills, and assess her progress by comparing the desired state of her logical reasoning ability with the actual state. There is no problem with this procedure. Compare Laura when she tries to increase her happiness by the means of critical feeling. Is it possible for her to aim to be happy and acquire the appropriate skills to achieve this outcome?

It seems that happiness, in contrast to proper reasoning, is a by-product of her actions. The term *by-product* denotes the fact that some states cannot be brought about intentionally (Elster 1983). Happiness is not the only state that seems to be a by-product. For example, Winston Churchill's charisma was essentially a by-product of his behavior. Had he tried to fake charisma, he would have risked being found out. Similarly, virtue is a by-product that cannot be brought about strategically, as we shall see in Chapter 10. Given that happiness is a by-product of actions performed for their own sake, the conscious pursuit of happiness – intentional activity aimed at achieving a state of happiness – may in fact be counterproductive (Schooler, Ariely, and Loewenstein 2003). Schooler and colleagues discuss three reasons why this may be the case.

First, people may lack explicit access to their experiences, making a precise assessment of their happiness impossible. For example, tourists want to be happy when they go on vacation. Wirtz, Kruger, Scollon, and Diener (2003) asked students before their spring break vacation how happy they thought they will feel on their vacation. During the vacation, the participants wore a pager on their wrist that beeped seven times per day, and they had to indicate their current feelings. They were asked four weeks later about the feelings they had experienced during their vacation and whether they would go on vacation again. It turned out that the participants had both more positive expectations and more positive memories of their vacations than their reports during the vacation indicated. They also had more negative expectations and memories than negative experiences during the vacation. Importantly, remembered experience, but not the actual experience, predicted the desire to repeat the experience. This study raises doubts about the ability of people to assess their own happiness because they seem to base the desire to repeat an experience on the wrong source (see Gilbert 2006 for other examples).

Second, gauging our own feelings may come at a hedonic cost: Thinking about happiness potentially undermines the very feeling state we think about. For example, Mauss, Tamir, Anderson, and Savino (2011) presented a film clip about relationship and intimacy after half of the all-female participants had read a text about the benefits of happiness whereas the other half had not. Self-reported loneliness was higher when the women read about the benefits of happiness than when they were in a control group that did not receive this information. This finding suggests that thinking about means to become happy may accentuate some negative aspects of our life, resulting in less happiness. It seems that spontaneity in experiencing happiness reaps more hedonic benefits than monitoring one's affective states.

Third, the pursuit of happiness may be self-defeating, in a manner analogous to striving to achieve the goal of not thinking about a problem (Wenzlaff and Wegner 2000) or attempting to re-experience a mood (Wegner et al. 1993). In other words, continuously thinking about happiness may deplete our ability to experience it. We should therefore not strive for happiness but for something we value in itself, such as doing a good job, being patient with our children, dining with friends, fixing a bike, exercising, writing a poem, or meditating. The ensuing well-being is a by-product of these activities done for their own sake.

In sum, happiness cannot be brought about directly through the use of conscious strategies. This is a pity because people often make decisions that are suboptimal for their happiness (see Hsee and Hastie 2006). The next section follows up the biases inherent in the pursuit of happiness and tells us how critical feeling could help to enhance positive experiences by advocating strategies that alleviate some of the biases when people assess their past, present, and future happiness.

The pursuit of happiness

You eat out once every week in the same restaurant, which prominently features clam chowder, your clear favorite, of a superb quality you could not get anywhere else. If you had to decide now on your dish for the next eight weeks, you probably would think that eight times clam chowder would be too uniform and hence go for a basil–tomato soup, the soup you like second best, for three of the weeks and maybe even once for a barley broth. However, if you dined at the restaurant and ordered the dish every week, you would probably always end up eating your clam chowder (see Simonson 1990), presumably because each new onset of an event results in a renewal of the positive experience (Nelson and Meyvis 2008). This is just one of many illustrations of the lack of ability to predict our future affective states (see Gilbert 2006 for an accessible summary of this research). Earlier, I discussed other examples of predictions about how exciting our vacations will be (Wirtz et al. 2003) and how happy we will be six months after winning a lottery (Brickman et al. 1978). These examples illustrate how poor predictions of affective states are. However, people rarely win the lottery; miscalculating my inclination for weekly clam chowder consumption seems trivial; and biased anticipation of enjoyment of a spring break trip may not affect our long-term well-being. In contrast, when people misestimate their happiness in the long term, they may make erroneous decisions that may have major impacts on their lives.

Earning money with feeling

Research has found that middle-class citizens often overestimate their future happiness if they were to become rich. Aspiring employees anticipate what they could buy and how they could spend time on the golf course or with their family on their yacht if they just earned enough money. They labour under a so-called *focusing illusion* by focusing on one facet of happiness (income) and neglecting other facets (Kahneman, Krueger, Schkade, Schwarz, and Stone 2006). These people then invest a lot of time in working harder, often in those years when their children are young and miss their mom or dad most. These social climbers are willing to sacrifice some happiness now in order to gain more happiness later. Alas, it turns out that being happier when one becomes rich is an illusion: Rich people often work harder than the average employee and do not have much time for playing golf or spending time with their family on their yacht. Of course, rich people can buy branded clothes and eat more sophisticated food than the average employee. Hard-working social climbers may one day find out that they sacrificed the enjoyments of daily life to get rich but are not much happier after all. Like the lottery winner, they adapt to their lifestyle. There is evidence from the United States that more money increases well-being up to a certain point, which lies at an income of about $75,000; beyond this point, there is hardly any increase in happiness (Kahneman and Deaton 2010). In other words, people who do not have a minimum of money at their disposal are unhappy because they cannot cover the essentials of daily life. A middle-class income is sufficient to become happy, and hard work to earn more money does not earn more happiness.

There is little research on how we could correct the focusing illusion. In principle, there are at least three ways critical feeling could contribute to refocusing life on the essentials. First, and trivially, through knowledge we can observe that the rich do not have more time to enjoy life than you and I, and that most of them are not happier than the average citizen. Much of the image of the rich comes through the press and from advertisements, where wealthy people are presented as happy, stylish – you name it. Therefore, *how* to change the image of the rich is not as trivial as the fact *that* we have to change it. The press quite often presents us with happy lottery winners (at least where I live), occasionally with lottery winners who have spent it all and fallen deep, but hardly ever with winners who spent their money wisely but nevertheless adapted to the new standard of life and are no longer happier than the average citizen.

A second way to feel critically about earning money consists of looking at how happy rich people are. People who focus on the rich confuse happiness with being rich. Refocusing means that we look at the category that really represents what we desire: to become happy. Based on research findings (Gilbert, Killingsworth, Eyre, and Wilson 2009), Gilbert (2006) proposed an alternative method of circumventing illusions that derive from wrong predictions of future happiness. Instead of trying to predict how we feel when we get rich, we should look at how happy rich people are. That is, instead of just knowing that it is an illusion, we should look at how *the rich* feel *now* instead of predicting how *we* would feel when we were rich in *the future*. We would then see that the rich do not feel happier than we do and we could draw the right conclusions: Getting rich is not worth the effort because it will not make us happier.

Daniel Gilbert introduced the term *surrogates* to denote people we look at – in this case the rich – in order to know how we will feel in the future. That is, when we want to determine happiness in the future, we should not look at how we might feel in the future but at how others feel now. Using this technique, we ground our predictions in facts, even though the information about the facts is derived from others. As a consequence, we are no longer influenced by our momentary state. For example, we no longer buy too much food because we are hungry when we look at how much a friend of ours is eating for lunch. In the end, Gilbert claimed that what is "so ironic about this predicament is that the information we need to make accurate predictions of our emotional futures is right under our noses, but we don't seem to recognize its aroma" (Gilbert 2006, p. 256).

I agree with Gilbert that, even if the information is under our noses, we might not recognize it and might therefore ignore it when making decisions. However, the usefulness of surrogates to predict feelings may have limitations. Some of them are discussed and dismissed by Daniel Gilbert himself, for example individual differences in tastes that make it difficult to draw comparisons. Moreover, Walsh and Ayton (2009) have shown that surrogates decrease error in affective forecasting, but this beneficial effect is diminished when event information is available in addition to information about surrogates. For example, when I compare myself to neighbors who have less income than I have, I may know about their housing and living conditions and neglect that they are nevertheless happy. In addition, is Gilbert's claim true that the surrogate information we need is readily available? How do I know that rich people are not happier than I am? We have already seen how positively they are depicted in the press. When I see rich people in person, I mostly see a thin slice of their life, and this looks more delectable than the average slices I experience of my life. This does not mean that they are happier. The problem is that rich people, like me, have their problems, their despairs, and their quarrels in private. They show themselves at their best, just as I do when I meet other people. Ironically, it may be easier for rich people to see that they are not happier than I am because, for them, the thin slices of my life look better than their life; yet, as we have seen above, they too see that my food is less delicate and my clothes less fashionable than theirs, which may alleviate the positive impression derived from the thin slices. In the end, empirical studies about our experiential ecology have to determine whether most information needed to make accurate predictions is available. Alternatively, much of the necessary information may be hidden because we only see thin slices that lead to biased judgments of the other person's happiness. Both hypotheses would predict that rich people know that they are not happier than people with an average income. After all, both fully available information and thin slices show them that people with average incomes are at least as happy as they are. However, people with average incomes need all information readily available to see that rich people are not happier than they are. Why, then, do not all people who could afford it aim to lead a more modest lifestyle?

Less is more

As we have seen, the happiness of lottery winners increases when they hear that they have won, but after about three months their happiness goes back to normal. What is the mechanism behind such adaptations? Immediately after winning the lottery, Sally, the lucky winner, compares her new lifestyle with her old need to turn every penny. As this comparison is favorable to the present state, she feels happy. However, after some months, she no longer spontaneously recalls how life was before she hit the jackpot. If she compares her life six months after the lottery win with her life some weeks ago, she arrives at the conclusion that life has not become better (see Gilbert 2006). While the change induces happiness, continuation does not. Comparably, patients adapt to disability or chronic illness. Again, chronically ill or disabled people get used to their new situation and may forget many details of their former life as a healthy person. According to the logic outlined above, this is especially the case where there is a sudden change in a person's condition, followed by stability or even some improvement, for example after an accident. In fact, people adapt better to negative conditions when they know that it is for life than when they know that the condition is reversible. Smith, Loewenstein, Jankovic, and Ubel (2009) have shown that patients adapt more fittingly to colostomy – a medical procedure in which the colon is rerouted through an artificial opening in the belly – when they know it is permanent than when they can hope that it will be time-limited. In general, people adapt better and feel less miserable when they cannot change a negative outcome than when they know that it is reversible (Gilbert 2006; Gilbert and Ebert 2002).

What can we learn from this observation? Certainly – when it comes to happiness – that less can be at least as good as more. When so many people who are forced to confront adversity remain happy, the question arises whether people might be able to embark on a more modest life and remain happy. There are good reasons to renounce material goods that make life comfortable but go beyond the basic needs. Beyond the beneficial effects that moderation has on the environment (because a modest lifestyle consumes less resources), we opt out to participate in the race to possess the most luxurious mansion, to play with the coolest gadgets, and to travel to the most exotic destinations. By renouncing luxury, we may detect the pleasures of the plain and simple and circumvent the tyranny of choice (see Schwartz 2004). Moreover, the observation that people adapt better to negative outcomes when they cannot change them suggests it is better to make a downward shift in living standards permanent and irreversible – for example by giving away material goods – than to keep all options open.

This is not to say that such a transition is easy. We certainly adapt better to becoming richer than to becoming poorer. Moreover, it is a more pleasurable experience to be the rich guy in the neighborhood than to be the poor one. What can be done about this? A contextual theory of happiness suggests that we could change our frame of reference in order to be happier with less (Parducci 1995). According to Parducci, happiness is a purely contextual phenomenon: We can be happy whether we are rich or poor. This theory suggests that lowering our aspiration level results in happiness despite our having fewer material goods. We have seen that people who have experienced adversity (e.g., becoming severely disabled in an accident) can regain average happiness after some time despite the fact that they are much worse off than the average person. The aspiration level theory predicts that we might in the same way become happy with a voluntarily adopted moderate lifestyle – that is, by changing our aspiration level.

What determines happiness, according to Parducci (1995), is the range of happiness we experience and the frequency with which happy events are experienced within sub-ranges. To illustrate the basic idea, I could have had experiences that ranged from extremely happy to moderately unhappy; I then can count the number of experiences within each sub-range, such as extremely happy, happy, moderately happy, neutral, and moderately unhappy. This theory makes some surprising predictions for which Parducci presents some empirical evidence. For example, if I have many happy experiences but also experience a few unhappy moments, I judge myself to be happier than, say, my uncle who has had the same happy experiences as I have but not the unhappy ones. Why? Because, for me, the range of experiences spans unhappy and happy experiences, I know how unhappy experiences feel and can contrast them with my many happy experiences close to the upper end of the range. I therefore think that I have a happy life. For my uncle, the range is narrow and includes just what are for me happy experiences. As most of his experiences will be average within his range, he will feel less happy than I do because he has not experienced unpleasant events. It seems that, in order to be really happy, we need a few very unhappy experiences that enable us to contrast our current happy state with what could have been. People without these contrasting cases just know their narrow range and think that their current state is average. This observation also explains why rich entrepreneurs do not feel happier than their middle-class employees.

The contextual theory of happiness predicts that, at the lower end of the happiness echelon, a person who experiences only miserable events may be happier than a person who has the same miserable experiences but also a few very happy ones. According to the same logic as presented above, people who have only miserable experiences do not know happier states and cannot compare the current miserable situation with happy memories; for them, misery is the average. A person who has a few happy memories, by contrast, can think of being much happier than the miserable state she experiences at present. However, such predictions need to be tested thoroughly in the real world. It has been shown that people can use positive reminiscing to boost their happiness (Bryant, Smart, and King 2005), and this could be an advantage for people who have at least some positive memories to recall. Finally, more recent research on the *peak-and-end effect* has shown that positive versus negative evaluations do not only depend on a person's average happiness within a range nor only on the frequency with which experiences at the higher or the lower end of the range occur.

Peak-and-end effect

Kahneman, Fredrickson, Schreiber, and Redelmeier (1993) and Fredrickson and Kahneman (1993) have demonstrated that judgments of positive and negative evaluations – and with them feelings – have two characteristics. First, they do not depend on time; this has been called *duration neglect*. The peak experience enters the equation to calculate the overall evaluation, regardless of whether we have experienced a pleasant or unpleasant state for a short or long time. Second, the end of the experience also enters the equation so that we obtain a peak-and-end rule, where the resulting overall evaluation of an experience is the average of the peak experience and the end experience of an emotional episode. The theory has received broad support, including for positive experiences (Do, Rupert, and Wolford 2008) and for pain during childbirth (Chajut, Caspi, Chen, Hod, and Ariely 2014).

 This theory leads to some counterintuitive predictions that can be supported experimentally. For example, people who undergo colonoscopy, a painful examination of the intestines, had similar negative overall feelings when one patient was examined for 40 minutes and the other for 20 minutes if both patients had approximately the same maximal intensity of pain and the same amount of pain at the end (Redelmeier and Kahneman 1996). Moreover, when both patients had the same maximum pain, the one who had less pain at the end judged his or her experience as less painful than the patient with more pain at the end. Indeed, when the medical doctor prolonged the procedure in such a manner that the patients experienced little pain at the end, the experience was overall seen as less painful even though the doctor added pain by not abruptly ending the examination (Redelmeier, Katz, and Kahneman 2003). These findings can be used to more mundane ends. Among the less gratifying duties of a father is washing the hair of his toddlers. Although I did a decent job most of the time, there were a few memorable instances when hair washing ended in a crying toddler who wanted to leave the bathtub. Before I realized the potential scope of the peak-and-end rule for my

Saturday afternoon duty, I acquiesced to the desire of my children to leave the bathtub, with the result that they were reluctant to enter the tub next time. This resistance can be explained by the peak-and-end rule because the most negative experience came at the end. The resistance vanished when I began to tell my children that they could not leave the bath now and that they should just play in the water with their toys, an activity they loved. When they grew a bit older, however, they entered the bathtub and pleaded, "But no hair washing, please." Apparently, and somewhat unfortunately for me, they were able to distinguish between playtime in the bathtub and daddy's sometimes less pleasant hair washing.

Eating and drinking with feeling

Remember the student who had to get up early but snoozed because the value of sleeping now exceeded the value of passing an exam in two months? There are related problems where the momentary value exceeds the long-term value. When I made an attempt to quit smoking about three decades ago, I gained weight that I later wanted to lose. At that time, I worked as a computer programmer for an industrial company. The staff canteen there offered weight-loss lunches. Nearby, there was a cafeteria that sold excellent mille-feuille. Often enough, I wandered to the cafeteria after my weight-loss lunch and met some other employees I had seen just 20 minutes ago in the weight-loss line. After some lunches, we greeted each other cheerily. Apparently, for them, too, the momentary value of the mille-feuille exceeded the long-term goal of losing weight.

How can we do better? Two variables determine whether a person overeats (Wansink 2010): food choice – including energy and nutrient composition, fiber, and water content – and serving sizes. Beyond self-control (see Stroebe, Van Koningsbruggen, Papies, and Aarts 2013), there are at least three solutions to increase variety of food choice and decrease serving size: implementation intentions, stopping rules, and change of environmental stimuli.

Implementation intentions

In the previous chapter, I discussed implementation intentions, such as getting up on time to attend a lecture, as a planning tool to increase the likelihood that we will achieve our goals. The same logic can be applied to prevent overeating. Instead of just having intentions – "from tomorrow onward, I shall eat healthy food" – dieters need to make an exact plan of what to eat. In one study, participants were told, "We want you to plan to eat a low-fat diet during the next month. You are free to choose how you will do this, but we want you to formulate your plans in as much detail as possible. Please pay particular attention to the situations in which you will implement these plans" (Armitage 2004, p. 320). Blank lines to write down the plan followed this instruction. Such precise plans helped employees to reduce fat intake (Armitage 2004) and students to eat more healthily (Verplanken and Faes 1999), to increase fruit and vegetable intake (Kellar and Abraham 2005), and to reduce the intake of snacks by planning to eat them only on particular occasions (see Sheeran, Milne, Webb, and Gollwitzer 2005 for a review).

Stopping when one has had enough

Instead of painstakingly abiding by a diet plan, people may monitor their feelings and listen to them (see Herbert, Blechert, Hautzinger, Matthias, and Herbert 2013). Many obese people do not seem to monitor their feelings of hunger. A study in the 1960s (Schachter and Gross 1968) manipulated clocks so that they displayed 12:00 when it was in fact 11:00. Overweight participants in this study went by the clock: 12:00 was lunchtime and they started eating. Participants with normal weight went with their inner clock and started eating when they were hungry, independently of what the clock displayed. More recent research has revealed that the French eat until they are no longer hungry while Americans eat until their plate is empty or until their TV show is over (Wansink, Payne, and Chandon 2007). Independent of nationality, however, overweight eaters relied less on internal cues than eaters with normal weight (see also Barkeling, King, Naslund, and Blundell 2007). This means that people can more successfully keep overeating at bay by using a subjective stop rule that terminates eating when they are full instead of an objective stop rule that asks for the plate to be empty. An obvious first step for people who want to lose weight is to check whether they are really hungry when they want to eat; if they are not hungry, they should not start eating. While eating, people should monitor whether they are sated and stop eating if this is the case. If eaters are able to listen to their feelings and therefore stop eating when full, they may, as a second step, influence their feeling of satiation. It has been observed that high-fat and low-fiber foods slow down satiation. As a consequence, people who feed on these nutrients eat more before the feeling of satiation sets in. In contrast, wholegrain products that are high in fiber accelerate satiation (Burton-Freeman 2000). Another means to accelerate satiation is to chew one's food slowly. Rozin, Kabnick, Pete, Fischler, and Shields (2003) observed that the French chewed their food more slowly and consequently ate less than their American counterparts. This finding helps to explain the *French paradox*: the fact that the French eat food that is apparently unhealthy but still have lower obesity rates than Americans.

Setting external cues

Stop rules seem to be an obvious method to follow in order to prevent overeating. Simply eat until you are satiated. However, there is a twist. What if the feeling of hunger is influenced by external cues that may result in automatic overeating? Unfortunately, this is exactly what has been observed to happen (see Wansink 2010; Wansink and Chandon 2006 for reviews). Large packages, plates, and serving bowls increase the amount a person serves by 15 to 45 percent. Similar biases apply to drinking: Bartenders with more than five years of experience poured an average of 29 percent more alcohol into tumblers (which are short but wide) than into highball glasses (which are narrow but tall; Wansink and Van Ittersum 2003). These influences remain largely unconscious. While people constantly overeat when they have bigger servings, they claim that they do not eat more and that they are not influenced by serving sizes.

It is therefore not optimal to attempt to prevent overeating by exclusively following your feeling of hunger because this feeling is influenced by external cues. Instead of setting stopping rules and obtaining information about your internal state, you may attempt to modify your environment by changing external cues. Wansink (2010) developed a database with 173 evidence-based recommendations on how to change external cues in order to prevent overeating. You begin by determining serving sizes in the grocery store by exploiting the projection bias, which denotes in this context the fact that people predict that their hunger will remain more stable over time than it is likely to be the case (Loewenstein, O'Donoghue, and Rabin 2003). When shopping for dinner, it has been shown that the amount of food people put in their cart depends on their hunger at the time of shopping. Consumers who shop before dinner and consistently buy too much food may try going shopping after lunch. This is effective because when they are satiated people predict that they will eat less. At home, people may decide how much – or how little – they cook, once again determining their serving size. Finally, the use of a smaller plate results in smaller serving sizes. As the eater is unaware of the effect of plate size on serving size, changing the external cue of the plate size (which is conscious) may over time lead to the right spontaneous behavior (eating less), presumably because the changes in serving size change the eater's feelings of satiation. Critical feeling consists of applying the knowledge that we buy more food when we are hungry, and in changing the external context in order to exploit the inclination to eat less when serving sizes are small.

Developing new tastes

So far in this section, we have dealt with healthy eating. We now turn to a more appealing topic, namely developing new culinary tastes by repeated exposure to new food. Moving to a new country often means that we cannot buy the food we consumed in our home country. We therefore have to become accustomed to the native food of our new place. Indeed, tastes for food – which also have a biological basis (see Rozin and Vollmecke 1986) – depend on repeated exposure (Crandall 1984; Pliner 1982). A case in point is chili, which at first provides an aversive experience. Preference increases after eaters have repeatedly tasted chili (Stevenson and Yeomans 1995). Furthermore, there is a positive correlation between spouses' food tastes, and this correlation tends to increase with the number of years a couple has been married (Price and Vandenberg 1980). Presumably, married couples eat the same food and therefore develop similar food tastes due to mere exposure. The message for critical feeling is simple: If you want to get accustomed to new food, just eat it!

Critical feeling and psychotherapy

Long existing techniques in psychotherapy may inspire strategies in critical feeling. Part of the arsenal that psychotherapists use for the treatment of psychological disorders can be seen as applications of critical feeling in the service of psychological improvement. Let's discuss two ways in which critical feeling is involved in psychotherapy. First, many of the psychological disorders include feelings that make people suffer, and psychotherapists aim via their treatment to bring these feelings back to normal. Second, psychotherapists use feelings as part of their interventions. By watching how psychotherapists work with feelings, we can learn about how to counter negative feelings or to use feelings to change behavior in everyday life. In addition to the two ways we are going to discuss, it has been observed that patients who are better able to tolerate and regulate affective activation show better outcomes in psychotherapy (Solbakken, Hansen, Havik, and Monsen 2012).

Many therapeutic interventions are aimed at negative feelings, such as anxiety. People who suffer from generalized social anxiety disorder have a constant fear of being judged, humiliated, or embarrassed (Stein and Stein 2008). This feeling is so intense that they experience bodily symptoms such as blushing, sweating, and trembling. In order to circumvent these feelings, people with social anxiety disorder avoid everyday activities that include a social component, such as working in small groups, going to restaurants or parties, talking to strangers, and dating. Needless to say, avoiding social activities hampers both professional and private life. Phobias are treated via a variety of methods that help either to reduce the elicitation of the feeling or to make the feeling bearable. One successful phobia treatment confronts people who are frightened by a certain stimulus. Therapists do not accustom patients to the frightening stimulus step by step, which might seem to be the most effective way to do it, but instead massively expose patients for a long duration to the object that elicits the extreme fear reaction (see Brewin 1996; Zarate and Agras 1994). For instance, people with social phobia have meals and drinks in busy restaurants, dive into a disco, attend parties, and go to other places full of people together with their therapist. These patients go through a three-day program of continuous social contact. Similarly, people with snake phobia are exposed to snakes non-stop. Indeed, after this massive intervention, many patients with social phobia have lower social anxiety, and many people with snake phobia lose their excessive fear of snakes. Critical feeling's strategy for reducing the intensity of excessive undesired feeling states can be seen in these cases, in which environments are selected or changed to expose the patient to the fear-eliciting stimulus.

The second way in which critical feeling is involved in psychotherapy is the use of feelings as part of a therapeutic intervention. The most prominent treatment is systematic desensitization, used to counter anxiety (Rachman 1967). Patients suffering from phobia are either confronted with the fear-inducing object, such as a snake; shown a picture of it; or asked to imagine the stimulus. Each time they are confronted with this stimulus, the patients are encouraged to relax. Based on a mixture of distraction and classical conditioning, the rationale of this technique consists of countering fear-inducing situations using the positive feelings that accompany relaxation. This therapy has been shown to be effective in treating phobias (Wolpe 1958).

Another technique, covert sensitization, is a form of aversion therapy. The rationale of aversion therapies is the opposite of that of systematic desensitization. If a person feels positive emotions at the sight of something she should avoid, such as alcohol abuse, gambling, or fingernail biting, therapists can make this a negative experience by combining it with a repulsive state, such as pain or vomiting. This seems a plausible technique. However, aversion therapies have several drawbacks. First, such methods are deemed outright unethical; a particular example is the use of electric shocks in so-called sexual orientation conversion therapies to "cure" homosexuality (Haldeman 1991). Second, such methods are only sometimes, and not always, successful at alleviating the symptoms. Finally, and crucially, they do not treat the underlying problem. The drug Antabuse, for example, is very effective at stopping drinking because the consumption of even small amounts of alcohol elicits vomiting. However, it does not stop the addiction: As soon as Antabuse is removed, drinking resumes (Witkiewitz and Marlatt 2011). As giving electric shocks and eliciting vomiting are inhumane, another technique has been invented in order to prevent overt negative reactions: covert sensitization. Instead of real electric shocks or vomiting, patients have to imagine that they have received a shock or vomited (Cautela 1967). Despite some effectiveness in alleviating symptoms, aversive therapies, including covert sensitization, are nowadays not widely used to treat addictions (Witkiewitz and Marlatt 2011).

There are at least three lessons critical feelers can learn from psychotherapy. First, there are methods to alleviate negative feelings; the most prominent of those is being repeatedly confronted with the aversive stimulus. Second, negative feelings may be alleviated by positive feelings elicited by relaxation. Third, aversive interventions are not commendable, on the one hand for ethical reasons and on the other hand because they often remove the symptom on the surface without affecting the deeper cause.

Managing negative feelings in everyday life

Psychotherapy treats extremely unpleasant feelings. However, you and I both have unpleasant feelings we would like to get rid of. We have to overcome disappointments. We may feel anger or fear, sadness or shame when it is not necessary and may even be harmful; we therefore would like to eliminate or at least attenuate these negative states. What can we do about such feelings and what can we learn from psychotherapy? This section and the next (about attaining positive feelings) are in the spirit of an old philosophical tradition of giving advice about the good life (see Nussbaum 1986) and of a similar tradition in non-Western cultures of *managing the heart* (Wikan 1990). The difference from the ancient philosophical tradition and from the ideas of non-Western societies lies in the reliance of psychologists on empirical evidence (see Kesebir and Diener 2008 for a similar approach).

Based on the empirical evidence reviewed in the previous section, one thing can be said at the outset: The lack of effectiveness of bringing about the desired outcome suggests that we should not rely on aversive interventions, such as self-punishment.

Sometimes, it helps to simply accept feelings, and individuals use this as a strategy for emotion regulation (see Parkinson and Totterdell 1999). I classify this strategy under meta-awareness because accepting an emotion requires that we reflect on it before we can accept it. Shallcross, Troy, Boland, and Mauss (2010) observed that acceptance of negative emotions from stressful events helps to reduce depressive symptoms in their study; people unwilling or unable to accept negative emotions, by contrast, showed an increase in feelings of depression. Accepting unpleasant emotions may be an easy way to avert sinking into further depressive states. Similarly, acceptance of obsessive thoughts helps to alleviate the negative feelings caused by them (Hannan and Tolin 2005). However, just accepting is often not enough. I shall now discuss three kinds of negative feeling and how to deal with them: fear and anxiety, shame and guilt, and grief.

Fear and anxiety

Some fears appear because we lack appropriate training. For example, a firefighter may not feel much in situations where many of us might tremble with fear. Proper training and planning to cope with a situation may help to alleviate some fears before they even appear. For example, people used to daily contact with dogs may not fear them, or fear them only when it is justified. However, we are not prepared for every situation, and we have to address fear when it appears.

Before people tackle their fear, they should ask whether the fear is unjustified and therefore inappropriate to the current situation. For example, if a girl has to pass a farm with a free-roaming snarling dog each time she walks to school, her fear is justified and her wish to take a detour on her way to school understandable. As it may be impossible to change the environment by removing the snarling dog, she changes her route, which is a version of the strategy in which we select environments such that we can attain positive feelings and circumvent negative ones. If a boy is afraid of every dog and goes to great lengths to avoid encounters with dogs, his fear seems excessive and not appropriate to the situation. In this case, selecting environments to circumvent fear is not sufficient.

After having achieved an understanding of the emotion and its justification (see Brady 2013), we have to decide which measures we will take to counter an inconvenient feeling. If fear is justified, as in the example with the girl and the dog, we should change the situation; a change of feelings is not appropriate. In contrast, the boy whose fear of every dog lacks justification may try to take measures to get rid of his anxiety. As a general lesson, it is important to understand the sensitivity of a person's feelings to a situation. When a person's fear is a reliable indicator of the situation, changing the feeling might lead to maladjustment in later situations. Only when a person's feelings provide unreliable information should we try to tune them.

Sometimes, I would like to change a disabling feeling, such as nervousness, even if it is justified. Nervousness could compromise my ability to demonstrate the competence I bring to an advertised position and therefore harm my prospects of getting the job. The same applies for test anxiety in students, and stage fright in actors. Such fears are often successfully treated with desensitization therapy (Kondaš 1967). A recent study has shown that reappraisal of pre-performance anxiety as excitement resulted in an opportunity-oriented mindset and in better performance (Brooks 2014). Given that the use of beta-blockers is common among professional musicians (27 percent of the performers in a study by Fishbein, Middlestadt, Ottati, Straus, and Ellis 1988), it is worth mentioning that psychological interventions compare well to medication because they reduce stage fright without interfering with performance (Lehrer 1987).

Shame and guilt

Shame and guilt are other examples of negative feelings in everyday life. In contrast to the previous section where I outlined how to get rid of negative feelings that are unjustified and harmful, this section illuminates the claim that one negative feeling might be less harmful than another, and that we should hence try to elicit the more beneficial feeling. Shame and guilt have been extensively examined by Tangney and her colleagues (see Tangney, Stuewig, and Mashek 2007). Both are negative, self-conscious, and moral emotions in that they bring to mind a transgression we have committed. Shame and guilt are often used interchangeably and are almost synonymous. However, there seems to be a decisive difference. The research by Tangney and colleagues revealed that feeling guilt is preferable to feeling shame after an inappropriate action. The decisive difference is the object of the negative evaluation (Lewis 1971). When people feel shame, they emphasize the negative aspects of their own person, or, as Tangney et al. (2007, p. 349) put it, "*I* did that bad thing." In contrast, when people feel guilt, they denigrate their own deeds – "I *did* that horrible *thing*" – with emphasis on the action.

The difference seems small but the effects are large. It turns out that people who denigrate themselves as people due to shame try to avoid that feeling by hiding, denying, or escaping the shame-inducing situation. This follows the logic that, if I want to keep others' and my own positive image of myself, I have to conceal or deny my wrongdoing. If I feel guilt, hiding or denying are not necessary because it is only the action that is wrong, not me as a person. People who feel shame, compared to people who feel guilt, show self-oriented distress and less empathy for others. How can I feel empathy for others when my sole objective is to avoid abasement? When I feel guilty, I can admit my wrongdoing and feel empathy for a potential victim. Shame-prone wrongdoers show destructive reactions to a victim's anger, such as externalization of blame and aggression. When they feel guilt, people focus on their action and respond with constructive behaviors toward correcting the wrongdoing. Only when constructive behavior that compensates for the wrongdoing is not possible may guilt-prone people respond with self-punishment, suggesting that guilt-prone people may disapprove of themselves as people if there is a lack of opportunity to make up for their guilt (Nelissen and Zeelenberg 2009).

People show a variety of physiological and psychological symptoms in response to shame and guilt (see Tangney et al. 2007). Shame, compared to guilt and negative affect in general, leads to increased activity of proinflammatory cytokines, which are proteins related to the immune response. Some psychological consequences of shame are low self-esteem, depression, anxiety, eating disorders, post-traumatic stress disorder, and suicidal ideation. Findings for guilt-prone individuals are more equivocal; they may show maladaptive guilt by chronic self-blame and obsessive rumination over their transgressions. Otherwise, guilt has adaptive functions, particularly for interpersonal behavior, and low levels of those negative consequences that shame-prone people experience.

This summary list of harmful consequences of shame, compared to guilt, leads to the recommendation that we attribute our wrongdoing not to us as a person but to the deed. This is a form of reappraisal. We do not necessarily feel better in the moment. However, by admitting what we have done and by initiating compensatory steps that help to amend the negative consequences of the deed, we can improve both our own well-being and the well-being of the victim of our wrongdoing in the long run.

A related feeling is embarrassment, which is "an aversive state of mortification, abashment, and chagrin that follows public social predicaments" (Miller 1995, p. 332). People who are embarrassed often feel that they are amiss, and that their behavior needs to be monitored, hidden, or changed (see Tangney et al. 2007). Embarrassment has all kinds of negative consequences, ranging from negative affect to fear of negative evaluations from others. This fear may render a person vulnerable to the influence of peer pressure, for example when buddies propose that everyone has another drink or when youths propose to take part in a dare.

How can we alleviate embarrassment? The first possibility is a variant of relaxation therapy: We can relax when we think of the embarrassing situation. Relaxation may be supported by thinking that we probably better remember situations where we were embarrassed than situations where others were embarrassed; therefore, others may remember their own embarrassments more than ours. I do not know of any empirical evidence that shows a memory superiority for our own embarrassments, but this seems plausible given that we remember information about ourselves better than information about others (Kuipers and Rogers 1979; Rogers, Kuiper, and Kirker 1977; see also Kihlstrom, Beer, and Klein 2003).

A second possibility applies to alleviating embarrassment caused by people who use the threat of this state as a means to take advantage of us. Knowing that another person is using the threat of embarrassment as an intentional strategy to subjugate our free will may make us less prone to comply with requests adverse to our interests. In terms of self-determination theory (Deci and Ryan 1985; Ryan and Deci 2000), we uphold a sense of autonomy at the cost of a sense of relatedness. We may still be the target of derision, and we may still feel embarrassed. However, at least we know that our action was self-determined. This makes us feel differently from those who comply. The latter may not feel embarrassed but they may notice that their action was not self-determined because it was done against their will. However, the effectiveness of such interventions needs to be proven in future research.

Grief

For a long time, most scholars believed that the loss of a spouse, child, parent, or close friend leads to deep and negative consequences. People who did not feel grief and be depressed in these moments were seen as pathological and cold. It was assumed that the bereaved needed to perform grief work in order to overcome this crisis. However, this is not what empirical research has normally found (see Bonanno 2004). Many studies have reported that a majority of people do not show intense negative responses to the death of a close family member or friend, and some negative responses and health problems were transient. The responses were only stronger when violence was involved as the cause of death, or when a child died. On average, people seem to be quite resilient in the face of loss. How can people become more resilient? There seem to be five characteristics of people who overcome severe loss without much harm.

First, resilient people possess hardiness, a trait that has been shown to alleviate illness caused by stressful life events (Kobasa, Maddi, and Kahn 1982). This trait consists of three dimensions. Such people have high control beliefs in that they are convinced that they can influence their surroundings and the outcome of events; they are committed to finding meaning and purpose in life; and they believe that they can learn and grow from both positive and negative experiences. While strategically increased self-efficacy might increase objective control of the environment (Bandura 1997) and therefore hardiness and resilience, the other two factors that make up hardiness may not be amenable to strategic control. It is an empirical question whether finding purpose in life for the sake of building up resilience is fruitless or not, as resilience may be a by-product of genuine meaning in life that cannot be brought about strategically. Meaning in life should be sought for its own sake. The same applies to the belief that we can learn and grow from both positive and negative experiences: Either we really believe it, which will bolster resilience, or we feign it as a means to an end, which will not suffice to increase resilience. We might actively elaborate on our positive or negative experiences and try to search for explanations for outcomes. Such a search is supposed to result in a genuine belief; we will experience that we learn and grow from trying to understand past events.

A second characteristic of people who show resilience in the face of loss is overconfidence. Again, this observation cannot lead to a recommendation for practice because resilience is just one of many consequences of overconfidence. As we shall see in the next chapter, overconfidence can have pronounced negative effects in incompetent performers (Kruger 1999). In sum, overconfidence helps people to remain resilient when they encounter loss but may incur costs when it comes to domains other than grief.

The third characteristic is repressive coping, which means that people suppress unpleasant thoughts, emotions, and memories. Repressive coping has been shown to be adaptive when it comes to extreme adversities such as the loss of a loved one (Bonanno et al. 1995), civil war (Bonanno, Field, Kovacevic, and Kaltman 2002), and sexual abuse in childhood (Bonanno, Noll, Putnam, O'Neill, and Trickett 2003). However, as we saw during the introduction of suppression of emotion as a strategy in the previous chapter, repressive coping has been shown to produce maladaptive outcomes under normal life circumstances, leading to more autonomous activation and to later health problems. Fortunately, there are enough other, less ambivalent strategies that bolster resilience.

Fourth, it has been found that telling others about negative experiences such as loss and trauma helps to improve well-being. At first, it seemed that sharing negative experiences with others had direct positive effects (Pennebaker 1997). Later research suggested that telling about loss does not directly benefit the bereaved or traumatized person. Rimé, Herbette, and Corsini (2004) proposed that the benefit does not come from sharing but from experiencing social integration when others respond with empathy to negative experiences. Indeed, Christophe and Rimé (1997) found that listeners responded less verbally but reduced social distance by hugging, kissing, or other physical signs of empathy. Sharing with others is positive, as long as the listener responds sensibly. What looked at the outset like changing an internal state by talking about negative feelings turned out to be changing the external context: By talking about negative feelings, bereaved people change the behaviors of the listeners toward them in a way that benefits them in coping with the loss.

Recent research has revealed the fifth and final characteristic of resilient people: positive emotion and laughter. On the one hand, this response helps people to reduce levels of distress, and on the other it helps them to connect to essential people in their social environment (Bonanno and Keltner 1997). Some earlier theorists thought that showing positive emotions and laughing during the period of grief are forms of unhealthy denial and therefore pathological (Bowlby 1980). This view was in line with the notion that such responses are inappropriate in a bereaved person. Critical feeling may take two forms when it comes to positive feelings and laughter to counter grief. The first is that life goes on, and that mourners should seek out situations that bring enjoyment and positive feelings if doing so does not completely counter their current feelings. Second, if ever bereaved family members or friends feel merry and joyous, whenever they laugh and feel cheerful, they should not feel ashamed because they think it to be inappropriate. In fact, this is quite normal and helps in finding one's way back to life. Positive emotions build a source of strength to overcome grief, in line with interventions in positive psychology.

Positive psychology

Positive psychology aims at measures that make people happier by emphasizing positive states, not by alleviating negative ones. A set of studies has been conducted by Seligman, Steen, Park, and Peterson (2005). They compared five simple interventions to a placebo intervention, which was to write down early memories every night before they went to sleep. From the five interventions tested, three worked in that they showed increased happiness and decreased depression. The first exercise that worked consisted of writing a letter and then paying a "gratitude visit" to a person who had been kind but whom we never properly thanked. This result reiterated other findings that gratitude boosts well-being (see Watkins 2013 for an overview). The second exercise involved each night writing down three good things that went well during the day and a causal explanation for each. For the third intervention, three key strengths of each individual were identified through an online assessment, and the participants were asked to use one of their key strengths in a new and different way every day for one week. Simply identifying the key strengths (another intervention the authors tested) was not enough. The further exercise that did not yield better results than the placebo condition was to write a story about a time when the participant was at his/her best and to reflect once every day about his/her strengths in this story. Other interventions have been tested since these studies; especially successful ones involved people vividly imagining future or past positive events or fully immersing themselves in the present moment, for example by savoring each bite of a tasty meal (see Quoidbach, Mikolajczak, and Gross 2015).

In another fascinating research program, Laura Carstensen and her colleagues found that long-term time perspective plays a crucial role in prioritizing goals, supporting the socioemotional selectivity theory (Carstensen, Isaacowitz, and Charles 1999). When the time perspective is open-ended, people prioritize knowledge goals; when the time perspective is restricted to the near future, they prioritize emotional goals. As age is naturally and inextricably related to years to live until death, time perspective is more limited for the elderly and more open-ended for the young. The authors predicted that younger respondents prefer to invest time in acquiring new knowledge and broaden their intellectual horizon while elderly respondents prefer emotional goals such as living a meaningful life and focusing on social relationships and on being interconnected with others. Indeed, younger people preferred to invest time in interactions where they gained new knowledge while elderly people preferred to invest in close relationships such as friendships with familiar people that provide emotional benefits (Fredrickson and Carstensen 1990). Such differences depend on time perspective and not on chronological age. When groups of young people differed in their life expectancy – one group being HIV-positive patients who suffered from symptoms – those with the shorter life expectancy prioritized social relationships with emotional rather than knowledge-related payoffs (Carstensen and Fredrickson 1998). In another study, elderly participants were asked to imagine that new technologies would enable them to live twenty years longer. By thus expanding their time perspective, the elderly participants did not dif-fer in their priorities from the young age group (Fung, Carstensen, and Lutz 1999).

These studies suggest new strategies for critical feeling. We must not only take the perspectives of others but also imagine different time perspectives. Changing perspectives brings a shift in viewpoints that result in reappraisal of a situation; the reappraisal, in turn, may lead to different priorities and decisions. In any decision we have to take, we may try to play with the different time perspectives. What goals would I pur-sue if I only had one more year to live? This may lead to a focus on more emotional goals, such as playing with our children or having dinner with friends instead of working day and night to maximize income or fame. When we are growing older, we may take a longer time perspective and ask ourselves, "What would I do if I were young?" In retirement we may choose not to start a big new project but we might understand why our children and grandchildren differ from us in the goals they wish to pursue and may themselves start a new project. In this case, changing time per-spective serves to enable us to understand another generation of people.

A different set of studies in positive psychology supports the notion that positive feelings help to build a strong person who is resili-ent in the face of adversity (see Fredrickson 2013 for an overview). First, positive emotions undo negative effects of negative emotions (Fredrickson and Levenson 1998). In fact, resilient people are profi-cient at using positive emotions to bounce back from negative emo-tional experiences (Tugade and Fredrickson 2014). Second, positive emotions *broaden* the scope of attention, thought, and action. For example, people in a positive mood think more broadly (Fredrickson and Branigan 2005; Rowe, Hirsh, and Anderson 2007), more flex-ibly (Dreisbach and Goschke 2004; Isen and Daubman 1984), more intuitively (Bolte, Goschke, and Kuhl 2003), and more creatively (Isen, Daubman, and Nowicki 1987). Broadening the scope of thought extends to the social realm. People who experience positive emotions are socially more inclusive in that they trust a larger circle of other people (Dunn and Schweitzer 2005), and are more likely to see "them" as "us" in that they form more inclusive group identities (Dovidio, Isen, Guerra, Gaertner, and Rust 1998). Finally, individuals who experience positive emotions are not prone to the own-race bias in face perception, which refers to the observation that people have a better recognition memory for faces of their own race, compared to faces of another race (Johnson and Fredrickson 2005). Such broadening feeds back on posi-tive emotions, as Fredrickson and Joiner (2002) observed in a study about the effects of broad-minded coping on affect.

According to Fredrickson (2013), the *build hypothesis* states that positive affect and personal resources support each other in an upward spiral that leads to better personal outcomes. In line with this hypothesis, it has been shown that people who regularly experience positive emotions show more resilience (Fredrickson, Tugade, Waugh, and Larkin 2003), can recruit more resources (Fredrickson, Cohn, Coffey, Pek, and Finkel 2008; Lyubomirsky, King and Diener 2005), and connect more easily with other people (Mauss, Shallcross, Troy, John, Ferrer, Wilhelm, and Gross 2011).

Although positive psychology is not the same as critical feeling (see the previous chapter), the interventions reviewed here could be classified as changing inner states by performing actions that have a known effect on feelings. Let us return to the pursuit of happiness. Effects of interventions in positive psychology may critically depend on whether a person shows gratitude or positive emotions for their own sake or for the sake of becoming happy or resilient. As I noted at the beginning of this chapter, happiness is probably a by-product of a person's actions, and actions aimed explicitly at becoming happy may backfire.

Let us look at how parents and teachers can increase the happiness of children and students through critical feeling. As Nel Noddings (2003) offers a book-length treatment of this question, we need just to give a brief overview. According to her, happiness is an important yet neglected educational goal. Making a home, parenting, attachment to a place, developing spirituality, developing an agreeable personality, making friends, finding a partner for life, and finding a suitable job are all ingredients conducive to happiness, but schools teach little about these topics. Noddings referred to empirical evidence when she noted that money in excess of what guarantees a minimal standard of life does not make us happy (see also Kahneman and Deaton 2010) and that having good friends is important in leading a happy life. She did not, however, refer to psychological literature when she recommended teaching certain ideas to increase the future happiness of students. Many of her recommendations were informed by common sense, not by empirical evidence. This is not necessarily her fault because empirical evidence is far from conclusive when it comes to interventions to advance happiness. When educators have to decide here and now how to bring up children so that they will be happy, they cannot wait until psychologists report research findings. Another important question is whether education for happiness interferes with the imparting of knowledge, the main task of schools.

Noddings' recommendations covered what to teach, such as homemaking and parenting. She provided a thoughtful analysis of how some learning happens incidentally and does not require formal education. Such education presumably is best provided at home, when taking walks, sitting at the dinner table, or playing games. Beyond the contents and methods recommended by Noddings, schools could teach various methods to cope with negative feelings, such as anxiety, shame, and grief. They could teach the joys of gratitude and of helping others. Finally, schools could provide room for discussion of whether happiness is a legitimate goal in itself or just a by-product of actions performed for other, more important purposes. Again, empirical research has yet to show whether schools can teach such topics without losing sight of their main task.

5 THE ROLE OF SENSORY AND BODILY FEEDBACK

When love and skill work together, expect a masterpiece.
(CHARLES READE 1895/1870, P. 48)

The first section of this chapter will take up the main theme of the previous chapter – happiness – and asks the question, "How can we exploit bodily feedback to become happier?" before I discuss a central idea that underpins the importance of critical feeling. If it could be shown that every thought is accompanied by an evaluation, trying to suppress feelings in order to think critically would turn out to be futile – we simply could not do it. Instead, we would need to complement critical thinking with critical feeling.

Observations about how bodily feedback influences affect support the notion that feelings are always with us. I shall review evidence for the claim that each percept, each thought, each action is accompanied by feelings. This view has important consequences for cognitive theories of skill acquisition and execution, as exemplified by the modification of a cybernetic model of action execution and monitoring. Skill learning is plagued by the paradox that smooth learning does not necessarily mean good learning outcomes; moreover, the assessment of skill is notoriously difficult. A final section deals with the role of the body in synchronous movement, a topic that leads to social interaction, which will be the topic of the next chapter.

Bodily feedback and affect

Common sense assumes that people smile when they are happy. However, there is also a commonsense notion that we can reverse this process, that we can make ourselves happy by smiling. "The world always looks brighter from behind a smile," as the saying goes, and this is indeed what can be shown by psychological research, for example on facial feedback and on feedback from postures (see Laird 2007). According to De Sousa (1987), people can use the expression of happiness as a bootstrap mechanism or shortcut to boost their own happiness. Indeed, facial affective feedback has been shown to be instrumental in judging humorousness (Strack et al. 1988) and in processing emotional language (Havas, Glenberg, Gutowski, Lucarelli, and Davidson 2010). Laird (2007) summarized other studies that provide compelling evidence that emotional expression through facial expressions, posture, breathing patterns, and vocal behavior influences emotional feeling. For example, speaking in a loud, harsh voice increases feelings of anger whereas speaking in a soft, low tone is more likely to result in sad feelings. The simplest explanation for why such techniques work is the self-perception theory (see Bem 1972). In the same way we think others are happy when we see their happy face or hear their happy voice, we think that we are happy when we get bodily feedback about our happy facial expression or when we hear ourselves talk in a happy voice.

Critical feeling in the context of bodily feedback comes into play when we try to cultivate a certain affective state. This will usually be a positive affective state, but sometimes it is appropriate to show compassion or sadness, and in such situations we may try to bring ourselves into a negative state. Trying to put on a positive emotional expression in order to get into a positive affective state is different from both suppressing negative emotions and from reappraising the situation. Although suppressing a negative emotion includes suppressing its emotional expression, it does not include putting on a positive emotional expression. In addition, putting on a positive emotional expression does not include suppression of the experience of a negative emotion. However, it remains to be seen whether laboratory findings on facial feedback will hold true for alleviating negative affect in everyday life. Reappraisal is different in that we reinterpret the situation in such a way that we withdraw the reason for feeling an emotion. Simulating the expression of a positive emotion, such as smiling, does not include such a cognitive reinterpretation.

However, there may be serious drawbacks of smiling as a means to become happy. One study has shown that businesspeople who have to smile for their customers felt less happy than when they were not forced to smile (e.g., Goldberg and Grandey 2007). How does this finding fit with the observation that putting on an emotion elicits this emotion? In laboratory studies that examined this effect, participants were not explicitly told to put on a certain emotion but were either instructed which muscles to move until they were in the position that the researchers wanted (see Laird 2007) or were asked to keep a pencil in their mouth in the same way as muscles are contracted in a certain emotional state (Strack et al. 1988). When the researchers wanted to induce a positive state, a person was instructed to hold the pencil between the teeth in order to activate the zygomaticus major, which is the *smiling muscle*.

When the experimenters aimed at a negative feeling state, they asked a person to hold the pencil between the lips, which led to the contraction of the corrugator, which lies between the eyebrows. Great care was taken that people did *not* know which emotions they were imitating with their face. The researchers intended to prevent demand effects – that is, that participants in their studies would report to be happy if they knew that they were expected to arrive at a happy state. Paradoxically, however, happiness may decrease if individuals intend to induce this state because positive feelings may be a by-product of an action, in this case to pose in such a way that certain muscles are activated. If people in their everyday life intend to bring about happiness by emulating a happy pose, they may undermine the achievement of their goal for the reasons I discussed at the beginning of the previous chapter. Again, the conscious pursuit of happiness may be self-defeating, and businesspeople who are forced to smile do not reap the benefit of activating the right muscles.

Some interventions aim to alleviate depressive symptoms through expressions of positive emotions via posture. Yet empirical evidence is mixed. Flack, Laird, and Cavallaro (1999) instructed depressed outpatients to assume postures that normally accompany anger, sadness, fear, and happiness. While assuming a negative posture led to more negative feelings than a neutral control condition, the happy posture did not discern any positive effect. Laird (2007) ascribed the failure to produce happy feelings through posture to the fact that an especially happy posture does not really exist. More research is needed to show whether postures or other means of bodily feedback, such as facial or vocal expression, could be used in psychotherapy or in everyday life.

In day-to-day life, it may sometimes work to tell people that they should not express their feelings if they are angry or sad. Duclos and Laird (2001) conducted a study with adults recruited from a mainstream Christian church in the United States. These participants were quite skeptical about psychological interventions. Nevertheless, their attempts to deliberately inhibit the expression of anger or sadness were effective in reducing the intensity of the respective feelings. This is an alternative to the therapy of addressing anger with relaxation techniques (Hazaleus and Deffenbacher 1986). However, the findings by Duclos and Laird do not seem to be in agreement with other studies that showed negative effects of suppressing emotions (Gross 1998; see also Chapter 3). Is it possible, for example, that telling people to suppress a negative emotion as a whole (including feeling, action tendencies, physiological effects, and expression) is counterproductive while telling them to suppress just the expression of the emotion would yield the desired result in that people would feel the negative affective state less intensely? Future research should examine whether there is a fine line between productive inhibition of emotional expression and counterproductive inhibition of emotional experience.

Acquisition and execution of skills

In a book about learning to stretch muscles, the authors instruct readers, "You will sense how far to stretch if you are paying attention to how the stretch feels" (Anderson and Anderson 2010, p. 14). This means that a learner stretches a muscle up to a certain point and monitors the strain on it. The resulting sensation is accompanied by an evaluation that the strain on the muscle is still within the comfort zone. When the stretch feels good, the learner stretches a bit more and then monitors the strain again. When it still feels good, he stretches even more, monitors the strain, evaluates its extent, and so on, up to a point where he notices that any further stretching would result in pain. Optimal stretching approaches the pain threshold without reaching or surpassing it.

The TOTE model

Stretching is a typical example of switching between acting and monitoring until we achieve a previously defined goal state. Miller et al. (1960) developed the TOTE model, in which T stands for test, O for operate, and E for exit. Their example was hammering a nail into a wall. We first test whether we have achieved the goal state. As the nail is not in the wall at the beginning, we have to operate – that is, to hit the nail with the hammer. Then we test again. If the nail is in the wall, we can exit the test-operate-test loop and stop hammering. If the nail is not yet in the wall, we hammer again, and so on until the test reveals that the nail is in the wall and we can exit the loop. Applying the TOTE model to the stretching example, we first test the strain on the muscle (test). If we feel that the strain is still comfortable, we stretch more (operate). We then again test the strain on the muscle (test). We repeat this cycle until we notice that more strain would cause pain; this is the point where we stop stretching (exit).

The classic TOTE model is a computational model, developed from cybernetics, where the aim is to bring the actual state to a goal state. When we hammer a nail into a wall, we have a well-defined target state and a well-defined actual state. However, this is not the case in our stretching example. While there are robot nailers, we could not develop a device that does my stretching for me. The goal state does not pertain to

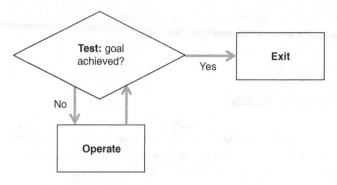

Figure 5.1 The TOTE model, by Miller et al. (1960).

the environment but to a sensation in my body. As I evaluate this bodily state, I *feel* whether I have achieved the goal state. Joëlle Proust (2013) therefore developed the idea that the evaluation of a goal state may be based on metacognitive experiences. Instead of test-operate-test-exit, we could also call this loop feel-operate-feel-exit. Many actions include feelings at the test phase. If Emily plays the flute, she has to coordinate her finger movements to the sounds she wishes to produce. She hears how well she hits the note and at the same time feels how smoothly her fingers move. Again, such high-level musical judgment seems to be an impossible feat for a robot, at least nowadays. A gymnast has to shape his exercises by experiencing whether his movements lead to the desired outcome. It may be relatively easy to evaluate body balance, but it is certainly more difficult to get a feeling for whether the movement is smooth and elegant to look at from the outside. Again, the feedback loop leading to the goal state includes feelings.

Couldn't we argue that hammering a nail into a wall also involves feelings? As long as the nail stands out, do we not feel worse than when it finally is in the wall? In this latter case, do we not feel some form of satisfaction? These are not intense feelings, but they should be measurable. If perceiving a nail in relation to the wall elicits affective feelings, we would have to ask whether perception in general is not only cognitive interpretation but also evaluation of the environment, amounting to the claim that feelings are behind every act of perception. To use an expression by Winkielman et al. (2003), perceptions are *hedonically marked*.

All cognitions are hedonically marked

The idea that all cognitions are hedonically marked is an old one in psychology (see Overskeid 2000). In the late nineteenth century, Wundt

(1893) claimed that every experience possesses a hedonic quality along a continuum from negative to positive. According to Petty and Cacioppo (1981), social psychologists agree "that the term attitude should be used to refer to a general and enduring positive or negative feeling" (p. 7). As most – if not all – objects elicit attitudes automatically, there is good reason to assume that we spontaneously experience affect whenever we interact with our environment. If correct, this assumption extends the applicability of critical feeling considerably.

Affective experiences seem to be involved in basic perceptual processes, as several studies show. Biases in perception lead to equivalent biases in liking (Chen and Scholl 2014), suggesting that perception and affect are in line. Successful perception of possible, compared to impossible, versions of the Necker cube elicits positive feelings (Topolinski, Erle, and Reber 2015). This finding suggests that the quality of perception is linked to affective valence. In line with this assumption, Chetverikov and Filippova (2014) found that participants liked degraded images more if they were able to categorize them correctly. According to Neisser (1976), perception includes the formation of hypotheses that will be tested in the subsequent examination of the object. Indeed, Chetverikov and Filippova (2014) showed that such hypothesis testing is not a purely cognitive affair and has also affective consequences.

What does this mean for the acquisition and execution of skill? If our hypothesis is true and all perception is inherently affective, perception of feedback from the environment or the body is also inherently affective. If so, every test stage in the TOTE loop not only is a computational process of comparison but also includes an evaluative experience. Indeed, Aarts, De Houwer, and Pourtois (2012, 2013) recently provided both behavioral and electrophysiological evidence that actions are automatically evaluated. If their findings can be generalized beyond the laboratory context, each action has an affective stamp and is therefore hedonically marked. We not only *compute* whether the current state deviates from the desired state; we *feel* it. This simple fact has been neglected by cognitive psychologists because they restricted themselves to building on the computer metaphor in order to explain human thought and behavior. While this metaphor was powerful in overcoming behaviorism and in introducing the concept of mind as an object of empirical inquiry in scientific psychology, it excluded feelings. When a carpenter looks at a nail in a wall, he does not only see it; his perception is accompanied by a spontaneous feeling. This feeling is positive, either of pleasure or of rightness, when the nail is in the wall. It feels neither pleasurable nor right if the nail still stands out when the goal is to have it in the wall. If the hypothesis advocated here is correct, even the act of hammering a nail includes affect. The more easily and smoothly we execute the act of hammering, the more positively we feel; and, the closer we come to the goal, the better.

Hammering a nail into a wall may be a boring affair. However, the hypothesis that cognitive analysis and affect are two sides of the same perceptual process has fascinating implications. We can find an abundance of examples of a feedback loop where the test phase includes feelings. An artist trys out arrangement of objects or forms within a painting until she can tell herself, "Yes, this looks like I want it to." Again, we could employ the TOTE loop to describe how the artist comes to the optimal arrangement, with the test stage being a feeling. Applying what we have learned to skill learning and training in sports, it is easy to see how learning proceeds from a conscious trying out to smoother automatic processes where we assess our feelings in order to monitor our progress. Whether we are learning to swim or to drive, we begin with a series of clumsy movements that we execute consciously. We control each of these movements in order to get them into the right order. Only after extensive training will we be able to execute an action automatically (Anderson 1982; Neves and Anderson 1981).

However, what does the transition from controlled to automatic behavior entail? Apart from making computational mechanisms work more smoothly and therefore faster, the transition increases the role of feelings. When behavior has become automatic, we no longer need to consciously compare the actual state to the target state because the comparison is made subconsciously and its result is experienced as a feeling. This view is certainly controversial until more evidence is available in favor of the assumption that perception is inherently affective. However, this view could explain two phenomena that are difficult to understand within a purely computational perspective. First, feelings may be a prerequisite for fast and efficient execution and monitoring of an action. Second, when we try to verbalize automated behaviors, such as riding a bicycle, we may stumble because we have problems verbalizing feelings that are part of evaluation. Anderson's (1982) theory of skill acquisition suggests a purely cognitive explanation in terms of unpacking schematic knowledge that might account for the lack of ability to verbalize automated behavior. It remains to be shown whether these two potential phenomena – difficulty to verbalize feelings versus difficulty to unpack schematic knowledge – can be separated empirically. Theoretically, they are not mutually exclusive. Despite the lack of empirical evidence, assuming that all cognition is colored by affect might advance our knowledge because it spurs new lines of inquiry. Capturing the TOTE loop as a feeling-operate-feeling-exit loop may open new pathways for both research and practice in skill learning and sports training.

I have argued that all cognition is accompanied by feelings. Generalizing from perception and thought, we may extend the claim to action. As discussed in Chapter 2, every thought is accompanied by an experience of ease, and this fluency is hedonically marked. Moreover, as briefly illustrated via the example of nailing earlier in this section, we not only execute an action and then see how far we have come in the test phase but also continually feel how smoothly we can execute the action in the operate phase. There has not been much research about this kind of action fluency (see Alter and Oppenheimer 2009). Nevertheless, from what we know about the evaluative effects of perceptual and conceptual fluency, there is reason to assume that action fluency is hedonically marked as well. Human beings not only think during their whole waking life; they also continuously evaluate what they see, think, and do (see Proust 2013).

The claim that all cognition is accompanied by evaluation opens up the opportunity to use feelings strategically. According to this view, proficiency in a skill includes automatic evaluation of an action through feeling. The goal of the action is perfection in execution assessed by bodily feedback, for example when we try to learn to do a somersault, or by multisensory feedback, for example when playing the flute.

Skills, virtue, and feelings

Feelings are ubiquitous. Every perception, every thought, every action is accompanied by some sort of feeling. We can use those feelings to assess our progress when learning a skill. These insights have important implications for virtue ethics (see also Chapter 10). Aristotle used a skill analogy when he described how we learn to be virtuous (see Annas 2011). This means that we can not only assess the progress of learning a skill but also the progress of learning to act morally.

However, there is a crucial difference between skill learning and acquisition of virtue. According to virtue ethicists, skill needs only knowledge whereas virtue needs the right feeling (Annas 2011; Sherman 1989). A rich woman may look generous by giving money to the poor. However, if she at the same time feels contempt for those who receive her money because she thinks they are not able to make their own living, her behavior does not mirror inner generosity. Therefore, the feelings that accompany an action are a necessary condition for its virtuousness. Virtue is in this view more than skillful action.

However, is it correct that skill just needs knowledge and no "right" feeling, unlike virtue? Philosophers have argued that a potter can shape a pot without love – he may even hate his profession – and he is still a skillful potter. So far, this is correct. Nevertheless, accompanying emotions may play a role in performing a skill too. First, empirical studies might examine whether the right feeling may give the product a different expression. Although the products of a potter who has the right feeling might be of the same technical quality as the products of a potter who has no or even ill tempered feelings, the happy potter may shape a pot that somehow looks more elegant or cheerful than the one by the unfeeling or even grumpy potter. The epigraph at the beginning of the chapter about love and skill working together seems to capture this notion. Second, further studies might show whether the relationship to the product changes. A potter who feels cheerful during the shaping of the pot certainly has a different experience from the potter who feels grouchy when seeing the final product. Even as a customer, I may enjoy the pot more if I know that the potter enjoyed making this piece, and I may miss this enjoyment when I either do not know the feelings of the potter (as is mostly the case nowadays) or when I know that the potter did it just to earn money; I might even entertain some vague negative feelings if I knew that the potter hated making that particular pot. Although a craftsman does not need the right feeling to exert his skill, it certainly helps to improve the relationship between him and his product, or between the customer and his product. In line with the psycho-historical framework (Bullot and Reber 2013a; see also Chapter 9), the emotional context in which the craftsman produces his work moderates the relationship between the artifact and the customer.

Desirable difficulties in skill learning

When learning a skill, we have to assess the proficiency with which we can exercise it. The most straightforward way to check our progress would be to assess the ease with which learning advances. This sounds plausible, but unfortunately it may be fraught with error. Monitoring the ease of performing a skill during the phase of acquisition may lead to systematic errors in our assessments because apparent ease of acquisition may be related to lower learning outcomes.

A study by Baddeley and Longman (1978) of postal workers in Britain illustrates this paradox nicely: In the 1960s, the Britain's Royal Mail introduced new postcodes with letters and numbers. In order to register the codes, postal workers had to learn to type on a new kind of typewriter especially designed for this task. The management of Royal Mail approached the researchers with the question of which training schedule would be optimal to learn most efficiently. The measure of efficiency was how many hours of training were necessary to attain proficiency with the typewriter. Is training many hours a day (a blocked schedule) superior such that learning is focused and can be finished within a short time? Or is it better to space learning, providing training for a relatively short period each day? The researchers did not know but offered to examine the question, assigning workers to different training schedules. For the sake of simplicity, let us look at the two extreme schedules. One group got four hours of training per day, the other group one hour per day. The group that learned for one hour per day needed fewer training hours than the group that trained for four hours per day. This observation suggests that spaced training is superior in terms of learning outcomes compared to training in a blocked schedule. Paradoxically, the group that trained one hour per day and showed superior performance liked the training *less* and thought that they were less efficient than the group that learned for four hours in a row. The impression that they were less efficient may have come from the fact that the postal workers who had longer training sessions each day made more progress while the one-hour group needed more days to accomplish the criteria for proficiency, despite their more efficient learning. This study yielded the paradoxical outcome that the better learning method led to less liking of the training than an inefficient method.

Bjork and his colleagues (Benjamin, Bjork, and Schwartz 1998; Simon and Bjork 2001, 2002) examined this tension further by assessing judgments of learning. In the experiment by Benjamin et al., participants had to respond to general knowledge questions. After they provided an answer, participants were instructed to indicate whether they would be able to recall the answer twenty minutes later. When an answer came to mind easily, participants thought that they would be likely to retrieve the answer. In contrast, when the answer came to mind after a lengthy search, participants predicted that they would do poorly in the recall session. In fact, the results were exactly opposite to the predictions: Participants recalled more answers that were difficult to find in the first round.

A study on perceptual–motor learning yielded similar results (Simon and Bjork 2001). These authors found that participants made fewer errors during acquisition of a skill if they were trained on a blocked rather than a random schedule. However, when it came to retention the next day, participants in the random condition fared significantly better than those in the blocked condition, in line with Baddeley and Longman's finding that the postal workers on the spaced schedule had the better learning outcomes in the long term. There was thus a discrepancy between the learners' experiences and learning outcomes: Ease of processing during the acquisition phase was related to poorer outcomes in the retention phase, and vice versa. In addition, Simon and Bjork required their participants to form a judgment on how well they had learned certain patterns in the acquisition phase of the perceptual–motor task. They found that participants in the blocked schedule rated their future retention more favorably than participants in the random schedule, mirroring the advantage in the acquisition phase but contradicting the actual outcome in the retention test.

Similarly, ease of learning gives people the misleading impression that they are competent (see Marteau, Wynne, Kaye, and Evans 1990; Reber et al. 2006); they have the erroneous intuition that they retrieve well what they learn with ease. Similarly, many education researchers and practitioners believe that reducing extraneous cognitive load and thus making learning easy is always beneficial for the learner (Sweller and Chandler 1994). In fact, some studies have shown that learning outcomes may be superior when learning is made more difficult, for example by presenting contents in a difficult-to-read font or making texts incoherent (Diemand-Yauman et al. 2011; McNamara, Kintsch, Songer, and Kintsch 1996). The phenomenon that difficulties lead to better learning outcomes has been given the name *desirable difficulties*.

Is there a way of rendering effortful training that includes some obstacles more pleasurable than it usually is? We could think about such difficulties and remember that, on similar occasions, we surmounted the obstacles and achieved our goal. Indeed, research by Oyserman and colleagues (Oyserman 2015; Oyserman, Bybee, and Terry 2006) suggests that students work harder if they link difficulties to the attainment of a personally meaningful goal and not to their lack of ability. Further research must show whether teachers could use instrumental conditioning as a strategy to help students persist in the face of difficulties: If difficulties are repeatedly followed by successful learning, learners may develop a positive attitude toward effortful training and therefore feel better when they encounter an obstacle. This does not seem to be the attitude people normally have: Learners often do not develop a positive attitude toward surmounting difficulties.

One reason why it is so difficult to see the connection between difficulties and training outcomes may be that many learners have always given up too early and have therefore never reaped the benefits of their effort by experiencing positive learning outcomes. Alternatively, they may have experienced the positive outcome but the difficulties and successes may have been too distant in time for them to make a connection between overcoming obstacles and outcome. Nevertheless, there seem to be people who have learned their lesson. If we look at successful athletes and musicians and also – to leave the realm of bodily activity – hard-working entrepreneurs, politicians, and academics, we see that there are people who know that they have to invest effort when they encounter obstacles, and they often do so with great enthusiasm and success. A study has shown that only experts tackle difficulties even when they do not like them, while learners at an intermediate level train in aspects they have already mastered (Coughlan, Williams, McRobert, and Ford 2014). Such behavior can be observed beyond mere skill learning. Moral role models examined by Colby and Damon (1992) treasure the chance to overcome difficulties instead of becoming frustrated and despairing. We may therefore learn how to confront and overcome difficulties in both skill learning and moral behavior from observing experts.

The speculations about persistence and success at an activity can be derived theoretically from simple principles of reinforcement. Persistence becomes associated with subsequent success, which also serves as reinforcement for persistence. If these assumptions were correct, it would be of utmost importance that children must be given the opportunity to persist in the face of difficulties and to experience immediate subsequent success that is then attributed to the effort they invested (for such attributional styles see Weiner 1986). Parents and teachers must arrange situations and tasks carefully in order to instill an experience of success after a child's persistence.

Self-assessment and feelings

A critic might object that persisting is meaningless when the obstacles are insurmountable, and that insistence on continuing such tasks could lead to learned helplessness (Peterson, Maier, and Seligman 1995). Therefore, it is an educator's task to teach the students when it is wise to persist and when not. If this prerequisite is met, learners can cultivate a positive feeling for difficult tasks after they have decided that they can and want to achieve a certain goal. Students also should learn to make realistic predictions about what they can achieve. Usually, people tend to be overly optimistic when a task is easy and overly pessimistic when a task is difficult (see Kruger 1999). Such regression to the mean does not only apply to the tasks but also to the performers. Extremely good people tend to underestimate their performance, and less competent people tend to overestimate their performance.

Perhaps the most extreme example of overestimation stems from university professors who were asked about the quality of their teaching compared to the teaching of their colleagues. If all professors answered accurately, the average performance judgments should have ended up at 50 percent because the professors had to indicate where they stood compared to their peers. The average judgments of the professors were at 94 percent, an astounding overestimation (Cross 1977). With professors, everything that encourages such overestimation comes together: An easy task, lack of immediate feedback, and lack of social competence (see Kruger 1999; Kruger and Dunning 1999). Talking in front of students is easy, but delivering a good lecture is hard. Even professors who are not well prepared and instead crack some jokes may think that they have managed the lecture quite well. The laughter of their students may reinforce this impression. Most often, however, professors lack immediate feedback, another source of overestimation. When they stand in front of students, there are always some who are enthusiastic, some who are bored, and the rest are quiet. When professors do not observe unanimous enthusiasm or students leaving their lectures in droves, they cannot figure out whether the lecture was good or bad. A final source of overestimation is lack of social competence regarding the likes and dislikes of their students. Some European universities began to collect student evaluations only ten to fifteen years ago, sometimes against resistance from the professors. More than once, I have encountered experienced professors who were flabbergasted when they saw the outcome of their first evaluation. They simply did not notice that the students did not like their teaching.

Another source of bias is processing fluency, combined with the comparative nature of the performance judgments. Working on easy tasks feels more fluent than working on difficult tasks (Reber et al. 2006). When we are able to perform a task easily, aren't we good at it? Yes, but others may perform well, too. That is why comparative performance judgments often go wrong, especially, as we have seen, with professors. People judge their own performance and do not look at what others do (Kruger and Dunning 1999). That is why they overestimate their performance when the task is easy but underestimate their performance on a difficult task. In this case, a performer observes that she did badly on a difficult task. Without taking the performance of others who suffer from the same constraints and limitations into account, she thinks that she did worse than other performers. These findings have important practical implications. I once read that there are restaurants in Switzerland that earn just enough money to pay their electricity bills. People think it is easy to manage a restaurant; it just needs some tables, some chairs, a kitchen, and a smile. This may indeed be enough to manage a middling restaurant. Yet, if it is easy for me to manage this kind of enterprise, it will be easy for you and also for everybody else; this is what hopeful novices often forget when they decide to open a restaurant. On the other hand, computer programming and doing mathematics are difficult. People are egocentric in that they look at how difficult these activities are for themselves without looking at how difficult they are for others. If prospective students decide which subject to take, they may end up with a suboptimal decision when they choose a subject that they consider easy and without obstacles, for example media studies, social anthropology, or psychology, which are incidentally also among the most popular subjects. On the other hand, students may miss an opportunity when they are interested in mathematics or computer science but think that these subjects are too difficult. Everybody has to think hard when solving mathematical problems or implementing algorithms in a computer program; this may also explain why only a few high school graduates decide to study mathematics or the other hard sciences (cf. McColm 2007).

The problem of underestimation is aggravated if a difficult activity, such as juggling, playing the violin, or computer programming, provides learners with immediate feedback. Again, people often underestimate how well they do because they fail to remember that others struggle with the same difficulties and get the same unfavorable feedback.

Critical feeling means that we know about the mechanisms described above and act accordingly. We might try to select tasks where we get immediate feedback. Where this is not possible, we might look for early indicators of our performance. Instead of just monitoring how difficult or easy the task is for us, we should take task difficulty into account and see how others solve the same problem. Being able to smoothly solve tasks that drive our friends and fellow students to desperation presumably indicates a special flair for a topic. In contrast, if we have difficulties at something everybody else masters with ease, this is probably not something in which we should invest much time (I am thinking of my dancing lessons…).

The power of synchronous movement

Drill is still widely used as part of military training despite the fact that close-order marching in military action would have been fatal since the invention of machine guns. Moreover, long-distance marching has lost its significance for moving troops since railroads and trucks came into use. The widespread use of close-order marching, which despite its apparent uselessness in modern warfare makes up a large part of military drill, puzzled military historian William McNeill (1995). Why do soldiers not revolt against this sweating in the sun? To answer this question, McNeill delved into historical documents and concluded that synchrony in drill results in interpersonal liking. This is supported by the observation that drill sergeants become surprisingly popular over time (Faris 1976), which suggests that moving in synchrony yields liking. McNeill pointed to the lack of sufficient scientific evidence and of a psychological theory that could explain why muscular bonding yields positive affect.

The fluency theory reviewed in Chapter 2 may help to explain the positive effects of drill. It predicts that synchrony results in higher fluency, which in turn increases affective positivity (Reber 2012a). Wilson and Knoblich (2005) argued that motor coordination increases the predictability of another person's actions. Earlier research documented correlations between behavioral coordination and positive rapport (Bernieri 1988; LaFrance and Broadbent 1976). Later research manipulated synchrony of movements between participants in an experiment and the experimenter. Participants preferred an experimenter who moved in sync to an experimenter who moved out of sync (Hove and Risen 2009). These findings are important because people frequently imitate their interaction partner's behavior (Ackerman and Bargh 2010; Wilson and Knoblich 2005). In line with these observations, Marsh, Richardson, Baron, and Schmidt (2006) examined a direct link between processing fluency and liking. Two participants had to coordinate their actions – swinging a pendulum – in coordination tasks of varying difficulty levels. Participants in the easy coordination task reported more liking for each other than participants in the difficult coordination task, which can be interpreted as a positive effect of interpersonal fluency on affect (Ackerman and Bargh 2010). Wiltermuth and Heath (2009) observed that synchronous activities of groups of three people resulted in greater trust, greater feelings of being in the same team, and more cooperation. Páez, Rimé, Basabe, Wlodarczyk, and Zumeta (2015) found that emotional synchrony through collective gatherings increased positive affect and positive social beliefs and strengthened collective identity and social integration. Together, these studies suggest that processing fluency from synchronous activity, such as marching but also dancing, increases the mutual liking of the participants (see Reber and Norenzayan 2010 for a more detailed analysis).

How can critical feeling be applied to synchronous activity? It is needless to say that dancing helps to build interpersonal bonds. In the light of twentieth-century history, however, it seems odd to recommend marching together with people whom we like to be with. As McNeill remarks, the popularity of synchronous movement declined after World War II because Nazi propaganda relied heavily on synchronous movement, such as marches and parades that increased the rapport both within the National Socialist movement and between the public and the National Socialist Party. The same holds true for the other big totalitarian system of the twentieth century, Stalinism. Beyond synchronous movement, both systems relied heavily not only on repetition of movement but also on other forms of synchronous activity, such as singing or music as an accompaniment to marching.

However, bad experiences in the past century may have prevented good uses of synchronous movement. McNeill concluded that our "contemporary disregard of this aspect of human sociality is unwise and probably also unsustainable over the long haul" (McNeill 1995, p. 157). Indeed, people who like to be part of a group activity, for example aerobics training, folk dance, or cheerleading, may seek out situations where they can move in synchrony, which increases interpersonal fluency and as a consequence interpersonal liking and social cohesiveness (see Reber and Norenzayan 2010).

Having discussed the ubiquity of feelings in skill acquisition and action monitoring, I would like to summarize how educators can make use of this knowledge.

We all learned skills at school, especially intellectual skills such as arithmetic, reading, writing, and later solving equations and the acquisition of a second language. Some schools provide courses in cooking, handicrafts, music, or swimming among other activities. I do not want to focus on which skills students learn but on how they learn them. Books that teach a skill often neglect feelings. Unlike the book on stretching (Anderson and Anderson 2010) mentioned earlier in this chapter, books on cooking, swimming, woodwork, or learning to play an instrument often do not encourage novices to assess their performance using sensory feedback. I am sure many teachers tell students to rely on their feelings to assess their performance while cooking, swimming, smoothing a board, or playing the violin. However, we then would need to provide teachers with some systematic knowledge on how their students could learn to use feelings as indicators of their progress. Feelings are ubiquitous in the acquisition and execution of skills, and sensory feedback plays a vital role in evaluating one's performance. The acquisition of skills may not only need good books but also practitioners who have experienced these feelings themselves. What is needed, then, is systematic work on how and when to convey such feelings to novices in order for them to benefit from the information provided by feelings.

The section on desirable difficulties showed that skills are sometimes better learned when performers go through periods of challenges. This might not have been a big problem some decades ago when children were taught – or even forced – to persist in the face of obstacles. Nowadays, however, we want children to be driven by intrinsic motivation. When they learn a skill, parents and teachers may well let them give up too early. One important discussion, especially in the light of low performance of Western students in international school assessment studies (OECD 2014), must address the question of to what degree we should demand our children to persist in a task. While advocates of autonomous learning might argue that children lose intrinsic motivation over time (e.g., Deci and Ryan 1985), persistence in the face of obstacles may be rewarded by smooth performance after the task has been learned.

Finally, schools might exploit the aesthetics of moving together in order to increase mutual liking and class cohesion. Group gymnastics and dance offer opportunities to move in synchrony with others. We have seen that such coordinated activities may increase trust (Wiltermuth and Heath 2009) and facilitate social interaction (Chartrand and Bargh 1999). Further research must determine whether synchronous movement consolidates the hierarchy between subordinates and leaders, a consequence that could be seen in a positive or negative light, depending on the objectives of the organization and on the importance one places on the personal autonomy of the individual student or employee. Nevertheless, it would be interesting to measure whether bullying in schools decreased and mutual respect among students increased if regular activities that included synchronous movement were introduced into the curriculum.

6 LIVING TOGETHER

Let me not to the marriage of true minds
Admit impediments. Love is not love
Which alters when it alteration finds,
Or bends with the remover to remove:
Oh no! It is an ever-fixèd mark
That looks on tempests and is never shaken;
It is the star to every wand'ring bark,
Whose worth's unknown, although his height be taken.
Love's not Time's fool, though rosy lips and cheeks
Within his bending sickle's compass come;
Love alters not with his brief hours and weeks,
But bears it out even to the edge of doom.
If this be error and upon me proved,
I never writ, nor no man ever loved.
(WILLIAM SHAKESPEARE 2003/1609, SONNET 116)

The previous chapter reviewed evidence that coordinated action increases social rapport. Even infants imitate the facial expression of their mothers (Meltzoff and Moore 1977). Mothers and infants synchronize their behavior (Trevarthen 1979) and coordinate their facial movements with each other's (Stern 1977, 1985). Children and adults may act in synchrony with others in order to increase social cohesion. The social functions of emotion are so pervasive (see Campos, Mumme, Kermoian, and Campos 1994) that Saarni (1999) claimed that emotions cannot be understood but in connection to social interaction. We learn emotions through social interaction, we employ them in social interaction, and we understand the emotions of others through social interaction. Moreover, using emotions strategically can be done not only for the sake of individual well-being and skill acquisition but also for the sake of collective concerns (see Wikan 1990 for an example from anthropology).

How much can we extend to feelings in general the idea that emotions are interwoven within their social context? Social interaction can determine feelings beyond emotions in several ways. First, from early childhood on, our preferences are shaped through instrumental conditioning. At the beginning parents, later peers, tell children what to like and what to dislike (see Bourdieu 1984/1979 for a sociological analysis). Although we may retain some autonomy in determining our tastes, preferences are embedded in our social ecology. Second, other people expose us to objects and experiences. As repeated exposure influences feelings in a positive direction – at least as long as we are not overexposed – parents have an opportunity to guide tastes by showing their son what they want him to like, and they may prevent their daughter from being exposed to music or movies they think harm her tastes (see Chapter 2). Third, subtle signals such as imitation and coordination of movements influence our feelings. We have already seen how military officers exploit such mechanisms to instill a sense of group identity within their units. Finally, feelings of knowing have been introduced as a metacognitive skill – based on fluency – that helps students to assess their knowledge. Such a skill could be seen in purely individualistic terms. To my knowledge, social psychologists have not yet examined the feeling of knowing other individuals. Quite certainly, we have an experience related to whether we can adequately appraise another person or not. The principal function of feelings of knowing in social contexts is not the assessment of how much we have to learn to pass an exam – like feelings of knowing at school – but getting an idea of the degree to which we can predict the behavior of our interaction partners.

   Although I do not explicitly follow up in detail the idea that most feelings are embedded in social contexts, this idea pervades most of this and the following chapters. Political views, interest in subject matter at school, understanding art, and belonging to religious communities are just some of the examples I shall discuss. In this chapter I begin with negative feelings in social interactions and turn to more and more positive feelings until I arrive at what is seen as the ultimate positive feeling: love. I end with a note on how to maintain marriage in the face of adversity.

Negative feelings in social interactions

Emotion expression has a social function; we communicate how we feel (see Kraut and Johnston 1979 for empirical evidence). While negative emotions are unpleasant for the person who experiences them, they may be useful in social interaction because they communicate to others what the person feels, which may give rise to action tendencies. I shall first review research on the positive social function of negative emotions and then discuss catharsis, the popular belief that watching aggressive sports or playing violent games serves as a valve to let off steam that is supposed to alleviate overt aggression.

The positive side of negative feelings

Negative emotions indicate that a person is not satisfied with the current state of affairs. Despite the disagreeable experience they elicit, negative feelings can have multiple positive consequences (see Parrott 2015). Negative affect improves memory, reduces judgmental biases, and attenuates negative effects of stereotyping (Forgas 2015). Beyond these benefits for the individual, negative affect improves interpersonal outcomes. Negative mood enables people to detect deception in videotaped statements by guilty or innocent defendants (Forgas and East 2008) and increases interpersonal fairness (Tan and Forgas 2010). These studies and others (see Schwarz 1990) should warn critical feelers that being in a positive affective state may make us careless and even egoistic. Although direct empirical evidence does not exist, the use of a rule of fairness in situations that require sharing might be a good method to enjoy a positive mood without its negative consequences. Such routines would prevent unfairness without making us unhappy.

In social interaction, the expression of negative feelings reveals a person's affective states to others. For example, if a man unintentionally violates a social norm, he may show embarrassment. While feeling embarrassment is unpleasant, expressing it signals to other group members that he is sorry for the transgression, which appeases the others in the group (Keltner and Buswell 1997). Similarly, guilt signals that we acknowledge our wrongdoing and may try to compensate the victim through action or an apology (see Baumeister, Stillwell, and Heatherton 1994; Tangney et al. 2007). The expression of negative emotions can also help in the workplace (see Van Kleef and Côté 2015 for a review). For example, an angry negotiator signals that she is committed to achieving an advantageous outcome and is therefore likely to elicit concessions in negotiations (e.g., Van Kleef, De Dreu, and Manstead 2004). Leaders in a negative mood have been shown to stimulate more effort among followers than leaders in a positive mood. However, teams with leaders in a positive mood developed a positive mood themselves and showed better coordination (Sy, Côté, and Saavedra 2005). Heerdink, Van Kleef, Homan, and Fischer (2013) showed that an angry leader can enforce conformity in groups, but, if participants in this study were given the alternative to leave a group headed by an angry leader, they did so.

While people in close relationships experience many positive emotions, negative feelings may positively influence partnerships by increasing interpersonal understanding, eliciting social support, and helping to resolve relationship problems (see Baker, McNulty, and Overall 2015 for a review). Disclosures of negative emotions may contribute to the partners' understanding, which in turn results in greater trust and closeness, as long as such emotions do not threaten the relationship (Simpson, Oriña, and Ickes 2003). Expressing negative emotions can initiate social support. Shimanoff (1987) showed that the quality of social support is associated with the extent to which spouses express negative emotions, such as vulnerabilities or hostilities toward a person other than the spouse. Finally, negative emotions may help in tackling marital problems and therefore increase long-term marital satisfaction. For example, Overall, Fletcher, Simpson, and Sibley (2009) observed that expressions of negative emotions, such as anger, blame, or derogation, in close relationships may be distressing in the short term but lead to greater reduction of problems over the course of the following year. Note that rational reasoning, a positive communication strategy, also led to positive long-term outcomes. To sum up, although positive emotions are important in close relationships, expression of negative feelings can be beneficial under some conditions. Doing so may foster mutual understanding, recruit social support, and initiate problem-solving attempts.

Beyond benefits of negative emotions and mood, Bastian, Jetten, Hornsey, and Leknes (2014) reviewed benefits of pain, such as enhancing the perceived value of endurance sports or the pleasure of eating spicy food. Although negative feelings may have positive consequences, they often do harm, for instance when they lead to aggressive behavior.

Reducing aggressive behavior

Aggression is probably the most disruptive behavior in social situations, and ways to suppress or regulate aggression would be welcome. Much has been done in this field; summaries of interventions to decrease or eliminate aggression can be found in Goldstein, Glick, and Gibbs (1998) and McGuire (2008). For example, McMurran, Fyffe, McCarthy, Duggan, and Latham (2001) developed a therapy program for offenders with personality disorders based on *stop and think*. Bad feelings, such as anger and fury, are taken as a cue that initiates a problem-solving process and encourages the belief that problems can be overcome. The problem-solving process begins with defining the problem and continues with setting goals for action, generation of alternative ways in which the goals could be achieved, examination of the advantages and disadvantages of each potential solution, and then action. The final step is evaluation of the action plan that has been implemented. This process is translated into six key questions that the target group can understand: (1) Bad feelings? (2) What's my problem? (3) What do I want? (4) What are my options? (5) What is my plan? (6) How did I do? These key questions are used in each session; the objective is to train people in the problem-solving process until its steps can be performed automatically, in analogy to driving lessons, which aim to automate the mental operations needed for driving. The rationale of this program is to make offenders interrupt their normal course of aggressive action after bad feelings. This interruption of anger and fury enables the initiation of thinking about the situation at hand in order to arrive at a solution.

Catharsis

Could offenders cool down aggressive impulses by watching aggression? Let us look at catharsis, which is the idea that by watching violence, we can "let off steam," calm down, and become at lower risk of committing violent acts. Influential thinkers from Aristotle (1997/ca. 350 BCE) to Sigmund Freud (Freud and Breuer 2004/1895) advocated catharsis as a way to regulate aggression. This idea is brilliant, ingenious – and wrong.

It turns out that people who watch aggressive acts become aggressive themselves. If catharsis really worked, we would predict that the perfect way to alleviate aggression would be watching violent movies. Contrary to this prediction, there is ample evidence that people who watch violent movies tend to become more violent themselves; letting our children play violent videogames increases their disposition to become violent themselves over time (Anderson, Berkowitz et al. 2003). Unfortunately, angry people who believe in catharsis may choose to play violent videogames (Bushman and Whitaker 2010). We do not have to limit our evidence to the findings of modern psychological studies. Historians have collected ample observations that public executions do not deter the public and may even stir violence. According to a report by the Massachusetts House of Representatives (1837; see also Rogers 2008), suicides were more common after a public execution. Acts of violence were not rare, according to this report. For example, after a public execution of a murderer who killed his wife, a spectator killed his own wife on the same day in the same manner as the executed man. Finally, a study cited in the report showed that, of a sample of 167 convicts who were sentenced to death, 164 had previously witnessed a public execution; this finding is difficult to reconcile with the idea that people let off steam by seeing violence or that the death penalty has a deterring effect. The report concluded that, beyond direct consequences, severe punishments have indirect effects, "by ministering to bad passions, and diminishing the natural sensibility of man for the sufferings of his fellow man," which "induce that hardness of heart which prepares the way for the commission of the most ferocious acts of violence" (Massachusetts House of Representatives 1837, p. 83).

Such findings have important consequences for critical feeling. Parents should be restrictive when it comes to violent videogames. The modern-time gladiators in the West include wrestlers, boxers, and hockey players. One move in North America might be to make hockey less aggressive. This would be a change in the environment that could affect the feelings of spectators. Alas, as parents, we cannot change the rules of the National Hockey League. Another move might aim to reappraise the situation by changing the image of boxers and hockey players. Adolescents may see them as strongmen. In fact, boxers and enforcers in North American hockey often suffer from concussions that cause depression and addiction to alcohol or psychoactive drugs (Förstl, Haass, Hemmer, Meyer, and Halle 2010; McCrory et al. 2013). Further research needs to examine whether knowledge about these facts helps to diminish the entertainment an audience gets from viewing aggressive sports – and whether the frequency of exposure to violence would be decreased.

Distance and feelings

Some time ago, I attended a talk with the title, "War: What Is It Good For?" The main thesis of the well-known historian Ian Morris (2014) is that the emergence of organized war enabled stable and peaceful organization of large societies. One historian in the audience asked whether it is an accident that such questions (which he ironically characterized as the *happy war hypothesis*) are discussed at such peaceful places as Harvard (where Morris gave the talk) or Stanford (where Morris teaches). As Morris himself admitted, he had never seen war up close, and it is virtually impossible to get a realistic idea of what war is from movies or computer games. Film director Samuel Fuller, who experienced bloody fighting as a young World War II soldier and later made war movies, objected to the idea that war could be depicted realistically in books or cinema. "If you really want to make readers understand a battle, a few pages of your book would be booby-trapped. For moviegoers to get the idea of real combat, you'd have to shoot at them every so often from either side of the screen" (Fuller, Fuller, and Rudes 2002, p.123). This example illustrates how remote most civilized people live from war and why most of us do not have a clue about how war feels.

However, with the growing distance of most people from war, the means to overcome distance in war also grew. Whereas a battle in the Middle Ages was a fight of man against man, later societies developed weapons that could be fired at a distance so that soldiers could not see the immediate consequences of their actions. One of the classic experiments on obedience, by Stanley Milgram (2009/1974), included a manipulation of distance between a so-called teacher, who was the participant in the study, and the putative victim.[1] The experiment examined whether participants were more likely to administer the highest shock level of 450 volts with increasing distance between them and the victim. This was indeed the case. If the participant did not hear anything other than the victim pounding on the wall after a shock of 300 volts, 65 percent of the participants administered shocks until they reached the maximum of 450 volts; if the participant heard the voice of the victim, 62 percent increased the shock to 450 volts; if the participant saw the suffering victim, 40 percent; if the participant had to put the victim's hand on a shock plate, 30 percent went to the maximum. Thus, a high percentage of participants still administered the highest shock level, but, with decreasing distance, the proportion fell by half. Presumably, the closer people were, the more pity they felt and the more reluctant they were to further increase the shock level.

The implications of these studies for modern warfare are obvious. For example, pilots do not see the consequences of releasing bombs from their planes. The crew of *Enola Gay*, the airplane that carried the first atomic bomb, did not see much more than the mushroom cloud and could probably not imagine the horror below in Hiroshima.

Distance is also growing in social relationships. Thanks to modern electronic devices, physical distance has increased between sellers and their customers, between fund managers and their clients, between politicians and their voters, and even between friends. There is a joke that, for an adolescent at a party, the best way to talk to a friend at the same party is via text messages. A fund manager who earns commissions on his sales may have an easier time persuading – and later staving off – his elderly client on the telephone than in his office. This means that it is easier to cheat another person at a distance than face to face. Distance may invite lying and cheating. What does this mean for critical feeling?

More closeness brings more feelings and therefore more natural defenses against letting others down. Although not foolproof, closeness presumably decreases the probability that fund managers will sell rotten financial products to their clients. However, in the same way some participants in Milgram's experiment went to the highest shock level even when they were close to the victim, there will always be some fund managers who sell rotten products even if they are able to look their client in the eye, and even if they have seen former clients suffer from losses. One example is Bernard Madoff, who socialized in the highest circles in New York and cheated those who considered him a friend without blinking. Critical feeling helps the honest to come closer to the fulfillment of their ideals in that they can reduce distance, but it does not prevent cheating by those who are either not able or not willing to feel empathy. That is why customers must recognize deceit.

Can critical feeling prevent us from being cheated?

Knowing how others feel seems to be a normal and healthy capacity in humans (see Saarni 1999). In fact, children who are good at reading the emotions of others are liked more than their peers who are worse at it (Denham, McKinley, Couchoud, and Holt 1990). If these findings were found to be generalizable to adolescents and adults, learning to read emotions would seem useful not only for getting an accurate picture of another person's emotion (e.g., Hall and Schmid Mast 2007; Ickes 1997) but also for connecting to others.

Understanding the emotions of others does not only mean accurately decoding emotions, for example from facial expression (see Ekman and Friesen 2003), but also understanding the causal history of events that lead to the emergence of an emotion, a topic recently examined in philosophy (Brady 2013; Deonna and Teroni 2012; Goldie 2004). As noted in Chapter 3, we only understand an emotion properly if we determine reasons for the emergence of the emotion that are indeed part of the causal history of events. One application of understanding emotions is the detection of cheating. There are huge individual differences in people's communicative behavior. As Ekman (1985) pointed out, what for some people is a quirk of behavior would be a sign of deceit in most people. For example, using circuitous language, speaking with many pauses between words, making many speech errors, accompanying speech with fewer hand movements, showing fear and distress while speaking, and using asymmetric facial expressions all usually signal that a person is trying to deceive us. However, we may mistake a true statement for a lie if we do not notice that a behavior is characteristic of a particular person. Proper understanding of a behavior – especially of the expression of an emotion – means that we can reliably link it to lying and deception or understand that it is characteristic of an individual.

Can we know when a person is telling us a lie in face-to-face interactions despite these individual differences? Usually, we are bad at detecting lies. A study by Ekman and O'Sullivan (1991) showed that most people, including judges and psychiatrists, detected lies at little above chance level. A later study showed that only experts whose task was detecting deception performed at above-chance level (Ekman, O'Sullivan, and Frank 1999). Seen from the viewpoint of critical feeling, people have to distance themselves from feelings of confidence, which most likely express overconfidence. Although there are clear differences in the face, the voice, and the body between truth telling and lying when videos are viewed in slow motion (Ekman, O'Sullivan, Friesen, and Scherer 1991), it is more difficult to discern lies when watching and hearing a person speak in real time.

Could we learn to detect lies? Ekman's (1985) work was directed at finding cues of lying in a person's face, body, language, and voice. Can we obtain accurate information from these cues? First, there are many facial signs of lying (see Ekman 1985 and the meta-analysis by DePaulo, Lindsay, Malone, Muhlenbruck, Charlton, and Cooper 2003 for details). People who want to detect lies often look at obvious signs in the face that can be feigned easily, such as smiles, but miss less obvious but reliable signs of lying in the body and voice. Instead of relying on our feelings or on obvious signs, we must learn how to interpret vocal, facial, and bodily expressions. In their meta-analysis, DePaulo et al. (2003) found several cues to deception related to voice. For example, liars sounded less involved, less immediate, and more uncertain than truth tellers did.

Second, people who are aware of high stakes usually feel strong emotions (DePaulo et al. 2003). These emotions are more difficult to control and may leak signs of lying. In fact, people who are subject to low or no stakes at all are less emotional and are better at deceiving and lying. Liars show three emotions. The first is detection apprehension; they feel anxiety about being caught. However, people may feel anxious about not being believed despite being honest. An innocent crime suspect who tells the truth presumably fears the serious consequences of not being believed. The second is deception guilt; liars have a bad conscience because they do not tell the truth. Finally, liars may feel enjoyment when duping another person. To deceive another person yields a feeling of one's own superiority as well as pleasure from demonstrating the dumbness of the victim. A recent study showed that people predicted they would experience deception guilt when they cheated. In fact, and contrary to their anticipation, they often experience positive feelings when they cheat (Ruedy, Moore, Gino, and Schweitzer 2013). The problem with the emotions that accompany lying is that people do not always express them openly. Moreover, we may interpret nervousness as detection apprehension where it is an honest fear that one will not be believed. This would again be an instance where we misunderstood the emotional expression of another person.

Why are people often so easily duped? When self-styled investment bankers maintain Ponzi schemes, they encounter the problem that customers begin to fear for their investments. However, the impostors are usually able to put off their customers with flimsy lies. Why do customers believe these lies? Customers have vested interests. If they did not believe the lie, they would have to admit that they had lost their money, which is unpleasant in itself, and that they had been duped by the alleged investment guru, which is humiliating. That is presumably why customers prefer to believe the guru instead of admitting that they have been hoodwinked. This social dynamic maintains an implicit collaboration between the customer and the banker in that the customer is motivated to believe the pretexts of the investor (see Ekman 1985). Customers may even become subject to a confirmation bias (e.g., Klayman and Ha 1987; Oswald and Grosjean 2004): They search for information that confirms their assumption, derived from their vested interests, that the statements of the investment banker are true. For example, when they find seemingly trustworthy information on the website of the guru's company, they calm down and believe the lie. There are other situations where the same dynamic plays out and where the victims of a lie are easy prey. Parents, for example, would be ashamed to hear that their offspring had committed a crime and are often more than willing to believe their son or daughter when they would better have doubted. Spouses may be motivated to believe a lie and not insist on getting further information because the truth would be too painful.

What can customers, parents, or spouses do to circumvent being duped over and over again? Despite a lack of research on this question, there is some general advice for people in this situation. First, they must ask what their interests are and what they would feel if they admitted that a statement were a lie. If they see that they have an interest in believing the lie, they should not look for information that confirms their assumptions derived from their interest but for information that *falsifies* their assumptions. For example, instead of visiting the investment guru's webpage, they could look for independent information about the past of the banker or about the reputation of the investments (see Makropoulos 2010 for early signs that Madoff was involved in a Ponzi scheme). Note that this method is different from that advocated by proponents of critical thinking, who advise people to suppress their feelings and attempt to take an impartial position. When one has vested interests, it is often difficult to abstract from one's own feelings. A better way to deal with this situation may be to ask directly what the feelings are and then turn to the consequences. While proponents of critical thinking propose to sweep feelings under the mat, critical feeling takes feelings into account and deals with them.

Loving your spouse

Falling in love

We think that falling in love is such an illogical event that is outside our control, and as a result we are tempted to deny the possibility that falling in love follows a logical path. Contrary to this folk belief, the Dutch psychologist Rombouts (1987, cited in Frijda 1988) found in interviews with students that there are four stages of falling in love. These steps seem to be invariant for most people. First, a person who meets another person has to be willing to fall in love. A settled man, a woman with a newborn baby, and a disappointed lover may not be willing to fall in love, and their journey ends here. If Homer is willing to fall in love, he may become interested in the other person, let's call her Sally, for minimal reasons, sometimes just because Sally "was there." Second, he now needs a minimal sign of interest from Sally, such as a smile or a nod of the head after he told her his opinion of President Obama. We now can proceed to step three, where we leave Homer alone for some hours or even some days so that his imagination and dreams can blossom. Now, Homer is ready to meet Sally again. At this final step, Sally only needs to provide another sign of apparent interest, for example a smile, and Homer's love is blooming.

If you have happened to fall in love lately, I do not wish to disrupt your rapture, and you may skip this and the next paragraph. The fact that there is logic behind falling in love may help out of misery those whose love has not been reciprocated. They can learn that they did not fall in love because the target of their affection was the one and only person who was suitable for them; they fell in love because they were willing to do so and interpreted (or, if they were unfortunate, over-interpreted) those minimal signs of interest. In the extreme, they could have fallen in love with any person who happened to cross their way when (1) they were ready to fall in love and (2) the other person possessed the attributes that meet their minimal criteria regarding sex, age range, personality, and looks.

What do we learn from the logic of falling in love? Perhaps the most important lesson is that people should not rely on it too much – many potential mates could be "the only one." The feeling may serve as a catalyst at the beginning of a relationship, but people should be cautious when making more far-reaching decisions about relationships and marriage.

The marriage decision

In order to make important decisions, managers are advised to employ decision tables where they write down advantages and disadvantages, to give a weight to each advantage and disadvantage and then to calculate the expected utility. Most people think that marriage is the most important decision they will make in their life. Who, however, would heed the wisdom of management when it comes to marriage decisions? I know of only one example, Charles Darwin (1838). He began, "This is the question," and continued:

Marry	*Not Marry*
Children – (if it Please God) – Constant companion, (& friend in old age) who will feel interested in one, – object to be beloved & played with. – better than a dog anyhow. – Home, & someone to take care of house – Charms of music & female chit-chat. – These things good for one's health. – *but terrible loss of time.* –	Freedom to go where one liked – choice of Society & *little of it.* – Conversation of clever men at clubs – Not forced to visit relatives, & to bend in every trifle. – to have the expense & anxiety of children – perhaps quarelling – **Loss of time.** – cannot read in the Evenings – fatness & idleness – Anxiety & responsibility – less money for books &c – if many children forced to gain one's bread. – (But then it is very bad for ones health to work too much)
My God, it is intolerable to think of spending ones whole life, like a neuter bee, working, working, & nothing after all. – No, no won't do. – Imagine living all one's day solitarily in smoky dirty London House. – Only picture to yourself a nice soft wife on a sofa with good fire, & books & music perhaps – Compare this vision with the dingy reality of Grt. Marlbro' St. Marry – Mary [sic.] – Marry Q.E.D.	Perhaps my wife wont like London; then the sentence is banishment & degradation into indolent, idle fool –

From what we know about Darwin's marriage, he made the right decision. By marrying, he not only reaped the fruits of marriage, as written down in the "Marry" column, but also circumvented some of the disadvantage of "Not forced to visit relatives" because his wife, Emma

Wedgwood, was his cousin so there was a negligible increase in the number of relatives.

At the time Darwin wrote down the advantages and disadvantages of marriage, love did not play a prominent role. His note "object to be beloved & played with – better than a dog anyhow" has an unfeeling tone, and his list sounds prosaic to modern ears, but his understanding of marriage was in line with his times while the notion that marriage should be founded on the passion of love was out of tune with most of history (see Coontz 2005). In some countries, such as Japan, arranged marriages have been common (Blood 1967), and even in the early 1940s a majority of American spouses remembered that their parents – especially the mothers – had influenced their decision on whom to marry (Bates 1941; see also Blood 1967). Until the nineteenth century, European parents had a say in the choice of the spouses of their children, despite the fact that parents were not allowed to coerce children into marriage (Borscheid 1983; Ozment 1983). Luther, for example, published a treatise in which he recommended parents neither to force children into unwanted marriages nor to hinder their offspring marrying a desired partner. On the other hand, the young people were told to get the consent of their parents before engagement (Ozment 1983). However, even if young men and women chose their spouse for themselves, financial considerations and status often played a more important role than love and passion (Borscheid 1983). Nowadays, loving a partner is the most prominent reason to marry a person, and parents are not given much opportunity to intervene.

At least in the West, most people want a marriage to be happy. It seems plausible to think that a couple will be happier when the partners chose freely than when the marriage is arranged. Such an assumption is reinforced by sentimental media reports in which a spouse – usually a woman from the Middle East – is unhappy with the choice of her parents because she loves another man. There are little data on this question, but the available data do not support the hypothesis that love marriages are happier than arranged marriages. One study from India (Gupta and Singh 1982) found that couples in arranged marriages became happier with time while couples in love marriages became less happy; in the end, the happiness in arranged marriages surpassed the happiness in love marriages. This finding may be explained by the fact that, at that time (during the 1980s), many marriages in India were arranged, and couples who decided to marry the partner they loved may have experienced exclusion and ostracism in their community. However, another study showed that Indian couples in the United States were not happier after love marriages than after arranged marriages, despite the fact that love marriages are the norm in the United States (Regan, Lakhanpal, and Anguiano 2012).

I do not want to advocate arranged marriages – there certainly are other reasons than happiness to let people choose their partner. However, the finding that more choice does not always make people happier (see Schwartz 2004) seems to apply to marriages, too. When it comes to happiness – presumably the most cherished outcome of a marriage in the West – arranged marriages are in no way inferior to love marriages. Taking the perspective of a person in an arranged marriage may at first lead us astray because we imagine how unhappy we would be if our parents had chosen the wrong partner for us, and how much pity we should feel for people in arranged marriages. Yet think twice: If we know that arranged marriages evoke feelings that are no more negative than feelings in love marriages, we may take the perspective of people who accept the convention that parents arrange their marriage. Maybe they are even relieved that they do not have to make a difficult choice, or that their parents have finally found an appropriate partner. In this case, critical feeling could contribute to intercultural understanding and the knowledge that the two kinds of marriages are equivalent when it comes to happiness. There is no need to feel pity for people in arranged marriages.

Keeping marriage together

Without endorsing the notion that parents should arrange marriages for their offspring, there is a point to the argument that founding marriage exclusively on the feeling of love is irrational, as marriages and intimate long-term relationships in general seem to undergo a characteristic temporal course. The beginning of a relationship is stormy and full of passion. After some time passes, however, many couples experience that rapture of love does not endure; they need a different grounding for their relationship. Sternberg (1986) distinguished between three components of love: intimacy, passion, and commitment. Although there are various conceptualization of the term *love* (see Berscheid 2010), it is important to note that all classifications distinguish between at least two main components. The first component includes passion and sexual attraction and is relatively short lived. The second component includes mutual understanding (part of Sternberg's intimacy component) and commitment and is relatively long lived. A study by Acker and Davis (1992) showed that the most powerful predictor of relationship satisfaction in long-term relationships is commitment. It seems that the conscious, rational decision to commit oneself to this and only this relationship helps people to overcome the relative lack of passion that creeps in after some time. The other component is the development of mutual understanding and a feeling of being secure. Recent research has shown that spouses can promote mutual understanding by taking the perspective of an impartial observer in a conflict, which stops the typical decline in marital satisfaction (Finkel et al. 2013). It seems that growing intimacy is often not manifested in a long-term relationship but is nevertheless important (Sternberg 1986). Intimacy is an aspect of love that probably develops after an arranged marriage has taken place. The assumption that intimacy grows unconsciously may explain why divorced couples may miss each other after they have been separated for some time, an observation that is difficult to account for by commitment (Weiss 1975). Commitment cannot play any role because it has been given up, and some divorcees even report to hate their ex-spouse.

In summary, the stormy beginning may be a kind of catalyst that helps to initiate the loving relationship and to maintain it for the first couple of months. During this time, mutual understanding and a sense of togetherness must develop, and these must be more long lasting than passion and attraction. An important ingredient in a long-term relationship is commitment. From the observation that people adapt better to a situation that is irreversible (see Chapter 4) we can derive the prediction that the commitment to be with the other person for life helps us to adapt to and overcome the difficulties characteristic of each relationship.

When your spouse fails

Diederik Stapel, from Tilburg, Netherlands, is a loving husband, a caring father, a wonderful son, a good friend, and a kind neighbor; he was seen as a successful social psychologist, a rising star in the field. He fell from fame to notoriety, however, when he hit the headlines because he had fabricated the data of more than fifty published articles. As he had fabricated data that had gone into the publications and theses of doctoral students, he ruined or at least hampered the careers of several academic hopefuls. Since then, Stapel has been seen as a conman by his friends and colleagues. His deceitful behavior eclipsed all the positive aspects of his personality. This is an instance of the negativity bias, which denotes the fact that we remember and weigh negative information more than positive information (see Baumeister, Bratslavsky, Finkenauer, and Vohs 2001; Rozin and Royzman 2001 for reviews). The negativity bias is especially salient when it comes to moral behavior and can be observed in many areas of life (Skowronski and Carlston 1987).

How can the immediate family cope with such a stain on the reputation of a loved one? Science writer Yudhijit Bhattacharjee (2013) described two responses: The parents of Stapel, both in their mid-eighties, denied any wrongdoing by their son and blamed the scientific system even though Stapel himself told them to accept that *he* had done what he was accused of doing. This denial is a convenient response that helps them to maintain a positive image of their beloved son. Eluding the facts and blaming others is convenient but in this case wrong. Stapel's wife, Marcelle, responded differently, as Bhattacharjee recounted in his article:

> Marcelle described to me how she placed Stapel inside an integrity scanner in her mind. "I sort of scanned his life in terms of being a father, being my husband, being my best friend, being the son of his parents, the friend of his friends, being a human being that is part of society, being a neighbor – and being a scientist and teacher," she told me. "Then I found out for myself that all of these other parts were really O.K."

Isn't this a fantastic response? From it we all could learn how to avoid negativity bias when our spouse fails in a domain. As negative information is more salient than positive information, we have to find ways to balance positive and negative aspects. One way of doing this – reminiscent of Thaler's (1985, 1999) mental accounting – is to divide a judgmental object, here Stapel, into different parts, such as spouse, child, friend, member of society, neighbor, and scientist, and then to find out that he failed on just one of six counts. Whereas most other people are swept away by the negative information, we can maintain a largely positive view of a person by looking at the different roles he or she plays. We then see that this person can be quite different in one role than in others. Such a response is critical in the sense that it maintains positive feelings toward a beloved person without negating the wrongdoing. The overall positive feeling is based on an honest assessment of the situation without negating the negative aspects of the target person.

Dividing a judgmental object into different parts, or looking at a person seen in a negative light from different perspectives, may help in other situations, too. Whenever there is stigma involved, we tend to focus on the negative characteristic instead of the whole person. We see a man living on the street as mentally ill, criminal, or addicted to drugs. While mental illness, a criminal record, and addiction can have severe effects on a person's functioning within the environment, we should not neglect his positive sides. The mental accounting approach may also help when we have mixed feelings about a person. I once made the observation that, when students work together on a project, a student may not learn from an academically superior fellow student simply because he does not like her. In this case, it may be justified for the student to suppress any negative feelings about the superior student in order to obtain better learning outcomes. Yet we should not stop at grudgingly giving in and learning from an unpopular fellow learner. This may even leave a doubly negative feeling in that we feel anger and envy toward the superior learner and at the same time shame and guilt that we gained benefit from that person. There is not much literature about dealing with feelings in this situation but we probably should try to look at the person from different viewpoints in order to see the positive sides as well. Such mindfulness is predicted to alleviate the negative feelings and to facilitate collaboration. As critical thinkers, we would merely maximize strategic rationality by looking for our advantage and neglecting feelings; only critical feeling enables people to reconcile opposing feelings without suppressing them.

How can parents teach their children about living together? The answer is simple: by living together! Living together means performing common activities, talking, negotiating, solving conflicts, making peace after quarrels, apologizing after wrongdoing, helping each other without immediate reward, and often just hearing the familiar footsteps in the house. Noddings (2003) provides plenty of examples of how we can make a happy home.

School may supplement the practice of living together with knowledge about this topic. Teachers may review some of the phenomena discussed in this chapter, such as the logic of falling in love, avoiding or alleviating negative feelings in social relationships, or building long-term intimacy through warm and stable friendships and loving relationships. However, little is won if children do not have the opportunity to observe and practice at home what the teacher preaches at school. To use an image inspired by Dewey (1909), teaching about social relationships without immersing the student in the experience would be like learning to swim on land. Although children can be taught about living together, and the classroom may provide an atmosphere where children flourish together, it will not replace a family.

Beyond social psychology, other subjects contribute to this important topic. Biology may provide children with examples of social interaction in animals. How does the social life of ants differ from the social life of chimpanzees, and the social life of the latter from that of humans? History may tell us how people lived together in the past. What did their families look like? How did they find friends and maintain friendships? How did marriage then differ from marriage now?

Finally, social studies may explore the distribution of rights and responsibilities in social relationships, for example across gender or age, including the relationship between children and adults. Should children make decisions about their education themselves? How do rights and responsibilities shift when a parent becomes severely ill? Should older siblings have more rights and responsibilities than younger ones?

7 CRITICAL FEELING IN BUSINESS AND POLITICS

> *It was Napoleon, I believe, who said that there is only one figure in rhetoric of serious importance, namely, repetition. ... The thing affirmed comes by repetition to fix itself in the mind in such a way that it is accepted in the end as a demonstrated truth.*
>
> (LE BON 1960/1895, P. 125).

When I moved into my new office, there were three books from my predecessor left on my desk, two about statistics and one titled *Behavior in Organizations* (Greenberg and Baron 2008). When I browsed the book, I found a section on the role of emotions in organizations that was partitioned into subsections. The first two subsections were titled "Are happier people more successful on their jobs?" and "Why are happier workers more successful?" Workers' happiness in these two sections is not seen as a value in itself but as a means to increase performance and success. Even when the authors later discuss the adverse effects of stress, they first discuss stress and task performance before they address physical health, desk rage, and burnout. The business literature too often presents issues from the viewpoint of employers or managers who have to keep their company up and running. When you browse marketing and consumer research journals it becomes obvious that many articles describe implications from the side of the marketer. Moreover, a new wave of psychologists and behavioral economists are helping governments "nudge" citizens into behaviors desired by the state authorities (Thaler and Sunstein 2008; see Burgess 2012 for a critique). There is a growing number of exceptions to the rule that marketing takes the side of industry or the state. An early example is an article by Kotler and Zaltman (1971), who examined how marketing techniques could be used for social causes. To nudge citizens to smoke less or to pay their taxes may be seen as a laudable enterprise. However, there may be examples of influencing people to show behavior desired by the state or the economy that amount to abuse rather than use. Does a scientist have the license to do research that helps a car dealer trick his customers into buying a more expensive car than they can afford? How could any responsible behavioral economist examine credit schemes that maximize consumption but increase consumer debt in unison? Should scientists support research into how to misinform citizens in order to bring public sentiment in line with the government? All three examples consider what some readers might see as flagrant abuses of nudging and marketing.

As discussed in Chapter 1, scientists have the right to do research into any question they like. White (1965) argued against the common misconception that a scientist who looks at a problem from a certain viewpoint has to adopt this viewpoint; from his argument follows, conversely, that a scientist has to take the perspective of salespeople in order to understand them. For example, when a marketing researcher looks at which kind of advertisement will yield the best sales outcomes, the researchers do not need to adopt the viewpoint that it is morally good to determine which will be the most effective advertisement. Research findings can be interpreted from multiple viewpoints, a fact that leads to plurality in social science research. Therefore, findings by marketing researchers could be used to educate consumers about how the industry is trying to influence them through advertisement. One example is Robert Cialdini (2006), who wrote an important book on social influence with recommendations for consumers on how to avoid undue influence. In this case, findings from consumer psychology were used in the service of human emancipation, which is the explicit goal of critical theory.

The main objective of a critical theory is "to liberate human beings from the circumstances that enslave them" (Horkheimer 1982, p. 244). Such a theory has first to analyze the circumstances to attain "the self-clarification of the struggles and wishes of the age" (Marx 1975/1843, cited in Fraser 1989, p. 2) before norms for political actions aimed at decreasing domination and increasing freedom can be developed (Bohman 2013). Critical theory has provided many insights into struggle and emancipation for class, gender, and race. Critical pedagogy was introduced in order to describe and counter dominance and oppression in education (Freire 1970). Finally, after criticizing the technicality of marketing research and its focus on need satisfaction, Alvesson (1994) advocated the use of critical theory in marketing.

This is not the place to develop an elaborate account of how psychological research could be embedded in critical theory. However, in line with Alvesson's (1994) work, future scholarship may develop new critical theories in order to counter the creation of artificial needs and the abuse of feelings, and a more systematic connection of experimental findings on feelings in psychology with critical theory would be of much merit. When we discuss psychological findings in business and politics, we can always elaborate issues from at least two viewpoints: on the one hand from the perspective of the business community or the political elite; on the other hand from the perspective of consumers and voters.

The following sections discuss how customers and voters can circumvent the undue influence of feelings on decisions. The first section reviews feelings used in business – more specifically, in marketing. The next section, on pluralistic ignorance, connects marketing and politics before the final section discusses political campaigns and feelings in war propaganda. The chapter coda outlines how schools could contribute to educating children to become thoughtful customers and responsible citizens.

Using feelings in product marketing

Marketers try to persuade consumers to buy their products. Therefore, they want potential customers to have a positive attitude. In the introduction to this book, we saw that an attitude has a cognitive, an affective, and a behavioral component. Marketers want consumers to think positively and to feel good about their product, and they want them to buy it at the highest possible price. In this book, we focus on the affective component: How do marketers induce positive feelings about their products? Below, I pick some of the methods mentioned in the literature (e.g., Cialdini 2006; De Houwer 2009; Mantonakis, Whittlesea, and Yoon, 2008) and explain how they are relevant to the use of critical feeling to emancipate consumers, as seen from the viewpoint of critical theory. The remainder of this section reviews various mechanisms underlying persuasion, such as repeated exposure and classical conditioning, and elaborates on how to counter these persuasive attempts by employing critical feeling strategies. At the end of this section, I introduce another, more radical method to circumvent being influenced by marketing methods.

Repeated exposure

Marketers try to exploit the mere exposure effect by familiarizing customers with a product (Zajonc 1968; see Chapter 2). The more we see a product or a message, at least up to a certain point, the more we begin to like it (e.g., Janiszewski and Meyvis 2001; see also Mantonakis et al. 2008). A study in marketing has shown that liking of packaged food influences purchase decisions, which means that liking is not just an unimportant side effect (e.g., Mueller and Szolnoki 2010). Similarly, Alter and Oppenheimer (2006) have shown that shares with familiar-sounding, easy-to-pronounce names achieved higher prices on the day of the initial public offering than shares with difficult-to-pronounce names. This fluency effect in the real marketplace shows that metacognitive feelings influence purchasing decisions.

In addition to effects of repeated exposure on liking, consumers assign messages they have heard a higher truth value than new messages. These findings support the insight of the French scholar Gustave Le Bon about repetition as a source of judged truth cited at the beginning of the chapter. Obviously, Napoleon possessed intuition about the effect of repetition and truth – an effect that was demonstrated empirically much later (Hasher, Goldstein, and Toppino 1977; see Dechene, Stahl, Hansen, and Wänke 2010 for a meta-analysis).

Finally, repeated exposure makes a person seem not only more agreeable but also more famous (e.g., Jacoby, Kelley, Brown, and Jasechko 1989). This finding can be neatly combined with a study where Weaver, Garcia, Schwarz, and Miller (2007) showed that a statement repeated three times by the same source was judged as being as true as statements uttered once by different sources. Obviously, we think that a message is more reliable if we hear it from three different sources than when we hear it only from one source. Comparably, it seems obvious that a person is more famous if three different sources know her name than when one source repeats her name three times. If we ask ourselves why a celebrity is famous, we may find out that it is just because the marketers make her appear omnipresent. Although we lack a study like Weaver et al.'s that explores how people use multiple versus single sources to make judgments of fame, we might plausibly predict that the same mechanisms are at play here, too.

The mere exposure effect on affect and judged truth is a prime example of the fact that we are often unaware of how feelings influence our choices. In order to sell products, marketers exploit precisely this subconscious route to decision making. One such route is to repeat information in order to render it familiar and to influence a whole range of judgments relevant to purchase, such as liking, truth, and fame. An obvious method to circumvent unconscious effects of mere exposure would be to avoid advertisements – a difficult endeavor in a modern society, where avoiding advertisements would amount to staying at home and turning off all media. Alternatively, consumers may try to become aware of the undue influence of repeated exposure. However, are consumers able to raise their awareness that they have seen or heard an advertisement repeatedly and correct their judgments accordingly? A study by Nordhielm (2002) suggests that this is possible but only when an advertisement is repeated often. In Nordhielm's experiment, a product advertisement was presented three, ten, or twenty-five times. When participants processed the advertisement shallowly, the product appeal increased linearly with number of exposures. By contrast, when participants processed the advertisements more deeply, an inverted U-shaped pattern was observed. Positive affective responses toward the product increased from zero (never seen) to three exposures, remained constant from three to ten exposures, and decreased from ten to twenty-five exposures. In fact, a difference in the affective responses between the two groups could only be seen after twenty-five exposures. It needs many repetitions of advertisements in order to reverse mere exposure effects.

A recent study on repeated exposure becomes relevant here. Unkelbach, Fiedler, and Freytag (2007) presented their participants with information about shares. Some shares were equally successful on the stock market, but information was repeated more often for shares of some companies than of others. A rational decision maker should be influenced by the success of a share but not by how often the share is mentioned. However, in contravention of normative decision rules, Unkelbach et al. (2007) found that participants in their experiment were influenced by the frequency of exposure to information about a share. Shares that were repeated more often were judged as more successful and were liked more. In some cases, repetition even overrode success. Crucially, people were able to distinguish which shares were presented most and hence could judge the amount of repetition, but they did not correct their judgments. Ideally, investors should not only monitor and recognize repeated exposure but also correct their judgments. Critical feeling may help us to prevent ourselves being unduly influenced by repeated exposure in purchase decisions by asking ourselves whether we have seen or heard a message repeatedly. If a message has been repeated, we may try to correct our preferences accordingly, in line with strategies to prevent unintentional plagiarism (Marsh, Landau, and Hicks 1997).

Alternatively, we might try to prevent an undue impact of repeated exposure by selecting environments in which we are only exposed to products we want to like. By watching certain TV channels but not others and by surfing web pages of high quality and ignoring those judged to be of low quality, we might at least exclude exposure to some advertisements that we do not want to encounter. However, we cannot prevent some exposure to undesired advertisements because a neat separation of desired and undesired advertisements is likely to be unrealistic. Perhaps the most effective way to circumvent being duped by the effects of mere exposure in the realm of consumer behavior is the mundane advice to plan ahead by making a shopping list at home and to stick to it at the shopping mall.

Finally, we might look at mechanisms underlying the effects of repeated exposure in order to prevent undue influence. In a series of experiments, Topolinski and Strack (2009c) have shown that the mere exposure effect depends on movements by the muscles involved in speech. If so, we could easily prevent the persuasive effects of repeated exposure to advertisements in cinema by suppressing these movements, for example by eating popcorn (see Topolinski, Lindner, and Freudenberg 2014 for a demonstration of this effect). However, motor-fluency effects seem to be subtle; some laboratories obtain them (Woltin and Guinote 2015) but others do not (Westerman, Klin, and Lanska 2015). Hence, more research is needed to establish the exact mechanism and to determine whether suppressing motor fluency, for example by eating popcorn, reliably prevents undue influence of repeated exposure in the real world.

Other mechanisms underlying persuasion

Marketers use methods of classical conditioning to associate the use of their product with positive affect (e.g., De Houwer 2009; Gorn 1982; Sweldens, Van Osselaer, and Janiszewski 2010). When I was young, advertisements for cigarettes were associated with positive feelings – either being attractive to the other sex or being adventurous and sporty. Nowadays, fear appeals have become popular to prevent smoking, and in some countries producers have to put warnings or disgusting images of corroded lungs on their packages. However, fear appeals only seem to be effective when the threat is moderate (Ray and Wilkie 1970). Hansen, Winzeler, and Topolinski (2010) have shown that mortality salience on cigarette packages may even favor smoking under certain conditions. It is easy for smokers to ignore what may seem to be exaggerated threats. After all, improved filter systems and the emergence of milder smoking tastes in the past few decades have decreased the probability that a smoker will develop lung cancer (Stellman, Muscat, Hoffmann, and Wynder 1997), making it easier to dismiss the message. Moreover, fear appeals are more effective when they are accompanied by the solution to a problem. Instead of telling smokers that their habit causes cardiovascular disease and lung cancer, health authorities should provide insights about how to quit smoking.

The other effective way to put across fear messages is to pair them with disgust (Morales, Wu, and Fitzsimons 2012). Marketers produce disgust not only by connecting it to the use of a product – such as cigarettes – but also by connecting it to its lack of use. This technique is used by producers of hygiene articles. Advertisers try to persuade consumers that they are dirty or smelly if they do not use the soap or deodorant on display. As the example of the early deodorant Odorono ("odor oh no") in the early twentieth century illustrates, puritanical British society was highly receptive to such campaigns because women in particular had to pretend that bodily odors did not exist (Sivulka 2007). Maybe simply knowing of conditioning as a technique may help people to discount some of the effects of conditioning; however, evidence concerning evaluative conditioning is mixed because conditioning effects also occur when people are aware of the relationship between the conditioned and the unconditioned stimuli (De Houwer, Thomas, and Baeyens 2001). Knowing that marketers want to elicit negative feelings about my own bodily odors might not prevent my feeling of disgust when I do not use deodorant. Similarly, using strategies known from emotion regulation research, such as suppression, reappraisal, or blocking of facial feedback, does not prevent attitude change due to evaluative conditioning (Gawronski, Mitchell, and Balas 2015).

Another path to persuasion consists in manipulating incidental affect. For example, by inducing positive feelings through a cozy atmosphere in a shopping mall (Donovan and Rossiter 1982), marketers persuade consumers no longer to evaluate a product on the basis of its quality (integral affect) but on the basis of the positive atmosphere in the mall (incidental affect; see Cohen, Pham, and Andrade 2008). According to the feelings-as-information theory (Schwarz 2012), consumers evaluate a product by asking themselves how they feel. When customers feel good, they evaluate the product positively, regardless of the source of the affect. Consumers may circumvent excessive buying by recalling that the whole atmosphere of a mall is created with the purpose of making consumers buy more. Even if such correction mechanisms are imprecise, we may at least save money.

A final persuasion technique builds on the observation that we like others who mimic us, without becoming aware of this effect. Salespeople may exploit this phenomenon to persuade their customers by mimicking them. Wieber, Gollwitzer, and Sheeran (2014) offered an antidote. One group had to form an implementation intention ("I want to be thrifty with my money! And, if I am tempted to buy something, then I will tell myself: I will save my money for important investments!"); another group had to form a general goal to be thrifty ("I want to be thrifty with my money! I will save my money for important investments!"). The authors showed that using implementation intentions to be thrifty reversed the persuasive effects of mimicking. It was not sufficient to have the goal to be thrifty; implementation intentions were a necessary requisite to remove the effects of mimicry.

There is a more radical and in the long term probably more effective way to counter the temptations of consumer society. Instead of fighting every attempt to change our attitudes, we may try to define values that emphasize modesty and social responsibility. Such a view deemphasizes comparison with and competition against others and replaces values that promote consumption with values that promote simplicity. In contrast to constantly monitoring whether we are being unduly influenced by means that we do not notice, such as repetition of advertisements, conditioning of attitudes, a positive atmosphere, or mimicry, changing values provides us with top-down guidance that prevents undue influence in the first place. This is at least an ideal we may want to achieve. Critical feeling consists of using a radical strategy to circumvent feelings related to desire and temptation. In the end, a change in aspiration level (see Chapter 4) may result in a loss of material comfort without loss of happiness. Indeed, there are reports of people who have simplified their life and withstood the temptations of wealth and consumerism, such as Diogenes of Sinope (Dorandi 2013), Mahatma Gandhi (Weber 2011), and many others whose names may be unknown to us (see Colby and Damon 1992). Not only individuals but also groups can relinquish mainstream values; prominent examples are religious communities such as the Amish (Kraybill 2001), Puritans, and Quakers (Shi 1985). These observations suggest that people may successfully resist the temptations of consumerism.

I have not discussed every possible mechanism of persuasion (see Cialdini 2006 for more "weapons of influence"). The reason is that we know about the power of some techniques, such as reciprocity, commitment, and social proof, but we do not know much about how these techniques play on our feelings. The principle of reciprocity, for example, says that, if you receive a gift, you have to give one in return. Gift exchanges and reciprocation build social relationships (Mauss 2000/1925). There is little psychological research, however, about the feelings related to gift exchange. How do people feel when they do not want to or cannot reciprocate? Similarly, commitment certainly implies feelings but they have not been well examined in scientific psychology. We know much about the behavioral consequences of commitment, as discussed in Cialdini, but it would be interesting to know about the experiential qualities related to the state of being committed. Finally, we again know more about behavior than feelings when it comes to social proof. We know little, for example, about the experience of not clapping one's hands when everybody around is applauding. However, there is one example of apparent social proof that is interesting for critical feeling: pluralistic ignorance.

Overcoming pluralistic ignorance

Every parent of a teenager knows how difficult it is to counter the argument that it is essential to get those fancy shoes because everybody else
has them and because, without those shoes, exclusion and stigma are
risked. Indeed, marketers benefit when teenagers think that everybody
else likes a product. This leads to the paradoxical situation that a teenager who perhaps does not even prefer the fancy shoes to their old ones
begs his or her parents for money in order not to become an outsider at
school. The situation might become even more paradoxical if most teenagers are not enthusiastic about the shoes but think that everybody else
really likes them. It is possible to imagine a town where all the teenagers
are at the same time urging their parents to give them money for the shoes
that apparently everybody else likes. This phenomenon is called *pluralistic ignorance*. This term, coined by Katz and Allport (1931), refers to
the phenomenon in which individuals falsely believe that the majority of
people in their community hold an opinion opposite to their own belief.
Early research on pluralistic ignorance was done on the group dynamics
of religious communities. In a now famous case study of a Texan community, Schanck (1932) observed beliefs among Methodists and Baptists.
These two religious denominations shared much in terms of belief and
liturgy but differed on one point that seemed essential: While Baptists
baptized their children by immersing them in water, Methodists sprinkled
the water. When asked, most members of the Methodist church thought
that a majority of Methodists believed that baptizing babies by sprinkling
water was essential. In addition, non-Methodist members of the community thought that most Methodists believed in the sprinkling form of
baptism. In other words, the belief of the Methodists about the majority
opinion of their church was the same as the belief of outsiders about the
opinion of typical Methodists. However, when asked in private, most
Methodists confided that, for them, the form of baptism was inessential.
Another instance where public opinion was falsely thought to contradict one's own convictions was playing with face cards. While members
of the community often played with so-called flinch cards, which had
only numbers printed on them, they eschewed playing with face cards
of the kind familiarly used in poker. Most Methodists, and again most
non-Methodist members of the community, believed that the majority of
Methodists objected to playing with face cards. In contrast, when asked
in private, most Methodists did not see playing with face cards as much
of a problem.

These instances of pluralistic ignorance may seem harmless and
inconsequential. However, pluralistic ignorance may be harmful, as in

the case of adherence to excessive drinking norms in university settings (Prentice and Miller 1993). At universities and fraternities, students are under pressure to consume an excessive amount of alcohol because they fear that they will otherwise not belong to the student community. Again, this is surprising given the fact that most students have had negative experiences or observed adverse consequences of alcohol in others, such as nausea, learning difficulties, absence from lectures, and goofy behavior. As is characteristic of pluralistic ignorance, most students in private disapproved of the drinking habits of other students in their university. However, despite this critical view of binge drinking, they thought that everybody else endorsed this custom, and they would have been embarrassed to admit they did not like it.

How can a student community overcome pluralistic ignorance regarding drinking norms? Schroeder and Prentice (1998) organized discussion groups in which they explained pluralistic ignorance and let students share their thoughts about alcohol consumption at parties. Pluralistic ignorance does not only have consequences for the beliefs of a community but also for feelings and action. This is where critical feeling comes into play. In order to turn negative feelings such as embarrassment into positive or neutral ones, people need to reappraise the situation by noting that their private opinion in fact corresponds to the majority opinion, and they need to know about pluralistic ignorance. Although this remains to be shown empirically, acquisition of knowledge of the mechanisms behind this phenomenon and free discussion about group norms should in theory attenuate or remove pluralistic ignorance in many domains, whether drinking, religion, politics, or purchase of shoes.

Let us go back to marketing. When adolescents believe that everybody else likes fancy shoe brands, parents run into the problem of explaining to their children that some no-brand shoes look as cool but cost only a quarter of the price. As long as teenagers believe that their peers don't find the shoes cool, they will be disappointed and insist that they must have the brand. Cool shoes are a problem that parents have to tackle, and overcoming disappointment in adolescence certainly contributes to an education for real life. There are adults who would rather buy expensive products and run into debt than swallow the disappointment that they cannot afford what their neighbors have. It is therefore important to address this state of false belief early on by conveying knowledge about pluralistic ignorance and by letting teenagers discuss attitudes toward trendy products.

Knowing what others really think can be liberating, in consumer behavior as well as in politics. No wonder that the proponents of restrictive social norms often want to shield their people from information that could lead them to believe that the norm is not as dominant as it seems. Dictators exercise censorship to prevent the propagation of attitudes that contradict the current norm. In order to get rid of constricting social norms, people need to talk to each other. This is why it is important, from the viewpoint of preventing pluralistic ignorance, not only to grant the right of freedom of speech but also to maintain a culture where people can openly express their concerns and thoughts.

Emotions in politics

There is a paradox in politics: On the one hand, politics founded on rational institutions is supposed to use reasoning about the advantages and disadvantages of planned measures in order to arrive at rational decisions. On the other hand, citizens would barely take the effort to engage in political activity, and politicians would stand little chance of winning an election, if reason alone ruled. Emotional topics are the ones that mobilize the masses (Le Bon 1960/1895) and attract voters to the ballot (see Groenendyk 2011). In 2014, the Swiss mass immigration vote, a hotly disputed topic, attracted more than 50 percent of the voters to the ballot, compared to the 30 percent voter turnout average. Many Americans vote only for a presidential candidate who shares their view on abortion, an emotionally charged topic (Jones and Saad 2012). Both sides, pro-choice and pro-life, resort to tactics that induce anger over the opposite side in their adherents. Another emotion kindled by politicians is fear. Political candidates, especially when they are challengers to the incumbent holder of an office, instill fear about war, terrorism, crime, or economic downturn with all their negative consequences. Some politicians try to induce enthusiasm whereas others try to mobilize their support base by using a confrontational style in political discussions. Such tactics are not new; Aristotle, in his *Rhetoric*, advised orators to arouse emotions that would be effective in that they would bring their listeners to the "appropriate beliefs," which of course means the beliefs of the orator (see Sherman 1989, p. 169). Recent research sheds light on how emotions shape political opinions. For critical feelers, it is relevant to know about these tactics not only to utilize their power to mobilize the citizenry but also to circumvent their undue influence. Findings reviewed in the following paragraphs suggest that the use of emotions and confrontational styles influences voter judgments and mobilization but undermines critical thinking and trust in politics.

A political campaigner wants to make people feel in order to make them act the way she wants them to. This is possible because the appeal to different emotions evokes different action tendencies. For example, a person who feels angry has an inclination to attack whereas a person who feels fear tends to withdraw. In the realm of politics, research has shown that voters are more likely to endorse risky and confrontational policies when they feel anger rather than fear (Nabi 2003), and they are also less willing to accept compromises in politics (MacKuen, Wolak, Keele, and Marcus 2010; Isbell 2012 provided an accessible summary of this research). Different emotions result in different risk assessments and in different measures to counter a state of affairs. In a study conducted in the weeks following the September 11th attack in 2001, Lerner, Gonzalez, Small, and Fischhoff (2003) showed that participants primed with anger perceived lower risks of being affected by future terrorist attacks than participants primed with fear. Presumably, participants primed with anger imagined aggressive counter-measures that would avert terrorist attacks whereas participants primed with fear responded more passively and could not imagine how to thwart future terrorism. Similar reasoning can be applied to the outcome of a study by Nabi (2003), in which participants favored harsher measures to punish drunk driving when primed with anger but preferred more precautionary measures, such as a state-subsidized taxi service for drunken partygoers, when primed with fear.

Emotions, like moods, elicit various processing styles. Fearful individuals, for example, become more careful, which leads to analytical processing in order to learn more about the fear-provoking situation (see Brader and Marcus 2013). Inducing fear is an effective strategy to weaken prior political convictions and political loyalties. Fearful individuals do not impulsively adhere to their political party but think carefully about their loyalties and political identities. Fearful citizens seem to be good citizens in that they act according to the democratic ideal of rational decision making and careful deliberation over political issues (MacKuen et al. 2010). Their considerations are impartial and their decisions even-handed, compared with those of people whose political action is kindled by anger. Angry citizens, by contrast, seem more loyal to political parties and rely on habit because their emotions are elicited by perceptions that their goals are threatened and their treatment by others is unfair. As a consequence, they tend to be unreceptive to viewpoints that do not agree with their own and they choose candidates according to superficial characteristics such as ideology (Parker and Isbell 2010).

Such mindless adherence is usually reinforced by a public press that aims to entertain its readership (see Norman 2004 for examples from Norway). In order to increase the entertainment value of an article, the press often uses emotional and confrontational styles when describing a scientific or a political debate. American presidential races often rely on negative statements about the competitor instead of raising the controversial issues in a sanguine way. In a recent study, Kienhues, Ferguson, and Stahl (2016) demonstrated that confrontational styles result in mindlessness (see also Reber 2014). They provided their participants with opposing scientific findings. In one condition, participants read a text about a scientific debate in a confrontational style that emphasized negative emotions between the two scientists. A control group received the same text with neutral descriptions of the debate. The researchers assessed both the degree to which participants thought that scientific findings (in general) are variable and their trust in the scientists. Compared to a neutral style, a confrontational style led to the belief that scientific findings are less variable, which can be taken as a sign of mindlessness because people do not consider different perspectives in the debate. However, people trusted experts less when the debate was confrontational; conditions that increase mindlessness decrease trust – or, viewed more positively, people trust experts who discuss opposing positions in an emotionally neutral way. This finding suggests that, when political debate becomes emotional, it may arouse enthusiasm in some adherents but undermine the trust of citizens more broadly. Interestingly, another experiment by the same authors revealed that a debate can be emotional as long as positive emotions are emphasized; only negative emotions do harm.

One way to summarize these findings consists of demanding that future empirical research examines how political debate can be brought back to reason. This is essential if we want politicians to try out schemes and to revise them if they turn out to have unintended harmful effects (see Popper 1945). On the other hand, we also need an analysis of where feelings in politics are justified. For example, undue fear of terrorist threat may result in wrong decisions, such as spending too much money on protection, but no fear may lead to too little protection. The question will in this case be what the optimal level of fear is. Too much anger in the abortion debate may lead to excessive aggression and violence, but how should we judge the justification of a political position if not by getting angry at the fact that people violate either the right to life or the right of choice? The feeling of anger serves as a signal of what an individual values. Again, we have to ask ourselves what the optimal level of anger is in order to enable us to signal the value without becoming violent.

Emotions, including enthusiasm, may have another positive side effect: participation. What is democracy worth without people taking part in political life, both as voters and as candidates for a political office? One problem in direct democracies, such as Switzerland, is low voter turnout, because referendums every three months fatigue people and only emotionally charged topics result in higher participation rates. Future research may tell us where the balance lies between the harmful influences of emotions and their beneficial effects, such as their signal value and mobilizing effects. Studies on the effect of emotions on political mobilization and voting behavior suggest that feelings play a crucial role in times of peace. Yet emotional propaganda seems to play an even greater role in times of war.

War propaganda

During war, a state requires the unconditional loyalty of its citizens. World War I unleashed the first war of modern propaganda. Interestingly, the approaches to propaganda for the home front differed between the two blocks. The Entente, especially the British Empire, relied on atrocity stories (Lasswell 1927; Sanders and Taylor 1982; see also Figure 7.1). Some of them later turned out to be exaggerated (Ponsonby 1928) and may be compared to modern urban legends. A scholar who certainly did not downplay German atrocities stated, "in the first World War British propaganda had to invent the stories of German soldiers bayoneting Belgian babies, because there were too few real atrocities to feed the hatred against the enemy" (Fromm 1973, p. 25).

In contrast, Germany and Austria-Hungary ridiculed the enemy armies (Weigel, Lukan, and Peyfuss 1983; see Figure 7.2). Adolf Hitler (1939/1925), a soldier in that war, contrasted the effects of the different approaches to propaganda by the Entente and by the Central Powers in his book *Mein Kampf*. He vividly described that the soldiers of the Central Powers did not encounter drunken Russians, sissy Frenchmen, and silly Brits as depicted in the German propaganda, but hard-fighting soldiers. This disappointment of expectations undermined the trust of the soldiers of the Central Powers in their own government. The Russian, French, and British soldiers, on the other hand, fought against a fierce German army, in line with what they anticipated after hearing the atrocity stories. Hitler concluded that the propaganda of the Entente succeeded in strengthening the home front while the Central Powers lost the propaganda war. In fact, the lost propaganda war by the Central Powers became part of the stab-in-the-back legend that the Nazis used to explain the defeat in World War I (see Taylor 2003). To sum up, the effectiveness of the propaganda of the Central Powers crumbled because it created erroneous expectations that were falsified. Inducing anger through atrocity propaganda was much more successful.

The implications for critical feeling are twofold, depending on the perspective we take. From the perspective of the state that wants to mobilize its population, it is important that the propaganda creates

Figure 7.1 Poster for the American propaganda movie *Hearts of the World* (1918).

expectations that are met later. Disappointed expectations lead to disillusionment, as on the side of the Central Powers in World War I. Moreover, we have seen that anger leads to impulsive reactions while fear leads to analytical thinking. Angry individuals want to attack while fearful individuals prefer to withdraw. In times of war, instilling anger seems to be the right thing to do. An angry home front neither fears nor underestimates the enemy but has the desire to attack and retaliate. From the perspective of the citizen, critical feeling means that we know about propaganda strategies and can prevent manipulation. However, a single

Figure 7.2 Propaganda of the Central Powers. Translation: "Each shot a Russian, each hit a Frenchman."

citizen cannot do anything against the emotions of the masses. We can only hope that the masses will never again be moved in the way they were in the twentieth century if the population as a whole – and on both sides – can circumvent being influenced by appeals to anger and outrage.

There is a contradiction between the claim that every adult is a mature citizen who can decide autonomously and the attempt to undermine this very autonomy by appealing to feelings. The tenet that marketing and campaigning are directed toward autonomous citizens only holds if one assumes that advertisements and political debate inform consumers and voters about the options from which they can choose. A well-informed consumer would then buy the products that yielded the highest benefit, and a well-informed citizen would vote for the candidate that best served the country. However, consumers and voters not only lack comprehensive information about products and politicians; they also have inferior knowledge about the effects of marketing on feelings. Even if consumers know how marketing works in principle, they may not notice an appeal to their feelings and therefore may undergo surreptitious influence. It is difficult to undo the influences of repeated exposure to a brand if we do not even remember having seen the product or heard the brand name.

There are two ways in which this contradiction could be resolved. We may realize that citizens are not as mature as we would like them to be and prohibit certain marketing practices. An instance of such a paternalistic solution is the prohibition of the advertisement of alcoholic beverages and tobacco products in many countries. A less obvious version of the paternalistic approach consists of nudging citizens toward desired behaviors (Thaler and Sunstein 2008). In doing so, the state employs the same means as marketers do in order to influence citizens to behave in the way most beneficial to the state. Such means may include incentives to use public transport or appeals to feelings to bring citizens to separate their waste for recycling.

As both industry and state use various means to appeal to feelings, an education aimed at fostering autonomy in future citizens should teach about the commonly used methods of persuasion (see Noddings 2003). Consumers may still only partly be able to elude the influence of advertisements, and voters may still be fascinated by emotional debates in politics. However, beyond counteracting attempts at surreptitious persuasion, such education provides future citizens with information that is necessary to make informed decisions about measures a state might take to shield citizens – especially children – from attempts at hidden influence. On the one hand, a mature citizen can figure out how propaganda influences gut feelings. On the other hand, an interesting discussion might ensue about being critical in times of war – should citizens act in accordance with their individual conscience or in accordance with the needs of their state? Questions of loyalty are not only relevant to war; loyalty to parents, to friends, at school or at work, plays a role in everybody's lives.

8 CRITICAL FEELINGS AT SCHOOL

From the standpoint of the child, the great waste in the school comes from his inability to utilize the experiences he gets outside the school in any complete and free way within the school itself; while on the other hand, he is unable to apply in daily life what he is learning in school. That is the isolation of the school – its isolation from life. When the child gets into the schoolroom he has to put out of his mind a large part of the ideas, interests and activities that predominate in his home and neighborhood. ...
A gap [exists] between the everyday experiences of the child and the isolated material supplied in such large measure in the school.
(JOHN DEWEY 1956/1899, P. 75–76)

John Dewey's (1956/1899) take-home message was that there exists a gap between school and home that makes school a bleak place without life. The take-home message of this chapter is that critical feeling can improve this state by employing strategies aimed at enhancing the experience of learning, by making learning interesting, and by fostering intuition and insight. The chapter has four sections. First, I review evidence that metacognitive feelings enhance the learning process, in line with the claim in Chapter 5 that each act of perception and thought – and therefore of learning – is accompanied by a feeling. Second, I discuss emotions in the classroom. The third section will address the closing of the gap between school and the life of the child. Knowledge about how to catch the attention of students enables teachers to make instruction lively and content interesting. The final section of this chapter reveals how school can be filled with life by fostering intuition and by eliciting aha-experiences.

Thus far I have addressed questions concerning education at the end of each chapter in Part II. I have looked at how parents and instructors may teach critical feeling in various domains, such as well-being, skill learning, living together, and marketing. This chapter looks at critical feeling *within* school education. Proponents of a liberal society may be skeptical about the role of schools in critical feeling; they may argue that parents educate their children while schools are institutions that impart the knowledge necessary for the future economic success of both

the students and the nation; they may encounter the notion of an education to happiness with skepticism, as Noddings proposes, and they may
bristle when they read Noddings' (2003, p. 250–251) idea that parents
may have too much power in education – that the state, for instance,
should limit the choice of schooling by religious fundamentalists who
would offer a curriculum that does not contribute to what modern educators see as intellectual growth.

   This chapter does not advocate a certain curriculum, nor does it
say much about how school could contribute to critical feeling in everyday life. It simply addresses the neglected questions of how children feel
at school and how feelings support learning. Even a liberal educator who
fears that the state might have assumed too much power in educating
children could accept that children should be supported in what they
learn; that they should be able to assess their own performance; and that
we are supposed to use feelings where doing so advances the goal of getting subject matter across. We could even go further and propose that
mathematics and science should not be purely cognitive exercises but
also opportunities to discover the beauty of scientific thinking. Such a
focus on feelings does not replace formal education; instead, exploring
the pleasures of thought and discovery is supposed to buttress formal
education in these topics. There may be beauty in the most formal exercises. Only a few children discover this beauty by themselves, or by the
guidance of a cheerful teacher. It is such a pity that many children miss
that experience during their education.

Feelings related to knowledge and performance

Feelings related to knowledge

When John Flavell (1979) introduced the term *metacognition*, he distinguished between *metacognitive knowledge* and *metacognitive experiences*. Among the metacognitive experiences I discussed in Chapter 2
were the tip-of-the-tongue phenomenon and the feeling of knowing.
Here, I focus on the implications of these feelings for critical feeling in a
learning situation.

   Let us first look at the tip-of-the-tongue phenomenon, in which
we have a feeling that we know a name but can only retrieve some elements of it. The effect of this feeling may be counterproductive in that
it encourages us to maintain our retrieval efforts. However, the harder
we try, the more we get stuck in our efforts to retrieve the name. The
best thing to do seems to be to abandon the retrieval efforts; after some

time, the name will appear to us spontaneously, at least in most cases (Brown 1991).

Like the tip-of-the-tongue phenomenon, the feeling of knowing tells us that we know a fact. Unlike the tip-of-the-tongue phenomenon, it lacks the retrieval of specific but incomplete elements of a name. Nevertheless, it has been shown that the feeling of knowing correlates with later retrieval (Koriat 2000). In terms of critical feeling, it seems commendable to trust feelings of knowing because students are likely to succeed in their retrieval attempts. There is one exception: if a student cheats at learning. Many students, when they have to learn vocabulary, use flashcards with the word in the foreign language on one side and the same word in the native language on the other side. Let's say Oliver is learning Spanish and sees the words "la mesa." If he does not cheat, he may become aware that he has no clue about the English translation of "la mesa." However, if he sneaks a look at the back side of the flashcard and reads that it means "the table," he may get the feeling that he knows this piece of vocabulary and can skip learning this item again – an assumption that may turn out to be plain wrong at the worst of all moments, namely in the exam.

Not all experiences that accompany the assessment and use of knowledge are metacognitive feelings. In test situations, students may feel anticipated regret because their intuitions have misled them. One dilemma in multiple-choice tests is whether students should stick with the first answer they provide or switch to another option. Numerous studies have found that switching response options benefits test performance and hence is superior to sticking with the first answer (see Kruger, Wirtz, and Miller 2005 for an overview). However, students do not seem to realize this. Kruger et al. found that students entertain the widespread belief that they should stick with the first answer and not switch. They found that switching from the right to the wrong answer leads to deeper regret than sticking with a wrong answer. Knowing that switching leads to better outcomes may help students to overcome the feeling of anticipated regret at committing a potential error. A further step might include building up a more positive attitude toward switching in order to encourage action that in fact is likely to improve performance.

Satisfaction with one's performance

We saw in Chapter 5 that learners can assess the appropriateness of their action by "listening" to their bodies. Athletes in sports competitions receive feedback not only from their bodies but also from their final ranking. However, the simple prediction that higher-ranked athletes are happier is misleading. What predicts the happiness of athletes with their performance? Expectations certainly play a role. An outsider placed sixth may be happier than a favorite placed fifth. Another source of happiness comes from counterfactual reasoning, which is thinking about what might have been. To take an example from everyday life, if you hurry to the airport and miss your plane by five minutes, you are probably angrier than when you miss your plane by an hour, because it is easier to imagine that you could have reached the plane in time (Kahneman and Miller 1986). The same logic applies to athletes' happiness about their performance in sports, as William James (1890) noted. The winner is expected to be happier than the athlete ranked second, who in turn should be happier than the athlete ranked third. In an illuminating study, Medvec, Madey, and Gilovich (1995) analyzed the smiles of silver- and bronze-medal-winning athletes at the 1992 Summer Olympics in Barcelona and at the 1994 Empire State Games. Surprisingly, bronze medalists appeared happier than silver medalists. In order to examine why the lower-ranked athletes were happier, the authors analyzed counterfactual thoughts in the TV interviews given by the medalists. Athletes who won a silver medal argued that they might have won the gold medal if only they had not made a certain mistake. Bronze medalists, on the other hand, imagined that they might have ended up fourth and were quite happy with their achievement. In addition, focus on almost finishing higher was related to a decrease in expressed happiness. In conclusion, the direction of counterfactual thought – upward comparisons by silver medalists and downward comparisons by bronze medalists – explains why the latter were happier than the former. In terms of critical feeling, imagining alternative scenarios that include downward comparisons might help to alleviate disappointment.

This finding on medalists in sports has a counterpart at school, where students at high-performing schools provide on average lower ratings of their own academic ability than students at low-performing schools. This phenomenon is called the *big-fish-little-pond effect* (Marsh and Parker 1984) and has been shown to be quite general (Marsh 1987; Marsh, Abduljabbar, Morin, Parker, Abdelfattah, Nagengast, and Abu-Hilal 2015; Marsh and Hau 2003). Affective consequences of academic self-concept and self-esteem result in lower satisfaction and happiness of students at high-performing schools than students at low-performing schools.

What could critical feeling do to improve the satisfaction of students at high-performing schools? We may suggest to these students that they are at a high-performing school and therefore have great reason to be proud and happy. A downside of this strategy may be that awareness of belonging to an elite might foster pejorative feelings toward students at low-performing schools. And, conversely, educators need to find evidence-based strategies to increase effort and performance of students at low-performing schools.

Emotions in the classroom

As discussed earlier, feelings do not play a major role in critical thinking and school curricula (Noddings 2003). There are some exceptions, though. For example, Matthew Lipman (2003) advocated that schools enhance thinking about emotions by broadening children's emotional vocabulary. Further research should explore the effects of a more fine-grained language in capturing emotions. Plausibly, a rich emotional vocabulary may increase both empathy and the ability to convey our feeling states in an intelligible way that helps others to understand our emotions (see Saarni 1999).

Teachers can do other things beyond broadening their students' emotional vocabulary; they can try to create an agreeable atmosphere in the classroom in order to provide the right emotional basis for school performance. For example, a bit of nervousness may give students the right amount of arousal to concentrate during an exam. Sweating and collywobbles are disagreeable, but students often become more relaxed after an exam has begun, when they are able to regulate negative emotions and focus on the task instead (Lyons and Beilock 2012). After having experienced several times that nervousness resolves itself within a few minutes into the exam, students may no longer be bothered by those signs before the test; they know the exam will go well. However, for some students, nervousness is crippling. They have learned well, maybe more than their fellow students, to be sure that they will not fail. Yet their anxiety is so overwhelming that their performance does not reflect their competence. This means that they may fail the exam not because there is something wrong with their learning but because of their feelings. They need the strategies discussed in Chapter 4 to overcome their test anxiety.

Much of the research on the emotions students feel at school has been conducted on test anxiety. Only recently have educational psychologists looked into the richness of emotional experience at school and to their surprise found that students feel positive emotions about as often as negative emotions (Pekrun, Goetz, and Perry 2002). For some students, school is a positive experience; they feel joy, hope, and pride. These positive emotions have positive consequences. They increase interest in a subject; they lead students to expend more effort and use strategies that benefit learning, for example elaboration; they reduce irrelevant thinking and mind wandering; and they facilitate self-regulated learning. The outcomes of negative emotions, such as anger, anxiety, and boredom, include low interest and effort; less frequent use of advantageous learning strategies; indulgence in irrelevant thinking and mind wandering; and learning that is less self-regulated and that depends more on external guidance. Boredom seems especially detrimental in the sense that negative correlations are particularly high with study interest, effort, and irrelevant thinking. Boredom and hopelessness also harm achievement outcomes.

Correlation is not causation. Although it seems plausible that hopelessness causes low achievement, it is as plausible that low achievement causes hopelessness. As much of the data have been obtained in cross-sectional studies, which are studies made with different groups at one point in time, the direction of causation is difficult to determine. In longitudinal studies, by contrast, researchers observe the same group at subsequent points in time and employ statistical analyses that address causation across time. In fact, longitudinal studies so far suggest reciprocal effects between emotion and achievement. That is, hopelessness harms achievement in exams, which in turn reinforces the feeling of hopelessness. These are simple feedback loops where positive emotions are related to positive outcomes and negative emotions to negative outcomes. In addition, there are more complex feedback mechanisms. For example, high test anxiety elicits support from parents and teachers, resulting in an alleviation of test anxiety, rendering such support less necessary.

How can teachers create an emotionally positive classroom? Pekrun and colleagues propose "designing educational environments in such ways that they foster students' psychological well-being and learning beyond perspectives of preventing and modifying negative emotions" (Pekrun et al. 2002, p. 103). This is a general statement that must be filled with content. A good starting point might be the distinction between incidental and integral affect mentioned in the previous chapter. First, school buildings and classrooms could create atmospheres that promote incidental positive affect. Second, teachers might try to promote integral positive affect, for example by creating enthusiasm in a subject. It has indeed been shown that enthusiastic teachers elicit student interest in their topics (Keller, Goetz, Becker, Morger, and Hensley 2014).

Some educators deny the possibility that a teacher could intentionally influence the subtle emotional exchanges during class (Aebli 2011/1983). This student of Piaget warns teachers against putting on emotions because students could easily – though unconsciously – recognize them as such; a teacher who faked emotions would therefore expose himself to ridicule. In contrast to Aebli's assumption, research has shown that emotions are not easy to recognize (Ekman 1985; see Chapter 6). Teachers might therefore try new expressions of their affect and look at the effect it has on their class. Let us come back to enthusiasm. Some teachers never convey their inner fire for a topic to their students. Why should such teachers not try to express this enthusiasm in incremental steps? I do not mean a glistening show that students may indeed discern, but trying to be more outgoing than usual. The teacher would act like a sculptor who improves an artwork a bit and checks whether the result looks fine. Although this may include some putting on of emotion at first, bodily feedback mechanisms might influence a teacher's enthusiasm positively. The teacher would shape his own behavior step by step in order to implement the desired state in the classroom, in our example enthusiasm to increase interest.

Making things interesting

There is often a gap between what students learn at school and what they are really interested in. Karl Popper (1945) described this gap as being the difference between the Platonic ideal of education and an ideal of education where students are encouraged to devote themselves to their studies for the sake of studying, for the real love for their subjects, and for inquiry. According to Plato's ideal, spelled out in his *Republic* and implemented in modern school as an institution, education has to serve the needs of the state, by educating both the ruling class, with the philosopher-king at the top, and members of the subordinate class, in order to provide them with the skills necessary to take their allotted places in society (see Popper 1945). This educational philosophy serves, according to Popper, a closed society in that students learn only what the state deems necessary. Such an education does not esteem creative students who pursue their own interests and therefore contributes to Dewey's (1956/1899) notion of a gap between school and a child's life cited as the epigraph of this chapter. This gap continues to exist, and a major challenge of education consists of motivating students to learn and to stay at school (Hidi and Harackiewicz 2000).

Mainstream research in educational psychology focuses on learning outcomes. In fact, I have experienced that it is difficult to publish research when it can be shown that interest increases but without a concomitant increase in learning. Obviously, the balance between the needs of the economy and the needs of the child leans heavily toward the needs of the economy. If one prefers to think of education in terms of its value for the state and economy, research on learning outcomes may be sufficient, and to invest in measures to increase interest would be a waste of money. The alternative view stresses that a student's interest is a value in its own right. If one thinks of education in terms of meeting the needs of the learner as a human being who strives for self-actualization (see Maslow 1943) and self-determination (Deci and Ryan 1985; Ryan and Deci 2000), research must include the personal experience of learning. Such research would follow Dewey's (1956/1899) educational philosophy in that it would aim to combine a society's need for a skilled workforce with individuals' need for self-actualization. Scientists and educators should see the utility of learning not only in terms of increased knowledge but also in terms of its personal value for the learner. Therefore, as long as an intervention enhances the learning experience by increasing interest in a field, without impairing learning outcomes, it is worth both the research effort and the implementation of the intervention in educational settings.

Interest does not just mean feeling pleasure at some stimulation (see Dewey 1975/1913), such as a computer game or a good joke told by a teacher. Interest has at least two components: liking a topic and the feeling that the topic is important and meaningful (Schiefele 1991). A person who is interested shows intrinsic long-term engagement in an activity in order to realize her potential. Intrinsic means that a person decides to engage in an activity, without the need of outside force or incentives. Of course, people may get a reward and still be interested. For example, academics receive a monthly salary for conducting research, but most of them are deeply interested in their scholarly activity. A good test for the intrinsic component of interest is whether an activity persists when the reward is taken away. Often, people who have received incentives stop an activity if they no longer receive the reward. For example, many people who are rewarded for environmentally responsible conservation behavior stop the behavior as soon as the reward is removed (De Young 1993; Vining and Ebreo 2002). Comparably, we would not claim that a student is interested in mathematics if she only reads math books when she gets an extra ten dollars for each A or B in math.

Interest seems to be a by-product of the learning process. We cannot just tell students to be interested. Instead, teachers must find ways to elicit interest in their students, either by adapting the contents in such a way that they fit pre-existing interests of their students or by teaching students how they can increase their interest in a topic in which they are not already interested. Such interventions lead to momentary interest elicited by characteristics of the situation, or situational interest, in contrast to enduring individual interests. How could teachers increase situational interest?

There is one popular but ineffective way to increase situational interest, so-called *seductive details*. These include glossy pictures in textbooks and presentations or fascinating biographical details about an author. However, when pictures do not illustrate a principle and when pictures or biographical details are irrelevant to the work of the author, they do not contribute to the connection between the subject matter and the learner. There is ample evidence that such seductive details increase interest but impair learning (Garner, Gillingham, and White 1989; Harp and Mayer 1997, 1998), especially for weak students (Magner, Schwonke, Aleven, Popescu, and Renkl 2014).

There are at least three effective ways to increase interest. First, *personalization*: With this method, materials are customized to the interests and preferences of the learner. Teachers may ask the students what they are interested in; alternatively, those interests may be registered over time by a computerized learning environment. Such a system may record the choices the students make or ask students about their personal interests; this information can later be used to give each student a personalized version of a formal task. For example, one student provides the information that she is interested in medicine and therefore gets the opportunity to learn probability calculus on a task about hereditary diseases whereas another student reports that he has watched all Indiana Jones movies and therefore receives the task of calculating the probability that Indiana Jones will survive an attack by his adversaries. Some experiments have found positive effects of personalization on both interest and learning (Ku, Harter, Liu, Thompson, and Cheng 2007; Ku and Sullivan 2002; Ross and Anand 1987; Walkington, Petrosino, and Sherman 2013). Other experiments have found effects of personalization on interest but not on learning outcomes (e.g., Bates and Wiest 2004; Cakir and Simsek 2010; Ku and Sullivan 2000). There seem to be differences between different kinds of personalization in terms of situational interest (Høgheim and Reber 2015). While Høgheim and Reber found positive effects of personalization based on middle school students' interests, such as music and sports, they found smaller effects of personalization based on everyday preferences and settings, such as a student's favorite drink or the name of the supermarket where the drink is purchased.

The second method, *choice*, also adapts the subject matter to the interests of the students but lets them choose. For example, if students have to present a novel in class, they can choose the book. Some teachers provide several options of topics for essay writing from which students can choose. However, it seems to be more difficult to provide choice in mathematics and science teaching (see Flowerday and Schraw 2000). A recently developed method makes choice in mathematics and science possible. Instead of being given a personal example, as in personalization, students are presented with multiple examples or topics. They then are instructed to choose the most interesting example. The formal principle, such as probability calculus with two independent events, is then explained via the example the student has chosen. This specific method is called *example choice*. Two studies have shown the effectiveness of example choice in increasing interest, one study with psychology students who had to learn the principle of confirmation bias (Reber, Hetland, Chen, Norman, and Kobbeltvedt 2009), the other with middle school students who were instructed in basic probability calculus (Høgheim and Reber 2015).

The third successful method of increasing interest is *relevance intervention*, developed by Judith Harackiewicz and her colleagues. There are two forms of this intervention: Passive relevance intervention provides students with reasons why the content they are learning could be relevant to their everyday life or to their future (Durik and Harackiewicz 2007). In contrast to personalization and example choice, instruction and tasks remain unchanged; that is, every student learns the same materials. Interest is increased by providing students with reasons why the content is relevant. Active relevance intervention is similar to passive relevance intervention, but the students have to list themselves the reasons why the topic could be relevant (Hulleman and Harackiewicz 2009). In summary, relevance intervention fulfills Dewey's postulate to unite the worlds inside and outside school not by adapting the contents to the interests, as the other interventions do, but by changing the mindset of the student in that they see the relevance of a topic.

The three interventions have all been tested and shown to increase situational interest. Although there are only a few studies on such interventions, it seems that not every method benefits every student. It has been found, for example, that students from Western cultures benefit most when they choose their own topic whereas East Asian students benefit most when a person important to them, such as their mother or their classmates, makes the choice for them (Iyengar and Lepper 1999). Furthermore, relevance interventions have been shown to benefit some groups but not others. For instance, passive relevance interventions benefits students with high initial interest (Durik and Harackiewicz 2007). Active relevance intervention, on the other hand, benefits those with low performance expectations (Hulleman and Harackiewicz 2009). Similarly, example choice increases interest most for students with low initial interest. This is an especially important finding because most interventions show the so-called Matthew effect in that they benefit those who are already well off but not those who need the intervention most (see

Bakermans-Kranenburg, Van IJzendoorn, and Bradley 2005). It seems that active relevance intervention and example choice are especially useful methods for weak students. All these methods require that *teachers* combine the learning materials with the interventions in order to kindle interest, and they have to employ the interventions. Could there be methods that allow *students* to increase interest on their own?

There is indeed not much research about how to make things interesting for ourselves. From what we know about interventions, we could derive some recommendations that then could be examined. For example, students could learn to regularly ask themselves how the contents they have encountered are relevant to their everyday life, or to their future. Students may try out different interventions in order to increase mindfulness (Langer 1997). For example, students mostly stop after they have found the "right" answer. This may be adaptive in terms of time management and minimal effort, but sticking with the first answer and therefore staying at the surface may make a topic less interesting. In mathematics, where there may be just one correct solution to a given task, students may try out whether there are different paths to the solution. Students often stop after they have found a solution even in domains where seeing different perspectives is important, such as politics, history, art, and literature. Encouraging students to try to find a different answer to the same question after they have found the first solution may increase both understanding and interest in students. As research on mindfulness focused on learning, these proposals to increase interest "from within" await further research.

A hitherto unexplored means to increase interest is by making the outcome of assignments relevant to the world outside school. Bronfenbrenner (1979) deplored that many children and adolescents never experience situations in which someone else depends on their work. Students do homework for their teachers and the teachers correct it to provide feedback to the students. It is a closed system, unless we think of the future benefits of instruction. It is hardly surprising that many students find this system meaningless and drop out of high school (see Hidi and Harackiewicz 2000; Oyserman 2015). We should therefore envision making education relevant in the sense that the immediate community or society at large depends on the students' work. There are some rare but encouraging examples. In a computer science course, students solved programming problems related to problems of everyday life, such as creating a computer-assisted device adapted to the individual needs of a stroke patient (Buckley 2009). The patient could not speak and could barely write. The device enabled him to express via a computer voice what he wanted to communicate. Buckley described how touching it was for both patient and students when the device was delivered; such learning outcomes count for others and are meaningful to students. Chen and Reber (2011) showed that writing Wikipedia articles is motivating for students. However, the possibilities for individual teachers within the current school system are limited. What is needed, in terms of strategies of critical feeling, is a radical change in the environment. Adapting education in such a way that communities depend on the products of school would require no less than a sweeping reform of curriculums and societies at large. As we have seen, few things seem to be more difficult than educational reform (Olson 2003; Ravitch 2000). The proposed vision that school outcomes be relevant to society is currently utopic and is limited by the current school system. Teachers therefore have to rely on interventions that increase interest within the constraints of the standard curriculum.

Some teachers confuse making their teaching interesting with making it funny. As discussed above, educational psychologists have shown that irrelevant embellishments of content distracts students' attention away from what is relevant and therefore harm learning. What, then, is a legitimate way to increase interest? John Dewey derived his answer from his critique of the state of schools in the United States in the late nineteenth and early twentieth centuries. He lamented that children lived in two separate worlds, one inside and one outside school. The solution to the problem consists of connecting the interests children bring from home to the topics children have to learn. Personalization, choice, relevance intervention, and mindfulness interventions all try to do exactly that, without embellishing the learning materials. Any method to increase interest has to guarantee that students will stay on track and not be distracted by seductive but irrelevant details.

Beyond interventions designed to increase situational interest, we may try to develop individual interests. Individual interests have been shown to increase with expertise (Alexander 2003; Hidi and Renninger 2006). When people become experts, they not only become more interested but can also begin to rely on intuition.

Cultivating intuition and insight

Cultivating intuition

Can we trust intuition or not? This old question is reminiscent of the question as to whether we can trust our feelings, discussed in Chapter 3. I then said that we can trust our feelings when the environment is stable and provides immediate and veridical feedback. The same applies to intuition (see Hogarth 2005; Kahneman and Klein 2009): Intuition seems to lead people astray in highly volatile environments that lack immediate feedback. Examples are the prediction of share prices that are inherently unstable or clinical judgment where feedback comes often after months and years. By contrast, master chess players store many chess positions in their minds – according to an estimate by Simon and Gilmartin (1973), more than 10,000 within their career. As the rules of chess remain stable and feedback often comes within a few moves, master players often find the two or three best options intuitively before they calculate which move is best (De Groot 1978). In the same way we can trust feelings, we can trust intuition – which is based on feelings (see Thompson 2014; Topolinski 2011) – in stable environments with immediate feedback. For critical feeling, this means that we select or build environments with stable rules and regular stimulus patterns. Teachers would have to carefully select teaching materials in order to provide students with stable outcomes and with instant feedback so that incorrect solutions were corrected immediately. As far as I know, there has been no research on how different learning methods or variety in the learning materials would foster intuitive judgment.

For the remainder of this section, I would like to focus on a particular heuristic in intuitive judgment, namely the assumption that beauty is truth. In his poem "Ode on a Grecian Urn," the Romantic poet John Keats (1999/1820) penned the lines:

> "Beauty is truth, truth beauty," – that is all
> Ye know on earth, and all ye need to know.

Although beauty and truth are two different concepts in philosophy, there seems to be an underlying correspondence between the two, something like a common denominator that makes it difficult for people to distinguish a depiction of something beautiful from a depiction of something true. In the medieval ages, an artist would not have been able to imagine producing a beautiful representation of something that was not true. Beauty and truth were intimately related (Eco 1988). Even scientists could not resist the temptation to think that a beautiful theory – a concept that is often related to a theory's simplicity and elegance – must be true. This thinking is exemplified by a quote from the mathematician Hermann Weyl: "My work always tried to unite the true with the beautiful; but when I had to choose one or the other, I usually chose the beautiful" (cited in Chandrasekhar 1987, p. 65). Chandrasekhar continued

> The example which Weyl gave was his gauge theory of
> gravitation, which he had worked out in his *Raum-Zeit-Materie*.
> Apparently, Weyl became convinced that this theory was not
> true as a theory of gravitation; but still it was so beautiful that
> he did not wish to abandon it and so he kept it alive for the
> sake of its beauty. But much later, it did turn out that Weyl's
> instinct was right after all, when the formalism of gauge
> invariance was incorporated into quantum electrodynamics.
>
> (CHANDRASEKHAR 1987, P. 65F)

Of course, this anecdote does not mean that all beautiful theories are true – there may have been as many beautiful theories that turned out to be wrong. Yet, it does illustrate that some scientists believe that, when a scientific proposition cannot be decomposed analytically, its truth can be revealed intuitively, by assessing its beauty. This suggests that beauty and truth must have some common underlying mechanism. Psychological research suggests that this is indeed the case, and that the common underlying mechanism is processing fluency. I discussed in Chapter 3 how processing fluency increases both affective preference and judged truth (Reber and Schwarz 1999; Reber et al. 1998; see Reber, Schwarz, and Winkielman 2004 for discussion). Reber and colleagues conducted experiments in which they manipulated the symmetry of patterns in a geometrical addition task in which participants had to indicate whether the presented solution to the task was correct or incorrect, a judgment similar to true and false. As symmetric patterns are seen as being more beautiful than asymmetric patterns (Jacobsen et al. 2006; Reber and Schwarz 2006), these experiments tested whether tasks with beautiful patterns are also seen as correct. The symmetry of the patterns was unrelated to whether the task solutions were correct. Nevertheless, participants were more likely to endorse solutions to tasks with symmetric patterns than solutions to tasks with asymmetric patterns (Reber et al. 2008). Although this is a situation remote from a mathematician having an intuitive hunch that a solution to a problem is the true one, the experiment shows that there is commonality between symmetry – which is both easier to process and seen as beautiful (see Makin, Pecchinenda, and Bertamini 2012) – and truth. The study is therefore a first step at demonstrating the mechanisms behind the hitherto anecdotal evidence about mathematicians and scientists using the beauty of a theory as a guide to its truth. Further research may examine more complex tasks, approaching – in a stepwise manner – situations that more closely correspond to what mathematicians experience when they solve problems.

What do such findings mean for critical feeling? When it comes to science, a careful analysis would have to demonstrate that more "beautiful" theories do indeed have a higher probability of being true. This would amount to a similar analysis of the ecology of knowledge to the analysis of fluency and judgments of truth reported by Reber and Unkelbach (2010; see also Chapter 3). When it comes to judgment, intuitions do not have the function of telling us whether a solution is true or false but rather guide our attention, one of the rational functions of feelings. The correctness of a solution has to be scrutinized after the solution has been found. Intuitive judgment tells us whether it is worth following up what we have found so far. However, do we not miss out on some correct solutions if we do not pursue them because they look ugly? Maybe, but beauty does not only signal that a solution might be true; beauty also signals that a solution is simple and elegant. A solution that is true and simple is likely to yield deeper insights and is therefore more important than a solution that is true but complex.

Cultivating insight

In Chapter 2, I discussed how the four characteristics of an aha-experience can be integrated into a unitary account. A sudden insight facilitates information processing related to the solution. This ease of processing, or fluency, in turn yields positive affect, and the problem solver is convinced that her solution is true. If an aha-experience provides positive affect, which is part of situational interest, such experiences might be deployed to increase interest in a topic. Indeed, the mathematics educator Peter Liljedahl (2005) looked at spontaneous aha-experiences during an undergraduate mathematics course. He found that students who had at least one aha-experience that accompanied an insight in the course of a semester reported to have a more positive attitude toward mathematics than students who did not have any aha-experiences. What facilitates such an experience? Liljedahl observed that aha-experiences were most frequent during group discussions about solving a problem. It seems that exchanging ideas facilitates sudden insights. Of course, Liljedahl's mostly qualitative study is only preliminary evidence that aha-experiences yield more positive attitudes and might therefore increase interest. It may well be that those who had a positive attitude beforehand were more likely to have an aha-experience, or that some unknown variable, such as persistence in problem solving, increased the probability of having both an aha-experience and a positive attitude toward mathematics.

What does Liljedahl's (2005) study mean for problem solvers and teachers? How could we instill aha-experiences? In order to provide an answer, we have to know more about the cognitive processing that goes on during sudden insights. Some psychologists claim that, in terms of cognitive processes, nothing special is involved in sudden insights compared to other forms of thinking, while other psychologists propose that insights activate processes that are not observed in more incremental forms of thinking (see Davidson 2003).

The *nothing-special approach* claims that solutions to insight tasks rely on cognitive processes that are not different from those involved in other problem-solving tasks (Weisberg and Alba 1981). These authors argued that there is no special cognitive psychology of insight because the observed phenomena could be explained by memory processes that are characteristic of all problem-solving attempts. This notion was supported by findings that (1) experts have a large, well-organized knowledge structure rather than unique mental processes that allow them to outperform novices (e.g., Chase and Simon 1973; De Groot 1978); (2) verbal reports about solving a typical insight problem showed that the majority of problem solvers used a series of incremental steps that involved ordinary understanding and reasoning skills (Perkins 1981); and (3) computer programs could reproduce major scientific discoveries by simulating recognition processes used to solve a wide variety of routine problems.

Beyond methodological problems identified with the nothing-special approach, some findings of abrupt transitions from ignorance to understanding that remain unconscious are difficult to reconcile with the notion that there are no special cognitive processes involved (see Siegler and Stern 1998). Note that the nothing-special approach is concerned with cognitive processes only, and therefore does not necessarily contradict the occurrence of aha-experiences, at least when one assumes that some of the usual processes related to the transition to understanding may happen abruptly. Moreover, Liljedahl (2005) found in his above-mentioned study that the contents of the insights were often inconsiderable when students felt an aha-experience. This means that aha-experiences may be connected to one of the incremental steps that are miniscule themselves but may be decisive in understanding the problem. In conclusion, the nothing-special approach to insight research may be correct insofar as no special cognitive processes are involved. On the other hand, the nothing-special approach may be wrong because what is special is not the cognitive processes involved in insight, but the experiences that accompany the sudden solution of a task, including the aha-experience.

The so-called *puzzle-problem approach* opposes the nothing-special approach by claiming that there are special cognitive processes involved in problem solving by insight. Researchers often use constrained puzzles and problems in well-controlled settings in order to examine these cognitive processes. These tasks are aimed at achieving two criteria for an insight to occur (Weisberg 1995). First, discontinuity; the solution to the task is not obvious to the students who are solving the problem, and they cannot proceed linearly up to the solution (as in so-called *incremental problems*; Metcalfe and Wiebe 1987). An example of a problem that is obvious to solve is an equation with two unknowns where a student knows the solution path. Although the solution of this problem needs time, the student knows how to proceed from the outset to arrive at the correct solution. An example of a task whose solution is not obvious to a novice is an equation used in pre-algebra instruction: $4 + 2 + 3 = 4 + ?$ (Hyde, Else-Quest, Alibali, Knuth, and Romberg 2006). Fourth graders who encounter this task for the first time often experience an impasse, which is a good starting point from which to experience an insight with the concomitant aha-experience. The second criterion for an insight to occur is restructuring; in order to elicit an aha-experience, a puzzle or problem cannot be solved by good reading or just retrieving knowledge but must lead to the formation of new mental representations.

The aha-experience provides positive outcomes and therefore seems to be desirable. For the French mathematician Henri Poincaré (1996/1913), aha-experiences even had an aesthetic quality. What do the accounts of insight mean for critical feeling in the service of eliciting such aha-experiences?

First, the study by Liljedahl (2005) suggests that, when we have to solve a problem, we should do what scientists do to make progress: talk to another person who knows the field. Exchanging ideas helps us to see a problem from different perspectives, a hallmark of mindful problem solving (Langer 1997). A new perspective may facilitate restructuring mental representations, for example by retrieving elements that were not obvious before. If you are alone, you may try to take a different perspective in order to recall new information. Taking multiple perspectives and being alert to distinctions – another feature of mindful thinking – may also help you to combine or compare facts and arguments in a new way.

Second, teachers may provide tasks that come close to the puzzles given in problem-solving studies focused on insight. A possible insight task, in which students are asked to solve pre-algebra problems, was given above. Creating and exploring insight tasks that could be used in mathematics and science education would be of much merit. There has hitherto been little research on how to instill insight and concomitant aha-experiences in educational settings, and the advice scientists can currently give to both problem solvers and teachers is preliminary.

This section has shown that critical feeling may play an important role in dry and rational topics such as mathematics. I have discussed aha-experiences in this chapter because most research is on insights in mathematics or science. However, people have insights and aha-experiences in many other domains, for example in preparing a speech, making art, reading a book, or during prayer. Aha-experiences are an unexplored phenomenon that yields much promise for increasing the fascination in any topic.

When it comes to educational applications of critical feelings, we have to ask what students and teachers should know. We may provide students with some hands-on experience about feelings of knowing and about the role of feelings in the assessment of their own performance. Students need to know that, if they learn French vocabulary from flashcards and cheat by turning the card over, they will feel that they know the word without really knowing it. Reiterating arguments on desirable difficulties in Chapter 5, we might provide students with experiences to teach them that some tasks require persistence in the face of difficulties, and that it is often rewarding to endure until the task is solved. When no solution is in sight, students may put the task to the side and return to it later in order to increase the chance that they will have an insight and to decrease the danger of boredom.

Students would also benefit from strategies to make their materials interesting. They may ask themselves how the content is relevant to their personal interests or future career (Hulleman and Harackiewicz 2009). Mindfulness interventions, as proposed by Langer (1997), may enhance the learning experience, but more research needs to be conducted to demonstrate the effectiveness of such interventions for enjoyment and interest. Often, however, it is not the students' mistake if materials are not interesting. Some learning materials are disconnected from the children's experience to a degree where students are unable even to ask (let alone answer) why the materials are relevant. In such cases it is the teacher's task to reveal the relevance of the materials beyond the generality that mathematics (or whatever the subject is) may one day help a student's career or – even worse in terms of intrinsic motivation – because it will be tested in the exam.

Teacher education should convey the knowledge necessary to create a positive classroom atmosphere, to improve learning outcomes and learning experiences, and to increase students' interest in the subject matter they instruct. To create a positive classroom atmosphere, teachers may benefit from many of the strategies of critical feeling discussed in this book. They should get information about and pay attention to the mood in their classroom. Teaching students strategies such as stop and think or reappraisal may help teachers to appease students. When it comes to improvement of learning outcomes and learning experiences, teachers certainly should know about desirable difficulties; if they think that learning should always be easy for their students, they may actually impair learning. It is astonishing to what degree learning still is amassed at school: a lesson, some tasks, a test. Learning outcomes might improve if textbooks implemented some distribution of the tasks over time. If textbooks do not distribute the exercises, the teacher should adhere to a spaced schedule (see Chapter 5). Every teacher should know that presenting some glossy pictures or fascinating biographical details about a scientist is likely to impair learning for weak students. However, teachers must not restrict themselves to attracting the attention of the disinterested. My experience as a university teacher is that it may be more demanding to teach for the interested than for those who lack interest. Those who are interested are eager to know more, and they often learn fast. If we do not ensure our instruction keeps up with their ambition, we may – in the worst case – extinguish the flame that sustains the interest of our best.

9 MUSIC, ART, AND LITERATURE

By nature, people are similar; they diverge as the result of practice.
(CONFUCIUS, *Analects*, §17.2,
CITED IN SLINGERLAND 2003B, P. 200)

The previous chapter emphasized the role of feelings when children learn at school, among them the role of beauty in judging a solution as true and the aesthetic quality of an aha-experience. When we think of aesthetics, we think of art. It amounts to common sense that aesthetic experiences may go beyond art and pertain to such different topics as beauty in nature, the attractiveness of a face, the melody of a foreign language, the arrangement of food on a plate, the elegance of a mathematical proof, or the sound of an engine. By contrast, art is often equated with aesthetics. This is a mistake made by many scholars and laypeople alike (see Carroll 1999; Danto 2003) and has been called the *artistic–aesthetic confound* (Bullot and Reber 2013b). The whole field of neuroaesthetics discusses its findings as if they could be applied to art in general. In a famous article, Ramachandran and Hirstein (1999) listed eight laws of artistic experience. The title of the article is "The Science of Art: A Neurological Theory of Aesthetic Experience" – as if aesthetics and art were interchangeable. This led to a narrow view of art as yielding aesthetic pleasure. In order to examine art appreciation, researchers in empirical aesthetics used the artwork as a stimulus and mainly used liking or aesthetic pleasure as dependent variables (see Bullot and Reber 2013a for a critique). We shall see that art appreciation consists of both understanding and evaluation, and that understanding depends on knowledge about the context in which the artwork has been created. Even an aesthetic theory of art (see Carroll 1999 for an overview) would have to consider understanding based on the art-historical context.

This chapter outlines critical feeling in art appreciation. Art encompasses the visual arts, literature, drama, poetry, music, dance, and architecture. This chapter begins with a review of how people interested in music develop certain tastes and continues with two ways of learning artistic styles. I next summarize the psycho-historical framework of art appreciation, which helps us to deal with the alienation effect, and connect ideas by the German playwright Bertolt Brecht to the most recent findings from cognitive psychology. The chapter ends with a review of research on emotion in art and how its findings may be used to develop critical feeling in understanding artworks that target our emotions.

Play it again, Sam: how to become a music lover

In line with the Confucius quote at the beginning of this chapter, research has found that newborns have similar musical preferences whereas adult audiences diverge in their tastes. How can we explain this phenomenon? Some years ago, Norbert Schwarz, Piotr Winkielman, and I (Reber, Schwarz, and Winkielman 2004) proposed a solution to this riddle by invoking fluency theory. This account starts from the fact that infants prefer consonant musical sequences to dissonant sequences (Trainor and Heinmiller 1998; Zentner and Kagan 1996), and they process consonant musical elements faster than dissonant ones (Schellenberg and Trehub 1996). The fluency theory of aesthetic pleasure can combine the two findings; consonant music is preferred because it can be more easily processed than dissonant music (see Reber 2012b).

When they are growing up, children are exposed to music and therefore acquire the taste of their culture. Repeated exposure to the music of their culture results in more fluent processing and therefore preference for the music the person heard repeatedly (see Gaver and Mandler 1987). Between 1958 and 2012, repetition of lyrics *within* a song increased the chance that a song would become a number-one hit in *Billboard* magazine's Hot 100 singles chart (Nunes, Ordanini, and Valsesia 2015), presumably through liking. In his classic study, Pierre Bourdieu (1984/1979) observed that members of the same social class shared tastes for music, fashion, or food, to name just a few. However, his conclusion was not in terms of processing fluency but in terms of social processes. He concluded that members of a social class become acquainted with what the taste of their class should be. The upper classes are especially socialized to express a refined taste that stands out against popular (and therefore vulgar) taste. According to Bourdieu, members of the upper class do not necessarily enjoy music when listening to it but feel satisfaction from playing well the game of society (Bourdieu 1984/1979) in which one has to distinguish the refined from the vulgar, the fine arts from popular art, and so on. In psychological terms, members of the upper class may not feel aesthetic pleasure from listening to opera but from pride due to having understood how to play the game of society.

According to fluency theory, a promising way to be at ease with refined taste is to expose oneself to the music one wishes to appreciate. For the upper class that means that they can play the game of society well and at the same time like the music suitable for their elevated class status. Note that it is not necessary to listen repeatedly to the same piece of music. Listening to Fugue No. 1 in C major by Bach, for example, not only increases familiarity with this particular piece but also contributes to implicit learning of a variety of musical attributes. Tillmann, Bharucha, and Bigand (2000) proposed that tonality and temporal characteristics of musical style are acquired through implicit learning, which is learning without awareness.

The proposed mechanism has an interesting consequence. There is ample evidence that implicit learning results in preference for stimuli that follow a rule. In a study by Gordon and Holyoak (1983), participants were presented with letter strings that followed a set of rules, a so-called *finite state grammar*. After this training trial, participants received new letter strings. Half of them followed the grammar and half did not. The participants had to judge how much they liked the letter strings, and it turned out that they liked grammatical letter strings more than ungrammatical ones. Kuhn and Dienes (2005) observed the same results for tunes that, unbeknownst to the participants in the experiment, followed a rule. First, participants listened to tunes that all were in accordance with the rule. Thereafter, participants listened to new tunes. New melodies that followed the same rule were preferred to new tunes that did not follow the rule. This study suggests that learning the principles of tonality presumably changes not only cognitive processing of music reception but also affective preference: Musical elements in accordance with the rules of tonality are preferred to irregular elements. What has been shown for music can also be observed for dance. Opacic, Stevens, and Tillmann (2009) exposed their participants to classical dance movements that were constructed in accordance with a rule. In a later trial participants preferred new sequences of dance movements that followed the rule from the learning session to sequences that did not follow the rule.

During their childhood, upwardly mobile members of the middle classes are often not exposed to the music of the upper classes. They therefore lack the taste of what is considered adequate by the upper classes. They are instead exposed to popular music, which leads to a taste that differs from the taste of the class they want to belong to. These middle-class listeners try to compensate for their subjectively felt deficit by explicitly learning all they can about "good" music and about what is the "right" musical taste. However, as Bourdieu (1984/1979) notes, members of the middle classes who want to mimic the taste of the elevated strata of society are much less at ease when expressing their taste than the upper classes, whose musical taste has been inculcated since early childhood. Moreover, acquiring musical knowledge is not always necessary. Bigand and Poulin-Charronnat (2006) reviewed evidence that various aspects of music processing do not depend on expertise; listeners may acquire them in a more implicit way. To acquire musical taste and some musical expertise, for example about musical styles, repeated listening to the music one wants to like in the future seems to be sufficient.

Pigeons as connoisseurs? The learning of artistic styles

Paintings have lines, texture, and composition but also coloring techniques and affective tones that characterize works of the same artist or of the same epoch, regardless of the subject matter of the artwork. This is the *style* of an artwork (Gardner 1970). A connoisseur should know the characteristics of distinct styles and the differences between styles of different epochs, such as Renaissance and Baroque. Such characteristics of these two styles have been analyzed by art historian Heinrich Wölfflin (1950). He found five differences between Renaissance art (in the sixteenth century) and Baroque art (in the seventeenth). First, Renaissance works have clear outlines whereas Baroque works do not, a difference he called *linear versus painterly*. Second, Renaissance paintings place objects parallel to the picture plane whereas the picture plane of Baroque paintings is diagonal, a dimension Wölfflin called *plane versus recession*. Third, Renaissance paintings are self-contained whereas Baroque paintings have looser boundaries, which is the difference between *closed versus open form*. Fourth, objects in Renaissance paintings tend to retain a certain independence whereas objects in Baroque are subsumed under a common theme; there is a development from *multiplicity to unity*. Fifth, Renaissance paintings achieved a clarity not seen the century before but Baroque voluntarily sacrificed this clarity; this is the difference between *clear and unclear*. Notice that these five differences apply across such attributes of a painting as subject matter, painter, and other features that were not relevant to distinguishing the two epochs, such as size or dominant color. Such an assessment of styles needs profound knowledge and thorough analytical thinking.

However, even non-experts in art are quite proficient at learning styles. No art expertise is necessary to learn to distinguish paintings according to artistic style; children aged below seven or eight classify paintings according to subject matter (people, churches, trees, etc.; Gardner 1970). At the age of twelve and older, they begin to classify paintings according to stylistic information. A surprising finding was presented by a team of scientists who examined discrimination learning of artistic styles in pigeons (Watanabe, Sakamoto, and Wakita 1995). They trained pigeons to discriminate specific paintings by Monet from specific paintings by Picasso. After this training session, the pigeons were presented with new paintings by Monet and Picasso, and they were quite good at distinguishing between the two styles. In addition, when they were presented with new paintings by Cézanne or Renoir, they classified them together with Monet, which makes sense given that all three artists were impressionists. Paintings by Braque and Matisse, on the other hand, were classified together with Picasso; again, artists of the same period were classified together. Similarly, pigeons have been shown to discriminate between the musical styles of Bach and Stravinsky (see Porter and Neuringer 1984). These studies suggest that distinguishing styles does not need much brain. This ability is astonishing, given the training connoisseurs need in order to distinguish styles. As pigeons are not well known for their profound knowledge of art or their thorough analytical thinking, there must be another mechanism that enables even birds to learn to discriminate styles. Let us again look at the characteristics that distinguish Renaissance and Baroque painting: linear, plane, closed form, multiplicity, and clear for the Renaissance paintings, versus painterly, recession, open form, unity, and unclear for the Baroque paintings. The characteristics of each epoch tend to occur together. It is likely to be this co-occurrence of characteristics that facilitates learning by people and animals alike. They are able to acquire stylistic information without being able to verbalize what the characteristics are. It seems that experiential information accounts for the fact that a certain painting is Renaissance and not Baroque, or Monet and not Picasso.

We have now two views of the connoisseur: on the one hand, the learned appreciator of art who knows exactly why one painting belongs to the Renaissance and the other to the Baroque, and on the other hand a viewer who feels that one must be Renaissance and the other Baroque, without being able to explain why this is so. In the first case, the connoisseur is in the possession of a sophisticated cognitive system; in the second case, he needs no more brain than a pigeon. But who is the real connoisseur? In the previous section, I discussed Bourdieu's notion that members of the upper classes cultivate the taste of their children from early on, while members of the upwardly mobile middle classes have to acquire the dominant taste later in life. This leads, according to Bourdieu, to a situation in which members of the middle class often acquire impressive factual knowledge about art but struggle to catch up in terms of a feeling for the different styles and for other attributes of art appreciation. Therefore, if we follow Bourdieu, knowledge alone is not sufficient to be a connoisseur. Although the person is knowledgeable, she lacks the refinement of feelings, based on implicit discrimination learning. But is it sufficient to have just learned the differences in style through discrimination learning? The idea that pigeons could be connoisseurs goes against the grain of every art lover, though it may elicit some wicked joy in those who despise the art world. Pigeons indeed possess the capacity to complete the first step of being a connoisseur, namely of learning different styles implicitly. This is what upper-class sons and daughters also do when they are young. The real connoisseur, however, needs something more. One cannot have a discussion informed by deeper understanding with a pigeon and rarely with a child, after all. Real connoisseurs have learned the distinctions implicitly but have also acquired explicit knowledge about the different styles. They come to understand what they have learned either way.

Understanding, however, means that a person can give reasons but also that those reasons are often accompanied by a feeling of knowing. The middle-class adult who diligently reads about art is not really proficient in automatically grasping a work because his learning is not informed by feeling. It is like having learned a second language as an adult. We may be able to speak it, to describe its grammar, and to write in it, but we lack the feeling that an utterance is correct, which we possess when speaking our native language. However, our discussion of critical feeling shows a way out: aspiring art lovers should not only learn about art and artistic styles but also expose themselves to it in order to learn styles through discrimination learning. They should not only look at works of art with an analytical mindset – specifically, to determine how to apply their recently acquired knowledge – but also just look at the paintings, like the upper-class child did. Although the middle-class adult may not as easily feel the distinction of styles as the upper-class child, there is still a chance that knowledge will be accompanied by some proficiency. And, if middle- or working-class parents want to educate their children to become art lovers, it is not enough to instill knowledge in them. Children have to see art around them in order to get the feeling.

Here I have followed Bourdieu's discussion about class and art. His discussion may give the impression that upper-class children are at an advantage in general. However, I do not think so. First, Bourdieu's observations convey a stereotypical image of how social classes appreciate art that may be true statistically but not in an absolute and deterministic sense. Second, many working-class children get a feeling for how an engine sounds if it works well; if an upper-class adult wants to learn the sound of engines, he looks as ignorant as the middle-class art viewer. Children who grow up on a farm may get a feeling for handling animals that one cannot acquire through learning about animals from books. Yet again, although brain plasticity is reduced in adults compared to children, and although adults learn more slowly, exposure to the objects one wants to get a feeling for – be they works of art, engines, or animals – combined with learning may be a better way to achieve feeling than pure learning from books.

The psycho-historical framework

Acquiring knowledge about the music or art one wants to appreciate is nevertheless useful in order to acquire the desired taste. Bullot and Reber (2013a) developed a psycho-historical framework for artistic understanding that they linked to the fluency theory of aesthetic pleasure. Let me first explain the art-historical framework and then connect it back to fluency theory.

The mainstream approaches to empirical aesthetics have assumed that art appreciation follows the laws of the brain (e.g., Ramachandran and Hirstein 1999; Zeki 1999). Surely, appreciating art does not work against the laws of the brain, but these laws are not sufficient to explain such a complex phenomenon. Many researchers in empirical aesthetics have seen artwork as a mere stimulus (Chatterjee 2011; Locher 2012). Even the most sophisticated theories on art appreciation (e.g., Chatterjee 2011; Leder, Belke, Oeberst, and Augustin 2004) lack a theory of the art-historical context. When a theory discussed the context in which an artwork was shown, it did not go beyond the artwork's immediate environment, such as a museum, a gallery, or an aesthetic experiment (Leder et al. 2004). However, to understand an artwork, the essential context is the one in which the artwork was created.

In order to illustrate why understanding is essential for evaluation, let me provide you with an analogy. When a student says that she likes calculus and judges a task as elegant, we expect her to understand what she is talking about. If the student told us that a problem was elegant without being able to solve the task, such ignorance would make her judgment unfounded. In the context of mathematical problem solving, evaluation is not possible without understanding. The same goes for art (Carroll 2001; Gilmore 2013). In order to evaluate a piece of art, we have to understand it. Yet, while it is obvious what understanding problems of calculus means (as measured, for example, by transfer tasks; see Mayer 2001), it is less clear what understanding a work of art means.

Bullot and Reber's (2013a) psycho-historical framework provides an answer to this problem. Let me lead you through Figure 9.1. The block labeled "Art-historical contexts" on the left includes trading places, institutions such as museums, historical processes at the time when the artist worked, and not least the intentions and actions of the artist (see Levinson 1979, 1989, 1993; Livingston 2005). All these contextual elements flow into the production of an artwork. The end product is an artifact that has functions and bears traces of its creation. For example, paintings by Lucio Fontana include a cut in the canvas that serves as a trace of the historical events during the creation of the artwork. The block "Appreciation of the work," on the right-hand side of the figure, contains three modes of appreciation. The first mode is *basic exposure*, in which a viewer, listener, or reader perceives the artwork as it presents itself, as a stimulus. The appreciator does not go beyond the information given in the artwork. The second mode is the *design stance*, which goes beyond mere exposure in that appreciators ask why an artwork has certain features. The responses can be found in the production of the artwork. This inquiry into causal information pertaining to the artwork leads to *artistic understanding*, which refers back to the art-historical context. Investigation into art appreciation has been done by two separate branches of inquiry. While researchers in empirical aesthetics limited their studies to basic exposure, which refers back to the artwork as a stimulus (the dark gray surface), scholars in the humanities and social sciences have focused on artistic understanding, which is related to the contexts in which the work was created (light gray area).

Basic exposure to an artwork may yield different experiences, among them aesthetic pleasures. However, these preferences are often based on shallow processing and lack proper understanding of the work of art. Such understanding is based on relevant facts from the art-historical context. As an appreciator may weigh such facts differently, artistic understanding is pluralistic – there is no one right understanding of an artwork. However, in line with White's (1965) philosophical arguments regarding historical thought, artistic understanding has to be grounded in facts about the history of a work.

The psycho-historical framework can explain phenomena that have eluded traditional empirical aesthetics. When experts find out that an artwork has been forged, the value of the work drops dramatically. This happened in the case of Han van Meegeren, who alleged to have found paintings by Johannes Vermeer that he had in fact painted himself (see Coremans 1949). A painting looks alike before and after the discovery that it was fabricated. An aesthetic approach limited to basic exposure of artworks cannot explain why an identical painting should

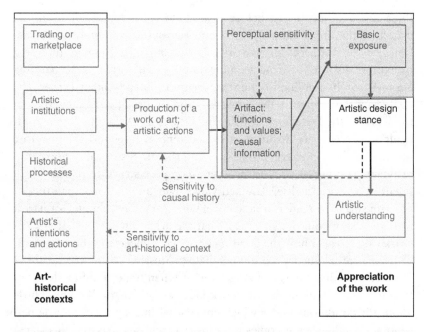

Figure 9.1 *The psycho-historical framework of the science of art appreciation. Solid arrows indicate relationships between causal and historical generation. Dashed arrows indicate information processing and representational states in the appreciator's mind that refer back to earlier historical stages in the production and transmission of a work. The dark gray area to the upper right covers the realm of empirical aesthetics (artifact as stimulus and basic exposure) while the light gray area to the left and bottom covers the realm of research in the humanities.*

all of a sudden cost only a fraction of what it cost before (Locher 2012). The psycho-historical framework explains this drop in value by the fact that a forged painting misleads the appreciator with regard to the causal history of the artwork. The forgeries by Van Meegeren undermined artistic understanding in that the works were not based on the original genius of a painter in the seventeenth century but on the emulation of old artistic ideas by a twentieth-century painter. A similar logic applies to look alikes such as Warhol's Brillo boxes (see Danto 1981). When appreciators understand the difference in causal history between artworks and everyday objects such as the Brillo soap boxes, they evaluate and valuate them differently.

The psycho-historical framework helps to explain another paradox. People normally like what they can process fluently. However, much art is disfluent and the audience likes it nevertheless. The fluency theory of aesthetic pleasure (Reber, Schwarz, and Winkielman 2004) cannot explain why people appreciate artworks that are difficult to process, and these are – as mentioned before – the kinds of artworks often appreciated by the upper classes. Bullot and Reber (2013a) analyzed several functions of disfluency in artworks. For example, artists may represent or express disorder or struggle; an example of the former is the painting *Snow Storm* by the English painter Joseph Mallord William Turner. The disfluency that supports the representation of struggle is exemplified in the work of the French painter Eugène Delacroix. Artworks that are difficult to perceive are disfluent at the perceptual level and are therefore disliked at first. However, understanding the art-historical context of a disfluent painting or of a novel with a complex structure renders them fluent at a conceptual level. When viewers encounter a new painting of the same artist or readers a new novel with the same technique of narration, they may immediately grasp what the artist intended, what the artwork expresses, or how the painting or novel connects to other artworks. This conceptual fluency from immediate processing of knowledge about the artwork contributes to liking, at least when understanding does not lead to the evaluation that the work lacks artistic merit. We know little about the conditions under which conceptual fluency may override perceptual fluency when it comes to liking. Current findings and theorizing (see Reber, Schwarz, and Winkielman 2004) suggest that an audience will like a perceptually fluent artwork by default, and people satisfied with what they see, hear, or read will continue to like it. However, in order to like an artwork that is complex and not comprehensible from what we perceive directly, an audience has to go beyond the information given. This account helps to explain the fact that experts like complex works more than novices do (see McWhinnie 1968 for visual art and Smith and Melara 1990 for music).

What does the psycho-historical framework tell us about critical feeling? Developing artistic taste requires that appreciators gather information that is relevant to the experience of the artwork . They do not need to learn encyclopedic knowledge that might be irrelevant. Most often, exact dates of birth and death of artists are irrelevant; for example, if one is interested in analyzing an artist's intentions according to formal criteria (see Bell 1914), knowledge of an artist's social background, marital life, or political opinions contributes little to the understanding of the work and in turn does not contribute to conceptual fluency. For this reason, knowing about the personal life of an artist in this case may be useless at best and a distraction from understanding the artwork at worst, at least when seen from the viewpoint of developing taste informed by the artwork.

The alienation effect: connecting Brecht to cognition

An art exhibition by best-selling contemporary artist Damien Hirst, titled *A Thousand Years*, shows the rotten head of a cow in a glass display case. Art philosopher Arthur Danto (2003, p. 49f.) writes how an art lover told him that "she found beauty in the maggots infesting the severed and seemingly putrescent head of a cow." He continues, "it gives me a certain wicked pleasure to imagine Hirst's frustration if hers were the received view. He intended that it be found disgusting, which was the one aesthetically unredeemable quality acknowledged by Kant in the *Critique of Aesthetic Judgment*." Danto's experience is a nice illustration of the popular belief that artworks have to be beautiful. So pervasive is this belief that art lovers often seek the beautiful in obviously ugly or disgusting artwork. However, not all art aims at beauty. It is plain wrong to try to find beauty in the rotten cow's head, and it is certainly not a sign of refined taste, to say the least, if someone thinks that this work of art is beautiful.

Beauty has been an aim of art in the past, and the eighteenth-century art historian Johann Jacob Winckelmann (1972) defined standards of beauty: order, harmony, simplicity, and calmness. There are works of art that are beautiful, music that is serene, and plays or movies we can just dive into and where we find we identify with the characters. These works of art are easy to look at, to listen to, or to watch. This changed, however, during the first half of the twentieth century: In drama, Bertolt Brecht (1964) introduced difficulties that prevented automatic identification with a character in a piece. These difficulties built into drama – called *Verfremdungseffekt* or *alienation effect* – were thought to make the audience think, to make them see a reality – such as the social conditions – that goes beyond mere identification with a character. The alienation effect is in line with what we know from philosophical insight and psychological research. Being able to process information from the environment with ease signals that the interaction between the person and environment is going smoothly, and no extra attention is needed to monitor the situation (Winkielman et al. 2003). By the same token, difficult processing may signal an ongoing problem that requires a person's attention and may elicit analytical thinking. Dewey (1910), for instance, proposed that the starting point of each act of reflective thinking is a difficulty. Contemporary artists might have a similar intuition when they believe that "if a work is to provoke serious thought, it must be ugly, disturbing, difficult to look at" (Lopes 2005).

In accordance with Dewey's (1910) notion, new psychological studies provide evidence that disfluent processing induces analytical thinking. In one study, the experimenters gave their participants a set of tasks whose intuitive answers contradicted the correct response (Alter et al. 2007; Song and Schwarz 2008). One example is, "On Day 1, there is one water lily on a pond. Every day, the surface covered by water lilies doubles, and the pond is fully covered by water lilies after forty-eight days. How many days does it take to cover half of the pond?" Spontaneously, people tend to respond twenty-four because the pond is fully covered after forty-eight days, and it seems obvious that half of the pond will be covered in half of the time. This is also a typical kind of school math task, and these often follow a linear function. However, the obvious answer is not the correct one because the growth of the water lilies follows an exponential function. You have by now probably found out that half of the pond is covered after forty-seven days, and it takes one day more until the whole pond is fully covered with water lilies. One group of participants in the experiment was presented with the tasks in easy-to-read, black Myriad Web twelve-point font, whereas another group was presented with the tasks in a difficult-to-read 10 percent gray italicized Myriad Web ten-point font. One would expect that people would be better at solving tasks that are easy to read because they would need less resources to read the task and could focus on solving it. Contrary to this intuition, people solved the tasks best if the font was difficult to read. How can we explain this result? As we have seen, easy processing indicates that everything is fine and that we can proceed without having to think too much. However, this attitude is counterproductive when people come up with an intuitive solution to the water lily task. The easy-to-read font indicates that things are fine, so they proceed with their spontaneous answer, which in this case is the wrong one. In contrast, the difficult-to-read font makes people think because it signals that something is wrong. It gives them the opportunity to find out that the spontaneous answer is the wrong one and then to look for the correct answer (see Thompson, Prowse Turner, Pennycook, Ball, Brack, Ophir, and Ackerman 2013 for exceptions, and Alter, Oppenheimer, and Epley 2013 for a reply).

Difficult tasks and difficult art make us think. Unfortunately, evoking analytical thinking comes at a price: We do not like things that are difficult to process. We would not like to read books that were written in a hardly readable font just to make us think. Many people do not watch a movie that is difficult to understand, and neither do they visit an exhibit featuring paintings that have no apparent meaning. This yields the paradoxical situation that artists make things difficult to understand in order to provide the audience with the opportunity to stop and think, but the audience rejects the artist's offer and instead gravitates to works whose meaning is more easily accessible.

How can museum educators bring these more complex works of art to an audience's attention, especially for novices in art? Here, acknowledging that lack of understanding is fine should be the starting point for further explorations into the work. The artist may support the audience in its search for deeper insight by leaving some hints that guide the audience's attention. As Brecht noted, difficulty in drama and other art is not an aim in itself, but should be resolved at the end in order to enable an audience to regain understanding and a sense of ease. In Brecht's own words: "When your work is complete, it must look light, easy. ... You mustn't leave out the difficulties, but must collect them and make them come easy through your work. For the only worthwhile kind of ease is that which is a victory of effort" (Brecht 1964, p. 174). It is like arriving at the peak of a beautiful mountain after a strenuous climbing tour. Look, for example, at Turner's painting *Snow Storm* : If you know the title, the difficulty of perceiving the scene depicted by the painting is made easy and you may focus on how Turner depicted the storm.

This leads us back to desirable difficulties (see Chapter 5). If an audience wants to refine its taste, it should not give up when difficulties emerge. There are various ways in which such difficulties can be understood, and viewers need some background knowledge about the painting, the artist, or the history of the times in order to understand more deeply what an artwork conveys. In a similar vein, critical feeling means that one is not mindlessly satisfied with the first impression in works that seem easy to grasp. The challenge is to see whether there are some deeper questions that lurk beneath the surface.

The role of emotions in art and literature

Emotions play an important role in the philosophy of art because many artists, most prominently during the era of Romanticism, have tried to express emotions in their work. Philosophers of art have always been puzzled by the question of who expresses an emotion in an artwork. It may be the artist, but this is not necessary. Remember that Beethoven is said to have known how music could bring his audience to tears, and that he laughed about it; if true, this almost cynical attitude contradicts the notion that the artist expresses his emotion (Carroll 1999). In a treatise on the role of emotions in art, Jenefer Robinson (2005) noted that the emotion in an artwork is expressed by a *persona*, which could either be the artist or an implied character not identical to the artist. In Beethoven's music, one can imagine how such an implied person feels despite the fact that Beethoven himself had quite different thoughts when composing his tear-provoking music.

Even if art theorists have provided potential solutions to the riddle of who expresses emotions in artworks, the question of what the audience feels still remains. We may be tempted to assume that emotions are elicited automatically, based on our physiology, when we read a novel, view an artwork, or hear music. This view is easy to refute, as Kant (2001/1790) noted (see Kivy 1990 for a discussion). People enjoy hearing a nightingale sing. However, if a human imitator produced the identical sound, people would not like it as much. If paintings or sounds elicit feelings automatically, we should not care whether an artwork has been forged or a bird sound is imitated. As long as the products are identical, they should elicit identical emotions, which apparently is not the case.

We have seen that Bullot and Reber's (2013a) psycho-historical framework can explain why this is not the case. Artworks are not simply stimuli we perceive but artifacts that have a history of creation (as outlined in Figure 9.1). Knowledge about the art-historical context may lead to completely new appraisals of an artwork that change the emotional experience. A series of paintings by Édouard Manet in which he depicts bullfighting nicely exemplifies the principle that we need to know about the context in order to have feelings informed by understanding of the artwork. Looking at a wounded bull, a contemporary audience may feel pity. However, Manet adored bullfighting (see Wilson Bareau 2001). Critical feeling would not deny that pity is an appropriate response to the scene depicted in the painting, but it would recommend taking the perspective of the artist in order to understand the feelings he wanted to express in the painting. Appreciation of Manet's depictions of bullfighting by a contemporary audience is an example of how emotions may change with time (see Elias 1969). In accordance with the principles of appraisal theory (see Chapter 2), appraisals derived from background knowledge about Manet's attitude to bullfighting differ from appraisals of a viewer without that knowledge. In order to enhance critical feeling in Romantic art, it is essential to acquire the relevant knowledge about the context in which the artwork was produced. Proper feeling derives from proper understanding. As outlined in the section on the psycho-historical framework, I follow White (1965) in arguing that proper understanding depends on the weighing of the facts of how we understand a work of art, which thereby ensures that plurality of proper understanding of artworks is maintained.

To sum up, an audience feels an emotion informed by a deeper understanding of an artwork only if the audience possesses the relevant information about the context and the conditions in which the artwork was made. For example, the reader of a novel from a time or culture other than their own may need to know the context in which it was written in order to be able to understand what the protagonists felt, especially if the same event triggers different feelings in the different times or cultures.

Most schools offer art education, and some high schools offer programs that focus on art and music. We can distinguish between two ways of educating a sense of art, and both are relevant to critical feeling.

First, the receptive sense can be educated through viewing art, listening to music, or reading poems and novels. A major problem is how to elicit positive feelings when students must analyze a painting, a piece of music, or a poem (see Noddings 2003). One reason for the lack of interest in art manifest in many children lies in art's lack of connection to the children's life. Poussin's paintings of Arcadia and the symbolism of religious painting in the Renaissance connect back to a past that is remote and unfamiliar. As Dewey (2005/1934) remarked, art has been put on a pedestal and been banned into museums. Only a chosen few, it seems, belong to the circles that regularly enjoy art while many children are excluded from both exposure to art and the acquisition of the knowledge necessary to understand art. The notion of high art is a relatively new invention, dating back to the eighteenth century (see Shiner 2001). Before this time, there was no clear distinction between arts and crafts. People in towns and villages were familiar with the products of local artists and craftsmen.

If teachers want to raise their students' interest in art, they could begin with the decoration of everyday objects – crafts – or with works of art that address topics of timeless interest. For elementary school children, such a topic could be the lives of children in the past or in other countries; for adolescents, love or rebellion; for adults, family life or decline and death. This would correspond to the techniques reviewed in the last chapter for connecting content to the life of the learner. Instead of analyzing a painting (or a poem or text) "to its ruin" (Noddings 2003, p. 103), a teacher may first show how art may tell students something interesting about life in the past, thereby conveying the art-historical context so useful for understanding an artwork.

Teachers may also encourage discussion of how an artwork is relevant to the conduct of life, for art and literature teach us about emotions and may thus provide us with a sentimental education (see Frevert et al. 2014; Nussbaum 1990; Robinson 2005; but see Landy 2012 for a differing viewpoint). When we read literature, we do not only experience pleasure from identifying with the hero and acquire beliefs about the characters and the events in the story; we also get educated in the vagaries of life. As we read, we feel with the characters and sometimes feel against them. If the artwork is close enough to our experience, these feelings may help us reassess parts or the whole of our life. Imagine a young man who cannot imagine loving a woman who is pregnant by another man, even if he is fond of her. A poem such as "Verklärte Nacht" ("Transfigured Night") by Richard Dehmel, later set to music by Arnold Schönberg, may transform his feelings and with them his attitudes more deeply than any scientific treatise about the topic. The moral derived from this poem requires a kind of sensibility that includes the experience of affective qualities to evaluate the situation. In this spirit, Carr (2005) advocates that moral education has to be freed from being purely based on reasoning. Moral knowledge is not merely propositional or factual knowledge but includes moral sensibility and therefore feelings. Thus, art and literature are well suited to educate moral sensibility, especially if a work matches a reader's life situation and therefore elicits interest.

Some teachers may not care about the interests of their students and only try to meet the standards set by classic curricula (Scruton 2007 advocates such an approach to education), based on the idea that at least some children might begin to understand the historical references of art. Such teaching objectives would be, for example, distinction of different styles and epochs; knowledge about art; and love of ancient art and culture. If a teacher aims to enable students to make distinctions between different styles or different eras, they may simply expose students to art, for example in the hallways of the school, promoting implicit learning of styles. However, even when a teacher aims at this more classic form of education, it seems sensible to enable students to connect an artwork to their everyday life or at least to what they already know or love. After having been familiarized with artworks, either through exposure or through discussion of how the work relates to life, students are more likely to be interested in art. Teachers may then begin with more formal training in art analysis. Finally, repeated exposure to art and conceptual fluency related to a rich semantic network due to understanding the artistic context seem to be prerequisites for the love of art and culture; thus, many educators try to convey these aspects to their students.

Teachers must consider how children appreciate art. Based on theories of cognitive development, Parsons (1987) devised a theory of how the understanding of art develops. He distinguished five stages that were roughly related to five phases of life. Preschool children see an artwork as an immediate source of delight. Subject matter begins to play a role for elementary school children: An artwork is beautiful if it is attractive and realistic. Adolescents begin to appreciate the expressive character of art: The more intense and the more interesting the experience that a painting provides, the better it is. Beauty and subject matter, on the other hand, become secondary to expressiveness. Adult viewers see a painting as a social rather than individual achievement. As artists and viewers share the cultural tradition, objective norms of appreciation come to the fore. Paintings have public significance as they become carriers of thoughts and feelings in culture and history. Neither beauty nor meaningfulness nor mere expression by the artist, but rather style and form, become relevant. The last stage is autonomy, where an appreciator weighs the various values of a tradition and provides judgments that are based on reasons. This theory gives teachers information on what kind of art education is appropriate at different stages of human development (see Smith 1988). Exercises relating to style and form may be too advanced for children, for example. Art education may be better started by asking preschool children about the subject matter of a work, which prepares them to consider the representation of objects in a painting, and then about the feelings an artwork elicits, which prepares school children to appreciate the expressive qualities of art.

The second method of educating the art sense comes from art production. Children not only learn to look at or to classify art but also to coordinate their different senses. As noted in Chapter 5, playing the flute depends on multimodal feedback from touching the instrument with mouth and fingers and from hearing the sound. Is it the sound I wanted to produce? The same can be achieved with drawing and writing. A child who draws a horse may execute the necessary movements and then evaluate the result. Is it a horse? This will most likely be a feeling, either of pleasure if the child has achieved the desired result or of disappointment if not (or of relief that the task is finished, regardless of the quality of the drawing). After writing an essay, students may read it and assess whether it achieves the desired effects. Of course, knowing one's intention when writing a text may bias such self-evaluations in a similar way as knowing the communicative intention biases the evaluation of whether an utterance is intelligible for the listener (see Keysar and Barr 2002). Nevertheless, art production, and even crafting artifacts or cooking, help students to develop the coordination of the execution of actions and their evaluation through the senses.

10   RELIGION AND MORALITY

Religion thus makes easy and felicitous what in any case is necessary.

(WILLIAM JAMES 1985/1902, P. 51)

I claimed in previous chapters that more knowledge enables a greater variety of feelings. This is certainly the case when people develop expertise. Wine experts have a wide spectrum of feelings because they have many years of experience in wine tasting and can therefore ground their evaluations in more fine-grained distinctions between different bouquets. A mechanic who understands the workings of an engine has more to enjoy and more to appraise than a novice who has no clue when it comes to engines. However, does richer knowledge broaden the spectrum of religious feelings? There are indications to the contrary. In the case of religion, history suggests that knowledge may overshadow experience, and psychological findings suggest that critical thinking undermines religious belief.

Knowing the workings of nature and technology may bring upon the diminishment of magical thinking and religious feelings. The German sociologist Max Weber (1946/1919) called this phenomenon *disenchantment*. He argued along the following lines: When humans did not understand the workings of nature, they felt awe for a world they did not understand. Nature was understood as the unfathomable work of a god or gods and therefore experienced with enchantment. However, as soon as people think that they understand what is going on inside nature and technology, they lose awe and religious attachment; they become disenchanted. Weber illustrated his theory with the following example: A person who understands the machinery that drives a streetcar – which in Weber's day was a major technical achievement, like smart phones nowadays – has a rational attitude toward this vehicle. Empirical evidence shows that people often overestimate the degree to which they understand technology (Rozenblit and Keil 2002) – who really understands the electronic machinery inside smart phones? However, it is not even necessary that a person understands the mechanics of streetcars or the electronics of smart phones in order to take this rational stance. It suffices that individuals have the impression that they might know how the technology inside a streetcar or a smart phone works to, in theory, become disenchanted.

Of course, one could argue that, the more a believer knows about *religion*, the richer their religious feelings despite their knowledge about the workings of nature and technology. There is certainly a point to this argument. However, the very way Westerners think may prevent many of them from fully appreciating the full and original meaning in religion. The problem has been discussed by Northrop Frye (1982), a scholar who used the tools of literary criticism to analyze the Bible. He distinguished three phases of meaning. In the first phase, statements were meant literally, despite the fact that we nowadays understand them as metaphors. For example, when Adam hid and God asked him, "Adam, where are you?" believers in this ancient mode believe that a physical person named Adam lived and hid and that God literally asked the physical person Adam where he was.

By contrast, later believers saw this story as an allegory of a question about our identity that all of us are confronted with at one time or another (see Buber 1994/1948). In this second phase, roughly from the time of Plato to the Enlightenment, religious language was metonymical in that a statement stood *for* something. It was the great time of allegories, both in religion and literature. For example, the bread stood for the body of Christ and the wine for the blood of Christ. This may also explain the power of medieval religious art, which was thought to convey the meaning of religious allegories. Proper understanding in the sense discussed in the previous chapter meant that believers were able to delve into the religious feelings emanating from depictions of Christ.

In the third phase, most prominent in the modern era, language became descriptive (Frye 1982). This was due to the influence of science, whose language and thought pervaded all domains of life. Statements that had previously had factual status, such as the creation myth and miracles, came under the scrutiny of people who asked the question "Is it true?" Religious feeling yielded to rational analysis. Beliefs in gods were explained with reference to cognitive mechanisms, for example a *hyperactive agency detection device* (Barrett 2004), a theory that posits that people look out for meaningful patterns and find them in the same way they see a face in a cloud (Guthrie 1993). The fact that some religious experiences can be explained by pattern-recognition mechanisms and other brain processes led some scholars (e.g., Dawkins 2006) to the conclusion that belief in god amounts to an illusion. However, religion may be useful for the maintenance of prosociality and of social order (Norenzayan 2013; Norenzayan and Shariff 2008). In terms of De

Sousa's (1987) distinction, religions can be seen as strategically rational but cognitively irrational because many statements in the Bible simply are not true from a scientific standpoint, a fact acknowledged by modern theologians (e.g., Tillich 2001/1957).

Is there empirical evidence for the claim that humans are less religious when language is descriptive? Although there is no direct evidence for this claim, a study by Gervais and Norenzayan (2012) suggests that critical thinking, which includes the ability to observe and describe, makes people less religious. This finding dovetails with results from other studies indicating that people who think more intuitively are more religious (Shenhav, Rand, and Greene 2012) and that healthy individuals who score high in an autism test are less religious (Norenzayan, Gervais, and Trzesniewski 2012), presumably because people prone to autism are less influenced by emotions. To sum up, theory and empirical evidence support the assumption that richer knowledge and the modern mode of critical thinking limit instead of broaden the spectrum of religious feelings. These findings help to explain the current disenchantment with religion and myth.

In contrast to earlier histories of religion, which saw monotheism as the pinnacle of religious development, Gauchet (1997) saw atheism as the endpoint. Early creation myths were superseded by a form of polytheism where the gods were present in everyday life. In the West, this led to a monotheism where one god became more and more distant, a slope that finally led to secularization (see also Tambiah 1990). For Gauchet, the history of religion ends with the absence of a god or gods. However, this does not mean that modern humans lack sensitivity regarding questions previously answered by religions. Even in an atheistic society, there will always be questions about whether there is a reality beyond what we see, problems of meaning, and our identity in the world and universe, or feelings related to the mysterious and numinous (see Gauchet 1997).

In the following section, I shall look at *re-enchantment*, a term used in this book to denote a development from seeing the universe in purely descriptive terms to adopting an affect-rich relationship with the world, including the belief that there are phenomena humans cannot know of in principle and that these phenomena pertain to our *ultimate concerns* (a term used by Tillich 2001/1957). In contrast to some works that delineate how modern humans can become re-enchanted via substitutes for religion, such as spectator sports (Gumbrecht 2009) or ideology (Edelstein 2009), I aim to delineate how believers could achieve re-enchantment not via surrogates of religion but via means that are genuinely religious. In contrast to believers who have to decide which values they want to endorse, scholars do not need to endorse religious aims in order to examine critical feeling for the sake of re-enchantment. In line with White (1965; see also Chapter 1), they may simply ask what course of action would lead to deep and sustainable religiosity if this were the superordinate goal.

Re-enchantment through rituals

In the Western hemisphere, secularization advances, which puts pressure on mainstream churches to become more and more liberal in the sense of loosening the strictness of their rules. Some Protestant churches have yielded to such pressure in the hope of keeping their members in the church. Paradoxically, however, churches that yield to the pressure to be liberal lose the most members whereas strict churches are strongest in terms of participation and commitment (Iannaccone 1994). How can we explain this observation? And how could we reverse this trend? Three variables might account for weakened bonds to religion in the West, and these could be employed in the service of re-enchantment: religious belief, mystic experience, and rituals.

Beliefs, especially in the Christian teachings, have changed in the Western hemisphere (e.g., Hamberg 1991). Scientifically educated people nowadays are less likely to believe in the devil and hell, in God-made creation that lasted one week in contrast to the evolution of earth and life, or in miracles performed by Christ or the saints. If people believe in these ideas, many do so not literally but allegorically. They believe that evil is more abstract in form than a personal devil; that hell is an abstract idea rather than a burning place; that creation can be framed in a manner that does not contradict evolution; and that the miracle of giving eyesight back to a blind person is meant to denote the fact that Jesus provided a religiously blind person with the capacity to see God. Turning back to the old literal faith may help adherents of evangelical churches to find re-enchantment (see Luhrmann 2012) but it would be an unpromising strategy for most others. Most people enlightened by modern education, including some religious scholars, think that religious beliefs should not contradict scientific facts (Baeck 1987/1928; Tillich 2001/1957).

One way in which believers seek re-enchantment is through mysticism, which includes individual experiences of the presence of or oneness with deities that often lead to enhanced sensory states (see Gellmann 2014). I will later look at an experiment on how meditation (Deikman 1963) might contribute to sensory enhancement, but I first focus on another promising strategy to achieve re-enchantment: communal rituals.

It has been shown, for example, that emotions within a relationship converge over time (Anderson, Keltner, and John 2003), suggesting that rituals might help to render emotional experiences within a community similar. Here I focus on research that helps us to understand how culturally shared rituals serve as the "cement" of a community (see Whitehouse and Lanman 2014). Rituals include rule-based actions that, first, are divorced from their usual goals. For example, washing already clean hands in a ritual context does not have the goal of cleaning a body part. Second, these actions are often seen as compulsory; a person has to perform a ritual in a certain cultural context. This may be one reason why rituals are often repeated. Third, rituals take place at special locations that are removed from the environment people live in, for example in a temple or on sacred ground (Boyer and Liénard 2006; Rappaport 1999; Rossano 2012).

How do rituals fit the architecture of the human mind, and what recommendations could we derive for critical feeling in the service of re-enchantment? To answer this question, I look at the functions of rituals and review research about potential mechanisms underlying ritual that are relevant to critical feeling.

The nature of rituals

Rituals are probably derived from ritualized behavior in the animal kingdom, where they signal a disposition to act without executing the action. For example, dogs signal their inferiority by exposing their neck and recognize the other dog's claim over a mate or territory without having to fight a superior adversary. The emotional significance of ritualized behavior in humans can be observed in the affective attunement between mother and infant (Stern 1985; Trevarthen 1985; see also Rossano 2012). If turn taking in face-to-face interaction between mother and child is interrupted, for example by showing the infant a still face of the mother or by disrupting the temporal characteristics of turn taking, the child feels distress.

Humans have the perhaps unique capacity to intentionally ritualize actions (Rossano 2012), and they can use rituals strategically, for example to help alleviate negative feelings due to loss (Norton and Gino 2014). In medieval history, sophisticated rituals were developed for negotiations, such as the surrender of a city and to beg pardon for its population (Althoff 2003). In this section, I am going to look at how, under certain circumstances, community rituals may be a key to re-enchantment because they lead to shared emotional responses, both toward the ritual and toward fellow believers. Moreover, I argue that processing fluency derived from various sources influences affective and cognitive evaluation of rituals and beliefs. The recommendations for instilling re-enchantment can be derived from these potential mechanisms.[1]

Harvey Whitehouse distinguished between two principal kinds of rituals (see Whitehouse and Laidlaw 2004). Infrequent rituals (called *imagistic*) feature intense emotions and high levels of sensory pageantry, including ordeal and mutilation; frequent, routinized rituals (called *doctrinal*) have quite ordinary actions, lower emotional commitment, and a high degree of repetitiveness, such as in the liturgies of the monotheistic religions. I focus here on frequent rituals, which are relevant to a fluency account and therefore to implications for critical feeling, even though saliency in rituals may be related to perceptual fluency and later retrieval fluency. However, infrequent but highly emotional and painful rituals are relatively rare in modern, large societies (Whitehouse and Laidlaw 2004). There are essentially four factors that make doctrinal rituals emotional and memorable. First, rituals are true, though not in the factual sense used in epistemology; second, rituals help to sanctify objects and actions; third, rituals are counterintuitive; and finally, despite a lack of instrumental value, rituals are seen as important (Reber and Norenzayan 2010). Let us discuss these points in turn.

Repetition and truth

The main characteristic of doctrinal rituals is their repetitiveness, which may serve various functions (see Boyer 1992; McCauley and Lawson 2002; Rappaport 1999), such as providing order in chaos or giving believers a sense of eternity, which can be seen as everlasting repetition of the same events. We saw in Chapter 7 that repeated exposure to statements makes them appear more likely to be true when we reviewed marketing and political campaigning. This plays a special role in rituals.

Rappaport (1999) distinguishes two kinds of truth: *factual truth*, where the truth of a belief depends on the correspondence of a belief with an empirical fact (see Kirkham 1992), and *ritual truth*, which is constructed by the exact repetition of religious texts and ritual acts such that every deviation feels wrong. Ritual truth related to religious beliefs, moral norms, or subjective values cannot be asserted through factual evidence. Such evidence can falsify factual truths but not ritual truths. Factual and ritual truths do not necessarily differ, however, in people's subjective experience of them (Shtulman 2013). People often believe in the truth of their religious beliefs in the same way they believe in the fact that tigers are predators. Many such beliefs have been inculcated in childhood and obtain a status of subjective truth similar to factual truth.

Repetition of religious beliefs may yield a sense of fluency if they are repeated often enough. This account helps to explain the observation that religious beliefs are often defended as vigorously as factual statements (see Gibbon 1994/1776–1781, chapter 21, for historical observations; Maio and Olson 1998 for how difficult it is to argue against truisms in the realm of facts). Although people could change their religious beliefs in principle, many believers keep them throughout their life.

So far, we have discussed the truth of beliefs. However, ritual truth does not only pertain to beliefs but also to the precise execution of a ritual action (Boyer 1992; Rappaport 1999). Any deviation from the prescribed way of acting feels wrong to believers. As the exact repetition of a sequence of sanctified actions is seen as the true one, rituals provide stability in the midst of change. This stability is attributed to the fact that the ritual is eternal; it has always been there and it will always be there (see Rappaport 1999).

History proves that it is not easy to change rituals and liturgy. In fact, many new religious movements build on the rituals of predecessors. For example, the *Sanctus*, which is still part of the liturgy of the Roman Catholic Church, is a version of the older Jewish *Kedusha* (Idelsohn 1995/1932, p. 303). In order to win adherents, the Catholic Church allowed groups who converted to Christianity to keep some of their liturgy, which blended with church rituals (Rappaport 1999, p. 339). In the seventh century, missionaries even allowed temples in East Anglia to have two altars, one for the Christian liturgy and the other for sacrifice to demons (Chaney 1970, p. 161). This practice of tolerating converts' liturgy continues to this day, as shown by a recent offer of the authorities of the Vatican to disaffected Anglican priests to keep central elements of their liturgy when they convert to the Catholic Church (Donadio and Goodstein 2009). Such practices demonstrate the importance of the stability of liturgies and show religious leaders and believers alike that it is judicious to keep rituals invariable and uniform.

Repetition in meditation and prayer

Religious beliefs and rituals are not only judged as true but also considered holy. Although such sanctification most probably depends on several factors beyond processing fluency, it may be possible that some forms of meditation and prayer – those that include repetition over a long period of time, such as mantras – increase fluency to a point that a stimulus may become so vivid that it facilitates sanctification. A study illustrates this phenomenon. In twelve sessions over three weeks, Deikman (1963) presented participants with a blue vase and recorded self-reports of their sensations. The participants were instructed to look at the vase without analyzing it, trying to see it as it exists in itself. Over the course of the experiment, participants experienced the blue of the vase as being more intense than at the beginning. Overall, the participants found the session pleasurable, valuable, and rewarding, and they began to be personally attached to the vase. They felt uncomfortable when the vase was removed during the final, thirteenth session. Finally, participants often reported that they were not able to capture their experience with words; this is reminiscent of the ineffability of many religious experiences. Of course, this study does not answer the question of how people sanctify objects and beliefs, but it captures characteristics often seen in ritual, such as heightened intensity of an experience, the positive value of the experience, and its ineffability. People may strategically expose themselves to ritual objects or perform repetitive activities in order to achieve such heightened experiences. For example, believers of an evangelical church reported an increase in the vividness of imagery after extensive practice of praying; this increase was similar to the sensory enhancement observed in Deikman's experiment (Luhrmann 2012). Little is known about how to optimize the effects of repeated exposure, but excessive repetition seems to be a key condition. Another open question pertains to the notion of lack of intentionality as a necessary condition for illumination, which seems to be a by-product of meditative practice that cannot be brought about strategically. Despite some progress in the research on the effects of meditation (see Sedlmeier, Eberth, Schwarz, Zimmermann, Haarig, Jaeger, and Kunze 2012), open questions about meditation's contribution to religious and spiritual experience remain.

Digitalization and simultaneity of stimulation

Passage from one stage of life to another may last several years. Rites of passage have the function of converting such a gradual transition into a digital one (see Rappaport 1999). Digitalization in this context means the conversion of a gradual (analog) state into an all-or-nothing state. An example is a rite of passage that defines an adolescent becoming an adult: In reality, this process is gradual and may last two years or more. In many cultures, rites to accelerate this transition exist. When a ritual defines a transition, the state of the adolescent becomes certain: Before the ritual, he is a child; after the ritual, an adult. In fact, the only period of uncertainty about the status of adulthood includes the duration of the rite. Without a rite of passage, believers have a vague feeling of being a child or an adult; when such rites exist, they know it for sure, and they may feel anticipatory joy (or – if the ritual is painful – fear) before the rite yet be proud of their new and elevated status after it. According to Reber and Norenzayan (2010), these observations suggest that members of a culture with clear boundaries should have a clear sense of their identity, and they should feel more positively about their identity than people in cultures with fuzzy boundaries. These assumptions about feelings before and after rites of passage await further research.

Another feature is the simultaneity of multimodal stimulation – for example, images, music, odors, and one's own body movements (Rappaport 1999, p. 257). It is plausible to assume that multimodal, coherent components in religious services facilitate communication and coordination among performers of the ritual (see Sosis 2003) and increase the ease with which beliefs and ritual actions can be retrieved. This increase in fluency presumably increases liking and the experienced accuracy of beliefs and actions. In addition, if stimulation in each modality results in the same affective response, such as awe, multimodality presumably enhances these effects.

Religious rituals that include praying, marching in processions, music, singing, and dancing result in synchronous behavior of the believers. These joint activities may increase memory for details of interaction partners (Macrae, Duffy, Miles, and Lawrence 2008), mutual liking (Marsh, Richardson, and Schmidt 2009), trust (Wiltermuth and Heath 2009), and strengthened collective identity (Páez et al., 2015). Synchrony results in higher interpersonal fluency, which, in turn, increases mutual liking (see Chapter 5). In sum, religious communities increase mutual bonds between their members by letting them act together.

Counterintuition in rituals

Stories, folktales, and ballads are transmitted orally and need to be memorized (Conway and Schaller 2007; Rubin 1995). What factors influence the transmission of religious rituals? Religious rituals often include counterintuitive agents that are believed to engage in actions involving special objects, in an otherwise ordinary process of an action-representation system (Boyer 2001; McCauley and Lawson 2002; Rappaport 1999, p. 289). One cognitive explanation for this phenomenon is derived from the observation that slightly counterintuitive content is better remembered. This led theorists to conclude that rituals with minimally counterintuitive contents are selected (Atran and Norenzayan 2004; Barrett and Nyhof 2001; Norenzayan, Atran, Faulkner, and Schaller 2006). Experimental demonstrations of the memory advantage of slightly counterintuitive stories fit the observation that information that is effortful to process elicits more active elaboration and leads to better memory performance (e.g.,

Benjamin et al. 1998; Diemand-Yauman et al. 2011; Gardiner, Craik, and Bleasdale 1973). Counterintuitive content, as long as it does not depart too much from common sense, at first may be moderately disfluent but may become more fluent with repetition.

Counterintuitive but fluent content may help to distinguish a group's own ritual from rituals of other groups. One way this could happen is as follows: If a group repeats counterintuitive rituals, it will obtain fluency advantages compared to members of outgroups that do not practice this specific ritual. As a consequence, interpersonal fluency increases among members of the ingroup. What members of the ingroup do feels right; what members of the outgroup do feels wrong. It therefore seems commendable for any religious group to develop rituals that are counterintuitive, but only slightly so. If the contents of rituals are excessively counterintuitive, this process may break down, as an overload of information would place too much strain on comprehension and memory in the first place (e.g., Atran and Norenzayan 2004; Boyer 2001).

The experienced importance of rituals

If the process of making a decision is surprisingly difficult, people infer that the decision must be important (Sela and Berger 2012). However, the effect of processing difficulty on judged importance is moderated by another variable. Labroo, Lambotte, and Zhang (2009) presented descriptions of law cases, mathematical theorems, and scientific findings in their study. For half of the participants, these descriptions were named (e.g., *Weierstrass theorem* in the case of the description of a mathematical theorem); for the other half, no name was given. Participants were furthermore assigned to a memorability condition and to an understandability condition: Participants in the memorability condition had to recall the description; participants in the understandability condition had to think about whether they understood the description. At the end of the experiment, participants provided a judgment of importance of a case, theorem, or finding. The authors found that, under the memorability condition, naming led to judgments of higher importance, and ease of processing mediated the effect between naming and importance judgments. In the understandability condition, by contrast, naming decreased judged importance, and ease of processing again mediated the effect. Labroo and colleagues concluded that judged importance is influenced by the ease with which information can be processed. This effect, however, depends on whether one tries to remember or to understand the information: Easy-to-remember information is seen as being important, whereas easy-to-understand information is seen as being unimportant.

Note how neatly this result explains the experienced importance of liturgy: Rituals often have a name and are highly memorable, either through salience or through frequent repetition (see Whitehouse and Laidlaw 2004). However, the beliefs behind the rituals are often mysterious and difficult to understand (Boyer 1992, p. 87–88). Both high memorability and low understandability contribute – if Labroo et al.'s (2009) finding can be generalized – to the experienced importance of rituals. Fluent but ineffable rituals are not only liked and feel right; they are also deemed important.

Other sources of re-enchantment

I have discussed processing fluency as a potential mechanism underlying re-enchantment. Fluency explains the effects of repetition on the experienced truth of beliefs and ritual actions, of regular practice in meditation, of digitalization and synchronization on positive affect, of the counterintuitiveness of rituals and beliefs on feelings toward the ingroup and the outgroup, and of the combined effects of memorability and lack of understanding on the perceived importance of rituals.

Phenomena and mechanisms other than fluency may contribute to re-enchantment. A first source of enchantment is belief in an afterlife and in communion with the dead, for example saints who exert their influence in this life (Jaeger 2012). This view requires that one doubts the principle that everything can be explained by science (see Weber, 1958a). This notion leads to a second source of re-enchantment: the mystery of what is and what cannot be explained by science. Dawkins (2006) wrote that people may feel awe regarding the workings of nature. However, given that people do not seem to feel enchantment regarding what they could know in principle, it is unlikely that a purely scientific worldview could ever lead to enchantment as a secular religion. Third, hypersensitivity in pattern recognition (Barrett 2004; Guthrie 1993) may be enchanting because suddenly recognizing a pattern from a disorderly array may yield aha-experiences in which people sometimes see mystical quality (see Noddings and Shore 1984). Although aha-experiences can be explained scientifically (Chapter 8) and the patterns could be explained away as illusions of the mind, people may still feel awe at the fact that they can associate those patterns with deeper meaning. In fact, some believers actively search for meanings of such patterns as signs of God (see Luhrmann 2012). Fourth, there is an aesthetic quality to religion. The beauty of the sea and the mountains, the subtlety of the designs of nature and the greatness of the overall design of the world, the naïve happiness of children, the musicality of interactions (Malloch 2000) – all contribute to a feeling that transcends scientific explanation. Fifth, people may experience unity with a deity or the universe – "that submergence of self in communion with Divine perfection" (Eliot 1994/1871, p. 20) – that believers see as a testimony for the possibility of overcoming the separation of mind and nature (e.g., Buber 2004/1923). Finally, people's questions about their place in the world may ever inspire looking for meaning even in a secular age. For many of these phenomena, we do not yet have satisfactory scientific explanations based on evidence. Factual truth plays a minor role for many experiences, even in a secular world. Things can be mysterious, awesome, beautiful, great, or full of meaning (see Gauchet 1997). These qualities transcend the power of reason and have led some scholars to claim that "religion is here to stay" (Markham 2010, p. 128).

Note that all of these phenomena have to do with form but not with belief. This may explain why people with vastly different beliefs may be enchanted, and why people with highly sophisticated beliefs may be disenchanted. As for the former, people with different beliefs may maintain the outer forms that are necessary to remain enchanted. Although these forms look very different from the outside, they share essential features, such as repetition, regularity, digitalization, synchrony, minimal counterintuitiveness, high memorability, and at the same time low intelligibility. By contrast, sophisticated systems of theology (such as the one by Tillich 1951–1963) may be in line with enlightened thought. However, they do not warm the heart of the individual and do not mobilize the masses. Modern humans in the West have apparently not only lost their beliefs but also the forms of those beliefs. Critical feeling in the service of re-enchantment means that, whatever the belief is, communities may try to build rituals that symbolize or enact what is sanctified. We may arrive at new beliefs, but the underlying mechanisms of the forms will remain the same; they are the only ones that enchant humans. One may ask whether any belief would do. Interestingly enough, rites of passage equivalent to baptisms and weddings have been known to strictly secular systems such as communism in Russia (where infants were *Octobered* instead of baptized; see Figes 1996, p. 747).

Yet do such rites really lead to enchantment? Could a purely scientific worldview be accompanied by rituals that illuminate adherents? It is an empirical question whether rituals have to be tied to the sacred in order to unfold their effects. This sanctification may require a form of unquestioned commitment and thus the acknowledgment of a mystery of faith that is foreign to the scientific worldview as scientists scrutinize every action, and asking why we have to perform an action spoils enchantment.

In summary, reintroducing rituals into our spiritual life may contribute to bringing back the enchantment many people long for. However, there seems to be an additional ingredient necessary to experience enchantment. We do not know exactly what this ingredient is, even though the various religions certainly propose the ones they think are most effective. I have outlined some necessary conditions for enchantment but they are certainly not sufficient.

Reducing religions to ritual would be too narrow a view. Believers not only long for enchantment but also for moral guidance from religion (e.g., Clark and Dawson 1996). The implementation of values plays an important role. Moral attitudes do not always translate into moral behavior, as the saying "the spirit is willing, but the flesh is weak" (Matthew 26:41) testifies. In the next section, I look at how people can implement the values they stand for so that the flesh is no longer weak when the spirit is willing.

The acquisition of moral habits

John Dewey (1909) distinguished between teaching morality and teaching about morality. Swimming lessons served as an analogy. A girl who learns to swim does this best in a pool where a teacher tells her how to move and how to breathe. Her practice provides her with immediate feedback about the success of her efforts. We do not generally ask children to practice swimming on land when we explain to them how to move. Although demonstrating some movements on land and repeating them before going into the water might be useful in some situations, it is usually best to swim in order to learn swimming. Correspondingly, moral dilemmas may be fun to discuss, but they do not provide us with the practical training we need in order to retrieve the right answer in any morally relevant situation.

Why is learning about morality not as useful as learning morality? One reason might be that we do not receive feeling-based feedback when moral judgment is the result of a mere exercise of reasoning. In the eleventh century, the Persian philosopher and theologian Al-Ghazzali (cited in James 1985/1902) noted that possessing all theoretical knowledge about being drunk is not the same as having the experience of being drunk. Although Al-Ghazzali applied the metaphor to religiosity, it can be used to illustrate moral emotions as well. Learning about feeling regret is not the same as feeling regret; theoretical knowledge about the emotion of guilt is not the same as the personal experience of guilt.

Western moral philosophy since Kant and Mill could be seen as instruction about morality. Kant introduced the idea that human beings should reason from a sense of duty. This has been called *deontological ethics*. In a famous example, Kant (2011/1785) noted that, when a merchant is honest and does not cheat his customers, his behavior is not ethical if he follows a natural inclination to be honest. His behavior is ethical only if he is honest out of a sense of duty. Mill (2002/1863) developed *utilitarianism* as an ethical theory. The basic idea is that people should behave in a way that brings the highest utility by maximizing benefits and minimizing harm, such as suffering. For example, if you have to decide to save the life of five people or the life of one, you should decide to save the life of five. This idea is intuitively unappealing if you would have to actively kill one person in order to save five lives. The famous example is a trolley that is rolling in the direction of five workers and that will kill them if nobody intervenes. Let's assume you have the opportunity to flick a switch in order to save the five lives, but then the trolley would kill one worker who is on another track. Despite the differences between deontological and utilitarian ethics, they share one important feature. Both approaches see moral decision making as the outcome of reasoning about rules (see Chapter 1); that is why moral education teaches about morality. This has not changed since Kant and Mill proposed their ethical theories (e.g., see the famous Neo-Kantian theory by Rawls in his *Theory of Justice*, 1971).

By contrast, virtue ethicists advocate the practice of morality in real situations. In his *Nicomachean Ethics*, Aristotle (2004/ca. 350 BCE) argued that we learn virtues like we learn skills (see Annas 2011 for a modern summary and extension of this theory). Comparably, Confucius saw moral education as training in cultural forms; morality in virtue ethics is not an intellectual exercise but embodied (Seok 2013; Sim 2007; Slingerland 2014). As discussed in Chapter 5, we know quite a bit about the acquisition of virtues if we use skill learning as an analogy. However, in contrast to China, where the system of Confucian virtue ethics was the foundation of the entrance exam for Chinese civil servants from 1313 until 1910, the currency of Aristotelian virtue ethics and its feeling component declined in Western thought and have been revived only in recent decades in Western philosophy. As outlined in Chapter 1, this book does not focus on character but on the right behavior in a given situation. The right action is the one that accords with one's values or the values of one's community. In line with both the action-centered approach and virtue ethics, we may ask how people over the course of their life come to reliably perform the right actions in a given situation.

The functions of feelings in moral judgment and action

Instead of eliminating feelings from moral decisions, we might aim to develop feelings in such a way that they assist us in making the right moral decisions and in acting virtuously. Feelings can have at least four functions in moral behavior.

First, as outlined in Chapter 3, feelings guide our attention. They tell us what is important (see De Sousa 1987 and Sherman 1989 for the same idea in Aristotelian ethics). For example, anger indicates that some-one else is about to harm us; outrage tells us that an action is trespass-ing on moral norms or social conventions. We then focus our attention to the relevant aspects of the situation in order to prevent harm in the case of anger, or to enforce compliance with norms and conventions in the case of outrage. Instead of suppressing feelings, people might better learn what feelings are appropriate in certain situations. There may be situations where anger is appropriate, but in most situations it is not. Reappraisal of past events that elicited the wrong feelings may help to shape our feelings as a response to similar future events. If we were able to acquire the ability to "recall" the right feelings in all or at least most situations, we could follow their lead to direct our attention and prepare for action. Moreover, as the appropriate response to an event depends on the contextual factors of the situation, we have to learn how to assess the situation flexibly.

This leads to the second function of feelings in ethics, which is motivating actions. Each emotion has an action tendency that people spontaneously follow unless they check their feelings and control their action, for example using a stop-and-think rule. Instead of preventing feelings from motivating our actions, we might better learn what actions are appropriate as a response to feelings such that we can implement our values – for example, so that we do not just snap and attack when we are angry but first communicate our anger in order to enable the other per-son to take remedial action. The trained response elicited by the feeling is not necessarily a rigid behavior bound to the feeling but could be an action plan that is derived from both the feeling and the assessment of the situation in order to enable us to respond flexibly. If we were able to associate the appropriate action with our feelings, we would need fewer cognitive resources to adapt the response in order to align our behavior with what is seen as adequate in the given situation. This means that we could act spontaneously and would have a good chance of acting rightly.

The third function of feelings in moral action is the assessment of whether the response is adequate. In Chapter 3, we saw that feelings may indicate that our actions do not correspond to our moral values and looked at various examples, such as feeling scruples, hiding information, and noting that our feelings stem from a source that is irrelevant as a guide to action. When we assess the moral appropriateness of an action, we can listen to feelings in addition to reason. Adherents of critical thinking might argue that we should set feelings aside and try to apply reasoning about moral rules to analyze whether our action was appropriate – for example, what would have been our duty, or what would have been the action that brought the greatest benefit to the most people. I noted above that it is difficult to exclude feelings, and many people justify their current action as being right a posteriori instead of conducting a balanced evaluation (see Chapter 1). As an alternative to the repression of feelings when assessing an outcome, we may learn to feel good when our action is virtuous and to feel bad when our action lacks virtue. The ability to accurately assess the outcomes of our actions by consulting our feelings would obviate the need for cumbersome analytic processing and lead to a smoother stream of thought and action.

All three of the functions of feelings discussed so far serve the purpose of enabling virtuous and spontaneous action. Although virtuous action is not warranted even if we learn what the right feelings are and how we should employ them, the use of feelings to guide attention, to motivate our action, and to assess outcomes increases the chances of virtuous action and saves cognitive resources so that they are available for other tasks.

There is a fourth function of feelings that seems unique to virtuous action in living together with others. When a friend suffers the loss of her spouse, it is appropriate to show compassion and warmth. We could do this in two ways, either by expressing what we know is appropriate or by expressing what we feel. It is easy to show empathy if our expressions derived from feeling correspond to our expressions derived from reason. We all know that this is not always the case. Sometimes, the disagreement between our own feeling and what we ought to feel stems from an outside event that colors our affect. For example, a young woman may be cheerful because she just heard that her beloved reciprocates her affection. She may have a hard time putting her feelings aside to show compassion for a bereaved friend.

Darker feelings that one should not tell a bereaved friend lurk beyond the joys of love and success. If I felt secret joy because I had a negative attitude toward the deceased person, or if I paradoxically and against my will felt *Schadenfreude* instead of compassion (see De Sousa 1987 for a discussion of such inappropriate feelings), I would have to resort to the expression of what I knew to be appropriate instead of the expression of what I felt in such a situation. However, lacking the feeling of compassion would lack virtue even if I could perfectly emulate the expression of compassion (see Annas 2011 for a detailed discussion).

Again, as for the other functions of feelings in moral action, removing feelings would be wrong. We may try to shape our feelings, both in the short term and in the long term. To address our feelings in the short term may help us to cope with the situation at hand. Before we visit our friend, we may turn our attention to the feelings we deem to be wrong; this leads to meta-awareness. If we had a negative attitude toward the deceased, we may accept that fact and focus on our bereaved friend, or try to look at the deceased from different perspectives in order to obtain a more positive attitude, enabling us to feel real compassion. In the long term, we may try to sort out the sources of our *Schadenfreude* or look into the triggers of paradoxical feelings. To my knowledge, there has been hardly any research about the best way to cope with such inappropriate feelings; the proposed measures thus await further research.

The paradoxes of Confucianism

As discussed in Chapter 5, proponents of virtue ethics since Aristotle have used a skill analogy for the learning of virtue (see Annas 2011). Even earlier than Aristotle in Greece, Confucius in China developed a virtue ethics based on the idea that a good citizen needs to learn the ritual forms of the old times. Such training enables a citizen to retrieve the right moral decision without mental effort (see Slingerland 2003a). Although one might object that the cultural forms acquired in ancient China, such as the odes, are outdated, Confucius is an excellent starting point for the role of critical feeling in moral action; I follow Reber and Slingerland's (2011) discussion of three paradoxes in Confucian virtue ethics.

The solutions to two paradoxes in Confucian thought involve processing fluency. The first paradox goes like this: Why do people have to overcome often great difficulties to learn to act with ease? Why can the state of effortless action only be attained through extended, effortful training in cultural forms (see Slingerland 2003a, 2003b, 2010)? The need to overcome this difficulty is, according to Confucius, the main reason why many people do not like learning to be a good person. He exposed a riddle of human learning that research could only unravel some 2500 years later when Baddeley and Longman (1978) observed a similar paradox in skill learning, as reviewed in Chapter 5. Let us remember that the group with distributed practice had superior learning outcomes but liked their learning experience *less* than the group with blocked practice, which resulted in inferior learning outcomes. However, learners lack insight into this phenomenon.

According to Confucius, people have to overcome morally insufficient natural or dominant responses in order to refine their behavior. By repeated training of cultural forms, which increases fluency, individuals acquire new habits that become dominant responses; they acquire a *second nature*. Confucius realized that intensive, lifelong practice is needed in order to internalize cultural forms, but he did not seem to have the knowledge or an intuition about the distribution of practice and its consequences for liking the learning process.

The second paradox pertains to the question "How one can force oneself to love something one does not already love?" (Slingerland 2003a, p. 13). The answer is provided by fluency theory, which assumes that ease of processing yields positive affect. This observation helps to explain not only the power of rituals but also how people come to like activities or readings they repeat because they deem them morally appropriate. Performing a duty may be tedious at the beginning; however, as discussed in Chapter 5, positive affect may be part of skill acquisition, depending on the learning schedule. Due to repeated exposure, liking the learning process is different from liking the retrieval process; while the learning process is disliked, ease of retrieval elicits positive effect. Disfluent and therefore disliked learning may yield fluent retrieval that is accompanied by positive feelings (Baddeley and Longman 1978; Simon and Bjork 2001, 2002). It is therefore of uttermost importance to persist in the face of these desirable difficulties during the learning process in order to later earn the fruits of fluent understanding and smooth execution of action (see the earlier mentioned study by Oyserman et al. 2006). Smooth execution and its ensuing positive affect are the rewards of persistence, in line with the finding on meditation by Deikman (1963).

Moreover, verbatim repetition of actions makes them true in the sense I discussed in the previous section, on rituals. We might thus use repetition of actions and events to enhance the feeling of the rightness and pleasure of moral actions. We do not have to force ourselves to love what we do not already love; we can still come to love what we do not love already. The secret is repetition of an activity even in the face of difficulty – by increasing the outcome fluency of the same action, we will begin to love what we have not loved before, to state this phenomenon in Confucius' terms. Such newly acquired habits do not need to be rigid and mindless. In fact, Vaughn, Dubovi, and Niño (2013) observed that processing fluency affected behavior more strongly when participants were high rather than low in trait mindfulness, supporting the notion of virtue ethics that moral habits can be mindful and flexible. An example of mindful repetition might include Bible studies in which the reader of the scriptures tries to extract new meanings from each new reading of the same passage (see Baeck 1987/1928).

A third paradox is related to what has been called the *paradox of virtue* (Nivison 1996, p. 31–43; see also Reber and Slingerland 2011): A deed is only virtuous if done without the intention of obtaining virtuousness, or even any conscious awareness of being virtuous. This is a crucial difference from skill acquisition: In contrast to virtuous action, a skill remains a skill even if done for extraneous or egoistic reasons. Although the question of intentional states and virtue has to my knowledge not been addressed directly in moral psychology, research on the conscious pursuit of happiness – intentional activity aimed at achieving a state of happiness – seems to become relevant here. I discussed these observations in Chapter 4, where we saw that trying to achieve happiness consciously is counterproductive. Like happiness, virtue seems to be a by-product of behavior that cannot be brought about consciously (Elster 1983).

The work of Jonathan Haidt (2001, 2007) testifies that people often do not have insights into their moral judgments. Essentially, when people have to reason about moral dilemmas such as eating dogs, they exhibit great difficulty in giving coherent reasons in favor of their moral intuition. As in the affective domain, people are not skilled at verbalizing the reasons behind their moral intuitions. Monitoring the virtuousness of actions may undermine real virtue because the outcome of reasoning processes undertaken in order to attain virtue may differ from the outcome of intuitive processes that happen when one is acting virtuously for its own sake. Paradoxically, moral agents may forego some of the positive affective consequences of virtuous deeds if they monitor their virtuousness too closely, because action then lacks spontaneity.

People can try to fake virtue by simulating virtuous behavior; this would not be virtuous because the deed would not be accompanied by the right feeling (Sherman 1989). However, according to Elster (1983), the act of faking can become self-defeating when a person does not intend to be virtuous but becomes so as a by-product of her behavior. In line with religious thought in Judaism, this phenomenon could be seen in a more positive light in that a person could begin to act in order to adopt moral beliefs (Baeck 1987/1928). However, neither Elster nor Baeck explored the psychological mechanism behind this phenomenon. In accordance with an analysis by Sosis (2003), the perception of one's own behavior might influence one's attitudes (e.g., Bem 1972). Reber and Slingerland's (2011) analysis of the paradox in Confucian thought suggests that repeated simulation of a behavior presumably increases its fluent execution, which increases both the positive affect and the experienced truth of the beliefs behind the simulated actions (see also the previous section, on rituals). Therefore, one strategy for acquiring virtue is just doing as if we acted virtuously, even if we hate to do it. However, such recommendations have to be made with caution. To my knowledge, there is no research about the self-defeating effects of simulating virtuous behavior.

The paradoxes and their solutions are as topical nowadays as they were in Confucius' time. Given that people choose to repeat experiences they like, as shown by research on selective exposure (Zillmann and Bryant 1985), it is not surprising that they circumvent the effortful training that is necessary to overcome their dominant responses. Surprisingly, people do not seem to have an intuition that what has been learned with effort may be retrieved with ease. Critical feeling begins with acknowledging the fact that difficulty with training is often desirable and results in ease of executing a skill. Overcoming the tendency of hedonic adherence to dominant responses means that people first need to explore what they want to strive for. Once they know what beliefs and actions they like to foster, they simply expose themselves to appropriate statements as a strategy to inculcate these beliefs or repeat actions in a ritualized manner until they become habit. When believers later encounter statements that correspond to their creeds, these assertions *feel right*. Essential to critical feeling, this feeling of rightness along with the ease and positive affect experienced when encountering the belief provide subjective criteria for the progress a person has made in the practice of the correct belief. Here we return to our discussion on ritual in the previous section. "The moral significance that makes an attitude or behavior normative is first *felt*, and this feeling is transmitted *ritualistically*," as Rossano (2012, p. 5, italics in the original) noted. In the same vein, when people encounter a situation in which they need to act rightly, the action will be elicited automatically because it has become a habit. That sounds promising but is prone to bias. Empirical research needs to examine to what degree and in what situations we can trust a feeling that either elicits an action or gauges its rightness.

To summarize, if people want to change their moral outlook, they may choose to expose themselves to the moral beliefs and practices that they want to adopt. Gradually, the adopted belief or practice will not only be represented in their cognitive and action systems but will also feel right. After some time of having been exposed to the right thoughts and acts, we can realistically hope to become good people by doing the right actions without effort – just by doing what feels right.

There is a downside, though. When I gave a talk at the University of Southern California, a listener in the audience asked whether the training of moral habits would not be a recipe for *un*critical feeling. The reason is that, when people repeat an action over and over again, it becomes a rigid habit that cannot be changed at will because the underlying thought becomes inaccessible (or intransparent; Carruthers 2011). There are two possible answers to this criticism. The first is that, yes, in the end, it is a rigid habit. Critical feeling does not come into play at this point – by then it is too late – but at the outset, when believers decide which values they want to implement and by what means. They can start flexibly but end up rigidly. Such practice requires commitment to a value and an understanding that a habit cannot easily be changed if believers happen to change their commitment. Deciding and then repeating applies to adult believers. Children, by contrast, do not choose their own values and therefore do not start flexibly. Religious educators may transmit beliefs by mere repetition in such a way that education indeed becomes indoctrination that leads to uncritical feeling and mindless creed. Likewise, moral attitudes may be drilled in such a way that they will be retrieved inflexibly when a relevant situation arises, leading to uncritical feeling.

The second answer negates that feeling needs to be uncritical even in the end. Dewey's (2012/1922) notion of habit is more flexible than the concept of habit as it is used in psychology (e.g., Ouellette and Wood 1998; Wood, Labrecque, Lin, and Ruenger 2015). In this understanding, one could develop mindful and complex habits of thinking. For example, if I hear an opinion, I may acquire the habit to always ask what the opposite would be. This view raises some questions. For example, are such apparently mindful habits in the end as rigid as habits of behavior? Could we be mindlessly mindful? Dual-processing theories (see Chaiken and Trope 1999) would suggest that we have to live with a tradeoff. We may be committed to a value and to developing fast but fixed response patterns that pop up spontaneously in the appropriate situations. The assessment of the outcome can be informed by feelings. Alternatively, we can maintain the flexibility of responses but remain slow because we have to analyze the outcome in order to assess our actions. Further theory and research will hopefully bridge the gap between these two modes of moral action but, at the moment, there is no magic bullet that enables us to act flexibly but fast and with the possibility of assessing the rightness of an action by using our feelings as information.

The role of friends

Friends may be seen as people who have the same interests as we do, and as people with whom we can have fun and whom we trust. Aristotle, by

contrast, saw the function of friendship in enhancing each other's morality. Indeed, Youniss (1985) found that adolescents saw one function of
friendship as being to learn from each other. If we assume that "learning
from each other" means mutual enhancement, be it of thought, feeling,
or action, adolescents ascribe to friendship, among other functions, the
moral function Aristotle had in mind.

Friends and other people may also serve to gauge our happiness
and virtue. I have discussed how people may gauge their future happiness
under the assumption that they are rich by observing *surrogates* who are
richer than they are (Gilbert 2006; see Chapter 4). Surrogates may also
provide information about how happy individuals are after acting morally or immorally. Friends may be well suited to be such surrogates. It
would be interesting to extend Gilbert's idea such that individuals gauge
not only happiness but also morality by observing surrogates. For example, Ellen, a university student, may not see the immorality of cheating
during an exam when she looks at herself. However, if she looked at her
friend Fred while he cheats during an exam, she would presumably see
that he is getting an advantage without merit. In other words, people may
be much better able to properly see immoral behavior in others than in
themselves. This idea is supported by Epley and Dunning's (2000) observation that people systematically overestimate their own morality when
they have to predict how they will act whereas predictions of the behavior of others are more accurate.

Being virtuous and being happy

Since Aristotle, philosophers have claimed that virtuous people are also
happy people. However, do we not all know people who at least looked
happy but lacked virtue? Do we not all know people who were virtuous
but died miserably? Or look at William James' (1985/1902) notion of
the moralist who adheres to moral norms out of a sense of duty. Kant
(2011/1785) saw this sense of duty as a necessary condition for moral
action, and one might argue that it elicits the feelings that have to accompany virtue. However, James distinguished between the moralist and the
religious person. While the moralist does the right thing out of a sense of
duty, the religious person does her duty with joy, as James put it in the
epigraph of this chapter.

One solution to the problem of virtue and happiness is redefining
the latter. After all, being virtuous is not the same as eating a juicy steak
or lying on the beach, which corresponds to the notion of happiness as
pleasure. When we talk about a virtuous person being happy, we rather
think of a deep contentment with life than of the satisfaction of vivid

but transient desires. Annas (2011) discusses at length the idea that psychologists and social scientists use the wrong notion of happiness when they define it as a state in which our desires are fulfilled. She proposes that Aristotelian *eudaimonia* (which can be translated as "happiness" or "flourishing") does not include the fulfillment of needs and desires but the actualization of a person, which means that a person also realizes his or her moral potential. Happiness thus requires a virtuous character. Such a person is a flourishing person (also Seligman 2011). The question arises whether this notion of happiness satisfies the requirements of a good definition. Happiness is defined in a way that is dependent on virtue; it would therefore be more accurate to define happiness in a way that is distinct from virtue. It would then become an empirical question whether virtue makes people happy or not. In fact, defining happiness not as short-term satisfaction of desires but as long-term contentment with life may be close to what Annas had in mind. Such a definition would meet the criterion that happiness is distinct from virtue and at the same time would help us to find a proper definition that leads to a testable hypotheses. Indeed, Diener and Kesebir (2013) reviewed evidence that virtue and happiness augment each other – that is, that virtue increases happiness and happiness increases virtue, in line with the broaden-and-build hypothesis (Fredrickson 2013) discussed in Chapter 4.

One could turn the question around and ask whether it is not happiness in the sense of desire satisfaction that prevents people from being virtuous. In fact, happiness in that sense may not even make us happy because our desires increase with their fulfillment, as discussed in Chapter 4. We get used to a certain standard of living and increase our aspiration level. It seems that desires stand in the way of both virtue and happiness – and, therefore, we would have to get rid of desire in order to become both virtuous and happy. We might heed the wisdom of the stoics that it is better to desire what we have instead of longing for what we desire (Epictetus 1991/ca. 125 CE).

This is easier said than done. Reports of temptations from early Christianity to modern times – most famously the temptation of St. Anthony (see Flaubert 2010/1874 for a literary account) – testify that desires are not easily kept at bay. What could critical feeling contribute to immunization against the tyranny of desires? We should certainly not suppress them. Empirical evidence suggests that suppressing thoughts backfires in that they come back with stronger force (Wegner et al. 1987). Even in solitude in the desert, desires and temptations were omnipresent in the early Christian monks who tried to suppress and overcome them (see Ward 1975). A better way may be meta-awareness: I am the one who has these desires; they are in no way objective. Accepting these desires as being my thoughts may alleviate some of the negative feelings stemming from not fulfilling them. Setting lower aspiration levels may help, too: Instead of dreaming about the upper limits of some desire, I may ask about the lower limits I am willing to accept, or about the lower limits that are sufficient for living. Finally, we may remove temptations from the environment or select environments that do not lead us into temptation. Early monks used this latter solution in a radical way by becoming eremites in the desert. In a less radical way, we may elude seductive environments in order to live in accordance with our best intentions.

The first part of this chapter looked at the role of rituals in maintaining or regaining enchantment and the second part at the implementation of moral action. Teachers at non-religious schools may educate pupils about religion from an anthropological viewpoint – but this amounts to swimming on land. To know religion, a person has to be immersed in religious life, ideally from childhood onwards.

I discussed Bourdieu's studies on the development of tastes in art. Reproduction of religious beliefs and practices is likely to work in a similar way (Stump 2008). Children learn through repeated exposure the rituals and the liturgy of their religion. Much of this learning is implicit. That is why some rituals lack symbolic meaning even though they are important to the person (Staal 1979). Rituals get their power from both repetition and uniformity. Practices that include synchronous activities, such as praying, walking in a procession, or singing, build up collective identity (Páez et al. 2015) and create social cohesion (see Reber and Norenzayan 2010). In a similar vein, orchestrating visual, auditory, motor, and other experiences within a liturgy stimulates all senses and provides an experience of unity (Rappaport 1999). Religious leaders have known this for a long time and exploited the susceptibility of humans to such experiences by providing both social and physical contexts that maximally support the activities during liturgy. As noted earlier, these contexts and activities become the truth (Boyer 1992; Rappaport 1999). In addition, they have a communal aspect in that believers who practice rituals become absorbed in a shared activity. Religious education may facilitate the experience of community without promoting dogmatic beliefs (see Carse 2008).

Religious or moral education should not result in mindless application of what has been inculcated. It should explain and build the meaning of beliefs and practices, looking at them from various angles, and then offer extended practice so that an activity can be executed smoothly. Practice has to be distributed and varied; that is, we have to apply a belief or moral action in various settings, under various conditions. Religious practices should not be simple stimulus–response pairings but include more and more complex habits for analyzing a situation in accordance with one's own creed, as envisioned by Dewey (2012/1922). This order of building a belief or practice, followed by taking different perspectives, extended practice, and flexible application, is inspired on the one hand by the stage pedagogy of Aebli (2011/1983), who derived it from Ziller (1876), and on the other hand by the mindfulness approach to learning advocated by Langer (1997; see Reber 2014 for a recent review). However, as mentioned earlier, further research should test the feasibility of learning to apply complex habits flexibly. Much would be gained if we were able to achieve this feat.

EPILOGUE

Building on critical thinking, I have developed the concept of critical feeling and reviewed some potential applications. This work lies at the intersection of philosophy, psychology, and education. I focused on psychology, which provides the empirical basis for interventions that make use of feelings in order to improve outcomes. As we have seen, there is already psychological research that informs critical feeling, but much more could be done.

In order to implement critical feeling, psychological research needs to be embedded in philosophical thought and implemented in educational practice. Insights from the philosophy of education, moral philosophy, theory of science, epistemology, and the philosophy of art provide us with the right questions for empirical research. Philosophy of education introduced the concept of critical thinking. Moral philosophy helped to anchor critical thinking in personal and communal values. This connection paved the way to establish a similar link between critical feeling and values. This conceptual work is important because research questions in psychology often derive from tacit assumptions and hidden values that must be made explicit. We have seen that clarifying the role of values behind a research question does not prevent scientists from doing value-free research. Beyond the distinction between value-free science and value-laden practice, theory of science needs to clarify the role of empirical psychology within the social sciences. Psychologists often like to see themselves as natural scientists, as the term *psychological science* testifies. That may be correct as long as they study basic processes. However, psychology as it is needed for critical feeling may be more akin to anthropology or sociology. There are anthropologies and sociologies of different cultures and classes. Likewise, we may develop psychologies of different groups by combining universal processes of perception, thought, and affect with various ecologies and historical contexts. The existing conceptual framework required for such integration is fragmentary at best. Epistemology asks questions to do with, for example, understanding the justification of feelings in certain situations. This perspective goes beyond existing psychological research about the interpretation of emotions and therefore opens new research questions. Answering these questions is crucial because critical feeling needs to be rooted in the understanding of one's own affective and metacognitive experiences. The philosophy of art teaches psychologists to go beyond measuring aesthetic preferences. A full picture of art appreciation requires that research examines the understanding of artworks as a prerequisite to their evaluation. This is essential for developing artistic tastes based on proper understanding. In order to conduct this research, universal processes of the mind need to be combined with contextual information about the artwork. Likewise, we must connect basic mental processes to their religious contexts in order to examine critical feeling in the service of re-enchantment and the acquisition of moral habits.

Regarding education, I have outlined some contents and methods that could help in the implementation of critical feeling. Yet, some important questions are left unanswered. While it seems obvious that the education of thinking skills falls within the responsibility of schools, it is much less clear who should deal with feelings – parents or schools. Some parents might lack the necessary knowledge about critical feeling to teach it to their children. This might lead to advantages for children who have more educated parents. On the other hand, although I noted that schools should teach *how* to feel but not *what* to feel, this distinction might be more clear-cut in theory than in practice. The question then arises how far a society accepts that an education system transmits values.

Beyond universal moral values, every community defines its own norms and derives duties for its members from them. William James (1985/1902) defined the religious person as one who does his or her moral duty with joy. Any responsible education should aim to teach children both the universal and community values, and how to implement them joyfully. Educating children to become adults who happily take their responsibilities seriously has always been a challenge, and it will be a challenge in the future. Evidence-based education supported by critical feeling has the promise to meet this challenge in various cultural, historical, and moral contexts.

NOTES

Introduction

1 The term *critical feeling* has been used a few times before but with different meanings. First, critical feeling has been captured as being pointed against another person. Psychiatrists, for example, have proposed that guilt is a self-critical feeling state (Prosen, Clark, Harrow, and Fawcett 1983); that a listener can be critical toward a social class or toward a person, for example toward a speaker in communicative situations (Jorgensen 1996); and that a psychotherapist can be critical toward his/her patient in psychoanalysis (Jacobs 1983). The term *critical feeling* as used in this book does not denote this adversarial meaning.

Second, in the therapy literature (Renneker 1990), a critical feeling can be a decisive feeling. In a state of despair, hope may be the decisive feeling that brings about a turnaround. This meaning can be applied to examples beyond psychotherapy. After some failures at school, Hannah despaired and gave up learning because she did not believe that she would achieve the grade point average needed to enter the school to which she aspired. When she regained hope that she could do it, she invested more time and finally did it. Hope turned out to be a critical feeling. Here, *critical* means that hope was a necessary condition for Hannah to achieve the positive outcome. This meaning of critical feeling comes closer to the term as defined in this book but it lacks the strategic component introduced here. In our example, Hannah did not decide that it would be good to hope for a positive outcome in order to obtain the necessary grade point average.

In an originally unpublished work, William James (1988) used the term *critical feeling* in a similar way when he delineated two ways to judge reality. James wanted to make clear that the more advanced feeling to judge reality is the decisive one, again without the strategic component essential to the critical feeling account presented in this book.

Third, the "critical" in critical feeling can be used like the "critical" in critical thinking: It is feeling based on foundations that allow us to question and to elaborate on the feelings at hand. Critical feeling in this sense has been used by Paul Haack in an article on feeling in music education. He used the term just once, at the end of his article, noting that "Critical feeling may be even more important than critical thinking for effective personal development and life in the century ahead" (Haack 1990, p. 32). He saw two reasons why school curricula emphasized discussion of subjective musical experiences less than discussion of the perceptual properties of music: First, it is easier to talk about objective realities, such as formal, elemental musical properties, than about subjective experiences, such as feelings in response to music. Second, scores of music educators have been instructed not to tell students what to feel. This led, according to Haack, to the misunderstanding among music educators that they should not discuss feelings. By contrast, he proposed that music educators not only address the musical object but also the perception of subjects and their interaction with the musical object. Students should learn about their reactions to music and scrutinize them, without having imposed on them a certain experience as the right feeling; it "must be critical thinking about feeling" (Haack 1990, p. 30). Similarly, Abrahams (2005) mentions critical feeling in the context of a critical theory of music without defining the term and without specifying mechanisms underlying it. The concept of critical feeling introduced in this book will be defined and goes beyond Haack's notion that critical feeling includes critical thinking, and looks at the underlying psychological mechanisms.

A preliminary outline of the term *critical feeling* as used in this book has been published in a book chapter on the strategic use of processing fluency (Reber 2012a).

1 Critical thinking

1   I am neither defending the number and kinds of values nor Spranger's typology. Typologies are old fashioned and have neither empirical support nor any currency in contemporary psychology. However, Spranger (1928/1914) himself was aware of the problems and thought of those types as ideal types that are always intermingled with each other rather than discrete types into which people can be classified according to a certain scheme. The important point here is to illustrate that different domains of values exist and that critical thinking and critical feeling go beyond the pursuit of truth or of subjective utility.

2   I have been fascinated by this example because it includes, from the standpoint of feelings, a real dilemma between, on the one hand, doing the right thing and losing the pension and, on the other, doing the wrong thing and saving the pension. As a father of three, Mr. Sauerland presumably could not simply renounce his pension claims. The tension here is between deontological morality (say sorry if something has gone wrong) and utilitarian considerations (the pension). This dilemma shows the importance of the institutional environment for our ability to apply critical feeling.

3 Critical feeling

1   Maybe De Sousa's (1987) notion of bootstrapping could be implemented in critical feeling. However, De Sousa's descriptions of this feedback mechanism – that we can arrive at feelings by doing as if we had that feeling – is descriptive rather than a guide to how we could use bootstrapping strategically.

6 Living together

1   Starting from Hannah Arendt's (2006/1963) notion of the "banality of evil," the research question of the classic Milgram experiment (2009/1974) was whether

average American citizens could be brought to commit cruelties, as the SS hench-men did during World War II. To this purpose, participants in the experiment had to administer an electric shock to a "student" who had to learn a word list. In reality, the "student" was a confederate of the experimenter and did not receive any real shocks. The "student" deliberately made mistakes, and the experimenter ordered the participant to administer a shock. The shock intensity was fifteen volts in the beginning, increased in fifteen-volt steps, and ended at a maximum intensity of 450 volts. The participant heard the "student" ask for the shocks to be stopped, express pain, scream, and finally, after pounding on the wall at 300 and 315 volts, showing no reaction to the learning task.

10 Religion and morality

1 There are alternative mechanisms underlying rituals. One such mechanism points to costly signals (Sosis 2003). Examples of such costly signals are actions that afflict pain on oneself, such as body scarification or self-flagellation, or that demand large investments of time. These rituals may enhance social cohesiveness by reducing the free-rider problem in religious groups whose stability depends on high levels of mutual trust. Another explanation emphasizes costly displays of belief, such as valuable sacrifices to the gods. Such *credibility-enhancing displays* are commonly found in rituals (Henrich 2009). Observers of these costly displays come to see the offerer of a sacrifice as a sincere believer, which may in turn inspire observers to be more receptive to these beliefs as well, which encourages further displays and thus the growth of the religious community (see Henrich 2009). I do not derive recom-mendations for critical feeling on the basis of these alternative mechanisms because it is unknown what effects on feelings they have – even though they presumably affect emotions and trust. In addition, some of the practices, such as body scarifica-tion and self-flagellation, are in a modern context neither desirable nor practicable.

REFERENCES

Aarts, K., De Houwer, J., and Pourtois, G. 2012. "Evidence for the automatic evaluation of self-generated actions," *Cognition* 124: 117–127.

Aarts, K., De Houwer, J., and Pourtois, G. 2013. "Erroneous and correct actions have a different affective valence: Evidence from ERPs," *Emotion* 13: 960–973.

Abrahams, F. 2005. "The application of critical pedagogy to music teaching and learning," *Update: Applications of Research in Music Education: A Literature Review* 23: 12–22.

Acker, M. and Davis, M. H. 1992. "Intimacy, passion and commitment in adult romantic relationships: A test of the triangular theory of love," *Journal of Social and Personal Relationships* 9: 21–50.

Ackerman, J. M. and Bargh, J. A. 2010. "Two to tango: Automatic social coordination and the role of felt effort," in *Effortless Attention*, B. Bruya (ed.). Cambridge, MA: MIT Press, 335–371.

Aebli, H. 2011/1983. *Zwölf Grundformen des Lehrens [Twelve basic forms of teaching]*. Stuttgart, Germany, Klett-Cotta.

Ajzen, I. 2001. "Nature and operation of attitudes," *Annual Review of Psychology* 52: 27–58.

Alexander, P. A. 2003. "The development of expertise: The journey from acclimation to proficiency," *Educational Researcher* 1:10–14.

Allison, T. S. and Allison, S. L. 1971. "Time-out from reinforcement: Effect on sibling aggression," *Psychological Record* 21: 81–86.

Allport, G. W., Vernon, P. E., and Lindzey, G. 1960. *Study of values*. Boston: Houghton Mifflin.

Allwood, C. M. 2011. "On the foundation of the indigenous psychologies," *Social Epistemology* 25: 3–14.

Alter, A. L. and Oppenheimer, D. M. 2006. "Predicting short-term stock fluctuations by using processing fluency," *Proceedings of the National Academy of Sciences of the United States of America* 103: 9369–9372.

Alter, A. L. and Oppenheimer, D. M. 2009. "Uniting the tribes of fluency to form a metacognitive nation," *Personality and Social Psychology Review* 13: 219–235.

Alter, A. L., Oppenheimer, D. M., and Epley, N. 2013. "Disfluency prompts analytic thinking – But not always greater accuracy: Response to Thompson et al. (2013)," *Cognition* 128: 252–255.

Alter, A. L., Oppenheimer, D. M., Epley, N., and Eyre, R. N. 2007. "Overcoming intuition: Metacognitive difficulty activates analytic reasoning," *Journal of Experimental Psychology: General* 136: 569–576.

Althoff, G. 2003. *Die Macht der Rituale. Symbolik und Herrschaft im Mittelalter*. Darmstadt, Germany: Primus Verlag.

Alvesson, M. 1994. "Critical theory and consumer marketing," *Scandinavian Journal of Management* 10: 291–313.

Anderson, C., Keltner, D., and John, O. P. 2003. "Emotional convergence between people over time," *Journal of Personality and Social Psychology* 84: 1054–1068.

Anderson, C. A., Berkowitz, L., Donnerstein, E., Huesmann, L. R., Johnson, J. D., Linz, D., Malamuth, N. M., and Wartella, E. 2003. "The influence of media violence on youth," *Psychological Science in the Public Interest* 4: 81–110.

Anderson, J. R. 1982. "Acquisition of cognitive skill," *Psychological Review* 89: 369.

Anderson, R. A. and Anderson, J. E. 2010. *Stretching*. Bolinas, CA: Shelter Publications.

Annas, J. 2011. *Intelligent virtue*. Oxford: Oxford University Press.

Arendt, H. 2006/1963. *Eichmann in Jerusalem: A report on the banality of evil*. London: Penguin.

Aristotle. 1997/ca. 350 BCE. *Poetics*. London: Penguin.

Aristotle. 2004/ca. 350 BCE. *The Nicomachean Ethics*. London: Penguin.

Armitage, C. J. 2004. "Evidence that implementation intentions reduce dietary fat intake: A randomized trial," *Health Psychology* 23: 319.

Armstrong, T. and Detweiler-Bedell, B. 2008. "Beauty as an emotion: The exhilarating prospect of mastering a challenging world," *Review of General Psychology* 12: 305–329.

Atran, S. 2006. "The moral logic and growth of suicide terrorism," *Washington Quarterly* 29: 127–147.

Atran, S. and Norenzayan, A. 2004. "Religion's evolutionary landscape: Counterintuition, commitment, compassion, communion," *Behavioral and Brain Sciences* 27: 713–770.

Audi, R. 2013. *Moral perception*. Princeton: Princeton University Press.

Babiak, P. and Hare, R. D. 2006. *Snakes in suits: When psychopaths go to work*. New York: Harper Business.

Baddeley, A. D. and Longman, D. J. A. 1978. "The influence of length and frequency of training session on the rate of learning to type," *Ergonomics* 21: 627–635.

Baeck, L. 1987/1928. *The essence of Judaism*. New York: Schocken.

Baker, L. R., McNulty, J. K., and Overall, N. C. 2015. "When negative emotions benefit close relationships," in *The positive side of negative emotions*, W. G. Parrot (ed.). New York: Guilford Press, 101–125.

Bakermans-Kranenburg, M. J., Van IJzendoorn, M. H., and Bradley, R. H. 2005. "Those who have, receive: The Matthew effect in early childhood intervention in the home environment," *Review of Educational Research* 75: 1–26.

Bandura, A. 1997. *Self-efficacy: The exercise of control*. New York: Freeman.

Bar, M. and Neta, M. 2006. "Humans prefer curved visual objects," *Psychological Science* 17: 645–648.

Barkeling, B., King, N. A., Naslund, E., and Blundell, J. E. 2007. "Characterization of obese individuals who claim to detect no relationship between their eating pattern and sensations of hunger or fullness," *International Journal of Obesity and Related Metabolic Disorders* 31: 435–439.

Barrett, J. L. 2004. *Why would anyone believe in God?* Walnut Creek, CA: Altamira.

Barrett, J. L. and Nyhof, M. 2001. "Spreading non-natural concepts: The role of intuitive conceptual structures in memory and transmission of cultural materials," *Journal of Cognition and Culture* 1: 69–100.

Bastian, B., Jetten, Y., Hornsey, M. J., and Leknes, S. 2014. "The positive consequences of physical pain: A biopsychosocial approach," *Personality and Social Psychology Review* 18: 256–279.

Bates, A. 1941. "Parental roles in courtship," *Social Forces* 20: 483.

Bates, E. T. and Wiest, L. R. 2004. "Impact of personalization of mathematical word problems on student performance," *Mathematics Educator* 14: 17–26.

Baumeister, R. F., Bratslavsky, E., Finkenauer, C., and Vohs, K. D. 2001. "Bad is stronger than good," *Review of General Psychology* 5: 323–370.

Baumeister, R. F., Campbell, J. D., Krueger, J. I., and Vohs, K. D. 2003. "Does high self-esteem cause better performance, interpersonal success, happiness or healthier lifestyles?" *Psychological Science in the Public Interest* 4: 1–44.

Baumeister, R. F., Stillwell, A. M., and Heatherton, T. F. 1994. "Guilt: An interpersonal approach," *Psychological Bulletin* 115: 243–267.

Bavelas, J. B., Black, A., Lemery, C. R., MacInnis, S., and Mullet, J. 1986. "Experimental methods for studying 'elementary motor mimicry'," *Journal of Nonverbal Behavior* 10: 102–119.

Bechara, A., Damasio, H., and Damasio, A. R. 2000. "Emotion, decision making and the orbitofrontal cortex," *Cerebral Cortex* 10: 295–307.

Bechara, A., Damasio, A. R., Damasio, H., and Anderson, S. W. 1994. "Insensitivity to future consequences following damage to human prefrontal cortex," *Cognition* 50: 7–15.

Bechara, A. T. F., Damasio, H., Tranel, D., and Damasio, A. R. 1997. "Deciding advantageously before knowing the advantageous strategy," *Science* 275: 1293–1295.

Begg, I. M., Anas, A., and Farinacci, S. 1992. "Dissociation of processes in belief: Source recollection, statement familiarity, and the illusion of truth," *Journal of Experimental Psychology: General* 121: 446–458.

Bell, C. 1914. *Art*. London: Chatto & Windus.

Bellah, R. N., Madsen, R., Sullivan, W. M., Swidler, A., and Tipton, S. M. 1985. *Habits of the heart: Individualism and commitment in American life*. Berkeley: University of California Press.

Bem, D. J. 1972. "Self-perception theory," *Advances in Experimental Social Psychology* 6: 1–62.

Benjamin, A. S., Bjork, R. A., and Schwartz, B. L. 1998. "The mismeasure of memory: When retrieval fluency is misleading as a metamnemonic index," *Journal of Experimental Psychology: General* 127: 55–68.

Bentham, J. 1988/1776. *A fragment on government*. Cambridge: Cambridge University Press.

Berlin, I. 1969. *Four essays on liberty*. Oxford: Oxford University Press.

Bernieri, F. J. 1988. "Coordinated movement and rapport in teacher–student interactions," *Journal of Nonverbal Behavior* 12: 120–138.

Berscheid, E. 2010. "Love in the fourth dimension," *Annual Review of Psychology* 61: 1–25.

Betsch, T., Plessner, H., Schwieren, C., and Gutig, R. 2001. "I like it but I don't know why: A value-account approach to implicit attitude formation," *Personality and Social Psychology Bulletin* 27: 242–253.

Bhattacharjee, Y. 2013, April 28. "The mind of a con man," *New York Times Sunday Magazine*: MM44.

Bigand, E. and Poulin-Charronnat, B. 2006. "Are we 'experienced listeners'? A review of the musical capacities that do not depend on formal musical training," *Cognition* 100: 100–130.

Blake, W. 1972/1810. "Vision of the last judgment," in *The complete writings of William Blake with variant readings*, G. Keynes (ed.). Oxford: Oxford University Press, 604–617.

Block, N. 1998. "On a confusion about a function of consciousness," in *The nature of consciousness: Philosophical debates*, N. Block, O. Flanagan, and G. Güzeldere (eds.). Cambridge, MA: MIT Press, 375–415.

Blood, R. O. 1967. *Love match and arranged marriage: A Tokyo–Detroit comparison.* New York: Free Press.

Bohman, J. 2013. "Critical theory," in *The Stanford encyclopedia of philosophy*, E. N. Zalta (ed.). http://plato.stanford.edu/entries/critical-theory (retrieved January 1, 2015).

Bolte, A. and Goschke, T. 2005. "On the speed of intuition: Intuitive judgments of semantic coherence under different response deadlines," *Memory & Cognition* 33: 1248–1255.

Bolte, A., Goschke, T., and Kuhl, J. 2003. "Emotion and intuition: Effects of positive and negative mood on implicit judgments of semantic coherence," *Psychological Science* 14: 416–421.

Bonanno, G. A. 2004. "Loss, trauma, and human resilience: Have we underestimated the human capacity to thrive after extremely aversive events?" *American Psychologist* 59: 20–28.

Bonanno, G. A., Field, N. P., Kovacevic, A., and Kaltman, S. 2002. "Self-enhancement as a buffer against extreme adversity: Civil war in Bosnia and traumatic loss in the United States," *Personality and Social Psychology Bulletin* 28: 184–196.

Bonanno, G. A. and Keltner, D. 1997. "Facial expressions of emotion and the course of conjugal bereavement," *Journal of Abnormal Psychology* 106: 126.

Bonanno, G. A., Keltner, D., Holen, A., and Horowitz, M. J. 1995. "When avoiding unpleasant emotions might not be such a bad thing: Verbal–autonomic response dissociation and midlife conjugal bereavement," *Journal of Personality and Social Psychology* 69: 975–989.

Bonanno, G. A., Noll, J. G., Putnam, F. W., O'Neill, M., and Trickett, P. 2003. "Predicting the willingness to disclose childhood sexual abuse from measures of repressive coping and dissociative experiences," *Child Maltreatment* 8: 1–17.

Bonanno, G. A. and Singer, J. L. 1990. "Repressor personality style: Theoretical and methodological implications for health and pathology," in *Repression and dissociation*, J. L. Singer (ed.). Chicago: University of Chicago Press, 435–470.

Bornstein, R. F. 1989. "Exposure and affect: Overview and meta-analysis of research 1968–1987," *Psychological Bulletin* 106: 265–289.

Børringbo, K., Buan, V., and Johanessen, R. B. 2012. "22. juli rettsaken [The 22th July case]," *Aftenposten online.* http://www.aftenposten.no/nyheter/iriks/22juli/article6810223.ece (retrieved July 26, 2014).

Borscheid, P. 1983. "Geld und Liebe: Zu den Auswirkungen des Romantischen auf die Partnerwahl im 19. Jahrhundert [Money and love: On the effects of the romantic on partner choice in the 19th century]," in *Ehe, Liebe, Tod: Zum Wandel der Familie, der Geschlechts- und Generationsbeziehungen in der Neuzeit [Marriage, love, death: On the transition of family and gender and generation relations in the modern era]*, P. Borscheid and H. J. Teuteberg (eds.). Münster, Germany: F. Coppenrath, 112–134.

Bourdieu, P. 1984/1979. *Distinction: A social critique of the judgment of taste.* Cambridge, MA: Harvard University Press.

Bowers, K. S., Farvolden, P., and Mermigis, L. 1995. "Intuitive antecedents of insight," in *The creative cognition approach*, S. M. Smith, T. B. Ward, and R. A. Finke (eds.). Cambridge, MA: MIT Press, 27–51.

Bowers, K. S., Regehr, G., Balthazard, C., and Parker, K. 1990. "Intuition in the context of discovery," *Cognitive Psychology* 22: 72–110.

Bowlby, J. 1980. *Loss: Sadness and depression, Vol. III: Attachment and loss.* New York: Basic Books.

Boyer, P. 1992. *Tradition as truth and communication: A cognitive description of traditional discourse.* Cambridge: Cambridge University Press.

Boyer, P. 2001. *Religion explained: The evolutionary origins of religious thought.* New York: Basic Books.

Boyer, P. and Liénard, P. 2006. "Precaution systems and ritualized behavior," *Behavioral and Brain Sciences* 29: 635–641.

Brader, T. and Marcus, G. E. 2013. "Emotion and political psychology," in *The Oxford Handbook of Political Psychology*, 2nd edition, L. Huddy, D. Sears, and J. Levy (eds.). Oxford: Oxford University Press, 165–204.

Brady, M. S. 2013. *Emotional insight: The epistemic role of emotional experience.* Oxford: Oxford University Press.

Brecht, B. 1964. *Brecht on theatre: The development of an aesthetic.* London: Methuen.

Brewin, C. R. 1996. "Theoretical foundations of cognitive-behavior therapy for anxiety and depression," *Annual Review of Psychology* 47: 33–57.

Brickman, P., Coates, D., and Janoff-Bulman, R. 1978. "Lottery winners and accident victims: Is happiness relative?" *Journal of Personality and Social Psychology* 36: 917–927.

Brinkmann, S. 2006. "Damasio on mind and emotions: A conceptual critique," *Nordic Psychology* 58: 366–380.

Brinkmann, S. 2011. *Psychology as a moral science: Perspectives on normativity.* New York: Springer.

Bronfenbrenner, U. 1979. *The ecology of human development: Experiments by nature and design.* Cambridge, MA: Harvard University Press.

Brooks, A. W. 2014. "Get excited: Reappraising pre-performance anxiety as excitement," *Journal of Experimental Psychology: General* 143: 1144–1158.

Brown, A. S. 1991. "A review of the tip-of-the-tongue experience," *Psychological Bulletin* 109: 204–223.

Brown, A. S. and Nix, L. A. 1996. "Turning lies into truths: Referential validation of falsehoods," *Journal of Experimental Psychology: Learning, Memory, and Cognition* 22: 1088–1100.

Brown, R. and McNeill, D. 1966. "The 'tip of the tongue' phenomenon," *Journal of Verbal Learning and Verbal Behavior* 5: 325–337.

Brunswik, E. 1955. "Representative design and probabilistic theory in a functional psychology," *Psychological Review* 62: 193–217.

Brunswik, E. 1956. *Perception and the representative design of psychological experiments.* Berkeley: University of California Press.

Brunswik, E. 1957. "Scopes and aspects of the cognitive problem," in *Contemporary approaches to cognition*, H. Gruber, K. R. Hammond, and R. Jessor (eds.). Cambridge, MA: Harvard University Press, 5–31.

Bryant, F. B., Smart, C. M., and King, S. P. 2005. "Using the past to enhance the present: Boosting happiness through positive reminiscence," *Journal of Happiness Studies* 6: 227–260.

Buber, M. 1994/1948. *The way of man.* New York: Citadel.

Buber, M. 2004/1923. *I and thou.* New York: Scribner.

Buckley, M. 2009. "Computing as social science," *Communications of the ACM* 52: 29–30.

Bullot, N. J. and Reber, R. 2013a. "The artful mind meets art history: Toward a psycho-historical framework for the science of art appreciation," *Behavioral and Brain Sciences* 36: 123–137.

Bullot, N. J. and Reber, R. 2013b. "A psycho-historical research program for the integrative science of art," *Behavioral and Brain Sciences* 36: 163–180.

Burgess, A. 2012. "'Nudging' healthy lifestyles: The UK experiments with the behavioural alternative to regulation and the market," *European Journal of Risk Regulation* 2012: 3–16.

Burnham, D. and Skilleås, O. M. 2012. *The aesthetics of wine.* Chichester, UK: Wiley-Blackwell.

Burton-Freeman, B. 2000. "Dietary fiber and energy regulation," *Journal of Nutrition* 130: 272S–275S.

Bushman, B. J. and Whitaker, J. L. 2010. "Like a magnet: Catharsis beliefs attract angry people to violent video games," *Psychological Science* 21: 790–792.

Cakir, O. and Simsek, N. 2010. "A comparative analysis of the effects of computer and paper-based personalization on student achievement," *Computers & Education* 55: 1524–1531.

Campos, J. J., Mumme, D. L., Kermoian, R., and Campos, R. G. 1994. "A functionalist perspective on the nature of emotion," *Monographs of the Society for Research in Child Development* 59: 284–303.

Carr, D. 2005. "On the contribution of literature and the arts to the educational cultivation of moral virtue, feeling and emotion," *Journal of Moral Education* 34: 137–151.

Carroll, J. S. 1978. "The effect of imagining an event on expectations for the event: An interpretation in terms of the availability heuristic," *Journal of Experimental Social Psychology* 14: 88–96.

Carroll, N. 1999. *Philosophy of art: A contemporary introduction.* London: Routledge.

Carroll, N. 2001. *Beyond aesthetics: Philosophical essays.* Cambridge: Cambridge University Press.

Carroll, N. 2002. "Aesthetic experience revisited," *British Journal of Aesthetics* 42: 145–168.

Carruthers, P. 2011. *The opacity of mind: An integrative theory of self-knowledge.* Oxford: Oxford University Press.

Carse, J. P. 2008. *The religious case against belief.* New York: Penguin.

Carstensen, L. L. and Fredrickson, B. F. 1998. "Socioemotional selectivity in healthy older people and younger people living with the human immunodeficiency virus: The centrality of emotion when the future is constrained," *Health Psychology* 17: 1–10.

Carstensen, L. L., Isaacowitz, D. M., and Charles, S. T. 1999. "Taking time seriously: A theory of socioemotional selectivity," *American Psychologist* 54: 165–181.

Cautela, J. R. 1967. "Covert sensitization," *Psychological Reports* 20: 459–468.

Chaiken, S. and Trope, Y. (eds.). 1999. *Dual process theories in social psychology.* New York: Guilford Press.

Chajut, E., Caspi, A., Chen, R., Hod, M., and Ariely, D. 2014. "In pain thou shalt bring forth children: The peak-and-end rule in recall of labor pain," *Psychological Science* 25: 2266–2271.

Chandrasekhar, S. 1987. *Truth and beauty. Aesthetics and motivations in science.* Chicago: University of Chicago Press.

Chaney, W. A. 1970. *The cult of kingship in Anglo-Saxon England: The transition from paganism to Christianity.* Manchester: Manchester University Press.

Chartrand, T. L. and Bargh, J. A. 1999. "The Chameleon effect: The perception-behavior link and social interaction," *Journal of Personality and Social Psychology* 76: 893–910.

Chase, W. G. and Simon, H. A. 1973. "Perception in chess," *Cognitive Psychology* 4: 55–81.

Chatterjee, A. 2011. "Neuroaesthetics: A coming of age story," *Journal of Cognitive Neuroscience* 23: 53–62.

Chen, W. and Reber, R. 2011. "Writing Wikipedia articles as course assignment," in *Proceedings of the 19th International Conference on Computers in Education: ICCE 2011*, T. Hirashima, G. Biswas, T. Supnithi, and F. Y. Yu (eds.). Chiang Mai, Thailand: Asia-Pacific Society for Computers in Education, 692–696.

Chen, Y.-C. and Scholl, B. J. 2014. "Seeing and liking: Biased perception of ambiguous figures consistent with the 'inward bias' in aesthetic preferences," *Psychonomic Bulletin & Review* 21: 1444–1451.

Chetverikov, A. and Filippova, M. 2014. "How to tell a wife from a hat: Affective feedback in perceptual categorization," *Acta Psychologica* 151: 206–213.

Christophe, V. and Rimé, B. 1997. "Exposure to the social sharing of emotion: Emotional impact, listener responses and secondary social sharing," *European Journal of Social Psychology* 27: 37–54.

Cialdini, R. B. 2006. *Influence: The psychology of persuasion*. New York: Harper Business.

Clark, C. M. 2006. *Iron kingdom: The rise and downfall of Prussia, 1600–1947*. Cambridge, MA: Harvard University Press.

Clark, J. W. and Dawson, L. E. 1996. "Personal religiousness and ethical judgements: An empirical analysis," *Journal of Business Ethics* 15: 359–372.

Cohen, D., Bowdle, B. F., Nisbett, R. E., and Schwarz, N. 1996. "Insult, aggression, and the southern culture of honor: An 'experimental ethnography'," *Journal of Personality and Social Psychology* 70: 945–960.

Cohen, J. B., Pham, M. T., and Andrade, E. B. 2008. "The nature and role of affect in consumer behavior," in *Handbook of Consumer Psychology*, C. P. Haugtvedt, P. Herr, and F. Kardes (eds.). Mahwah, NJ: Lawrence Erlbaum, 297–348.

Colby, A. and Damon, W. 1992. *Some do care: Contemporary lives of moral commitment*. New York: Free Press.

Conway, L. G. and Schaller, M. 2007. "How communication shapes culture," in *Social Communication*, K. Fiedler (ed.). New York: Psychology Press: 107–127.

Cook, K. J. 1998. *Divided passions: Public opinions on abortion and the death penalty*. Boston: Northeastern University Press.

Coontz, S. J. 2005. *Marriage, a history: How love conquered marriage*. London: Penguin.

Coremans, P. B. 1949. *Van Meegeren's faked Vermeers and De Hooghs: A scientific examination*. Amsterdam: J. M. Meulenhoff.

Cosmides, L. and Tooby, J. 2013. "Evolutionary psychology: New perspectives on cognition and motivation," *Annual Review of Psychology* 64: 201–229.

Côté, S., DeCelles, K. A., McCarthy, J. M., Van Kleef, C. A., and Hideg, I. 2011. "The Jekyll and Hyde of emotional intelligence: Emotion-regulation knowledge facilitates both prosocial and interpersonally deviant behavior," *Psychological Science* 22: 1073–1080.

Coughlan, E. K., Williams, A. M., McRobert, A. P., and Ford, P. R. 2014. "How experts practice: A novel test of deliberate practice theory," *Journal of Experimental Psychology: Learning, Memory, and Cognition* 40: 449–458.

Crandall, C. S. 1984. "The liking of foods as a result of exposure: Eating doughnuts in Alaska," *Journal of Social Psychology* 125: 187–194.

Cross, P. 1977. "Not can but will college teaching be improved?" *New Directions for Higher Education* 17: 1–15.

Cuddy, A. J. C., Fiske, S. T., and Glick, P. 2007. "The BIAS map: Behaviors from intergroup affect and stereotypes," *Journal of Personality and Social Psychology* 92: 631–648.

Currie, G., Kieran, M., Meskin, A., and Moore, M. 2014. *Philosophical aesthetics and the sciences of art*. Cambridge: Cambridge University Press.

Cutting, J. E. 2003. "Gustave Caillebotte, French impressionism, and mere exposure," *Psychonomic Bulletin & Review* 10: 319–343.

Damasio, A. R. 1994. *Descartes' error: Emotion, reason, and the human brain*. New York: G. P. Putnam.

Damasio, A. R. 1996. "The somatic marker hypothesis and the possible functions of the prefrontal cortex," *Transactions of the Royal Society (London)* 351: 1413–1420.

Danto, A. C. 1981. *The transfiguration of the commonplace: A philosophy of art*. Cambridge, MA: Harvard University Press.

Danto, A. C. 2003. *The abuse of beauty: Aesthetics and the concept of art*. Chicago: Open Court.

Darwin, C. R. 1838. "This is the question: Marry; Not marry [Notes on marriage]." https://www.darwinproject.ac.uk/darwins-notes-on-marriage#_edn14 (retrieved May 14, 2015).

Davidson, J. E. 2003. "Insights about insightful problem solving," in *The psychology of problem solving*, J. E. Davidson and R. J. Sternberg (eds.). Cambridge: Cambridge University Press, 149–175.

Davies, M. I. and Clark, D. M. 1998. "Thought suppression produces a rebound effect with analogue post-traumatic intrusions," *Behaviour Research and Therapy* 36: 571–582.

Dawkins, R. 2006. *The God delusion*. Boston: Houghton Mifflin.

DeCasper, A. J. and Fifer, W. P. 1980. "Of human bonding: Newborns prefer their mothers' voices," *Science* 208: 1174–1176.

DeCasper, A. J. and Spence, M. J. 1986. "Prenatal maternal speech influences newborns' perception of speech sounds," *Infant Behavior and Development* 9: 133–150.

Dechene, A., Stahl, C., Hansen, J., and Wänke, M. 2010. "The truth about the truth: A meta-analytic review of the truth effect," *Personality and Social Psychology Review* 14: 238–257.

Deci, E. L. and Ryan, R. M. 1985. *Intrinsic motivation and self-determination in human behavior*. New York: Plenum Press.

De Groot, A. D. 1978. *Thought and choice in chess*. New York: Mouton de Gruyter.

De Houwer, J. 2009. "Conditioning as a source of liking: There is nothing simple about it," in *Frontiers of Social Psychology: The Social Psychology of Consumer Behavior*, M. Wänke (ed.). New York: Psychology Press, 151–166.

De Houwer, J., Thomas, S., and Baeyens, F. 2001. "Association learning of likes and dislikes: A review of 25 years of research on human evaluative conditioning," *Psychological Bulletin* 127: 853–869.

Deikman, A. J. 1963. "Experimental meditation," *Journal of Nervous and Mental Disease* 136: 329–343.

Denes-Raj, V. and Epstein, S. 1994. "Conflict between intuitive and rational processing: When people behave against their better judgment," *Journal of Personality and Social Psychology* 66: 819–829.

Denham, S. A., McKinley, M., Couchoud, E. A., and Holt, R. 1990. "Emotional and behavioral predictors of preschool peer ratings," *Child Development* 61: 1145–1152.

Deonna, J. A. and Teroni, F. 2012. *The emotions: A philosophical introduction.* Abingdon, UK: Routledge.

DePaulo, B. M., Lindsay, J. J., Malone, B. E., Muhlenbruck, L., Charlton, K., and Cooper, H. 2003. "Cues to deception," *Psychological Bulletin* 129: 74–112.

DePaulo, B. M. and Morris, W. L. 2006. "The unrecognized stereotyping and discrimination against people who are single," *Current Directions in Psychological Science* 15: 251–254.

De Sousa, R. 1987. *The rationality of emotions.* Cambridge, MA: MIT Press.

Devine, P. G. 1989. "Stereotypes and prejudice: Their automatic and controlled components," *Journal of Personality and Social Psychology* 56: 5–18.

Dewey, J. 1909. *Moral principles in education.* Boston: Houghton Mifflin.

Dewey, J. 1910. *How we think.* Lexington, MA: D. C. Heath.

Dewey, J. 1938. *Experience and education.* New York: Kappa Delta Pi.

Dewey, J. 1956/1899. *The child and the curriculum and the school and society.* Chicago: University of Chicago Press.

Dewey, J. 1975/1913. *Interest and effort in education.* Boston: Riverside.

Dewey, J. 2005/1934. *Art as experience.* New York: Penguin.

Dewey, J. 2012/1922. *Human nature and conduct.* Mineola, NY: Dover.

De Young, R. 1993. "Changing behavior and making it stick: The conceptualization and management of conservation behavior." *Environment and Behavior* 25: 485–505.

Dickie, G. 1962. "Is psychology relevant to aesthetics?" *Philosophical Review* 71: 285–302.

Diemand-Yauman, C., Oppenheimer, D. M., and Vaughan, E. B. 2011. "Fortune favors the bold (and the italicized): Effects of disfluency on educational outcomes," *Cognition* 118: 111–115.

Diener, E. and Kesebir, P. 2013. "A virtuous cycle: The relationship between happiness and virtue," in *The philosophy and psychology of virtue: An empirical approach to character and happiness*, N. Snow and F. Trivigno (eds.). New York: Routledge, 287–306.

Do, A. M., Rupert, A. V., and Wolford, G. 2008. "Evaluations of pleasurable experiences: The peak–end rule," *Psychonomic Bulletin & Review* 15: 96–98.

Donadio, R. and Goodstein, L. 2009, October 21. "Vatican bidding to get Anglicans to join its fold," *New York Times*: A1.

Donovan, R. J. and Rossiter, J. R. 1982. "Store atmosphere: An environmental psychology approach," *Journal of Retailing* 58: 34–57.

Dorandi, T. 2013. *Diogenes Laertius: Lives of eminent philosophers.* Cambridge: Cambridge University Press.

Doris, J. and Stich, S. 2005. "As a matter of fact: Empirical perspectives on ethics," in *The Oxford handbook of contemporary philosophy*, F. Jackson and M. Smith (eds.). Oxford: Oxford University Press, 114–152.

Doris, J. M. 2002. *Lack of character: Personality and moral behavior.* New York: Cambridge University Press.

Dovidio, J. F., Isen, A. M., Guerra, P., Gaertner, S. L., and Rust, M. 1998. "Positive affect, cognition, and the reduction of intergroup bias," in *Intergroup cognition and intergroup behavior*, C. Sedikides (ed.). Mahwah, NJ: Lawrence Erlbaum, 337–366.

Dreisbach, G. and Goschke, T. 2004. "How positive affect modulates cognitive control: Reduced perseveration at the cost of increased distractibility," *Journal of Experimental Psychology: Learning, Memory, and Cognition* 30: 343–353.

Duarte, J. L., Crawford, J. T., Stern, C., Haidt, J., Jussim, L., and Tetlock, P. E. 2015. "Political diversity will improve social psychological science," *Behavioral and Brain Sciences* 38: e130.

Duclos, S. E. and Laird, J. D. 2001. "The deliberate control of emotional experience through control of expressions," *Cognition and Emotion* 15: 27–56.

Dunn, J. R. and Schweitzer, M. E. 2005. "Feeling and believing: The influence of emotion on trust," *Journal of Personality and Social Psychology* 88: 736–748.

Durik, A. M. and Harackiewicz, J. M. 2007. "Different strokes for different folks: How individual interest moderates the effects of situational factors on task interest," *Journal of Educational Psychology* 99: 597–610.

Easterbrook, J. A. 1959. "The effect of emotion on cue utilization and the organization of behavior," *Psychological Review* 66: 183–201.

Eco, U. 1988. *Art and beauty in the middle ages.* New Haven, CT: Yale University Press.

Edelstein, D. 2009. "The birth of ideology from the spirit of myth: Georg Sorel among the idéologues," in *The re-enchantment of the world: Secular magic in a rational age*, J. Landy and M. Saler (eds.). Stanford: Stanford University Press, 201–224.

Eich, E. and Metcalfe, J. 1989. "Mood dependent memory for internal versus external events," *Journal of Experimental Psychology: Learning, Memory, and Cognition* 15: 443–455.

Eisenberg, N. 2000. "Emotion, regulation, and moral development," *Annual Review of Psychology* 51: 665–697.

Ekman, P. 1985. *Telling lies: Clues to deceit in the marketplace, marriage, and politics.* New York: W. W. Norton.

Ekman, P. and Friesen, W. V. 2003. *Unmasking the face: A guide to recognizing emotions from facial clues.* Cambridge, MA: Malor Books.

Ekman, P. and O'Sullivan, M. 1991. "Who can catch a liar?" *American Psychologist* 46: 913–920.

Ekman, P., O'Sullivan, M., and Frank, M. G. 1999. "A few can catch a liar," *Psychological Science* 10: 263–266.

Ekman, P., O'Sullivan, M., Friesen, W. V., and Scherer, K. R. 1991. "Face, voice, and body in detecting deceit," *Journal of Nonverbal Behavior* 15: 125–135.

Elias, N. 1969. *The civilizing process: The history of manners.* Oxford: Blackwell.

Eliot, G. 1994/1871. *Middlemarch.* London: Penguin.

Elster, J. 1983. *Sour grapes: Studies in the subversion of rationality.* Cambridge: Cambridge University Press.

Ennis, R. H. 1962. "A concept of critical thinking," *Harvard Educational Review* 32: 81–111.

Ennis, R. H. 1987. "A taxonomy of critical thinking dispositions and abilities," in *Teaching thinking skills: Theory and practice*, J. Baron and R. J. Sternberg (eds.). New York: Freeman, 9–26.

Epictetus. 1991/ca. 125 CE. *Enchiridion.* New York: Prometheus.

Epicurus. 2012. *The art of happiness.* New York: Penguin.

Epley, N. and Dunning, D. 2000. "Feeling 'holier than thou': Are self-serving assessments produced by errors in self- or social prediction?" *Journal of Personality and Social Psychology* 79: 861–875.

Erickson, P., Klein, J. L., Daston, L., Lemov, R., Sturm, T., and Gordin, M. D. 2013. *How reason almost lost its mind: The strange career of Cold War rationality.* Chicago: University of Chicago Press.

Faris, J. H. 1976. "The impact of basic combat training: The role of the drill sergeant," in *The social psychology of military service,* N. Goldman and D. R. Segal (eds.). Newbury Park, CA: Sage, 13–24.

Feinberg, M., Willer, R., Antonenko, O., and John, O. P. 2012. "Liberating reason from the passions overriding intuitionist moral judgments through emotion reappraisal," *Psychological Science* 23: 788–795.

Fiedler, K. 2000. "Beware of samples! A cognitive-ecological sampling approach to judgment biases," *Psychological Review* 107: 659–676.

Fiedler, K. 2013. "Fluency and behavior regulation: Adaptive and maladaptive consequences of a good feeling," in *The experience of thinking,* C. Unkelbach and R. Greifeneder (eds.). Hove, UK: Psychology Press, 234–254.

Figes, O. 1996. *A people's tragedy: Russian revolution 1891–1924.* London: Jonathan Cape.

Finkel, E. J., Slotter, E. B., Luchies, L. B., Walton, G. M., and Gross, J. J. 2013. "A brief intervention to promote conflict reappraisal preserves marital quality over time," *Psychological Science* 24: 1595–1601.

Fischer, B., Biscaldi, M., and Gezeck, S. 1997. "On the development of voluntary and reflexive components in human saccade generation," *Brain Research* 754: 285–297.

Fishbein, M., Middlestadt, S. E., Ottati, V., Straus, S., and Ellis, A. 1988. "Medical problems among ICSOM musicians: Overview of a national survey," *Medical Problems of Performing Artists* 3: 1–8.

Fisher, A. 2011. *Critical thinking: An introduction.* Cambridge: Cambridge University Press.

Flack, W. F., Laird, J. D., and Cavallaro, L. A. 1999. "Emotional expression and feeling in schizophrenia: Effects of specific expressive behaviors on emotional experiences," *Journal of Clinical Psychology* 55: 1–20.

Flaubert, G. 2010/1874. *The temptation of St. Anthony.* Whitefish, MT: Kessinger.

Flavell, J. H. 1979. "Metacognition and cognitive monitoring," *American Psychologist* 34: 906–911.

Flowerday, T. and Schraw, G. 2000. "Teacher beliefs about instructional choice: A phenomenological study," *Journal of Educational Psychology* 92: 634–645.

Forgas, J. P. 2015. "Can sadness be good for you? On the cognitive, motivational, and interpersonal benefits of negative affect," in *The positive side of negative emotions,* W. G. Parrot (ed.). New York: Guilford Press, 3–36.

Forgas, J. P. and Bower, G. H. 1987. "Mood effects on person–perception judgments," *Journal of Personality and Social Psychology* 53: 53–60.

Forgas, J. P. and East, R. 2008. "On being happy and gullible: Mood effects on skepticism and the detection of deception," *Journal of Experimental Social Psychology* 44: 1362–1367.

Forster, M., Leder, H., and Ansorge, U. 2013. "It felt fluent, and I liked it: Subjective feeling of fluency rather than objective fluency determines liking," *Emotion* 13: 280–289.

Förstl, H., Haass, C., Hemmer, B., Meyer, B., and Halle, M. 2010. "Boxing – Acute complications and late sequelae: From concussion to dementia," *Deutsches Ärzteblatt International* 107: 835–839.

Forsyth, D. R. 2009. *Group dynamics.* Belmont, CA: Wadsworth.

Fortenbaugh, W. W. 1975. *Aristotle on emotion.* London: Duckworth.

Fowers, B. J. 2005. "Psychotherapy, character, and the good life," in *Critical thinking about psychology: Hidden assumptions and plausible alternatives*, B. D. Slife, J. S. Reber and F. C. Richardson (eds.). Washington, DC: American Psychological Association, 39–59.

Frank, R. H. 1988. *Passions within reason: The strategic role of the emotions*. New York: W. W. Norton.

Fraser, N. 1989. *Unruly practices: Power, discourse and gender in contemporary social theory*. Minneapolis: University of Minnesota Press.

Freddi, S., Tessier, M., Lacrampe, R., and Dru, V. 2013. "Affective judgement about information relating to competence and warmth: An embodied perspective," *British Journal of Social Psychology* 53: 265–280.

Fredrickson, B. L. 2013. "Positive emotions broaden and build," *Advances in Experimental Social Psychology* 47: 1–53.

Fredrickson, B. L. and Branigan, C. 2005. "Positive emotions broaden the scope of attention and thought–action repertoires," *Cognition and Emotion* 19: 313–332.

Fredrickson, B. L. and Carstensen, L. L. 1990. "Choosing social partners: How old age and anticipated endings make us more selective," *Psychology and Aging* 5: 335–347.

Fredrickson, B. L., Cohn, M. A., Coffey, K. A., Pek, J., and Finkel, S. M. 2008. "Open hearts build lives: Positive emotions, induced through loving-kindness meditation, build consequential personal resources," *Journal of Personality and Social Psychology* 95: 1045–1062.

Fredrickson, B. L. and Joiner, T. 2002. "Positive emotions trigger upward spirals toward emotional well-being," *Journal of Personality and Social Psychology* 65: 45–55.

Fredrickson, B. L. and Kahneman, D. 1993. "Duration neglect in retrospective evaluations of affective episodes," *Journal of Personality and Social Psychology* 65: 45–55.

Fredrickson, B. L. and Levenson, R. W. 1998. "Positive emotions speed recovery from the cardiovascular sequelae of negative emotions," *Cognition and Emotion* 12: 191–220.

Fredrickson, B. L., Tugade, M. M., Waugh, C. E., and Larkin, G. R. 2003. "What good are positive emotions in crises? A prospective study of resilience and emotions following the terrorist attacks on the United States on September 11th, 2001," *Journal of Personality and Social Psychology* 84: 365–376.

Freire, P. 1970. *Pedagogy of the oppressed*. New York: Herder and Herder.

Freud, S. and Breuer, J. 2004/1895. *Studies in hysteria*. London: Penguin.

Frevert, U. 1995/1991. *Men of honour: A social and cultural history of the duel*. Cambridge, MA: Blackwell.

Frevert, U., Eitler, P., Olsen, S., Jensen, U., Pernau, M., Brückenhaus, D., Beljan, M., Gammerl, B., Laukötter, A., Hitzer, B., Plamper, J., Brauer, J., and Häberlen, J. C. (eds.). 2014. *Learning how to feel: Children's literature and the history of emotional socialization 1870–1970*. Oxford: Oxford University Press.

Frijda, N. H. 1986. *The emotions*. Cambridge: Cambridge University Press.

Frijda, N. H. 1988. "The laws of emotion," *American Psychologist* 43: 349–358.

Frijda, N. H. 1994. "Varieties of affect: Emotions and episodes, moods, and sentiments," in *The nature of emotions: Fundamental questions*, P. Ekman and R. J. Davidson (eds.). New York: Oxford University Press, 197–202.

Fromm, E. 1973. *The anatomy of human destructiveness*. New York: Holt, Rinehart, & Winston.

Frye, N. 1982. *The great code: The Bible and literature*. Orlando, FL: Harcourt.

Fuller, S., Fuller, C. L., and Rudes, J. 2002. *Third face: My tale of writing, fighting, and filmmaking*. New York: Alfred A. Knopf.

Fung, H. H., Carstensen, L. L., and Lutz, A. 1999. "The influence of time on social preferences: Implications for life-span development," *Psychology and Aging* 14: 599–604.

Garcia-Marques, T., Silva, R. R., Reber, R., and Unkelbach, C. 2015. "Hearing a statement now and believing the opposite later," *Journal of Experimental Social Psychology* 56: 126–129.

Gardiner, J. M., Craik, F. I. M., and Bleasdale, F. A. 1973. "Retrieval difficulty and subsequent recall," *Memory & Cognition* 1: 213–216.

Gardner, H. 1970. "Children's sensitivity to painting styles," *Child Development* 41: 813–821.

Garner, R., Gillingham, M. G., and White, C. S. 1989. "Effects of 'seductive details' on macroprocessing and microprocessing in adults and children," *Cognition and Instruction* 6: 41–57.

Garrod, S. and Pickering, M. J. 2004. "Why is conversation so easy?" *Trends in Cognitive Sciences* 8: 8–11.

Gauchet, M. 1997. *The disenchantment of the world: A political history of religion*. Princeton: Princeton University Press.

Gaver, W. W. and Mandler, G. 1987. "Play it again, Sam: On liking music," *Cognition and Emotion* 1: 259–282.

Gawronski, B., Mitchell, D. G. V., and Balas, R. 2015. "Is evaluative conditioning really uncontrollable? A comparative test of three emotion-focused strategies to prevent the acquisition of conditioned preferences," *Emotion* 15: 556–568.

Gellmann, J. 2014. "Mysticism," in *The Stanford encyclopedia of philosophy*, E. N. Zalta (ed.). http://plato.stanford.edu/archives/spr2014/entries/mysticism (retrieved May 1, 2015).

Gervais, W. M. and Norenzayan, A. 2012. "Analytic thinking promotes religious disbelief," *Science* 336: 493–496.

Ghirlanda, S., Jansson, L., and Enquist, M. 2002. "Chickens prefer beautiful humans," *Human Nature* 13: 383–389.

Gibbon, E. 1994/1776–1781. *The history of the decline and the fall of the Roman Empire, Vol. I*. London: Penguin.

Gibbon, E. 1995/1788. *The history of the decline of fall of the Roman Empire, Vol. III*. London: Penguin.

Gibson, J. J. 1979. *The ecological approach to visual perception*. Boston: Houghton Mifflin.

Gifford, R. 1976. "Environmental numbness in the classroom," *Journal of Experimental Education* 44: 4–7.

Gifford, R. 2002. *Environmental psychology: Principles and practice*. Colville, WA: Optimal Books.

Gigerenzer, G., Todd, P. M., and ABC Research Group. 1999. *Simple heuristics that make us smart*. New York: Oxford University Press.

Gilbert, D. 2006. *Stumbling on happiness*. New York: First Vintage Books.

Gilbert, D. T. and Ebert, J. E. J. 2002. "Decisions and revisions: The affective forecasting of changeable outcomes," *Journal of Personality and Social Psychology* 82: 503–514.

Gilbert, D. T., Killingsworth, M. A., Eyre, R. N., and Wilson, T. D. 2009. "The surprising power of neighborly advice," *Science* 323: 1617–1619.

Gilmore, J. 2013. "Normative and scientific approaches to the understanding and evaluation of art," *Behavioral and Brain Sciences* 36: 144–145.

Glaser, E. 1942. "An experiment in the development of critical thinking," *Teachers College Record* 43: 409–410.

Goldberg, L. S. and Grandey, A. A. 2007. "Display rules versus display autonomy: Emotion regulation, emotional exhaustion, and task performance in a call center simulation," *Journal of Occupational Health Psychology* 12: 301–318.

Goldie, P. 2004. "Emotion, reason, and virtue," in *Emotion, evolution, and rationality*, D. Evans and P. Cruse (eds.). Oxford: Oxford University Press, 249–267.

Goldman, A. I. 1986. *Epistemology and cognition*. Cambridge, MA, Harvard University Press.

Goldstein, A. P., Glick, B. G., and Gibbs, J. C. 1998. *Aggression replacement training: A comprehensive intervention for aggressive youth*, revised edition. Champaign, IL: Research Press.

Goleman, D. 1995. *Emotional intelligence*. New York: Bantam.

Gollwitzer, P. M. 1999. "Implementation intention: Stong effects of simple plans," *American Psychologist* 54: 493–503.

Gopnik, B. 2012. "Aesthetic science and artistic knowledge," in *Aesthetic science: Connecting minds, brains, and experience*, A. P. Shimamura and S. E. Palmer (eds.). New York: Oxford University Press, 129–159.

Gordon, P. C. and Holyoak, K. J. 1983. "Implicit learning and generalization of the 'mere exposure' effect," *Journal of Personality and Social Psychology* 45: 492–500.

Gorn, G. J. 1982. "The effects of music in advertising on choice behavior: A classical conditioning approach," *Journal of Marketing Research* 46: 94–101.

Gracian, B. 1991/1653. *The art of wordly wisdom*. Madrid / Radford, VA: A & D Publishing.

Graf, L. K. M. and Landwehr, J. R. 2015. "A dual-process perspective on fluency-based aesthetics: The pleasure-interest model of aesthetic liking," *Personality and Social Psychology Review* 19: 395–410.

Greenberg, J., and Baron, R. A. 2008. *Behavior in organizations*. Upper Saddle River, NJ: Prentice Hall.

Greifeneder, R., Alt, A., Bottenberg, K., Seele, T., Zelt, S., and Wagener, D. 2010. "On writing legibly: Processing fluency systematically biases evaluations of handwritten material," *Social Psychological & Personality Science* 1: 230–237.

Grob, A., Little, T. D., Wanner, B., and Wearing, A. J. 1996. "Adolescents' well-being and perceived control across 14 sociocultural contexts," *Journal of Personality and Social Psychology* 71: 785–795.

Groenendyk, E. W. 2011. "Current emotion research in political science: How emotions help democracy overcome its collective action problem," *Emotion Review* 3: 455–463.

Gross, J. J. 1998. "Antecedent- and response-focused emotion regulation: Divergent consequences for experience, expression, and physiology," *Journal of Personality and Social Psychology* 74: 224–237.

Gumbrecht, H. U. 2009. "'Lost in focused intensity': Spectator sports and strategies of re-enchantment," in *The re-enchantment of the world: Secular magic in a rational age*, J. Landy and M. Saler (eds.). Stanford: Stanford University Press, 149–158.

Gupta, U. and Singh, P. 1982. "An exploratory study of love and liking and type of marriages," *Indian Journal of Applied Psychology* 19: 92–97.

Guthrie, S. 1993. *Faces in the clouds*. New York: Oxford University Press.

Haack, P. 1990. "Beyond objectivity: The feeling factor in listening," *Music Educators Journal* 77: 28–32.

Hackforth, R. 1972. *Plato's Phaedrus*. Cambridge: Cambridge University Press.

Haffner, S. 1980. *The rise and fall of Prussia*. London: Weidenfeld and Nicolson.

Haidt, J. 2001. "The emotional dog and its rational tail: A social intuitionist approach to moral judgment," *Psychological Review* 108: 814–834.

Haidt, J. 2007. "The new synthesis in moral psychology," *Science* 316: 998–1002.

Haldeman, D. C. 1991. "Sexual orientation conversion therapy for gay men and lesbians: A scientific examination," in *Homosexuality: Research implications for public policy*, J. C. Gonsiorek and J. D. Weinrich (eds.). Newbury Park, CA: Sage Publications, 149–160.

Hall, J. A. and Schmid Mast, M. 2007. "Sources of accuracy in the empathic accuracy paradigm," *Emotion* 7: 438–446.

Hamberg, E. M. 1991. "Stability and change in religious beliefs, practice, and attitudes: A Swedish panel study," *Journal for the Scientific Study of Religion* 30: 63–80.

Hamill, R., Wilson, T. D., and Nisbett, R. E. 1980. "Insensitivity to sample bias: Generalizing from atypical cases," *Journal of Personality and Social Psychology* 39: 578–589.

Hannan, S. E. and Tolin, D. F. 2005. "Mindfulness- and acceptance-based behavior therapy for obsessive-compulsive disorder," in *Acceptance and mindfulness-based approaches to anxiety*, S. M. Orsillo and L. Roemer (eds.). New York: Springer, 271–299.

Hansen, J., Dechêne, A., and Wänke, M. 2008. "Discrepant fluency increases subjective truth," *Journal of Experimental Social Psychology* 44: 687–691.

Hansen, J., Winzeler, S., and Topolinski, S. 2010. "When the death makes you smoke: A terror management perspective on the effectiveness of cigarette on-pack warnings," *Journal of Experimental Social Psychology* 46: 226–228.

Hargus, E., Crane, C., Barnhofer, T., and Williams, J. M. G. 2010. "Effects of mindfulness on meta-awareness and specificity of describing prodromal symptoms in suicidal depression," *Emotion* 10: 34–42.

Harman, G. 1999. "Moral philosophy meets social psychology: Virtue ethics and the fundamental attribution error," *Proceedings of the Aristotelian Society* New Series 99: 315–331.

Harp, S. F. and Mayer, R. E. 1997. "The role of interest in learning from scientific text and illustrations: On the distinction between emotional interest and cognitive interest," *Journal of Educational Psychology* 89: 92–102.

Harp, S. F. and Mayer, R. E. 1998. "How seductive details do their damage: A theory of cognitive interest in science learning," *Journal of Educational Psychology* 90: 414–434.

Harrison, A. A. 1977. "Mere exposure," *Advances in Experimental Social Psychology* 10: 39–83.

Hart, J. T. 1965. "Memory and the feeling-of-knowing experience," *Journal of Educational Psychology* 56: 208.

Hasher, L., Goldstein, D., and Toppino, T. 1977. "Frequency and the conference of referential validity," *Journal of Verbal Learning and Verbal Behavior* 16: 107–112.

Havas, D. A., Glenberg, A. M., Gutowski, K. A., Lucarelli, M. J., and Davidson, R. J. 2010. "Cosmetic use of botulinum toxin-A affects processing of emotional language," *Psychological Science* 21: 895–900.

Hazaleus, S. L. and Deffenbacher, J. L. 1986. "Relaxation and cognitive treatments of anger," *Journal of Consulting and Clinical Psychology* 54: 222.

Heerdink, M. W., Van Kleef, G. A., Homan, A. C., and Fischer, A. H. 2013. "On the social influence of emotions in groups: Interpersonal effects of anger and happiness on conformity versus deviance," *Journal of Personality and Social Psychology*, 105: 262–284.

Heider, F. 1958. *The psychology of interpersonal relations*. New York: Wiley.

Henrich, J. 2009. "The evolution of costly displays, cooperation and religion: Credibility enhancing displays and the implications for the evolution of culture," *Evolution and Human Behavior* 30: 244–260.

Herbert, B., Blechert, J., Hautzinger, M., Matthias, E., and Herbert, C. 2013. "Intuitive eating is associated with interoceptive sensitivity: Effects on body mass index," *Appetite* 70: 22–30.

Hertzke, A. D. 1998. "The theory of moral ecology," *Review of Politics* 60: 629–659.

Hickok, G. 2009. "Eight problems for the mirror neuron theory of action understanding in monkeys and humans," *Journal of Cognitive Neuroscience* 21: 1229–1243.

Hidi, S. and Harackiewicz, J. M. 2000. "Motivating the academically unmotivated: A critical issue for the 21st century," *Review of Educational Research* 70: 151–179.

Hidi, S. and Renninger, K. A. 2006. "The four-phase model of interest development," *Educational Psychologist* 41: 111–127.

Hitchcock, D. 1983. *Critical thinking: A guide to evaluating information*. Toronto: Methuen.

Hitler, A. 1939/1925. *Mein Kampf*. London: Hurst and Blackett.

Hoffman, M. L. 2001. *Empathy and moral development: Implications for caring and justice*. Cambridge: Cambridge University Press.

Hogarth, R. M. 2005. "Deciding analytically or trusting your intuition? The advantages and disadvantages of analytic and intuitive thought," in *The routines of decision making*, T. Betsch and S. Haberstroh (eds.). Mahwah, NJ: Lawrence Erlbaum, 67–82.

Høgheim, S. and Reber, R. 2015. "Supporting interest of middle school students in mathematics through context personalization and example choice," *Contemprary Educational Psychology* 42: 17–25.

Holmes, E. A., Crane, C., Fennell, M. J. V., and Williams, J. M. G. 2007. "Imagery about suicide in depression: 'Flash-forwards'," *Journal of Behavioral Therapy and Experimental Psychiatry* 38: 423–434.

Holmes, E. A. and Mathews, A. 2010. "Mental imagery in emotion and emotional disorders." *Clinical Psychology Review* 30: 349–362.

Horkheimer, M. 1982. *Critical theory*. New York: Seabury Press.

Hove, M. J. and Risen, J. L. 2009. "It's all in the timing: Interpersonal synchrony increases affiliation," *Social Cognition* 27: 949–960.

Hsee, C. K. and Hastie, R. 2006. "Decision and experience: Why don't we choose what makes us happy?" *Trends in Cognitive Sciences* 10: 31–37.

Hugdahl, K. and Kärker, A. C. 1981. "Biological vs. experiential factors in phobic conditioning," *Behavioural Research and Therapy* 19: 109–115.

Hulleman, C. S. and Harackiewicz, J. M. 2009. "Promoting interest and performance in high school science classes," *Science* 326: 1410–1412.

Hume, D. 1888/1738. *A treatise of human nature*. Oxford: Clarendon Press.

Hunter, P. G., Schellenberg, E. G., and Griffith, A. T. 2011. "Misery loves company: Mood-congruent emotional responding to music," *Emotion* 11: 1068–1072.

Hunter, P. G., Schellenberg, E. G., and Schimmack, U. 2008. "Mixed affective responses to music with conflicting cues," *Cognition and Emotion* 22: 327–352.

262 / References

Hursthouse, R. 1999. *On virtue ethics*. Oxford: Oxford University Press.

Hyde, J. S., Else-Quest, N. M., Alibali, M. W., Knuth, E., and Romberg, T. 2006. "Mathematics in the home: Homework practices and mother–child interactions doing mathematics," *Journal of Mathematical Behavior* 25: 136–152.

Hyman, J. 2006. "In search of the big picture," *New Scientist* 191: 44–45.

Iannaccone, L. 1994. "Why strict churches are strong," *American Journal of Sociology* 99: 1180–1211.

Ickes, W. J. (eds.). 1997. *Empathic accuracy*. New York: Guilford Press.

Idelsohn, A. Z. 1995/1932. *Jewish liturgy and its development*. Mineola, NY: Dover.

Isbell, L. M. 2012. The emotional citizen: How feelings drive political preferences and behavior. *APS Observer* 25: 13–16.

Isen, A. M. and Daubman, K. A. 1984. "The influence of affect on categorization," *Journal of Personality and Social Psychology* 47: 1206–1217.

Isen, A. M., Daubman, K. A., and Nowicki, G. P. 1987. "Positive affect facilitates creative problem solving," *Journal of Personality and Social Psychology* 52: 1122–1131.

Iyengar, S. S. and Lepper, M. R. 1999. "Rethinking the role of choice: A cultural perspective on intrinsic motivation," *Journal of Personality and Social Psychology* 76: 349–366.

Jacobs, T. J. 1983. "The analyst and the patient's object world: Notes on an aspect of countertransference," *Journal of the American Psychoanalytic Association* 31: 619.

Jacobsen, T., Schubotz, R. I., Hofel, L., and von Cramon, D. Y. 2006. "Brain correlates of aesthetic judgment of beauty," *Neuroimage* 29: 276–285.

Jacoby, L. L. and Dallas, M. 1981. "On the relationship between autobiographical memory and perceptual learning," *Journal of Experimental Psychology: General* 110: 306–340.

Jacoby, L. L., Kelley, C., Brown, J., and Jasechko, J. 1989. "Becoming famous overnight: Limits on the ability to avoid unconscious influences of the past," *Journal of Personality and Social Psychology* 56: 326–338.

Jaeger, C. S. 2012. *Enchantment: On charisma and the sublime in the arts of the West*. Philadelphia: University of Pennsylvania Press.

James, H. W. 1929. "The effect of handwriting upon grading," *English Journal* 16: 180–185.

James, W. 1884. "What is an emotion?" *Mind* 9: 188–205.

James, W. 1890. *The principles of psychology*. New York: Holt.

James, W. 1985/1902. *The varieties of religious experience*. New York: Penguin.

James, W. 1988. *Manuscript essays and notes*. Cambridge, MA: Harvard University Press.

Janiszewski, C. and Meyvis, T. 2001. "Effects of brand logo complexity, repetition, and spacing on processing fluency and judgment," *Journal of Consumer Research* 28: 18–32.

Johnson, K. J. and Fredrickson, B. L. 2005. "'We all look the same to me': Positive emotions eliminate the own-race in face recognition," *Psychological Science* 16: 875–881.

Jones, D. A. 2007. *Approaching the end: A theological exploration of death and dying*. Oxford: Oxford University Press.

Jones, J. and Saad, L. 2012, September 24–27. "Abortion is threshold issue for one in six U.S. voters." http://www.gallup.com/poll/157886/abortion-threshold-issue-one-six-voters.aspx (retrieved October 14, 2015).

Jones, R. P., Cox, D., and Navarro-Rivera, J. 2012. *The 2012 American Values Survey: How Catholics and the religiously unaffiliated will shape the 2012 election and beyond*. Washington, DC: Public Religion Research Institute.

Jorgensen, J. 1996. "The functions of sarcastic irony in speech," *Journal of Pragmatics* 26: 613–634.

Jung, C. G. 1971/1921. *Psychological types*. Princeton: Princeton University Press.

Juslin, P. N. and Västfjäll, D. 2008. "Emotional responses to music: The need to consider underlying mechanisms," *Behavioral and Brain Sciences* 31: 559–621.

Kagan, J. 2009. *The three cultures: Natural sciences, social sciences, and the humanities in the 21st century*. Cambridge: Cambridge University Press.

Kahn, H. 1960. *On thermonuclear war*. Princeton: Princeton University Press.

Kahneman, D. and Deaton, A. 2010. "High income improves evaluation of life but not emotional well-being," *Proceedings of the National Academy of Sciences* 107: 16489–16493.

Kahneman, D., Fredrickson, B. L., Schreiber, C. A., and Redelmeier, D. A. 1993. "When more pain is preferred to less: Adding a better end," *Psychological Science* 4: 401–405.

Kahneman, D. and Klein, G. 2009. "Conditions for intuitive expertise: A failure to disagree," *American Psychologist* 64: 515–526.

Kahneman, D., Krueger, A. B., Schkade, D., Schwarz, N., and Stone, A. A. 2006. "Would you be happier if you were richer? A focusing illusion," *Science* 312: 1908–1910.

Kahneman, D. and Miller, D. T. 1986. "Norm theory: Comparing reality to its alternatives," *Psychological Review* 93: 136–153.

Kahneman, D. and Tversky, A. 1982. "The simulation heuristic," in *Judgment under uncertainty: Heuristics and biases*, D. Kahneman, P. Slovic, and A. Tversky (eds.). New York: Cambridge University Press, 201–208.

Kaltman, S. and Bonanno, G. A. 2003. "Trauma and bereavement: Examining the impact of sudden and violent deaths," *Journal of Anxiety Disorders* 17: 131–147.

Kant, I. 2001/1790. *Critique of the power of judgment*. Cambridge: Cambridge University Press.

Kant, I. 2011/1785. *Groundwork of the metaphysics of morals: A German–English edition*. Cambridge: Cambridge University Press.

Katz, D. and Allport, F. H. 1931. *Student attitudes*. Syracuse, NY: Craftsman.

Keats, J. 1999/1820. "Ode on a Grecian urn," in *The Oxford Book of English Verse*, C. Ricks (ed.). Oxford: Oxford University Press, 401–403.

Keehner, M., Mayberry, L., and Fischer, M. H. 2011. "Different clues from different views: The role of image format in public perceptions of neuroimaging results," *Psychonomic Bulletin & Review* 18: 422–428.

Kellar, I. and Abraham, C. 2005. "Randomized controlled trial of a brief research-based intervention promoting fruit and vegetable consumption," *British Journal of Health Psychology* 10: 543–558.

Keller, M. M., Goetz, T., Becker, E. S., Morger, V., and Hensley, L. 2014. "Feeling and showing: A new conceptualization of dispositional teacher enthusiasm and its relation to students' interest," *Learning and Instruction* 33: 29–38.

Keltner, D. and Buswell B. N. 1997. "Embarrassment: Its distinct form and appeasement functions," *Psychological Bulletin* 122: 250–270.

Kendler, H. H. 2006. "Views from the inside and outside," *American Psychologist* 61: 259–261.

Kesebir, P. and Diener, E. 2008. "In pursuit of happiness: Empirical answers to philosophical questions," *Perspectives on Psychological Science* 3: 117–125.

Keysar, B. and Barr, D. J. 2002. "Self-anchoring in conversation: Why language users do not do what they 'should'," in *Heuristics and biases: The psychology of intuitive judgment*, T. Gilovich, D. Griffin, and D. Kahneman (eds.). Cambridge: Cambridge University Press, 150–166.

Kienhues, D., Ferguson, L. E., and Stahl, E. 2016. "Diverging information and epistemic change," in *Handbook of epistemic cognition*, J. Greene, W. Sandoval, and I. Bråten (eds.). London: Routledge.

Kihlstrom, J. F., Beer, J. S., and Klein, S. B. 2003. "Self and identity as memory," in *Handbook of self and identity*, M. R. Leary and J. R. Tangney (eds.). New York: Guilford Press, 68–90.

Kim, U. and Berry, J. W. 1993. *Indigenous psychologies, research and experience in cultural context*. Newbury Park, CA: Sage Publications.

Kirkham, R. L. 1992. *Theories of truth*. Cambridge, MA: MIT Press.

Kivy, P. 1990. *Music alone: Philosophical reflections on the purely musical experience*. Ithaca, NY: Cornell University Press.

Klayman, J. and Ha, Y. W. 1987. "Confirmation, disconfirmation, and information in hypothesis testing," *Psychological Review* 94: 211–228.

Kobasa, S. C., Maddi, S. R., and Kahn, S. 1982. "Hardiness and health: A prospective study," *Journal of Personality and Social Psychology* 42: 168–177.

Koenig, M. A., Clément, F., and Harris, P. L. 2004. "Trust in testimony: Children's use of true and false statements," *Psychological Science* 15: 694–698.

Kohlberg, L. 1981. *The philosophy of moral development: Moral stages and the idea of justice*. New York: Harper & Row.

Kondaš, O. 1967. "Reduction of examination anxiety and 'stage-fright' by group desensitization and relaxation," *Behaviour Research and Therapy* 5: 275–281.

Koole, S. L. 2009. "The psychology of emotion regulation," *Cognition and Emotion* 23: 4–41.

Koriat, A. 1993. "How do we know that we know? The accessibility model of the feeling of knowing," *Psychological Review* 100: 609–639.

Koriat, A. 1997. "Monitoring one's own knowledge during study: A cue-utilization approach to judgments of learning," *Journal of Experimental Psychology: General* 126: 349–370.

Koriat, A. 2000. "The feeling of knowing: Some metatheoretical implications for consciousness and control," *Consciousness and Cognition* 9: 149–171.

Kosfeld, M., Heinrichs, M., Zak, P. J., Fischbacher, U., and Fehr, E. 2005. "Oxytocin increases trust in humans," *Nature* 435: 673–676.

Kotler, P. and Zaltman, G. 1971. "Social marketing: An approach to planned social change," *Journal of Marketing* 35: 3–12.

Kraut, R. E. and Johnston, R. E. 1979. "Social and emotional messages of smiling: Ethological approach," *Journal of Personality and Social Psychology* 37: 1539–1553.

Kraybill, D. B. 2001. *The riddle of Amish culture*. Baltimore: Johns Hopkins University Press.

Krech, D., Crutchfield, R. S., and Ballachey, E. L. 1962. *Individual in society*. New York: McGraw-Hill.

Kristjánsson, K. 2013. *Virtues and vices in positive psychology*. Cambridge: Cambridge University Press.

Kruger, J. 1999. "Lake wobegon be gone! The 'below-average effect' and the egocentric nature of comparative ability judgments," *Journal of Personality and Social Psychology* 77: 221–232.

Kruger, J. and Dunning, D. 1999. "Unskilled and unaware of it: How difficulties in recognizing one's own incompetence lead to inflated self-assessments," *Journal of Personality and Social Psychology* 77: 1121–1134.

Kruger, J., Wirtz, D., and Miller, D. T. 2005. "Counterfactual thinking and the first instinct fallacy," *Journal of Personality and Social Psychology* 88: 725–735.

Kruglanski, A. W., Chen, X., Dechesne, M., Fishman, S., and Orehek, E. 2009. "Fully committed: Suicide bombers' motivation and the quest for personal significance," *Political Psychology* 30: 331–357.

Ku, H.-Y., Harter, C. A., Liu, P.-L., Thompson, L., and Cheng, Y.-C. 2007. "The effects of individually personalized computer-based instructional program on solving mathematics problems," *Computers in Human Behavior* 23: 1195–1210.

Ku, H.-Y. and Sullivan, H. J. 2000. "Personalization of mathematics word problems in Taiwan," *Educational Technology Research & Development* 48: 49–60.

Ku, H. Y. and Sullivan, H. J. 2002. "Student performance and attitudes using personalized mathematics instruction," *Educational Technology Research & Development* 50: 21–34.

Kuhn, G. and Dienes, Z. 2005. "Implicit learning of non-local musical rules," *Journal of Experimental Psychology: Learning, Memory, and Cognition* 31: 1417–1432.

Kuipers, N. A. and Rogers, T. B. 1979. "Encoding of personal information: Self–other differences," *Journal of Personality and Social Psychology* 37: 499–514.

Kull, S., Ramsay, C., and Lewis, E. 2003. "Misperceptions, the media, and the Iraq war," *Political Science Quarterly* 118: 569–598.

Kunst-Wilson, W. R. and Zajonc, R. B. 1980. "Affective discrimination of stimuli that cannot be recognized," *Science* 207: 557–558.

Kvale, S. 2003. "The church, the factory and the market: Scenarios for psychology in a postmodern age," *Theory & Psychology* 13: 579–603.

Labroo, A. A., Dhar, R., and Schwarz, N. 2008. "Of frog wines and frowning watches: Semantic priming, perceptual fluency, and brand evaluation," *Journal of Consumer Research* 34: 819–831.

Labroo, A. A., Lambotte, S., and Zhang, Y. 2009. "The 'name-ease' effect and its dual impact on importance judgments," *Psychological Science* 20: 1516–1522.

Lafortune, L. and Robertson, A. 2006. "A reflection on the relationship between emotions and critical thinking," in *Toward emotional competences*, F. Pons, M.-F. Daniel, L. Lafortune, P.-A. Doudin, and O. Albanese (eds.). Aalborg: Aalborg University Press, 131–153.

LaFrance, M. and Broadbent, M. 1976. "Group rapport: Posture sharing as a nonverbal indicator," *Group & Organization Management* 1: 328–333.

Laird, J. D. 2007. *Feelings: The perception of self.* New York: Oxford University Press.

Lakin, J. L. and Chartrand, T. L. 2003. "Using nonconscious behavioral mimicry to create affiliation and rapport," *Psychological Science* 14: 334–339.

Lakoff, G. and Johnson, M. 1980. *Metaphors we live by.* Chicago: University of Chicago Press.

Landwehr, J. R., Labroo, A. A., and Herrmann, A. 2011. "Gut liking for the ordinary: Incorporating design fluency improves automobile sales forecasts," *Marketing Science* 30: 416–429.

Landy, J. 2012. *How to do things with fictions.* Oxford: Oxford University Press.

Langer, E. J. 1989. *Mindfulness.* Cambridge, MA: Da Capo Press.

Langer, E. J. 1994. "The illusion of calculated decisions," in *Beliefs, reasoning, and decision making: Psycho-logic in honor of Bob Abelson*, R. C. Schank, and E. J. Langer (eds.). Hillsdale, NJ: Lawrence Erlbaum, 33–53.

Langer, E. J. 1997. *The power of mindful learning*. Cambridge, MA: Perseus Books.

Langlois, J. H. and Roggman, L. A. 1990. "Attractive faces are only average," *Psychological Science* 1: 115–121.

Lasswell, H. D. 1927. *Propaganda technique in the world war*. New York: Alfred A. Knopf.

Le Bon, G. 1960/1895. *The crowd: A study of the popular mind*. New York: Viking.

Leder, H., Belke, B., Oeberst, A., and Augustin, D. 2004. "A model of aesthetic appreciation and aesthetic judgments," *British Journal of Psychology* 95: 489–508.

Lee, A. Y. 2001. "The mere exposure effect: An uncertainty reduction explanation revisited," *Personality and Social Psychology Bulletin* 27: 1255–1266.

Lee, A. Y. and Labroo, A. A. 2004. "The effect of conceptual and perceptual fluency on brand evaluation," *Journal of Marketing Research* 41: 151–165.

Lehrer, P. M. 1987. "A review of the approaches to the management of tension and stage fright in music performance," *Journal of Research in Music Education* 35: 143–153.

Lerner, J. S., Gonzalez, R. M., Small, D. A., and Fischhoff, B. 2003. "Effects of fear and anger on perceived risks of terrorism: A national field experiment," *Psychological Science* 14: 144–150.

Lerner, J. S., Li, Y., Valdesolo, P., and Kassam, K. 2015. "Emotion and decision making," *Annual Review of Psychology* 66: 799–823.

Lev-Ari, S. and Keysar, B. 2010. "Why don't we believe non-native speakers? The influence of accent on credibility," *Journal of Experimental Social Psychology* 46: 1093–1096.

Leventhal, H. and Scherer, K. 1987. "The relationship of emotion to cognition: A functional approach to a semantic controversy," *Cognition and Emotion* 1: 3–28.

Levinson, J. 1979. "Defining art historically," *British Journal of Aesthetics* 19: 232–250.

Levinson, J. 1989. "Refining art historically," *Journal of Aesthetics and Art Criticism* 47: 21–33.

Levinson, J. 1993. "Extending art historically," *Journal of Aesthetics and Art Criticism* 51: 411–423.

Lewis, H. B. 1971. *Guilt and shame in neurosis*. New York: International Universities Press.

Libby, L. K., Shaeffer, E. M., Eibach, R. P., and Slemmer, J. A. 2007. "Picture yourself at the polls: Visual perspective in mental imagery affects self-perception and behavior," *Psychological Science* 18: 199–203.

Lick, D. J. and Johnson, K. L. 2015. "The interpersonal consequences of processing ease: Fluency as a metacognitive foundation for prejudice," *Current Directions in Psychological Science* 24: 143–148.

Liljedahl, P. G. 2005. "Mathematical discovery and affect: The effect of AHA! experiences on undergraduate mathematics students," *International Journal of Mathematical Education in Science and Technology* 36: 219–234.

Lipman, M. 2003. *Thinking in education*. Cambridge: Cambridge University Press.

Livingston, P. 2005. *Art and intention*. Oxford: Oxford University Press.

Locher, P. J. 2012. "Empirical investigation of an aesthetic experience with art," in *Aesthetic science: Connecting minds, brains, and experience*, A. P. Shimamura and S. E. Palmer (eds.). New York: Oxford University Press, 163–188.

Loewenstein, G., O'Donoghue, T., and Rabin, M. 2003. "Projection bias in predicting future utility," *Quarterly Journal of Economics* 118: 1209–1248.

Lopes , D. 2005. *Sight and sensibility*. Oxford: Oxford Univerity Press.

Lopez, S. J. and Snyder, C. R. 2011. *The Oxford handbook of positive psychology*. Oxford: Oxford University Press.

Lord, C. 2013. *Aristotle's* Politics, 2nd edition. Chicago: University of Chicago Press.

Luhrmann, T. M. 2012. *When God talks back*. New York: Alfred A. Knopf.

Lyons, I. M. and Beilock, S. L. 2012. "Mathematics anxiety: Separating the math from the anxiety," *Cerebral Cortex* 22: 2102–2110.

Lyubomirsky, S., King, L., and Diener, E. 2005. "The benefits of frequent positive affect: Does happiness lead to success?" *Psychological Bulletin* 131: 803–855.

MacIntyre, A. 1985. *After virtue*. London: Duckworth.

Mackie, D. M. and Worth, L. T. 1989. "Processing deficits and the mediation of positive affect in persuasion," *Journal of Personality and Social Psychology* 51: 27–40.

Mackie, J. 1977. *Ethics: Inventing right and wrong*. New York: Penguin.

MacKuen, M., Wolak, J., Keele, L., and Marcus, G. E. 2010. "Civic engagements: Resolute partisanship or reflective deliberation," *American Journal of Political Science* 54: 440–458.

Macrae, C. N., Bodenhausen, G. V., Milne, A. B., and Jetten, J. 1994. "Out of mind but back in sight: Stereotypes on the rebound," *Journal of Personality and Social Psychology* 67: 808.

Macrae, C. N., Duffy, O. K., Miles, L. K., and Lawrence, J. 2008. "A case of hand waving: Action synchrony and person perception," *Cognition* 109: 152–156.

Magner, U. I. E., Schwonke, R., Aleven, V., Popescu, O., and Renkl, A. 2014. "Triggering situational interest by decorative illustrations both fosters and hinders learning in computer-based learning environments," *Learning and Instruction* 29: 141–152.

Maio, G. R. and Olson, J. M. 1998. "Values as truisms: Evidence and implications," *Journal of Personality and Social Psychology* 74: 294–311.

Makin, A. D. J., Pecchinenda, A., and Bertamini, M. 2012. "Implicit affective evaluation of visual symmetry," *Emotion* 12: 1021–1030.

Makropoulos, H. 2010. *No one would listen: A true financial thriller*. Hoboken, NJ: Wiley.

Malloch, S. N. 2000. "Mothers and infants and communicative musicality," *Musicae Scientiae* 3: 29–57.

Mandler, G. 1975. *Mind and emotion*. New York: Wiley.

Mangan, B. 1993. "Taking phenomenology seriously: The 'fringe' and its implications for cognitive research," *Consciousness and Cognition* 2: 89–108.

Mantonakis, A., Whittlesea, B. W. A., and Yoon, C. 2008. "Consumer memory, fluency, and familiarity," in *Handbook of consumer psychology*, C. P. Haugtvedt, P. Herr, and F. Kardes (eds.). Hove, UK: Lawrence Erlbaum, 77–102.

Markham, I. S. 2010. *Against atheism: Why Dawkins, Hitchens, and Harris are fundamentally wrong*. Chichester, UK: Wiley-Blackwell.

Markham, L. R. 1976. "Influences of handwriting quality on teacher evaluation of written work," *American Educational Research Journal* 13: 277–283.

Marsh, H. W. 1987. "The big-fish-little-pond effect on academic self-concept," *Journal of Educational Psychology* 79: 280–295.

Marsh, H. W., Abduljabbar, A. S., Morin, A. J. S., Parker, P., Abdelfattah, F., Nagengast, B., and Abu-Hilal, M. M. 2015. "The big-fish-little-pond effect: Generalizability of social comparison processes over two age cohorts from Western, Asian, and Middle Eastern Islamic countries," *Journal of Educational Psychology* 107: 258–271.

Marsh, H. W. and Hau, K. T. 2003. "Big-fish-little-pond effect on academic self-concept: A cross-cultural (26-country) test of the negative effects of academically selective schools," *American Psychologist* 58: 364–376.

Marsh, H. W. and Parker, J. W. 1984. "Determinants of student self-concept: Is it better to be a relatively large fish in a small pond even if you don't learn to swim as well?" *Journal of Personality and Social Psychology* 47: 213–231.

Marsh, K. L., Richardson, M. J., Baron, R. M., and Schmidt, R. C. 2006. "Contrasting approaches to perceiving and acting with others," *Ecological Psychology* 18: 1–38.

Marsh, K. L., Richardson, M. J., and Schmidt, R. C. 2009. "Social connection through joint action and interpersonal coordination," *Topics in Cognitive Science* 1: 320–339.

Marsh, R. L., Landau, J. D., and Hicks, J. L. 1997. "Contributions of inadequate source monitoring to unconscious plagiarism during idea generation," *Journal of Experimental Psychology: Learning, Memory, and Cognition* 23: 886–897.

Marteau, R. A., Wynne, G., Kaye, W., and Evans, T. R. 1990. "Resuscitation: Experience without feedback increases confidence but not skill," *British Medical Journal* 300: 849–850.

Martin, J. R. 1992. "Critical thinking for a humane world," in *The generalizability of critical thinking*, S. P. Norris (ed.). New York: Teachers College Press, 163–180.

Martin, L. L., Ward, D. W., Achee, J. W., and Wyer, R. S. 1993. "Mood as input: People have to interpret the motivational implications of their moods," *Journal of Personality and Social Psychology* 64: 317–326.

Marx, K. 1975/1843. "Letter to A. Ruge, September 1843," in *Karl Marx: Early writings*. New York: Vintage Books, 209.

Maslow, A. H. 1943. "A theory of human motivation," *Psychological Review* 50: 370–396.

Massachusetts House of Representatives. 1837. *Reports on the abolition of capital punishment*. Boston: Dutton and Wentworth.

Mauss, I. B., Shallcross, A. J., Troy, A. S., John, O. P., Ferrer, E., Wilhelm, F. H., and Gross, J. J. 2011. "Don't hide your happiness! Positive emotion dissociation, social connectedness, and psychological functioning," *Journal of Personality and Social Psychology* 100: 738–748.

Mauss, I. B., Tamir, M., Anderson, C. L., and Savino, N. S. 2011. "Can seeking happiness make people unhappy? Paradoxical effects of valuing happiness," *Emotion* 11: 807–815.

Mauss, M. 2000/1925. *The gift: The form and reason for exchange in archaic societies*. New York: W. W. Norton.

Mayer, R. and Wittrock, M. C. 1996. "Problem-solving transfer," in *Handbook of educational psychology*, D. Berliner and R. Calfee (eds.). New York: Macmillan, 45–61.

Mayer, R. E. 2001. *Multimedia learning*. Cambridge: Cambridge University Press.

Mazur, J. E. 2006. *Learning and behavior*, 6th edition. Upper Saddle River, NJ: Pearson Prentice Hall.

McCabe, D. P. and Castel, A. D. 2008. "Seeing is believing: The effect of brain images on judgments of scientific reasoning," *Cognition* 107: 343–352.

McCauley, R. N. and Lawson, E. T. 2002. *Bringing ritual to mind: Psychological foundations of cultural forms*. Cambridge: Cambridge University Press.

McColm, G. 2007. "A metaphor for mathematics education," *Notices of the American Mathematical Association* 54: 499–502.

McCrory, P., Meeuwisse, W. H., Aubry, M., Cantu, R. C., Dvořák, J., Echemendia, R. J. et al. 2013. "Consensus statement on concussion in sport: The 4th international conference on concussion in sport, Zurich," *Journal of Athletic Training* 48: 554–575.

McGuire, J. 2008. "A review of effective interventions for reducing aggression and violence," *Philosophical Transactions of the Royal Society B: Biological Sciences* 363: 2577–2597.

McMurran, M., Fyffe, S., McCarthy, L., Duggan, C., and Latham, A. 2001. "'Stop & think!': Social problem-solving therapy with personality-disordered offenders," *Criminal Behaviour and Mental Health* 11: 273–285.

McNamara, D. S., Kintsch, E., Songer, N. B., and Kintsch, W. 1996. "Are good texts always better? Interactions of text coherence, background knowledge, and levels of understanding in learning from text," *Cognition and Instruction* 14: 1–43.

McNeill, W. H. 1995. *Keeping together in time: Dance and drill in human history.* Cambridge, MA: Harvard University Press.

McPeck, J. E. 1981. *Critical thinking and education.* Oxford: Martin Robertson & Company.

McWhinnie, H. J. 1968. "A review on aesthetic measure," *Acta Psychologica* 28: 363–375.

Medvec, V. H., Madey, S. F., and Gilovich, T. 1995. "When less is more: Counterfactual thinking and satisfaction among Olympic medalists," *Journal of Personality and Social Psychology* 69: 603–610.

Meltzoff, A. N. and Moore, M. K. 1977. "Imitation of facial and manual gestures by human neonates," *Science* 198: 75–78.

Menninghaus, W. 2003. *Disgust: The theory and history of a strong sensation.* Albany: SUNY Press.

Mercier, H. and Sperber, D. 2011. "Why do humans reason? Arguments for an argumentative theory," *Behavioral and Brain Sciences* 34: 57–111.

Metcalfe, J. and Wiebe, D. 1987. "Intuition in insight and noninsight problem solving," *Memory & Cognition* 15: 238–246.

Mikhail, J. 2009. "Is the prohibition of homicide universal? Evidence from comparative criminal law," *Brooklyn Law Review* 75: 497–515.

Milgram, S. 2009/1974. *Obedience to authority: An experimental view.* New York: Perennial Classics.

Mill, J. S. 2002/1863. *Utilitarianism.* Indianapolis: Hackett.

Miller, G. A., Galanter, E., and Pribram, K. H. 1960. *Plans and the structure of behavior.* New York: Holt.

Miller, R. S. 1995. "Embarrassment and social behavior," in *Self conscious emotions,* J. P. Tangney and K. W. Fischer (eds.). New York: Guilford Press, 322–339.

Mischel, W. and Shoda, Y. 1995. "A cognitive-affective system theory of personality: Reconceptualizing situations, dispositions, dynamics, and invariance in personality structure," *Psychological Review* 102: 246–268.

Moore, B. N. and Parker, R. 2012. *Critical thinking.* New York: McGraw-Hill.

Morales, A. C., Wu, E. C., and Fitzsimons, G. J. 2012. "How disgust enhances the effectiveness of fear appeals," *Journal of Marketing Research* 49: 383–393.

Morris, I. M. 2014. *War! What is it good for? Conflict and the progress of civilization from primates to robots.* New York: Farrar, Straus and Giroux.

Mueller, S. and Szolnoki, G. 2010. "The relative influence of packaging, labelling, branding and sensory attributes on liking and purchase intent: Consumers differ in their responsiveness," *Food Quality and Preference* 21: 774–783.

Munsinger, H. and Kessen, W. 1964. "Uncertainty, structure, and preference," *Psychological Monographs* 78: 1–24.

Muraven, M. and Baumeister, R. F. 2000. "Self-regulation and depletion of limited resources: Does self-control resemble a muscle?" *Psychological Bulletin* 126: 247–259.

Muth, C. and Carbon, C. C. 2013. "The aesthetic aha: On the pleasure of having insights into Gestalt," *Acta Psychologica* 144: 25–30.

Myers, D. G. 1993. *The pursuit of happiness*. New York: Avon Books.

Nabi, R. L. 2003. "Exploring the framing effects of emotion: Do discrete emotions differentially influence information accessibility, information seeking, and policy preference?" *Communication Research* 30: 224–247.

Neisser, U. 1976. *Cognition and reality: Principles and implications of cognitive psychology*. New York: W. H. Freeman.

Nelissen, R. M. A. and Zeelenberg, M. 2009. "When guilt evokes self-punishment: Evidence for the existence of a Dobby effect," *Emotion* 9: 118–122.

Nelson, L. D. and Meyvis, T. 2008. "Interrupted consumption: Disrupting adaptation to hedonic experiences," *Journal of Marketing Research* 45: 654–664.

Nelson, T. O. and Dunlosky, J. 1991. "When people's judgments of learning (JOLs) are extremely accurate at predicting subsequent recall: The 'delayed-JOL effect'," *Psychological Science* 2: 267–270.

Neumann, R. and Strack, F. 2000. "'Mood contagion': The automatic transfer of mood between persons," *Journal of Personality and Social Psychology* 79: 211–223.

Neves, D. M. and Anderson, J. R. 1981. "Knowledge compilation: Mechanisms for the automatization of cognitive skills," in *Cognitive skills and their acquisition*, J. R. Anderson (ed.). Hillsdale, NJ: Lawrence Erlbaum: 57–84.

Newell, B. R. and Shanks, D. R. 2014. "Unconscious influences on decision making: A critical review," *Behavioral and Brain Sciences* 37: 1–61.

Newman, E. J., Garry, M., Bernstein, D. M., Kantner, J., and Lindsay, D. S. 2012. "Nonprobative photographs (or words) inflate truthiness," *Psychological Bulletin & Review* 19: 969–974.

Nisbett, R. E. 2003. *The geography of thought: How Asians and Westerners think differently... and why*. New York: Free Press.

Nisbett, R. E. and Wilson, T. D. 1977. "Telling more than we can know: Verbal reports on mental processes," *Psychological Review* 84: 231.

Nivison, D. 1996. *The ways of Confucianism*. La Salle, IL: Open Court.

Noddings, N. 2003. *Happiness and education*. Cambridge: Cambridge University Press.

Noddings, N. 2012. *Philosophy of education*. Boulder, CO: Westview Press.

Noddings, N. and Shore, P. J. 1984. *Awakening the inner eye: Intuition in education*. New York: Teachers College Press.

Nordhielm, C. L. 2002. "The influence of level of processing on advertising repetition effects," *Journal of Consumer Research* 29: 371–382.

Norenzayan, A. 2013. *Big gods: How religion transformed cooperation and conflict*. Princeton: Princeton University Press.

Norenzayan, A., Atran, S., Faulkner, J., and Schaller, M. 2006. "Memory and mystery: The cultural selection of minimally counterintuitive narratives," *Cognitive Science* 30: 531–553.

Norenzayan, A. and Gervais, W. M. 2013. "The origins of religious disbelief," *Trends in Cognitive Sciences*, 17: 20–25.

Norenzayan, A., Gervais, W. M., and Trzesniewski, K. H. 2012. "Mentalizing deficits constrain belief in a personal God," *PLoS ONE* 7: e36880.

Norenzayan, A. and Shariff, A. F. 2008. "The origin and evolution of religious prosociality," *Science* 322: 58–62.

Norman, V. 2004. *Blue notes: Politikkens paradokser [Blue notes: The paradoxes of politics]*. Bergen, Norway: Fagbokforlaget.

Norton, M. L. and Gino, F. 2014. "Rituals alleviate grieving for loved ones, lovers, and lotteries," *Journal of Experimental Psychology: General* 143: 266–272.

Nunes, J. C., Ordanini, A., and Valsesia, F. 2015. "The power of repetition: Repetitive lyrics in a song increase processing fluency and drive market success," *Journal of Consumer Psychology* 25:187–199.

Nussbaum, M. C. 1986. *The therapy of desire: Theory and practice in hellenistic ethics*. Princeton: Princeton University Press.

Nussbaum, M. C. 1990. *Love's knowledge: Essays on philosophy and literature*. Oxford: Oxford University Press.

Ochsner, K. N. and Gross, J. J. 2008. "Cognitive emotion regulation: Insights from social cognitive and affective neuroscience," *Current Directions in Psychological Science* 17: 153–158.

OECD (Organisation for Economic Co-operation and Development). 2014. *PISA 2012 technical report*. Paris: OECD.

Öhman, A. and Mineka, S. 2001. "Fears, phobias, and preparedness: Toward an evolved module of fear and fear learning," *Psychological Review* 108: 483–522.

Olson, D. R. 2003. *Psychological theory and educational reform: How school remakes mind and society*. Cambridge: Cambridge University Press.

Opacic, T., Stevens, C., and Tillmann, B. 2009. "Unspoken knowledge: Implicit learning of structured human dance movement," *Journal of Experimental Psychology:Learning, Memory, and Cognition* 35: 1570–1577.

Ornaghi, V., Brockmeier, J., and Grazzani, I. 2014. "Enhancing social cognition by training children in emotion understanding: A primary school study," *Journal of Experimental Child Psychology* 119: 26–39.

Oswald, M. E. and Grosjean, S. 2004. "Confirmation bias," in *Cognitive illusions*, R. F. Pohl (ed.). Hove, UK: Psychology Press, 79–94.

Ouellette, J. and Wood, W. 1998. "Habit and intention in everyday life: The multiple processes by which past behavior predicts future behavior," *Psychological Bulletin* 124: 54–74.

Overall, N. C., Fletcher, G. J., Simpson, J. A., and Sibley, C. G. 2009. "Regulating partners in intimate relationships: The costs and benefits of different communication strategies," *Journal of Personality and Social Psychology* 96: 620–639.

Overskeid, G. 2000. "The slave of the passions: Experiencing problems and selecting solutions," *Review of General Psychology* 4: 211–237.

Oyserman, D. 2011. "Culture as situated cognition: Cultural mindsets, cultural fluency, and meaning making," *European Review of Social Psychology* 22: 164–214.

Oyserman, D. 2015. *Pathways to success through identity-based motivation*. Oxford: Oxford University Press.

Oyserman, D., Bybee, D., and Terry, K. 2006. "Possible selves and academic outcomes: How and when possible selves impel action," *Journal of Personality and Social Psychology* 91: 188–204.

Ozment, S. 1983. *When fathers ruled: Family life in Reformation Europe*. Cambridge, MA: Harvard University Press.

Páez, D., Rimé, B., Basabe, N., Wlodarczyk, A., and Zumeta, L. 2015. "Psychosocial effects of perceived emotional synchrony in collective gatherings," *Journal of Personality and Social Psychology* 108: 711–729.

Palmer, S. E. 1999. *Vision science: Photons to phenomenology*. Cambridge MA: MIT Press.

Palmer, S. E., Schloss, K. B., and Sammartino, J. 2013. "Visual aesthetics and human preference," *Annual Review of Psychology* 64: 77–107.

Parducci, A. 1995. *Happiness, pleasure, and judgement: The contextual theory and its applications*. Mahwah, NJ: Lawrence Erlbaum.

Parker, M. T. and Isbell, L. M. 2010. "How I vote depends on how I feel: The differential impact of anger and fear on political information processing," *Psychological Science* 21: 548–550.

Parkinson, B. and Totterdell, P. 1999. "Classifying affect regulation strategies," *Cognition and Emotion* 13: 277–303.

Parks, C. M. and Toth, J. P. 2006. "Fluency, familiarity, aging, and the illusion of truth," *Aging, Neuropsychology, and Cognition* 13: 225–253.

Parr, W. V., Heatherbell, D., and White, K. G. 2002. "Demystifying wine expertise: Olfactory threshold, perceptual skill and semantic memory in expert and novice wine judges," *Chemical Senses* 27: 747–755.

Parrott, W. G. (ed.). 2015. *The positive side of negative emotions*. New York: Guilford Press.

Parsons, M. L. 1987. *How we understand art: A cognitive developmental account of aesthetic experience*. Cambridge: Cambridge University Press.

Pascal, B. 1995/1660. *Pensées*. London: Penguin.

Paul, R. W. and Elder, L. 2002. *Critical thinking: Tools for taking charge of your professional and personal life*. Upper Saddle River, NJ: Pearson Education.

Pekrun, R., Goetz, T. W. T., and Perry, R. P. 2002. "Academic emotions in students' self-regulated learning and achievement: A program of qualitative and quantitative research," *Educational Psychologist* 37: 91–105.

Pennebaker, J. W. 1997. "Writing about emotional experiences as a therapeutic process," *Psychological Science* 8: 162–166.

Perkins, D. N. 1981. *The mind's best work*. Cambridge, MA: Harvard University Press.

Perkins, D. N., Farady, M., and Bushey, B. 1991. "Everyday reasoning and the roots of intelligence", in *Informal reasoning and education*, J. F. Voss, D. N. Perkins, and J. W. Segal (eds.). Hillsdale, NJ: Erlbaum, 83–105.

Perrett, D. I., May, K. A., and Yoshikawa, S. 1994. "Facial shape and judgments of female attractiveness," *Nature* 368: 239–242.

Peterson, C., Maier, S. F., and Seligman, M. E. P. 1995. *Learned helplessness: A theory for the age of personal control*. New York: Oxford University Press.

Peterson, C. and Seligman, M. E. P. 2004. *Character strengths and virtues: A handbook and classification*. Oxford: Oxford University Press.

Petrie, K. J., Booth, R. J., and Pennebaker, J. W. 1998. "The immunological effects of thought suppression," *Journal of Personality and Social Psychology* 75: 1264–1272.

Petty, R. E. and Cacioppo, J. T. 1981. *Attitude and persuasion: Classic and contemporary approaches*. Dubuque, IA: William C. Brown.

Pham, L. B. and Taylor, S. E. 1999. "From thought to action: Effects of process- versus outcome-based mental simulations on performance," *Personality and Social Psychology Bulletin* 25: 250–260.

Piaget, J. 1970. "Piaget's theory," in *Carmichael's manual of child psychology*, P. H. Mussen. New York: Wiley, 703–732.

Plassmann, H., O'Doherty, J., Shiv, B., and Rangel, A. 2008. "Marketing actions can modulate neural representations of experienced pleasantness," *Proceedings of the National Academy of Sciences* 105: 1050–1054.

Pliner, P. 1982. "The effects of mere exposure on liking for edible substances," *Appetite* 3: 283–290.

Poincaré, H. 1996/1913. *Science and method*. London: Routledge/Thoemess Press.

Pons, F., Harris, P. L., and Doudin, P. A. 2002. "Teaching emotion understanding," *European Journal of Psychology of Education* 17: 293–304.

Ponsonby, A. 1928. *Falsehood in wartime: Propaganda lies of the First World War*. London: George Allen and Unwin.

Popper, K. 2002/1963. *Conjectures and refutations*. London: Routledge & Kegan Paul.

Popper, K. R. 1945. *The open society and its enemies* (2 vols). London: Routledge.

Porter, D. and Neuringer, A. 1984. "Musical discriminations by pigeons," *Journal of Experimental Psychology: Animal Behavior Processes* 10: 138–148.

Prentice, D. A. and Miller, D. T. 1993. "Pluralistic ignorance and alcohol use on campus: Some consequences of misperceiving the social norm," *Journal of Personality and Social Psychology* 64: 243–256.

Price, R. A. and Vandenberg, S. G. 1980. "Spouse similarity in American and Swedish couples," *Behavior Genetics* 10: 59–71.

Prinz, J. J. 2004. *Gut reactions: A perceptual theory of emotion*. Oxford: Oxford University Press.

Pritchard, M. 2014. "Philosophy for children," in *The Stanford encyclopedia of philosophy*, E. N. Zalta (ed.). http://plato.stanford.edu/entries/children (retrieved October 19, 2015).

Prosen, M., Clark, D. C., Harrow, M., and Fawcett, J. 1983. "Guilt and conscience in major depressive disorders," *American Journal of Psychiatry* 140: 839–844.

Proust, J. 2013. *The philosophy of metacognition*. Oxford: Oxford University Press.

Proust, J. 2014. "The representational structure of feelings," in *Open MIND*, T. Metzinger and J. M. Windt (eds.). Frankfurt: MIND Group.

Quoidbach, J., Mikolajczak, M., and Gross, J. J. 2015. "Positive interventions: An emotion regulation perspective," *Psychological Bulletin* 141: 655–693.

Rachman, S. 1967. "Systematic desensitization," *Psychological Bulletin* 67: 93–103.

Rajagopalan, M. S., Khanna, V., Stott, M., Leiter, Y., Showalter, T. N., Dicker, A., and Lawrence, Y. R. 2010. "Accuracy of cancer information on the Internet: A comparison of a Wiki with a professionally maintained database," *Journal of Clinical Oncology* (Meeting Abstracts).

Rakoczy, H., Warneken, F., and Tomasello, M. 2008. "Sources of normativity: Young children's awareness of the normative structure of games," *Developmental Psychology* 44: 875–881.

Ramachandran, V. S. and Hirstein, W. 1999. "The science of art: A neurological theory of aesthetic experience," *Journal of Consciousness Studies* 6: 15–51.

Rappaport, R. A. 1999. *Ritual and religion in the making of humanity*. Cambridge: Cambridge University Press.

Ravitch, D. 2000. *Left back: A century of failed school reforms*. New York: Simon & Schuster.

Rawls, J. 1971. *A theory of justice*. Cambridge, MA: Belknap Press of Harvard University Press.

Ray, M. L. and Wilkie, W. L. 1970. "Fear: The potential of an appeal neglected by marketing," *Journal of Marketing* 34: 54–62.

Reade, C. 1895/1870. *The work of Charles Reade, D.C.L.: Put yourself in his place, Vol. I*. New York: Metropolitan.

Reber, R. 2008. "Art in its experience: Can empirical psychology help assess artistic value?" *Leonardo* 41: 367–372.

Reber, R. 2012a. "Critical feeling: The strategic use of processing fluency," in *The experience of thinking*, C. Unkelbach and R. Greifeneder (eds.). Hove, UK: Psychology Press, 169–184.

Reber, R. 2012b. "Processing fluency, aesthetic pleasure, and culturally shared taste," in *Aesthetic science: Connecting mind, brain, and experience*, A. P. Shimamura and S. E. Palmer. New York: Oxford University Press, 223–249.

Reber, R. 2014. "Mindfulness in education," in *Handbook of mindfulness*, A. Ie, C. Ngnoumen and E. Langer. Oxford: Wiley-Blackwell, 1054–1070.

Reber, R., Brun, M., and Mitterndorfer, K. 2008. "The use of heuristics in intuitive mathematical judgment," *Psychonomic Bulletin & Review* 15: 1174–1178.

Reber, R. and Flammer, A. 2002. "The development of gender differences in affective expression and in the relationship between mood and achievement-related self-judgments," *European Journal of Psychology of Education* 17: 377–392.

Reber, R., Hetland, H., Chen, W., Norman, E., and Kobbeltvedt, T. 2009. "Effects of example choice on interest, control, and learning," *Journal of the Learning Sciences* 18: 509–548.

Reber, R., Meier, B., Ruch-Monachon, M. A., and Tiberini, M. 2006. "Effects of processing fluency on comparative performance judgments," *Acta Psychologica* 123: 337–354.

Reber, R. and Norenzayan, A. 2010. "The shared fluency theory of social cohesiveness." http://papers.ssrn.com/sol3/papers.cfm?abstract_id=1702407 (retrieved October 19, 2015).

Reber, R., Ruch-Monachon, M.-A., and Perrig, W. J. 2007. "Decomposing intuitive components in a conceptual problem solving task," *Consciousness and Cognition* 16: 294–309.

Reber, R. and Schwarz, N. 1999. "Effects of perceptual fluency on judgments of truth," *Consciousness and Cognition* 8: 338–342.

Reber, R. and Schwarz, N. 2006. "Perceptual fluency, preference, and evolution," *Polish Psychological Bulletin* 37: 16–22.

Reber, R., Schwarz, N., and Winkielman, P. 2004. "Processing fluency and aesthetic pleasure: Is beauty in the perceiver's processing experience?" *Personality and Social Psychology Review* 8: 364–382.

Reber, R. and Slingerland, E. G. 2011. "Confucius meets cognition: New answers to old questions," *Religion, Brain & Behavior* 1: 135–145.

Reber, R. and Unkelbach, C. 2010. "The epistemic status of processing fluency as source for judgments of truth," *Review of Philosophy and Psychology* 1: 563–581.

Reber, R., Winkielman, P., and Schwarz, N. 1998. "Effects of perceptual fluency on affective judgments," *Psychological Science* 9: 45–48.

Reber, R., Wurtz, P., and Zimmermann, T. D. 2004. "Exploring 'fringe' consciousness: The subjective experience of perceptual fluency and its objective bases," *Consciousness and Cognition* 13: 47–60.

Redelmeier, D. A. and Kahneman, D. 1996. "Patients' memories of painful medical treatments: Real-time and retrospective evaluations of two minimally invasive procedures," *Pain* 66: 3–8.

Redelmeier, D. A., Katz, J., and Kahneman, D. 2003. "Memories of colonoscopy: A randomized trial," *Pain* 104: 187–194.

Regan, P. C., Lakhanpal, S., and Anguiano, C. 2012. "Relationship outcomes in Indian–American love-based and arranged marriages," *Psychological Reports* 110: 915–924.

Reisenzein, R. 2007. "What is a definition of emotion? And are emotions mental–behavioral processes?" *Social Science Information* 46: 424–428.

Renneker, R. E. 1990. "Cancer and psychotherapy," in *The psychotherapeutic treatment of cancer patients*, J. G. Goldberg (ed.). New Brunswick, NJ: Transaction, 131–166.

Rhodes, G. 2006. "The evolutionary psychology of facial beauty," *Annual Review of Psychology* 57: 199–226.

Rimé, B., Herbette, G., and Corsini, S. 2004. "The social sharing of emotion," in *Emotional expression and health: Advances in theory, assessment and clinical applications*, I. Nykliček, L. Temoshok, and A. Vingerhoets (eds.). Hove, UK: Brunner-Routledge, 29–42.

Robinson, J. 2005. *Deeper than reason: Emotion and its role in literature, music, and art*. Oxford: Clarendon Press.

Rogers, A. 2008. *Murder and the death penalty in Massachusetts*. Amherst: University of Massachusetts Press.

Rogers, T. B., Kuiper, N. A., and Kirker, W. S. 1977. "Self-reference and the encoding of personal information," *Journal of Personality and Social Psychology* 35: 677–688.

Rokeach, M. 1973. *The nature of human values*. New York: Free Press.

Rombouts, H. 1987. "Grondslagen voor verliefdheid [The basics of falling in love]," *Tijdschrift voor Seksuologie* 11: 200–214.

Rosch, E. 1996. "The environment of minds: Toward a noetic and hedonic ecology," in *Cognitive ecology*, M. P. Friedman and E. C. Carterette (eds.). San Diego: Academic Press, 3–27.

Roseman, I. J., Antoniou, A. A., and Jose, P. E. 1996. "Appraisal determinants of emotions: Constructing a more accurate and comprehensive theory," *Cognition and Emotion* 10: 241–278.

Rosenberg, M. J. and Hovland, C. I. 1960. "Cognitive, affective, and behavioral components of attitudes," in *Attitude organization and change*, C. I. Hovland and M. J. Rosenberg (eds.). New Haven: Yale University Press, 1–14.

Ross, L., Lepper, M. R., and Hubbard, M. 1975. "Perseverance in self-perception and social perception: Biased attributional processes in the debriefing paradigm," *Journal of Personality and Social Psychology* 32: 880–892.

Ross, L. and Nisbett, R. E. 1991. *The person and the situation: Perspectives of social psychology*. New York: McGraw-Hill.

Ross, S. M. and Anand, P. G. 1987. "A computer-based strategy for personalizing verbal problems in teaching mathematics," *Educational Communication and Technology Journal* 35: 151–162.

Rossano, M. J. 2012. "The essential role of ritual in the transmission and reinforcement of social norms," *Psychological Bulletin* 138: 529–549.

Rothman, A. J. and Schwarz, N. 1998. "Constructing perceptions of vulnerability: Personal relevance and the use of experiential information in health judgments," *Personality and Social Psychology Bulletin* 24: 1053–1064.

Rouse, J. 2002. *How scientific practices matter: Reclaiming philosophical naturalism*. Chicago: University of Chicago Press.

Rowe, G., Hirsh, J. B., and Anderson, A. K. 2007. "Positive affect increases the breadth of attentional selection," *Proceedings of the National Academy of Sciences* 104: 383–388.

Rozenblit, L. and Keil, F. 2002. "The misunderstood limits of folk science: An illusion of explanatory depth," *Cognitive Science* 26: 521–562.

Rozin, P. 2006. "Domain denigration and process preference in academic psychology," *Perspectives on Psychological Science* 1: 365–376.

Rozin, P., Kabnick, K., Pete, E., Fischler, C., and Shields, C. 2003. "The ecology of eating: Smaller portion sizes in France than in the United States help explain the French paradox," *Psychological Science* 14: 450–454.

Rozin, P. and Royzman, E. 2001. "Negativity bias, negativity dominance, and contagion," *Personality and Social Psychology Review* 5: 296–320.

Rozin, P. and Vollmecke, T. A. 1986. "Food likes and dislikes," *Annual Review of Nutrition* 6: 433–456.

Rubin, D. C. 1995. *Memory in oral traditions: The cognitive psychology of epic, ballads, and counting-out rhymes.* Oxford: Oxford University Press.

Rubin, M., Paolini, S., and Crisp, R. J. 2010. "A processing fluency explanation of bias against migrants," *Journal of Experimental Social Psychology* 46: 21–28.

Ruedy, N. E., Moore, C., Gino, F., and Schweitzer, M. E. 2013. "The cheater's high: The unexpected affective benefits of unethical behavior," *Journal of Personality and Social Psychology* 105: 531–548.

Ryan, R. M. and Deci, E. L. 2000. "Self-determination theory and the facilitation of intrinsic motivation, social development, and well-being," *American Psychologist* 55: 68–78.

Saarni, C. 1999. *Development of emotional competence.* New York: Guilford Press.

Salovey, P. and Mayer, J. D. 1990. "Emotional intelligence," *Imagination, Cognition, and Personality* 9: 185–211.

Sanders, M. L. and Taylor, P. M. 1982. *British propaganda during the First World War, 1914–18.* London: Macmillan.

Schachter, S. and Gross, L. P. 1968. "Manipulated time and eating behavior," *Journal of Personality and Social Psychology* 10: 98–106.

Schanck, R. L. 1932. "A study of a community and its groups and institutions conceived of as behaviors of individuals," *Psychological Monographs* 43: 1–133.

Schellekens, E. and Goldie, P. 2011. *The aesthetic mind: Philosophy and psychology.* Oxford: Oxford University Press.

Schellenberg, E. G. and Trehub, S. E. 1996. "Natural music intervals: Evidence from infant listeners," *Psychological Science* 7: 272–277.

Scherer, K. R. 1984. "On the nature and function of emotion: A component process approach," in *Approaches to emotion,* K. R. Scherer and P. Ekman (eds.). Hillsdale, NJ: Lawrence Erlbaum, 293–317.

Scherer, K. R. 2005. "What are emotions? And how can they be measured?" *Social Science Information* 44: 695–729.

Schiefele, U. 1991. "Interest, learning, and motivation," *Educational Psychologist* 26: 299–323.

Schooler, J. W., Ariely, D., and Loewenstein, G. 2003. "The pursuit and assessment of happiness can be self-defeating," *Psychology of Economic Decisions* 1: 41–70.

Schroeder, C. M. and Prentice, D. A. 1998. "Exposing pluralistic ignorance to reduce alcohol use among college students," *Journal of Applied Social Psychology* 28: 2150–2180.

Schubert, T. W. 2005. "Your highness: Vertical positions as perceptual symbols of power," *Journal of Personality and Social Psychology* 89: 1–21.

Schubert, T. W., Waldzus, S., and Seibt, B. 2008. "The embodiment of power and communalism in space and bodily contact," in *Embodied grounding: Social, cognitive, affective, and neuroscientific approaches,* G. R. Semin and E. R. Smith (eds.). Cambridge: Cambridge University Press, 160–183.

Schurz, G. 2013. "Wertneutralität und hypothetische Werturteile in den Wissenschaften [Value neutrality and hypothetical value judgments in science]," in *Werte in den*

Wissenschaften: Neue Ansätze zum Werturteilsstreit [Values in science: New Approaches tot he value judgment dispute], G. Schurz and M. Carrier (eds). Berlin: Suhrkamp, 305–334.

Schwartz, B. 2004. *The paradox of choice: Why more is less.* New York: HarperCollins.

Schwartz, B. L. 1994. "Sources of information in metamemory: Judgments of learning and feelings of knowing," *Psychonomic Bulletin & Review* 1: 357–375.

Schwartz, S. H. 1992. "Universals in the content and structure of values: Theory and empirical tests in 20 countries," *Advances in Experimental Social Psychology* 25: 1–65.

Schwarz, N. 1990. "Feelings as information: Informational and motivational functions of affective states," in *Handbook of motivation and cognition: Foundations of social behavior, Vol. II*, E. T. Higgins and R. M. Sorrentino (eds.). New York: Guilford Press, 527–561.

Schwarz, N. 1998. "Accessible content and accessibility experiences: The interplay of declarative and experiential information in judgment," *Personality and Social Psychology Review* 2: 87–99.

Schwarz, N. 2004. "Metacognitive experiences in consumer judgment and decision making," *Journal of Consumer Psychology* 14: 332–348.

Schwarz, N. 2012. "Feelings-as-information theory," in *Handbook of theories of social psychology, Vol. I*, P. A. M. Van Lange, A. W. Kruglanski, and E. T. Higgins (eds.). London: Sage, 289–308.

Schwarz, N., Bless, H., Strack, F., Klumpp, G., Rittenauer-Schatka, H., and Simons, A. 1991. "Ease of retrieval as information: Another look at the availability heuristic," *Journal of Personality and Social Psychology* 61: 195–202.

Schwarz, N. and Clore, G. L. 1983. "Mood, misattribution, and judgments of well-being: Informative and directive functions of affective states," *Journal of Personality and Social Psychology* 45: 513–523.

Schwarz, N. and Clore, G. L. 2007. "Feelings and phenomenal experiences," in *Social psychology: Handbook of basic principles*, A. Kruglanski and E. T. Higgins (eds.). New York: Guilford Press, 385–407.

Schwarz, N., Sanna, L. J., Skurnik, I., and Yoon, C. 2007. "Metacognitive experiences and the intricacies of setting people straight: Implications for debiasing and public information campaigns," *Advances in Experimental Social Psychology* 39: 127–161.

Scruton, R. 2007. *Culture counts: Faith and feeling in a world besieged.* New York: Encounter Books.

Seamon, J. G., Brody, N., and Kauff, D. M. 1983. "Affective discrimination of stimuli that are not recognized: Effects of shadowing, masking, and central laterality," *Journal of Experimental Psychology: Learning, Memory, and Cognition* 9: 544–555.

Sedlmeier, P., Eberth, J., Schwarz, M., Zimmermann, D., Haarig, F., Jaeger, S., and Kunze, S. 2012. "The psychological effects of meditation: A meta-analysis," *Psychological Bulletin* 138: 1139–1171.

Sela, A. and Berger, J. 2012. "Decision quicksand: How trivial choices suck us in," *Journal of Consumer Research* 39: 360–370.

Seligman, M. E. P. 2002. *Authentic happiness: Using the new positive psychology to realize your potential for lasting fulfillment.* New York: Free Press.

Seligman, M. E. P. 2011. *Flourish: A visionary new understanding of happiness and well-being.* New York: Free Press.

Seligman, M. E. P., Steen, T. A., Park, N., and Peterson, C. 2005. "Positive psychology progress: Empirical validation of interventions," *American Psychologist* 60: 410.

Selznick, P. 1992. *The moral commonwealth*. Berkeley: University of California Press.

Seok, B. 2013. *Embodied moral psychology and Confucian philosophy*. Lanham, MA: Lexington Books.

Shakespeare, W. 2003/1609. "Sonnets," in *Shakespeare's romances and poems*, D. Bevington (ed.). New York: Pearson, 1713–1744.

Shallcross, A. J., Troy, A. S., Boland, M., and Mauss, I. B. 2010. "Let it be: Accepting negative emotional experiences predicts decreased negative affect and depressive symptoms," *Behaviour Research and Therapy* 48: 921–929.

Shalvi, S., Gino, F., Barkan, R., and Ayal, S. 2015. "Self-serving justifications: Doing wrong and feeling moral," *Current Directions in Psychological Science* 24: 125–130.

Sheeran, P., Milne, S., Webb, T. L., and Gollwitzer, P. M. 2005. "Implementation intentions and health behaviour," in *Predicting health behaviour: Research and practice with social cognition models*, M. Conner and P. Norman (eds.). Maidenhead, UK: Open University Press.

Shenhav, A., Rand, D. G., and Greene, J. D. 2012. "Divine intuition: Cognitive style influences belief in God," *Journal of Experimental Psychology: General* 141: 423.

Sherman, N. 1989. *The fabric of character: Aristotle's theory of virtue*. Oxford: Oxford University Press.

Shi, D. 1985. *The simple life*. Athens: University of Georgia Press.

Shimamura, A. P. and Palmer, S. E. (eds.). 2012. *Aesthetic science: Connecting minds, brains, and experience*. New York: Oxford University Press.

Shimanoff, S. B. 1987. "Types of emotional disclosures and request compliance between spouses," *Communications Monographs* 54: 85–100.

Shiner, L. 2001. *The invention of art: A cultural history*. Chicago: University of Chicago Press.

Shtulman, A. 2013. "Epistemic similarities between students' scientific and supernatural beliefs," *Journal of Educational Psychology* 105: 199–212.

Siegler, R. S. and Stern, E. 1998. "Conscious and unconscious strategy discoveries: A microgenetic analysis," *Journal of Experimental Psychology: General* 127: 377–397.

Silvia, P. J. 2005. "What is interesting? Exploring the appraisal structure of interest," *Emotion* 5: 89–102.

Silvia, P. J. 2012. "Human emotions and aesthetic experience: An overview of empirical aesthetics," in *Aesthetic science: Connecting minds, brains, and experience*, A. P. Shimamura and S. E. Palmer (eds.). Oxford: Oxford University Press, 250–275.

Sim, M. 2007. *Remastering morals with Aristotle and Confucius*. New York: Cambridge University Press.

Simon, D. A. and Bjork, R. A. 2001. "Metacognition in motor learning," *Journal of Experimental Psychology: Learning, Memory, and Cognition* 27: 907–912.

Simon, D. A. and Bjork, R. A. 2002. "Models of performance in learning multisegment movement tasks: Consequences for acquisition, retention, and judgments of learning," *Journal of Experimental Psychology: Applied* 8: 222–232.

Simon, H. A. 1956. "Rational choice and the structure of the environment," *Psychological Review* 63: 129–138.

Simon, H. A. 1967. "Motivational and emotional controls of cognition," *Psychological Review* 74: 29–39.

Simon, H. A. and Gilmartin, K. J. 1973. "A simulation of memory for chess positions," *Cognitive Psychology* 5: 29–46.

Simonson, I. 1990. "The effect of purchase quantity and timing on variety-seeking behavior," *Journal of Marketing Research* 27: 150–162.

Simpson, J. A., Oriña, M. M., and Ickes, W. 2003. "When accuracy hurts, and when it helps: A test of the empathic accuracy model in marital interactions," *Journal of Personality and Social Psychology* 85: 881–893.

Sivulka, J. 2007. "Odor, oh no! Advertising deodorant and the new science of psychology, 1910 to 1925," in *Proceedings of the 13th Conference on Historical Analysis & Research in Marketing (CHARM): Marketing history at the center*, B. J. Branchik (ed.). Durham, NC: Duke University Press, 212–220.

Skinner, E. A., Chapman, M., and Baltes, P. B. 1988. "Control, means-ends, and agency beliefs: A new conceptualization and its measurement during childhood," *Journal of Personality and Social Psychology* 54: 117–133.

Skowronski, J. J. and Carlston, D. E. 1987. "Social judgment and social memory: The role of cue diagnosticity in negativity, positivity, and extremity biases,' *Journal of Personality and Social Psychology* 52: 689–699.

Slater, A., von der Schulenburg, C., Brown, E., Badenoch, M., Butterworth, G., Parsons, S., et al. 1998. "Newborn infants prefer attractive faces," *Infant Behavior & Development* 21: 345–354.

Slingerland, E. G. 2003a. *Effortless action: Wu-wei as conceptual metaphor and spiritual ideal in early China*. Oxford: Oxford University Press.

Slingerland, E. G. 2003b. *Confucius: Analects – With selections from traditional commentaries*. Indianapolis: Hackett.

Slingerland, E. G. 2008. *What science offers the humanities: Integrating body and culture*. Cambridge: Cambridge University Press.

Slingerland, E. G. 2010. "Toward an empirically-responsible ethics: Cognitive science, virtue ethics, and effortless attention in early Chinese thought," in *Effortless attention: A new perspective in the cognitive science of attention and action*, B. Bruya (ed.). Cambridge, MA: MIT Press, 247–286.

Slingerland, E. G. 2011. " The situationist critique and early Confucian virtue ethics," *Ethics* 121: 390–419.

Slingerland, E. G. 2014. *Trying not to try: The art and science of spontaneity*. New York: Crown.

Smith, D. M., Loewenstein, G., Jankovic, A., and Ubel, P. A. 2009. "Happily hopeless: Adaptation to a permanent, but not to a temporary, disability," *Health Psychology* 28: 787–791.

Smith, J. D. and Melara, R. J. 1990. "Aesthetic preference and syntactic prototypicality in music: 'Tis the gift to be simple'," *Cognition* 34: 279–298.

Smith, N. R. 1988. "How we understand art by Michael J. Parsons," *Studies in Art Education* 29: 318–320.

Solbakken, O. A., Hansen, R. S., Havik, O. E., and Monsen, J. T. 2012. "Affect integration as a predictor of change: Affect consciousness and treatment response in open-ended psychotherapy." *Psychotherapy Research* 22: 656–672.

Song, H. J. and Schwarz, N. 2008. "Fluency and the detection of misleading questions: Low processing fluency attenuates the Moses illusion," *Social Cognition* 26: 791–799.

Sosis, R. 2003. "Why aren't we all Hutterites? Costly signalling theory and religious behaviour," *Human Nature* 14: 91–127.

Speisman, J. C., Lazarus, R. S., Mordkoef, A., and Davison, L. 1964. "Experimental reduction of stress based on ego-defense theory," *Journal of Abnormal and Social Psychology* 68: 367–380.

Spranger, E. 1928/1914. *Types of men: The psychology and ethics of personality.* New York: G. E. Stechert.

Sroufe, L. A. 1977. "Wariness of strangers and the study of infant development," *Child Development* 48: 731–746.

Staal, F. 1979. "The meaninglessness of ritual," *Numen* 26: 2–22.

Stein, M. B. and Stein, D. J. 2008. "Social anxiety disorder," *The Lancet* 371: 1115–1125.

Stellman, S., Muscat, J., Hoffmann, D., and Wynder, E. 1997. "Impact of filter cigarette smoking on lung cancer histology," *Preventive Medicine* 26: 451–456.

Stern, D. N. 1977. *The first relationship: Infant and mother.* Cambridge, MA: Harvard University Press.

Stern, D. N. 1985. *The interpersonal world of the infant.* New York: Basic Books.

Sternberg, R. J. 1986. "A triangular theory of love," *Psychological Review* 93: 119–135.

Sternberg, R. J. and Davidson, J. E. (eds.). 1995. *The nature of insight.* Cambridge, MA: MIT Press.

Stevenson, R. J. and Yeomans, M. R. 1995. "Does exposure enhance liking for the chilli burn?" *Appetite* 24: 107–120.

Strack, F. and Deutsch, R. 2004. "Reflective and impulsive determinants of social behavior," *Personality and Social Psychology Review* 8: 220–247.

Strack, F., Martin, L. L., and Stepper, S. 1988. "Inhibiting and facilitating conditions of the human smile: A nonobtrusive test of the facial feedback hypothesis," *Journal of Personality and Social Psychology* 54: 768–777.

Stroebe, W., Van Koningsbruggen, G. M., Papies, E. K., and Aarts, H. 2013. "Why most dieters fail but some succeed: A goal conflict model of eating behavior," *Psychological Review* 120: 110.

Stump, R. W. 2008. *The geography of religion: Faith, place, and space.* Lanham, MD: Rowman & Littlefield.

Suri, G., Whittaker, K., and Gross, J. J. 2015. "Launching reappraisal: It's less common than you might think," *Emotion* 15: 73–77.

Sutton, R. I. and Rafaeli, A. 1987. "Characteristics of work stations as potential occupational stressors," *Academy of Management Journal* 30: 260–276.

Sweldens, S., Van Osselaer, S. M. J., and Janiszewski, C. 2010. "Evaluative conditioning procedures and the resilience of conditioned brand attitudes," *Journal of Consumer Research* 37: 473–489.

Sweller, J. and Chandler, P. 1994. "Why some material is difficult to learn," *Cognition and Instruction* 12: 185–233.

Sy, T., Côté, S., and Saavedra, R. 2005. "The contagious leader: Impact of the leader's mood on the mood of group members, group affective tone, and group processes," *Journal of Applied Psychology* 90: 295–305.

Tambiah, S. J. 1990. *Magic, science and religion and the scope of rationality.* Cambridge: Cambridge University Press.

Tan, H. B. and Forgas, J. P. 2010. "When happiness makes us selfish, but sadness makes us fair: Affective influences on interpersonal strategies in the dictator game," *Journal of Experimental Social Psychology* 46: 571–576.

Tangney, J. P., Stuewig, J., and Mashek, D. J. 2007. "Moral emotions and moral behavior," *Annual Review of Psychology* 58: 345–372.

Taylor, C. 1989. *Sources of the self.* Cambridge: Cambridge University Press.

Taylor, P. M. 2003. *Munitions of the mind: A history of propaganda from the ancient world to the present day*. Manchester: Manchester University Press.

Teasdale, J. D., Moore, R. G., Hayhurst, H., Pope, M., Williams, S., and Segal, Z. V. 2002. "Metacognitive awareness and prevention of relapse in depression: Empirical evidence," *Journal of Consulting and Clinical Psychology* 70: 275–287.

Thaler, R. H. 1985. "Mental accounting and consumer choice," *Marketing Science* 4: 199–214.

Thaler, R. H. 1999. "Mental accounting matters," *Journal of Behavioral Decision Making* 12: 183–206.

Thaler, R. H. and Sunstein, C. R. 2008. *Nudge: Improving decisions about health, wealth, and happiness*. New Haven: Yale University Press.

Thompson, V. A. 2014. "What intuitions are…and are not," *Psychology of Learning and Motivation* 60: 35–75.

Thompson, V. A., Prowse Turner, J. A., Pennycook, G., Ball, L. J., Brack, H., Ophir, Y., and Ackerman, R. 2013. "The role of answer fluency and perceptual fluency as metacognitive cues for initiating analytic thinking," *Cognition* 128: 237–251.

Tillich, P. 1951–1963. *Systematic theology*. Chicago: University of Chicago Press.

Tillich, P. 2001/1957. *Dynamics of faith*. New York: HarperCollins.

Tillmann, B., Bharucha, J. J., and Bigand, E. 2000. "Implicit learning of tonality: A self-organizing approach," *Psychological Review* 107: 885–913.

Topolinski, S. 2011. "A process model of intuition," *European Review of Social Psychology* 22: 274–315.

Topolinski, S., Erle, T. M., and Reber, R. 2015. "Necker's smile: Immediate affective consequences of early perceptual processes," *Cognition* 140: 1–13.

Topolinski, S., Likowski, K., Weyers, P., and Strack, F. 2009. "The face of fluency: Semantic coherence automatically elicits a specific pattern of facial muscle reactions," *Cognition and Emotion* 23: 260–271.

Topolinski, S., Lindner, S., and Freudenberg, A. 2014. "Popcorn in the cinema: Oral interference sabotages advertising effects," *Journal of Consumer Psychology* 24: 169–176.

Topolinski, S., and Reber, R. 2010. "Gaining insight into the 'aha' experience," *Current Directions in Psychological Science* 19: 402–405.

Topolinski, S. and Strack, F. 2009a. "The architecture of intuition: Fluency and affect determine intuitive judgments of semantic and visual coherence and judgments of grammaticality in artificial grammar learning," *Journal of Experimental Psychology: General* 138: 39–63.

Topolinski, S. and Strack, F. 2009b. "The analysis of intuition: Processing fluency and affect in judgements of semantic coherence," *Cognition and Emotion* 23: 1465–1503.

Topolinski, S. and Strack, F. 2009c. "Motormouth: Mere exposure depends on stimulus-specific motor simulations," *Journal of Experimental Psychology: Learning, Memory, and Cognition* 35: 423–433.

Trainor, L. J. and Heinmiller, B. M. 1998. "The development of evaluative responses to music: Infants prefer to listen to consonance over dissonance," *Infant Behavior & Development* 21: 77–88.

Trevarthen, C. 1979. "Communication and cooperation in early infancy: A description of primary intersubjectivity," in *Before speech: The beginning of interpersonal communication*, M. Bullowa (ed.). Cambridge: Cambridge University Press, 321–347.

Trevarthen, C. 1985. "Facial expressions of emotions in mother–infant interactions," *Human Neurobiology* 4: 21–32.

Triandis, H. C. and Gelfand, M. J. 1998. "Converging measurement of horizontal and vertical individualism and collectivism," *Journal of Personality and Social Psychology* 74: 118–128.

Troy, A. S., Shallcross, A. J., Davis, T. S., and Mauss, I. B. 2013. "History of mindfulness-based cognitive therapy is associated with increased cognitive reappraisal ability," *Mindfulness* 4: 213–222.

Tugade, M. M. and Fredrickson, B. L. 2014. "Resilient individuals use positive emotions to bounce back from negative emotional experiences," *Journal of Personality and Social Psychology* 86: 320–333.

Tversky, A. and Kahneman, D. 1973. "Availability: A heuristic for judging frequency and probability," *Cognitive Psychology* 5: 207–232.

Unkelbach, C. 2007. "Reversing the truth effect: Learning the interpretation of processing fluency in judgments of truth," *Journal of Experimental Psychology: Learning, Memory, and Cognition* 33: 219–230.

Unkelbach, C., Bayer, M., Alves, H., Koch, A., and Stahl, C. 2010. "Fluency and positivity as possible causes of the truth effect," *Consciousness and Cognition* 20: 594–602.

Unkelbach, C., Fiedler, K., and Freytag, P. 2007. "Information repetition in evaluative judgments: Easy to monitor, hard to control," *Organizational Behavior and Human Decision Processes* 103: 37–52.

Unkelbach, C. and Stahl, C. 2009. "A multinomial modeling approach to dissociate different components of the truth effect," *Consciousness and Cognition* 18: 22–38.

Vandenberg, D. 1983. *Human rights in education*. New York: Philosophical Library.

Van Kleef, G. A. and Côté, S. 2015. "On the social influence of negative emotional expression," in *The positive side of negative emotions*, W. G. Parrot (ed.). New York: Guilford Press, 126–145.

Van Kleef, G. A., De Dreu, C. K., and Manstead, A. S. 2004. "The interpersonal effects of anger and happiness in negotiations," *Journal of Personality and Social Psychology* 86: 57–76.

VanLehn, K. 1990. *Mind bugs: The origins of procedural misconceptions*. Cambridge, MA: MIT Press.

Vaughn, L. A., Dubovi, A. S., and Niño, N. P. 2013. "Processing fluency affects behavior more strongly among people higher in trait mindfulness," *Journal of Research in Personality* 47: 782–788.

Velanova, K., Wheeler, M. E., and Luna, B. 2008. "Maturational changes in anterior cingulate and frontoparietal recruitment support the development of error processing and inhibitory control," *Cerebral Cortex* 18: 2505–2522.

Velten, E. 1968. "A laboratory task for induction of mood states," *Behaviour Research and Therapy* 6: 473–482.

Verplanken, B. and Faes, S. 1999. "Good intentions, bad habits, and effects of forming implementation intentions on healthy eating," *European Journal of Social Psychology* 29: 591–604.

Vining, J. and Ebreo, A. 2002. "Emerging theoretical and methodological perspectives on conservation behavior," in *New handbook of environmental psychology*, R. Bechtel and A. Churchman (eds.). New York: Wiley, 541–558.

Walkington, C., Petrosino, A., and Sherman, M. 2013. "Supporting algebraic reasoning through personalized story scenarios: How situational understanding mediates performance," *Mathematical Thinking and Learning* 15: 89–120.

Walsh, E. and Ayton, P. 2009. "My imagination versus your feelings: Can personal affective forecasts be improved by knowing other peoples' emotions?" *Journal of Experimental Psychology: Applied* 15: 351–360.

Walton, G. M. 2014. "The new science of wise psychological interventions," *Current Directions in Psychological Science* 23: 73–82.

Wänke, M., Bohner, G. and Jurkowitsch, A. 1997. "There are many reasons to drive a BMW: Does imagined ease of argument generation influence attitudes?" *Journal of Consumer Research* 24: 170–178.

Wänke, M., Schwarz, N., and Bless, H. 1995. "The availability heuristic revisited: Experienced ease of retrieval in mundane frequency estimates," *Acta Psychologica* 89: 83–90.

Wansink, B. 2010. "From mindless eating to mindlessly eating better," *Physiology & Behavior* 100: 454–463.

Wansink, B. and Chandon, P. 2006. "Can 'low-fat' nutrition labels lead to obesity?" *Journal of Marketing Research* 43: 605–617.

Wansink, B., Payne, C. R., and Chandon, P. 2007. "Internal and external cues of meal cessation: The French paradox redux?" *Obesity* 15: 2920–2924.

Wansink, B. and Van Ittersum, K. 2003. "Bottoms up! The influence of elongation on pouring and consumption volume," *Journal of Consumer Research* 30: 455–463.

Ward, B. 1975. *The sayings of the desert fathers.* London: Mowbrays.

Watanabe, S., Sakamoto, J., and Wakita, M. 1995. "Pigeons' discrimination of paintings by Monet and Picasso," *Journal of the Experimental Analysis of Behavior* 63: 165–174.

Waterhouse, L. 2006. "Multiple intelligences, the Mozart effect, and emotional intelligence: A critical review," *Educational Psychologist* 41: 207–225.

Watkins, P. C. 2013. *Gratitude and the good life: Toward a psychology of appreciation.* Dordrecht, Netherlands: Springer.

Weaver, K., Garcia, S. M., Schwarz, N., and Miller, D. T. 2007. "Inferring the popularity of an opinion from its familiarity: A repetitive voice sounds like a chorus," *Journal of Personality and Social Psychology* 92: 821–833.

Weber, M. 1946/1919. "Science as a vocation," in *From Max Weber: Essays in sociology,* H. H. Gerth, and C. Wright Mills (eds.). Oxford: Oxford University Press, 129–156.

Weber, M. 1949/1917. "The meaning of 'ethical neutrality' in sociology and economics," in *The methodology of the social sciences,* E Shils and H. A. Finch (eds.). Piscataway, NJ: Transaction, 1–49.

Weber, M. 1958a. *From Max Weber: Essays in sociology.* Oxford: Oxford University Press.

Weber, M. 1958b. *The religion of India: The sociology of Hinduism and Buddhism.* New York: Free Press.

Weber, M. 1967. *Ancient Judaism.* New York: Free Press.

Weber, M. 1968/1916. *The religion of China: Confucianism and Taoism.* New York: Free Press.

Weber, M. 1992/1905. *The Protestant ethic and the spirit of capitalism.* London: Routledge.

Weber, T. 2011. "Gandhi's moral economics: The sins of wealth without work and commerce without morality," in *The Cambridge companion to Gandhi*, J. M. Brown and A. Parel (eds.). Cambridge: Cambridge University Press, 135–153.

Wecker, C. 2013. "How to support prescriptive statements by empirical reserarch: Some missing parts," *Educational Psychology Review* 25: 1–18.

Wegner, D. M., Erber, R., and Zanakos, S. 1993. "Ironic processes in the mental control of mood and mood-related thought," *Journal of Personality and Social Psychology* 65: 1093–1104.

Wegner, D. M., Schneider, D. J., Carter, S. R., and White, T. L. 1987. "Paradoxical effects of thought suppression," *Journal of Personality and Social Psychology* 53: 5.

Weigel, H., Lukan, W., and Peyfuss, M. D. 1983. *Jeder Schuss ein Russ, jeder Stoss ein Franzos: Literarische und graphische Kriegspropaganda in Deutschland und Österreich 1914–1918 [Each shot a Russian, each stab a Frenchman: Literary and visual war propaganda in Germany and Austria 1914–1918]*. Vienna: Edition Christian Brandstätter.

Weinberger, D. A., Schwartz, G. E., and Davidson, R. J. 1979. "Low-anxious, high-anxious, and repressive coping styles: Psychometric patterns and behavioral and physiological responses to stress," *Journal of Abnormal Psychology* 88: 369–380.

Weiner, B. 1985. "An attributional theory of achievement motivation and emotion," *Psychological Review* 92: 548–573.

Weiner, B. 1986. *An attributional theory of motivation and emotion*. New York: Springer.

Weisberg, R. W. 1995. "Prolegomena to theory of insight," in *The nature of insights*, R. J. Sternberg and J. E. Davidson (eds.). Cambridge, MA: MIT Press, 157–196.

Weisberg, R. W. and Alba, J. W. 1981. "An examination of the alleged role of 'fixation' in the solution of several 'insight' problems," *Journal of Experimental Psychology: General* 110: 169–192.

Weiss, R. S. 1975. *Marital separation*. New York: Basic Books.

Wenzlaff, E. M. and Wegner, D. M. 2000. "Thought suppression," *Annual Review of Psychology* 51: 59–91.

Wenzlaff, R. M. and Bates, D. E. 1998. "Unmasking a cognitive vulnerability to depression: How lapses in mental control reveal depressive thinking," *Journal of Personality and Social Psychology* 75: 1559–1571.

Westerman, D. W., Klin, C. M., and Lanska, M. 2015. "On the (elusive) role of oral motor-movements in fluency-based memory illusions," *Journal of Experimental Psychology: Learning, Memory, and Cognition* 41: 1003–1013.

Westermann, R., Spies, K., Stahl, G., and Hesse, F. W. 1996. "Relative effectiveness and validity of mood induction procedures: A meta-analysis," *European Journal of Social Psychology* 26: 557–580.

White, M. G. 1965. *Foundations of historical knowledge*. New York: Harper & Row.

Whitehouse, H. and Laidlaw, J. A. 2004. *Ritual and memory: Towards a comparative anthropology of religion*. Walnut Creck, CA: Rowman Altamira.

Whitehouse, H. and Lanman, J. A. 2014. "The ties that bind us," *Current Anthropology* 55: 674–695.

Whittlesea, B. W. A. 1993. "Illusions of familiarity," *Journal of Experimental Psychology: Learning, Memory, and Cognition* 19: 1235–1253.

Whittlesea, B. W. A., Jacoby, L. L., and Girard, K. 1990. "Illusions of immediate memory: Evidence of an attributional basis for feelings of familiarity and perceptual quality," *Journal of Memory and Language* 29: 716–732.

Whittlesea, B. W. A. and Williams, L. D. 2000. "The source of feelings of familiarity: The discrepancy–attribution hypothesis," *Journal of Experimental Psychology: Learning, Memory, and Cognition* 26: 547–565.

Wicker, A. W. 1969. "Attitudes versus actions: The relationship of verbal and overt behavioral responses to attitude objects," *Journal of Social Issues* 25: 41–78.

Wieber, F., Gollwitzer, P. M., and Sheeran, P. 2014. "Strategic regulation of mimicry effects by implementation intentions," *Journal of Experimental Social Psychology* 53: 31–39.

Wikan, U. 1990. *Managing turbulant hearts: A Balinese formula for living.* Chicago: University of Chicago Press.

Wilson, M. and Knoblich, G. 2005. "The case for motor involvement in perceiving conspecifics," *Psychological Bulletin* 131: 460–473.

Wilson, T. D., Lisle, D. J., Schooler, J. W., Hodges, S. D., Klaaren, K. J., and Lafleur, S. J. 1993. "Introspecting about reason can reduce post-choice satisfaction," *Personality and Social Psychology Bulletin* 19: 331–339.

Wilson Bareau, J. 2001. *Manet by himself.* New York: Little, Brown.

Wiltermuth, S. S. and Heath, C. 2009. "Synchrony and cooperation," *Psychological Science* 20: 1–5.

Winckelmann, J. J. 1972. *Winckelmann: Writings on art,* ed. D. G. Irwin. London: Phaidon.

Winkielman, P. and Cacioppo, J. T. 2001. "Mind at ease puts a smile on the face: Psychophysiological evidence that processing facilitation elicits positive affect," *Journal of Personality and Social Psychology* 81: 989–1000.

Winkielman, P., Halberstadt, J., Fazendeiro, T., and Catty, S. 2006. "Prototypes are attractive because they are easy on the mind," *Psychological Science* 17: 799–806.

Winkielman, P. and Schwarz, N. 2001. "How pleasant was your childhood? Beliefs about memory shape inferences from experienced difficulty of recall," *Psychological Science* 12: 176–179.

Winkielman, P., Schwarz, N., Fazendeiro, T. A., and Reber, R. 2003. "The hedonic marking of processing fluency: Implications for evaluative judgment," in *The psychology of evaluation: Affective processes in cognition and emotion,* J. Musch and K. C. Klauer (eds.). Mahwah, NJ: Lawrence Erlbaum, 189–217.

Wirtz, D., Kruger, J., Scollon, C. N., and Diener, E. 2003. "What to do on spring break? The role of predicted, on-line, and remembered experience in future choice," *Psychological Science* 14: 520–524.

Witkiewitz, K. and Marlatt, A. 2011. "Behavioral therapy across the spectrum," *Alcohol Research & Health* 33: 313–319.

Wölfflin, H. 1950. *Principles of art history: The problem of the development of style in later art.* New York: Dover.

Wolpe, J. 1958. *Psychotherapy by reciprocal inhibition.* Stanford: Stanford University Press.

Woltin, K.-A. and Guinote, A. 2015. "I can, I do, and so I like: From power to action and aesthetic preferences," *Journal of Experimental Psychology: General,* 144, 1124–1136.

Wood, W., Labrecque, J., Lin, P.-Y., and Ruenger, D. 2015. "Habits in dual process models," in *Dual process theories of the social mind,* J. Sherman, B. Gawronski, and Y. Trope. New York: Guilford Press, 371–385.

Wundt, W. 1893. *Grundzüge der physiologischen Psychologie [Essentials of physiological psychology].* Leipzig: Wilhelm Engehnann.

Youniss, J. 1985. *Adolescent relations with mothers, fathers and friends*. Chicago: University of Chicago Press.

Zajonc, R. B. 1968. "Attitudinal effects of mere exposure," *Journal of Personality and Social Psychology* 9: 1–27.

Zanna, M. P. and Rempel, J. K. 1988. "Attitudes: A new look at an old concept," in *The social psychology of knowledge*, D. Bar-Tal and A. W. Kruglanski (eds.). Cambridge: Cambridge University Press, 315–334.

Zarate, R. and Agras, W. S. 1994. "Psychosocial treatment of phobia and panic disorders," *Psychiatry* 57: 133–141.

Zeki, S. 1999. *Inner vision: An exploration of art and the brain*. Oxford: Oxford University Press.

Zentner, M. R. and Kagan, J. 1996. "Perception of music by infants," *Nature* 383: 29.

Ziller, T. 1876. *Vorlesungen zur allgemeinen Pädagogik [Lectures on general education]*. Leipzig: Matthes.

Zillmann, D. and Bryant, J. 1985. "Affect, mood, and emotion as determinants of selective exposure," in *Selective exposure to communication*, D. Zillmann and J. Bryant (eds.). Mahwah, NJ: Lawrence Erlbaum, 157–190.

Zillmann, D., Katcher, A. H., and Milavsky, B. 1972. "Excitation transfer from physical exercise to subsequent aggressive behavior," *Journal of Experimental Social Psychology* 8: 247–259.

INDEX